FINAL C...

FINAL CUT

Dreams and Disaster in the making of *Heaven's Gate*

STEVEN BACH

faber and faber

LONDON · BOSTON

First published in Great Britain in 1985 by
Jonathan Cape Ltd
This paperback edition first published in 1986 by
Faber and Faber Limited
3 Queen Square London WC1N 3AU

Printed in England by Clays Ltd, St Ives plc

Portions of this book have appeared in *Vanity Fair* and *American Film*.

Selections from *The Cattle Barons' Rebellion Against Law and Order: First Eyewitness Accounts of the Johnson County War in Wyoming 1892* appear here courtesy of the Rare Books and Manuscripts Division, New York Public Library, Astor, Lenox and Tilden Foundations.

Selection as noted from *The New York Times* reprinted here by permission. © New York Times Company 1978, 1980, 1981, 1984.

From *D. W. Griffith: An American Life* by Richard Schickel © Gideon Productions, Inc. 1984. Reprinted by permission of Simon & Schuster, Inc.

From *Adventures in the Screen Trade* © William Goldman 1983.
Published by Warner Books.

From "Michael Cimino's Battle to Make a Great Movie" by Jean Vallely. Reprinted from the December 1978 issue of *Esquire*. Esquire Associates 1978.

From "Michael Cimino's Way West" by Rex McGee, reprinted by permission of *American Film* from the October 1980 issue. © The American Film Institute 1980.

From *Taking It All In* by Pauline Kael. © Pauline Kael 1980, 1981, 1982, 1983, 1984. Reprinted by permission of Holt, Rinehart & Winston, Publishers.

From "Behind the Cameras on *Heaven's Gate*" by Vilmos Zsigmond. © *American Cinematographer* 1980. Reprinted by permission.

"Hollywood's War" by Tom Buckley appeared in the April 1980 issue of *Harper's* magazine. Quotations that appear here from the article are reprinted by permission of the author.

Line from "Me and Bobby McGee" by Kris Kristofferson and Fred Foster © Combine Music Corporation 1969. International Copyright Secured. All Rights Reserved.

Selections as noted from *The Los Angeles Times* reprinted here by permission. © *The Los Angeles Times* 1979, 1982, 1983.

Selections from Claudia Cohen's column, which appeared in the November 21, 1980 issue of the New York *Daily News*, are reprinted here by permission, New York *Daily News*. © 1980.

A CIP record for this book is available from the British Library.

4 6 8 10 9 7 5 3

This book is for my mother and father

CONTENTS

AUTHOR'S FOREWORD

Orson Welles once observed that a poet needs a pen, a painter a brush, and a filmmaker an army. This has never been more true (or more expensive) than it is today; nor has the military analogy ever been more apt. Wars, metaphorical and real, are hell we know, not only for the foot soldiers who slog through the trenches but also for the generals and chiefs of staff who get the glory or the sack.

Heaven's Gate was a movie about a war and was one itself; it had many battlefields. One was literal, in Montana; another was economic, mainly in New York; some were political in both Hollywood and New York; and all of them were informed by personality.

More than a little havoc was wreaked, and more than a little rubble was left. Falling debris from the collapse of a once-great company dazed participants and onlookers alike, including many civilian bystanders, as unsure of what had happened as were those correspondents gamely sending confused dispatches back to the motion-picture and financial and, eventually, worldwide press.

Rebecca West once said she wrote to find out what she thought, and in some measure the pages that follow are my attempt to find out what sense I can draw from events that seemed as senseless at times to myself as they did to the press and the general public. As both participant and witness to the non-sense I do not shrink from the admission that I lobbed the occasional grenade into the chaos or participated in skirmishes back on the home front that did nothing to improve conditions in the theater of war. It is hoped that the tone is less "confessional" than frank and that the glimpses of life at staff headquarters and in the trenches may reveal, now that the smoke has cleared, what happened and how, and maybe even why.

These pages do not claim to be without personal viewpoint or to be exhaustive. There is another war story that might well be written about *Heaven's Gate* by its chief general: that of the unwieldy war to create art from technology and ambition and will. It's a tough battle to try to touch the human spirit with money, machinery, and matériel. Victory or defeat in that war is in the eye or the heart of the beholder, and the reader as viewer can decide for himself.

In the meantime, however, here are the spent shell casings, the bombs exploded, the duds waiting or never to go off, the broad landscape of debris, the narrower one of souvenir, all collected by a once shell-shocked observer and participant after sifting through the rubble.

ACKNOWLEDGMENTS

When I first went to work for United Artists in May 1978, William Goldman urged me to keep a diary. I took his advice, and his appearance in those (and these) pages is therefore his own fault. Not so, many others.

I also kept daily business journals, notes on telephone calls, meetings, and other professional miscellany, usually in the sort of spiral notebooks favored, appropriately enough, by students. The cost of my education was high and borne by many.

My two secretaries—Rita Joelson in the West and Anne Harkavy in the East—devotedly maintained calendars, travel itineraries, and records of phone calls made and received and saw to it that my personal files covering the events narrated in this book were as orderly and as complete as I would ever want them as memorabilia. I owe Anne and Rita much for their friendship and aid over the years, but for nothing so much as their having unwittingly compiled the basic documentation on which this book is based.

I owe others, too. These pages could not have been written without the aid and support, both factual and friendly, of many who, like the author, were participants in or witnesses to the events here related. Some of them shared those years on condition they not be thanked by name, a condition I hereby acknowledge and respect. They know who they are and also, I hope, my gratitude to them. Others, whose names follow, were in varying ways helpful in clarifying issues, dates, moments, moods, and sometimes motives. They include from United Artists and the movie: Andreas "Andy" Albeck, Joann Carelli, Bart

Farber, Joseph Farrell, Robert French, Gene Goodman, Tom Gray, James Harvey, Allen Highfill, Lehman Katz, Derek Kavanagh, Roz Komack, Tambi Larsen, Nan Leonard, Charles Okun, Kathi Page, Gerald Paonessa, Richard Parks, Gary Schrager, Robert Schwartz, Hy Smith, Lois Smith, Dean Stolber, and Anthea Sylbert.

Others who were helpful include Tom Buckley, Les Gapay, Sabrina Grigorian, Leticia Kent, Paul Schumach, Fred Schuler, Sybelle Schuler, Gene Shalit, Kevin Thomas, Johannes Waltz, and Jim Watters. Special help and support came from Robert Doggett and James Kellerhals, and my gratitude and debt to them are great.

Conversations are re-created in this book, reconstructed from memory, both mine and others, and from the basic research materials already cited. In all but the obvious one or two I was either participant or witness.

There are two important omissions to the sources utilized, both major participants in the drama who chose not to cooperate in its chronicling. David Field wrote me after long consideration that he did not want to read or even to be in the book. Michael Cimino was unresponsive to requests for interviews. Each of them would perhaps write a substantially different account from the one found here.

I also wish to thank the following people and organizations for their generous extensions of time and help: Dan Black and Frank Miele of the *Daily* (Kalispell) *InterLake;* William F. Conrod of the National Park Service; Mary Corliss of the Museum of Modern Art Film Library; Dick Harms of Michigan State University in East Lansing, Michigan; Kathleen Kimble of the (Montana) *Missoulian;* Carmelita Pope of the American Humane Association; Chief Martin Stefanic of the Kalispell, Montana, Police Department; and the staffs of the following libraries: Amerika Haus in Munich; Margaret Herrick Library of the Academy of Motion Picture Arts and Sciences in Los Angeles; New York Public Library, particularly the Rare Books department; and the Österreichisches Filmmuseum in Vienna.

At William Morrow I am indebted to Sherry Arden, Lisa Drew, Laurie Lister, and Deborah Baker for their encouragement and attentiveness to this project. Robert J. Wunsch (without whom this book would never have been written) not only led me to the typewriter, but to my agent, Robert Lescher, who was both spiritual father to the book and to its author as well.

And finally, for the kind of support, encouragement, patience, and loyalty that go beyond definition and certainly beyond my ability to repay, two people who lived through these events in different ways and who shared the burdens and the occasional exultations: Maurice Pacini and Werner Röhr.

CAST OF PRINCIPAL CHARACTERS

Unless otherwise indicated, corporate positions listed below are those held by the individuals named as they enter the text.

ALBECK, ANDREAS ("ANDY")	*President of United Artists*
ALLEN, WOODY	*Actor, filmmaker*
AUERBACH, NORBERT	*Head of foreign distribution, UA*
BACH, STEVEN	*Head of East Coast and European production, UA*
BECKETT, JOHN ("JACK")	*Chairman, Transamerica*
BROWN, DAVID	*Film producer*
BROWN, DENNIS	*Production management executive, UA*
CAPOTE, TRUMAN	*Writer*
CARELLI, JOANN	*Film producer*
CHARTOFF, ROBERT	*Film producer*
CIMINO, MICHAEL	*Filmmaker*
COHN, SAM	*Agent*
COPPOLA, FRANCIS	*Filmmaker*
FARBER, BART	*Head of ancillary sales, UA*
FIELD, DAVID	*Production executive, UA*
FITTER, AL	*Head of domestic distribution, UA*
GOLDMAN, WILLIAM	*Writer*

GOODMAN, GENE	*Head of domestic distribution, UA*
HARVEY, JAMES ("JIM")	*Executive vice-president, Transamerica;*
	chairman, UA
HUPPERT, ISABELLE	*Actress*
HURT, JOHN	*Actor*
JOFFE, CHARLES	*Film producer*
KAMEN, STAN	*Agent*
KATZ, LEHMAN ("LEE")	*Production management executive, UA*
KAVANAGH, DEREK	*Production management executive, UA*
KRIM, ARTHUR	*Chairman UA, later Orion*
KRISTOFFERSON, KRIS	*Actor*
MANKIEWICZ, CHRISTOPHER	*Production executive, UA*
MANSFIELD, DAVID	*Musician, composer*
NASATIR, MARCIA	*Production executive, UA*
OKUN, CHARLES	*Production manager*
PAONESSA, GERALD ("JERRY")	*Production executive, UA*
PARKS, RICHARD	*Production executive, UA*
PERSKY, LESTER	*Film producer*
PLESKOW, ERIC	*President UA, later Orion*
REYNOLDS, WILLIAM	*Film editor*
RISSNER, DANTON ("DANNY")	*Head of production, UA*
ROLLINS, JACK	*Film producer*
ROSENFELT, FRANK	*Chairman, MGM*
SELLERS, PETER	*Actor*
SMITH, HY	*Advertising executive, UA*
SMITH, LOIS	*Production executive, UA*
STOLBER, DEAN	*Head of business affairs, UA*
STREISAND, BARBRA	*Actress*
SYLBERT, ANTHEA	*Production executive, UA*
TOWNSEND, CLAIRE	*Production executive, UA*
UGLAND, RUDY	*"Boss wrangler"*
WALKEN, CHRISTOPHER	*Actor*
WEISSMANN, ERIC	*Lawyer*
WILLIAMS, JEREMY	*Lawyer*
WINKLER, IRWIN	*Film producer*
WUNSCH, ROBERT	*Production executive, UA*
ZADAN, CRAIG	*Production executive, UA*

FINAL CUT

PROLOGUE: MAIN TITLE

The modern corporation depends for its effectiveness . . . on the quality of its internal organization, which is to say the extent and depth of the submission of its employees. . . . High salaries are collected for such submission, but it would be wrong to suggest that these are the decisive factor. Belief in the purposes of the corporation—conditioned power—is almost certainly more important.

—John Kenneth Galbraith,
The Anatomy of Power
(1983)

The old United Artists doesn't exist today, but on August 26, 1980, a hot, hazy day in Los Angeles, it did, and 79 percent of the American people knew it did, and 66 percent of them knew its principal occupation was the making of motion pictures.

The figures were in a shiny dark green folder stamped "CONFIDENTIAL" in red, which had been assembled and prepared by the National Research Group, Inc. for an audience of two. One copy was spread open on the coffee table in an office in the wing of MGM's Irving Thalberg Building occupied by United Artists' West Coast operations.

I was trying to memorize these and other figures between spoonfuls of cottage cheese and grapefruit sections ordered from the studio commissary. They had been delivered by a white-coated Oriental waiter, a kindly, stooped man rumored to have been hired as an extra in *The Good Earth*, whose English was inadequate to his ever getting directions out of Culver City. It was partly as an antidote to such Hollywood apocrypha that the market research firm had been hired to compile the hard statistics before me.

The only other copy of the confidential report entitled "Public Recognition of Motion Picture Corporate Names" was, I knew, being scrutinized from behind large corrective lenses by Andreas ("Andy") Albeck, president and chief executive officer of United Artists, now somewhere over the Great Plains approaching the Rocky Mountains. Knowing Andy, I assumed he had already committed the figures to memory, analyzed and weighed them, and found them no more cheering than I. The figures concerned not only United Artists but all the major motion-picture companies. Twentieth Century-Fox was best known (90 percent), followed by Paramount (70 percent). But knowing the name was one thing; knowing what it meant was something else again. The percentage of people polled by the survey who were not absolutely sure what these famous companies did for a living was substantial. Of the survey's sample 34 percent had no idea that United Artists was making movies, not to mention the 21 percent, the more than 45 million people in America who had never heard of us at all. The numbers were humbling, as hard to swallow as my "Luciano Pavarotti Diet Special."

My secretary, Rita, came in quietly and slid an airplane ticket into the breast pocket of the blazer I had left hanging on the doorknob. Clipped to the ticket envelope was an itinerary: "Western Airlines Flight 723, dep. LAX 12:35, arr. SFO 1:40." Phone numbers I might need were neatly typed below that, followed by the late-afternoon return flight information. She stole a piece of melba toast from the lunch tray and announced through high-fiber, low-cal crumbs, "The car." Her thumb jerked outside. She then closed the confidential report I had continued to study, stuck it in my script bag, a handsome canvas and leather affair that had been a gift from Michael Cimino the previous Christmas, a "consolation prize" for the movie he was supposed to have delivered at the same time, which wasn't ready yet. I used to joke when complimented on the bag, "Yes, and it cost me only thirty-five million dollars." It was meant as an ironic wisecrack, but it became gallows humor in time. Rita thrust the bag into my hand and steered me to the door, looping the blazer over my free arm, and walked with me to the hallway beyond the outer office.

As I walked backward, calling out last-minute reminders, I passed the two- by three-foot still enlargements from famous movies made or owned by United Artists that marched down the corridor in chromium-framed cadence. It was a pleasant passage, long and cool and crowded with familiar faces: John Wayne, Woody Allen, Bette Davis, Diane Keaton, Paul Muni, Liza Minnelli, Spencer Tracy, Robert De Niro, Gloria Swanson, Jack Nicholson, Marlene Dietrich, the Beatles. And at the end of the corridor, just before the heavy glass entrance doors, were two other photographs, not *from* movies but *about* them. The first pictured Arthur Krim and Robert Benjamin and their associates, posed around Krim's desk in 1951; the second, grainy and fuzzy, revealed Mary Pickford seated at hers, basking in the smiles of Charlie Chaplin, D. W. Griffith, and Douglas Fairbanks in 1919. Corporate photographs, both . . . *united artists.*

I emerged from the Thalberg Building into an oppressive yellowish smog through which even the wind-whipped palm trees half a block away on West Washington Boulevard were dim shapes in the haze. Escaping for only a few hours would be a relief. The car was at the curb, air conditioning roaring, and the driver bullied his way through the back streets of Culver City to have me at the Western Airlines terminal in ten minutes. On the way something nagged at me, something dark and stately just outside the periphery of my memory's vision. Of course. Crossing the building lobby, I had glimpsed, as I did several times each day, the bronze bust of Irving Thalberg, pedestaled there in memoriam. *Use that?* I wondered. *How about the name of the building, too, and the dopey street and bungalow names: Ince Way, the Gable Building, the Garland Building? Or "Mrs. Mayer's Chicken Soup" and "The Luciano Pavarotti Diet Special"? Hell, I might as well claim Griffith Park is named after D.W. because it should be, even though it isn't.*

As I strapped myself into the seat on flight 723, the $35 million script bag under the seat in front of me, I realized this was grasping at pretty flimsy straws. But flimsy straws were all I had. The figures from the National Research Group weren't going to help, and I needed help: I was flying to San Francisco to keep them from changing the name of the company I worked for, United Artists.

In mid-flight I read the following:

Although United Artists and these other companies are well-known to the general public, very few people are able to associate specific movies with the producing companies. For example, only 4% knew who brought the God-father movies to the screen; only 6% knew who brought out Star Wars and

The Empire Strikes Back; 7% *could identify who made* The James Bond *movies and* 6% Rocky I *and* Rocky II; *and only* 3% *could correctly identify the makers of* Smokey and the Bandit *I or II.* The Pink Panther *movies drew the highest correct identification of moviemaker on our list, with* 8% *correctly identifying United Artists.*

That was sobering enough, but an accompanying table indicated that fully 73 percent of the American public could not associate any movie at all with its releasing company.

Well, what did it really matter? I wondered as the plane banked in over San Francisco International Airport. The sky was blue and clear except for some low clouds or fog nuzzling hilltop houses, where people were getting on with their lives just fine without knowing who released what. What difference did it make if Paramount or Warner Brothers or the Acme Widget Company had produced and released *Casablanca? Casablanca* was *Casablanca* was *Casablanca,* I reminded myself as the plane taxied to a stop.

I looked at my watch. Andy would now be somewhere over the Nevada desert, and I had a good two hours before the four-thirty meeting.

Inside the terminal a driver in a dark blue chauffeur's uniform held a sign chalked with my name. I introduced myself and told him where we were going. We pushed through the crowded shuttle gate to the exit, got into the car, and headed for the city. As we passed Candlestick Park and the Cow Palace, I roused myself from gloom and asked the driver, who would have looked equally competent behind the wheel of a Mack truck or tractor, "You ever heard of United Artists?"

"The movie people?" He glanced into the rearview mirror.

"That's right," I said, encouraged.

"Sure." He nodded. Then, after a moment of eyeing me in the mirror, he asked, "You in the movies?"

"Movie business."

"Yeah?" he said, brightening. "I drive a lot of you movie people. We have premieres here all the time and a film festival. A lot of you people come up for sneak previews and productions and I don't know what all. I drove, oh, you know—what's his name?—that big producer for a whole week once, twenty-four hours a day." He thought of the name. *"That* was a blast! You movie people!" he said, chuckling loudly in memory of the shenanigans of what's his name. I knew what's his name; I could just imagine. Twenty-four hours a day. On whose tab? I wondered.

As the car proceeded toward the city, I listened with half an ear to a discourse about Francis Ford Coppola and George Lucas, who lived there or nearby and *The Streets of San Francisco* television show and more. I was concentrating on the skyline, dominated by the chalk white exclamation point of the pyramid in the financial district, gliding behind intervening buildings only to reappear in some new alignment to them. If ever a city's topography made a skyline superfluous, it is San Francisco's, but I found the combination of sea and sky and bay and hills and buildings exciting. I even liked the pyramid, a structure of some civic controversy, which the driver pointed out with "There it is—the Transamerica Building. We'll be there in ten minutes."

I changed my mind and decided not to go there immediately. I still had plenty of time before the meeting and asked the driver to loop through Golden Gate Park on the way, to give me some time to think. He nodded, swerved away from downtown, and turned his curiosity from a question to a statement: "I can't figure why a movie person would be going to an insurance company anyway."

"Transamerica owns United Artists," I explained.

"No kidding?" he said. Then: "What do you do in the movies?"

"I'm head of production for the company."

"Is that like a production manager?"

"Yeah, I guess so. Something like that. Yeah."

My mind started rehearsing. *Metro-Goldwyn-Mayer will always be linked to Louis B. Mayer and Irving Thalberg, businessmen; Warner Brothers, to the Warners; Columbia, to the Cohns; Paramount, to Zukor. But United Artists will forever be Mary Pickford—*

Bad beginning. Suppose Transamerica's chairman didn't want to identify with Mary Pickford?

Tradition, I began again. *Company pride* . . . Wait a minute. That might connote pride in United Artists but none in Transamerica. Not brilliant. Much less than perfect. Tradition was too abstract, anyway, sentimentally so at that. It might have some meaning for the thousands of UA employees in 113 offices in fifty-nine countries around the world, but if it had any sympathetic force with Transamerica, we wouldn't be having this meeting in the first place. Tradition wasn't marketable; that was the point I would hear in rebuttal, a point I could myself reinforce with the National Research Group's unpleasant statistics.

As the car circled slowly through the park, I pulled the shiny green folder again from my script bag. Inside, Rita had clipped an article two or three weeks old from the *New Yorker*: Pauline Kael, answering her own question "Why Are Movies So Bad?" with "The Numbers." Oversimplifying every step of the way, she trashed the conglomerates—exactly like Transamerica—that owned the movie companies. Their pernicious influence, from executive suite to mail room, Explained It All. Still, maybe there was an argument to be made here, that a conglomerate's respect for a sixty-one-year-old name would give the lie to Kael's thesis. No. Not unless I was prepared to recommend we announce we were letting Pauline Kael guide corporate policy. Besides, her sweeping denunciations seemed unlikely to lighten the mood at a meeting I hoped would remain tactful. How tactful could it be with "Part of what has deranged American life in this past decade is the change in book publishing and in magazines and newspapers and in the movies as they have passed out of the control of those whose lives were bound up in them and into the control of conglomerates, financiers, and managers who treat them as ordinary commodities." Perhaps perfectly true, but not much help. Transamerica's chairman was a strong-willed, proud man, who had plaques and scrolls testifying to his contributions to American life, not to his derangement of it. The strength of Pauline Kael's argument, possibly even its correctness, precluded my using it.

I closed the folder, took a fresh shirt out of my script bag, and as I tied a sincere tie around my sincere button-down collar, I reflected there was simply no argument I could advance that was not sentimental. Who besides me, or film cranks, cared about a name? Pickford, Chaplin, Fairbanks, and Griffith were dead. So I feared was I as the car headed back to the city and 600 Montgomery Street. There was no way sentiment was going to keep them from calling it Transamerica Films.

Albeck was already meeting privately with UA's Chairman (and President of Transamerica) James Harvey by the time I left the elevator on the pyramid's twenty-fifth floor. Harvey's secretary, Jeannette McGinley fixed me a cup of black coffee, which I allowed to grow cold. I watched Jeannette at her hushed and efficient work, silhouetted against the windows and the late-afternoon clouds rolling in to mask the blue. Her orderly calm was so different from the telephone-jangling circus on West Washington Boulevard that it seemed a reproach to my overreaction to the name change and to the movie business itself.

I glanced at a copy of the glossy, colorful annual report casually positioned for visitor perusal. As I read the figures for airlines and rent-a-cars and insurance policies and turbines, I realized I couldn't care less. I didn't scorn them; I just didn't want to identify with Mr. DeLaval of DeLaval Turbine, whoever he might be. I wanted to identify with Griffith and Chaplin and that crowd. Yes, Krim and that crowd, too. Being head of worldwide production for Transamerica Films instead of United Artists would induce some kind of corporate identity crisis that

I knew I would not be alone in feeling. Changing the company's name was to cut us off from the company's history, a kind of moral (and morale) sustenance derived from its past and from its function as well. Most important, it would deprive us of the perhaps illusory but nonetheless effective belief that what we were doing had continuity and permanence.

I studied the sleek graphs and multicolored charts and the glossy corporate smiles beaming up at me from the pages on my lap; there was Mr. Beckett, chairman, smart and rich and decent, too. He knew a hell of a lot that I didn't know: He knew that I didn't make the product at all; *he* did. I just made—or caused to be made—the penultimate product. And all along, I mused as I watched Jeannette's immaculate calm, I thought I had been hired to make movies.

At four-thirty or a few minutes before, Jim Harvey and Andy Albeck emerged from Jim's office, Jim tall and friendly and capable-looking in shirt sleeves and silk rep tie. He radiated Princeton and the Bohemian Club and success. Andy looked efficient, crisp, and well organized, showing not a trace of his five-hour flight from New York.

We went into a small conference room, where we waited for Mr. Beckett and, to kill time, discussed the plans for the new offices UA would occupy sometime during the coming year. Three floor plans had been prepared by a go-go New York and Los Angeles design firm, which liked to demonstrate its oh-wow verve. The first plan was a simple grid, boxes in a row that made conventional sense and would have been equally suitable on a not very reduced scale for a kennel. The second was slightly more daring but without distinction. The third plan, the drop-dead prizewinner, was radically different, with broad corridors running along the perimeter of the space, giving window views of the courtyard gardens to all secretaries and visitors. Executive offices were designed as interior islands, diagonally placed glass enclosures which could be opened to the view or curtained and shuttered off for privacy. Elsewhere floating panels could alter space and function. It was the least orthodox, hardest to "read," and costliest of the plans. Jim found it "bizarre" but "different"; Andy thought it "radical and uneconomical" and announced his selection of the simple, logical grid on grounds of cost and practicality. The designs would be shown as a courtesy to Beckett after the meeting.

John Beckett arrived: tall, rangy, white-haired, with a crooked grin that angled beneath eyes so sharp they seemed honed and polished. In the movies he could have been played by Arthur O'Connell, I thought, and found it hard to imagine, except for his air of easy authority that his unpretentious manner had for twenty years commanded a multi-billion-dollar corporation that owned not only UA but also Occidental Life, Budget Rent-A-Car, TransInternational Airlines, among other companies. He had real power and took it for granted you knew it and respected it as much as he did. He had given Harvey his own president's desk in January, and it was understood that Harvey would assume Beckett's duties as chief executive at the end of the year and the chairmanship when Beckett decided to relinquish it. That wasn't to be quite yet, and the fact made even more curious the easy, folksy tone of his speech.

He took a seat with the rest of us around a small table and thanked me for coming up from Los Angeles. "What do you think of our little idea?" He grinned, getting directly to business with cracker-barrel crispness.

"Not much," I answered, as flatly as I could.

"Tell me why," he said, unstartled. I thought for a moment he hadn't heard me, but he had and was listening.

"It's the creative community," I answered, hoping to focus the argument someplace outside myself. "There is a tradition that creative people like to feel part of. Whether it's sentimental or even romantic, it's real. United Artists is the only major company founded by creative people. The name is one of the oldest and most important in movie history, and with all due respect, the company would *not* smell as sweet bearing the name of a financial institution. They don't call Paramount Gulf and Western Pictures, and they don't call Random House RCA Books. *Transamerica Films* will say to the creative community only that the corporation regards itself as more important than the tradition behind it and the people who make the product that makes the money. It's not the name per se; it's what changing the name implies about the company's attitude toward the people who do the work. And if they don't question the attitude, the press will. Loudly."

It was a windy mouthful, and Beckett listened politely. Andy nodded support at my side, and Jim remained attentively silent.

"What effect will it have on business?" Beckett asked.

"The business of selling or the business of attracting talent?"

"Marketing," he said. "I prefer to call it marketing. That's where our emphasis should be."

"Probably none," I admitted, disliking question and answer.

Beckett nodded. "I understand what you're saying," he replied in a tone subdued enough to indicate he did. "I know how . . . *emotional* Hollywood people can be. God knows they're up here fast enough to complain to Jim every time they don't like *your* attitude." He let it sink in gently, then brushed it aside as something pesky and unimportant. "But we depend on you to handle the creative people. That's your job, and we're confident you'll do it well." He looked into the clouds over San Francisco as if collecting there a final thought, then twisted in his chair back into the room and leaned both forearms heavily on the table.

"Gosh," he said with a shake of the head, "the reason we bought the darn company in the first place was we hoped it would have some effect on the Transamerica stock, and it never has. I don't know why. Paramount gooses Gulf and Western, and Universal pushes up MCA, but even at our most successful you boys—and the previous gang, too— have just never had any effect on our stock. That's a *shame* because the stock ought to reflect your successes. You're a stockholder, too," he reminded me. "We all are." His gesture around the table made us a club.

"You boys will be down a little this year. Can't be helped. Nobody expects anybody to bat a thousand. You'll come in somewhere between twenty and twenty-five million dollars net, down some from last year. Not what we'd hoped, but with interest rates what they are . . . *And,* you'll see, it won't affect TA's stock at all. Up or down, it doesn't seem to matter. And darn it, I think it's because the general public just doesn't know we're in bed with you fellas. We've tried everything. Those annual analysts' meetings in New York, for example. All we get is lunch and time away from the office that would be better spent *in* the office." He turned to Harvey. "What was that line we used on the logo?"

"'Entertainment from Transamerica Corporation,'" Jim quoted.

"That's it. It was too long to register or something, so we simplified it to 'A Transamerica Company' and used the TA logo alongside, and that hasn't worked either. People just don't associate United Artists with Transamerica."

I didn't say that maybe the problem was that Transamerica was such a colorless, generic name that *it* was the one that should be changed (its public recognition score was 67 percent, but only 18 percent could correctly identify any business it was in). I had a more important point. "You make it hard for me. My job is not easier if I have to explain to people who are, as you point out, emotional that a respected name is being changed because of some effect it might have on the Transamerica stock."

He gave a slight shrug and bent over to retrieve a large piece of heavy cardboard leaning against the wall in the corner. He placed it faceup on the table before us, and we could see through the translucent protective covering that it was some kind of storyboard. He lifted the cover, and there it was: an almost frame-by-frame rendering of the new leader, the five or six seconds of film before the movie starts that identify the releasing company. It was beautifully, expensively prepared, perhaps twenty separate drawings illustrating the movement of the current logo: the words *United Artists* followed by *A Transamerica Company* in smaller type. As the words began mechanically to alter in size, the *United Artists* grew smaller and smaller and the sub line grew larger and larger until the word *Transamerica* filled the screen.

"This is how we'll begin," he explained. "We'll use this to get people used to the idea of Transamerica, and then, say, eighteen months from now we'll drop the United Artists, or maybe we'll begin before that to reverse the order." His hands moved right over left, illustrating his point. "It will read 'Transamerica' first, with 'United Artists' underneath. I don't know. We can play with it. But finally we'll switch to Transamerica Films. *Gradually.* That's the key. What do you say to eighteen months?"

"Two years," I said automatically.

"I think eighteen months will do it," he answered, and I wondered exactly when he would be stepping down as chairman.

It had all been decided. I had flown up from Los Angeles for nothing but a courtesy meeting, probably urged on Beckett by Andy at that. The market survey had been a shot in the dark, a misfire that would serve Beckett's purposes, not mine, if he knew about it, and no figures or polls or discussions or sentimental arguments were going to alter a *fait accompli. That's what you get to do when you're the boss,* I reflected as Beckett turned swiftly to the matter of the offices, looking over the plans with lively interest, chuckling when he saw the layout of the diagonal glass islands and surrounding corridors giving onto the courtyard.

"What do you say, Andy?" he asked without looking up.

Andy briskly pointed out the cost efficiency of the grid plan which had been approved.

Beckett listened, nodded, considered. He then turned to me. "And you?"

I didn't care much at this point, but I looked at the renderings and said, "Plan One is boring. Plan Two is just an attempt not to look like Plan One. Plan Three has some drama."

"Drama!" exclaimed Beckett. "I think so, too. You fellas are in a business that's supposed to have some drama, aren't you?" He turned to Andy. "What do you say?"

Andy recognized a fiat when he heard one. He glanced at me and said simply, "Plan Three. We want Steve to be happy."

"You're the one who'll be living there," Beckett drawled to me cheerfully, and in spite of my surprise, I realized how predictable it was. The man who had reshaped San Francisco's skyline with a controversial white pyramid and was about to change a company's name to memorialize his own career—not Mary Pickford's or Arthur Krim's—would, of course, opt for the most dramatic, most attention-riveting design. And he would feel he had given me something, even as he had taken something away.

To soften the blow of "Transamerica Films" and because he had pride in his domain, he offered to show me around the pyramid because it was my first time inside in the more than two years I had worked for the company. The interior was modern but not stark, functional but not without personality. The walls were hung with contemporary paintings, each by a California artist, each personally selected by Beckett. He commented on his selections with almost fervent precision and feeling. The taste was not folksy. The sharp eyes could see.

He took me up to the twenty-sixth floor, the topmost, one large room with a 360-degree view of San Francisco below. It was possible to stand in the middle of the room and, with a simple turn, survey the horizon in every direction. No wonder he wanted to show it off.

"We use this room for small gatherings, cocktail parties, that sort of thing," he said. "Feel free to use it. Just call Jim's secretary anytime you're in town and want to give a party. This isn't *our* room; it's for all of Transamerica, the 'family,'" he stressed, "and we want you to feel that."

I nodded, doubting I would ever invite anyone there but mollified that he had had the courtesy to make the offer. He knew he had steamrollered me and, quite apart from his right to do so, he seemed to be paying deference to my disappointment.

We went downstairs, where I excused myself to catch the Western Airlines shuttle back to Los Angeles. Just before I left, Beckett said, "There's one other thing I should add about this company name thing." The easy cadence crept back in his speech. "I'm just sick and tired of all the rumors about United Artists. Sick and tired of all the things I read in the press. It just seems to me that when we call the company Transamerica Films, that will shut up those rumors once and for all. Then they'll *know*," he said with evident and earnest sincerity, "this company is *not for sale*."

CHAPTER I

MOVIE PEOPLE

The fish stinks from the head.

**—variously attributed to Adolph Zukor
and Samuel Goldwyn (circa 1930)**

There is an antique strip of silent film barely two minutes long that is perhaps unique in motion-picture and business history. It is in two parts, two simple cuts. The first records the ritual signing of incorporation papers, and there is an appropriate solemnity as signatures are affixed to documents dated February 5, 1919. The scene is artlessly composed and shot and would be of no visual interest whatever were it not that the four signatories, the founding partners of the newly formed United Artists Corporation, were perhaps the four most famous people on earth.

One of them, known as America's Sweetheart, was romantically involved with another (the swashbuckling one) in a courtship that would soon thrill whole continents as few celluloid fictions ever would. The third, the tall, craggy one, is generally regarded as the single most seminal figure in film history (at the very least the father of American film), and the fourth created a persona who, twirling his cane as he lurches off bravely to confront capricious fate, may have become the most beloved and best-known film image of all time.

In this documentary snippet all is entrepreneurial sobriety. Mary Pickford's famous curls are pulled up and back, and she wears a tasteful black dress and a single strand of discreet pearls; Chaplin, without mustache or cane, wears a dark tie with three-piece suit of somber cut and looks the circumspect gentleman of means. D. W. Griffith, too, wears dark tie and vested suit; but the fabric is a relaxed pale tweed, and of all of them, his hawklike face would most suggest movie star dash were it not for the somewhat portly Douglas Fairbanks (soon to become the bridegroom of the female founder-partner), actorishly attired like the Broadway dandy he recently was, in natty striped tie and double-

breasted suit coat with soaring eagle-wing lapels. Lawyers hover solic-
itously as this celebrated quartet primly sign their brainchild into being.

Abruptly the film cuts to its second part, a studio back lot where the
Big Four (the papers called them that) shed their corporate poses to
become camera creatures: The hair of America's Sweetheart cascades in
glinting curls, and she beams the ingenuous, world-winning smile;
Chaplin, got up now as the Little Tramp, burlesques Fairbanks's swashbuckling acrobatics; Fairbanks returns the compliment, imitating the
Tramp's splay-footed walk; and Griffith, paternalistically amused, allows
the hollows of his craggy face to fill with smiles as he fondly observes
actors who (at this moment anyway) require no direction.

It is only newsreel and publicity footage to launch the hopeful new
company they named after themselves; for the first time a group of
motion-picture artists had banded together to control their creative and
economic destinies. Richard Schickel has called it their "bold venture,"
but a wag of the day famously wisecracked, "The lunatics have taken
charge of the asylum." Today, more than six decades later, it is tempting to read into these two minutes of fuzzy, grainy film not merely the
balancing of the first cut's tycoon gravity by the second's antic exuberance but that more difficult and delicate balance these four hoped to
bring to their art, which happened to be—then as now—also an industry and very big business.

They formed United Artists in hopes of resolving the "art versus
business" conflict under which all four had until now chafed, a conflict
which seemingly began with the first nickel's plunk into the first nickelodeon. That they did not resolve it, that it has remained stubbornly
resistant to resolution and remains the dominating central issue of
American motion pictures to the present day suggest that the conflict
may, in fact, be irresolvable, a false dichotomy, less "either/or" than
"both/and." Perhaps that scrap of film hints at this. Did the anonymous
cameraman freeze in time artists playing at enterprise or entrepreneurs
playing at art? Or subtly varied gradations of both? The image is
blurred. On film and in fact.

The business of the art the Big Four united to serve began with
machines, gadgets really, and its history is crowded with claimants for
the invention of the many and various mechanical devices or processes
which permitted the photographing and projection of images that
seemed to move as they flickered by at so many frames per second (now
twenty-four). The most famous, Thomas A. Edison, actually invented
his process to provide pictorial accompaniment for the sounds re-

produced by his earlier invention, the talking machine, having in effect invented talking pictures a generation before Al Jolson forever shattered the silence of the novelty Edison thought negligible anyway. Even the most visionary of these early inventors and gadgeteers seem to have seen none of the global and social impact these light and shadow machines would produce. It fell rather to young, hustling (often immigrant) junk dealers, furriers, glove salesman to spy, if not the ultimate potential of a new medium, a new and exciting way to make a buck. And as those bucks began to accumulate from the nickels proliferating in the scores, then in the hundreds, then in the thousands of nickelodeons springing up as the century turned, mere flickers of light inspired flickers of greed. The novelty machines, or the patents governing their design and manufacture, seemed suddenly not negligible at all.

The storied early days of motion pictures in America were days of sternly enforced monopoly by the controllers of those patents. The furriers and junk dealers went on scrambling, ignominiously securing their pieces of the action in storefront movie parlors or as itinerant projectionists, moving from town to town with projectors, reels of film, and bedsheets for screens. They hustled and schlepped and gypsied cross country and ignored patent law; what they didn't ignore were the customers. These renegade showmen (pioneers we call them today) were learning not only to make money catch as catch could but also their audiences' rapidly changing tastes, expectations, and dreams.

The patent holders were not much interested in dreams. Instead, they formed the Motion Picture Patents Company, which they called (with refreshing frankness) the Trust, to monopolize and control the burgeoning novelty. Monopoly meant just that: No film could legally be made, distributed, or exhibited without licensing agreements with the Trust. Eastman Kodak colluded with other Trust members to sell its raw film stock only to Trust licensees; finished film of a length decreed by the Trust (perhaps the first-known instance of final cut) could be exhibited only in theaters bound by Trust agreements, could be projected only on projectors covered by Trust patents, and only so long as those projectors remained undefiled by celluloid which, in some renegade fashion, had evaded the Trust's tentacles.

It worked with a merry vengeance from about 1908 to 1912, with energetic, sometimes violent enforcement of Trust dictates by federal marshals or hired goons, who not only swept up the little competitors but also kept licensees in line when they showed signs of wandering. Police prevention of unauthorized use of Trust equipment—equipment essential to the whole process—forced many outlaw producers farther and farther from the Trust's most effective area of domination, the East.

In legend, at least, it was Southern California's proximity to the Mexican border and consequent safety from prosecution that accounted for movies' establishing their foothold on the West Coast, although the easy accessibility of mountains, sea, and desert was probably an equal lure. "A tree's a tree," someone pointed out.

These fugitive early filmmakers were in a sense the first auteurs, and there were hundreds of them, creating their own action in Chicago, Cuba, Florida, California—anywhere there was something to shoot and light to shoot it in. They behaved with all the circumspection of uninhibited pirates.

The Trust, meanwhile, widened its net and began in 1910 to buy up rival film exchanges in an effort to stem this buccaneer bravado by controlling not only the manufacture and exhibition of movies but also their distribution. After a single year the Trust's distribution subsidiary was with only one exception the sole film distributor in America. It was the perfect vertical monopoly. Antitrust action was eventually successful when pressed, but the restraints of the Trust were ultimately undone less by the provisions of the Sherman Antitrust Act than by the very success of the nickel-spinning novelty itself.

Audiences by the tens of thousands craved flickers and couldn't have cared less if the flicker was blessed with patent legitimacy or not. This rapacious audience hunger was not only growing but changing. The early thrill, when any piece of film depicting anything that moved—a parade, a fire engine, a train pulling into a station, a sneeze, a kiss—was gone, and it was the outlaw producers who were there to see and hear and sense the change. The members of the Trust were in touch with their lawyers; the early filmmakers and exhibitors were in touch with their audiences.

By this time, around the start of World War I, story films had achieved dominance as the preferred entertainment. Since Edwin S. Porter's *The Great Train Robbery* just after the turn of the century, stories—stories about people, which meant actors, which meant new and vexing problems ahead—grew longer and more complex in the telling, until D. W. Griffith's *The Birth of a Nation* in 1915 forever altered the way film would be made and viewed. *The Birth of a Nation*'s more than two-hour length dealt a deathblow to the standard one-reel (about ten minutes) product of the Trust. Griffith's masterpiece not only would hold for two hours it would (a contemporary reviewer promised) "make you laugh . . . make you cry . . . make you angry . . . make you glad . . . make you hate . . . make you love." In just over two hours D. W. Griffith turned a lunatic whisper into a battle cry. This upstart, lower-class peep show pastime, this mute flicker of shadow play, this—this

. . . *novelty* had become, of all things, the art form of the twentieth
century.

In the early and mid-1910s, small production companies numbered
in the hundreds in America. The sheer volume of their activity, coupled with their audiences' indifference to patent credentials—or more
relevantly, to the entertainment offered in the Trust's standardized
product—busted the Trust. As Europe lurched into armed conflict, another war was being fought in America, a ruthless combat for box office.

The key to the box office was not production but distribution, and
the great pioneers who were to become moguls and tycoons and czars
were almost never producers (though they often called themselves
that). Rather, they were exhibitors or distributors who had a clear,
simple need that continues to the present day: product.

Of the major motion-picture companies, almost all began production as a means of supplying product to the distribution or exhibition
arms of then vertically structured companies embracing all phases of the
process, from production to exhibition. The great exception was United
Artists, which was founded not as a production company at all but as a
pure distribution company because distribution was where the money,
the really *big* money was. (Some would say *is*.)

The economics have hardly changed during the century, though the
numbers are now larger and what the government will allow has radically modified actual operations. A distributor charges a fee, normally
around 30 percent of the box-office gross, for the services he renders in
getting the film from theater to theater, providing advertising campaigns, promotion, and so on. This 30 percent is before profits (if any),
in which the distribution company's production or financing arm may
share typically another 50 percent or more. The great majority of films
today never achieve profit—that is, a level of financial return at which
the filmmaker will share in revenues. But the distributor's 30 percent is
inviolate and in what is called first position. The distributor is simply
closer to the well, and once the machinery for film distribution was in
place, the great controlling fact of the movie business as business became and remains: the machine must be fed.

Hardly any of this was lost on the smartest of the independents
during the heyday of the Trust. Their often maverick approach to material, their fringe positions left them unfettered by whatever standards or
formulas for "entertainment" the gentlemen of the Trust had con-
cocted. The independents noticed something else, too: Their custom-

ers, "those wonderful people out there in the dark" (as a famous movie later called them), had stars in their eyes.

Early in the 1910s one of the first and strongest opponents of the Trust, Adolph Zukor, imported a French film starring Sarah Bernhardt as *Queen Elizabeth*, an experiment so prestigious and successful it led Zukor into production on his own with well-known stage personalities of the day. (His aptly named Famous Players in Famous Plays would evolve into Paramount Pictures.) Zukor probably did as much as anyone in these still early but wildly lucrative days to introduce the much feared star system. Whether he and others, seeking exploitable values in their films, actually created the system or merely bowed to its inevitability is moot; it was a system whose time had come for tens of millions of weekly moviegoers.

As these loyal, avid spectators responded more and more reliably to certain kinds of stories, certain kinds of actors found more and more work, and public curiosity about them inevitably followed. Satisfying this curiosity later proved to have enormous economic consequences for producers, who painted themselves as helpless victims of a spontaneous and inexorable public phenomenon. Maybe so, but it was a phenomenon eagerly exploited by Zukor and others, who used it to attract or even guarantee an audience for the product. Thus, Carl Laemmle, head of IMP (a predecessor of the present Universal), lured a popular but anonymous actress from the Trust's Biograph Studios (who had neatly identified her only as "The Biograph Girl") and broadcast her name to the general public, creating in effect the first Movie Star: the euphoniously named Florence Lawrence. Public response was immediate, and so was that of other players, many of them bravely prepared to follow Miss Lawrence's lead and sacrifice anonymity for fame. *Après Florence le déluge.*

Before there were any stars and especially during the unlamented days of the Trust, most pictures were rented or sold at a flat rate regardless of content or cast. Suddenly the entire structure of pricing individual pictures changed, with higher prices demanded for bigger star names and, in some cases, director names in much the same manner that prevails today.

For the luckiest distributors, those with a Pickford, a Chaplin, a Fairbanks under contract, the vehicles of these stars were used to guarantee playing time for the companies' lesser product in a scheme known as block booking. Under this system an exhibitor might be forced to accept five or six as yet unmade pictures of uncertain quality to get the "new Pickford." This leverage would become vital when a company like Paramount began churning out pictures at the rate of 2 a week, an A and a B, or 104 per year, about the entire output of all Hollywood studios as this is written.

The biggest stars then were pulling not only their own expensive weight but everybody else's as well and were in effect subsidizing the distribution companies to which they were under contract. Some of the stars were actually smart enough to figure this out and, having shed along with privacy and anonymity any inhibitions they might have had about demanding remuneration commensurate with these sacrifices, escalated the salary game still higher. The early moguls now found themselves being wagged by what had seemed the most negligible of tails: *actors*. And no mogul was being wagged more vigorously than Zukor, by a petite blond Canadian girl named Gladys Smith, whose name in lights was spelled Mary Pickford. Who had friends.

If her pictures were so important to Mr. Zukor, she reasoned, how important might they be for her on her own or with a few close friends to lend encouragement and clout, like Fairbanks (a friend getting closer and closer), Chaplin, and Griffith? Why should Zukor keep half the profits and all the distribution fee? Who was earning the money anyway? It was time for art for artists' sake.

Pickford, Fairbanks, Chaplin, and Griffith all had, it happens, participated in a phenomenally successful Liberty loan tour near the end of the war, along with William S. Hart, who almost made the Big Four the Big Five but pulled out at the last moment. Perhaps it was on this tour, when they confronted at first hand the living, breathing, cheering human proof of their popularity, shelling out record sums for war bonds at the stars' urging, that the idea of United Artists was born. (It seems likely, though there is some dispute. B. P. Schulberg, later head of production at Paramount, said it was his idea and won an out-of-court settlement when he said so to a judge.) However or wherever the idea arose, it has over the years become encrusted with romance: Art would prevail; business would bow; creative freedom would out.

The interesting reality is that by 1919 each of the founders already had his (or her) own production company within one of the existing major companies, each operated with an astonishing degree of creative freedom, and each was as famous and adored and well paid as it had been the good fortune of very few people in history, and no one else at all in the movies, to be. Not only that, but they were young. What they didn't have was autonomy.

• • •

Mary Pickford had been inveigled into movie acting ten years earlier, in 1909, by young D. W. Griffith for $5 a day, working for the Trust's Biograph Studios on Fourteenth Street in New York (which both would soon leave over just such Trust issues as those described above). Lillian Gish was to relate over dinner at Lüchow's (just down the street from Biograph) some seventy years after the fact that one of the reasons she and Gladys Smith were willing to forsake the stage for flickers was Griffith's habit of inviting them to lunch at the very same Lüchow's, which neither young actress could then afford.

Ten years later Mary Pickford was producing her own films and making $10,000 a week when the income tax was 6 percent and the buying power of the dollar such that she could no doubt have *bought* Lüchow's had she cared to, and at a good price, too, for she was no mean negotiator. When she prepared to sign her contract with Zukor, she balked at the last minute, insisting she be paid for the four weeks in which the two had wrangled over terms. Zukor paid the $40,000.

Chaplin's rise was even swifter. An unknown English vaudevillian in 1913, by 1916 he, too, was earning $10,000 weekly (plus lavish bonuses), and at the time of the formation of United Artists, not ten years after his obscure arrival in the United States, he had a contract with Zukor's chief rival, First National (a forerunner of Warner Brothers), to produce and star in eight pictures over an eighteen-month period, for which he was to receive $1 million and 50 percent of the profits.

Fairbanks, unlike Pickford and Chaplin, had already achieved some celebrity on the stage before reluctantly succumbing to movie money in 1915, but by the end of the following year his pictures were being made by the Douglas Fairbanks Picture Corporation and were being distributed by Zukor.

Griffith at forty-four was the oldest of the quartet and senior to them in experience. A former actor and playwright, he entered films in 1908 as a scenario writer and actor for the same $5 a day he offered Mary Pickford a year later, when he himself was making only double that. The swiftness of his rise is properly overshadowed by the transformation of the medium which it accomplished; still, it is worth noting that between 1908 and 1915 he had completed 451 films, including *The Birth of a Nation,* and, in the words of the Museum of Modern Art's Iris Barry, had "established the motion picture once and for all as the most popular and persuasive of entertainments and compelled the acceptance of the film as art." By 1919 he had added *Intolerance* and *Hearts of the World* (and others) to the canon and was releasing through

Zukor, who had meanwhile lost Pickford to a better offer from First National.

All the money and fame and freedom and "film as art" were fine, but they were subject to the pleasure of the distributors like Zukor and First National, a pleasure that showed signs of strain from ever-escalating artistic demands. Rumor was rife, in fact, in 1919 that Zukor and First National were plotting a merger, which would virtually eliminate competition for stars and directors, would be in effect a new Trust, and would end the very system that had done so much to enhance the lives of the Big Four. Whether ending the star system might or might not have been possible or a good thing is debated still, but any threat to the star marketplace was not to be taken lightly by *stars*—or star directors. If by creating their own company they could remove themselves from and even thwart a Zukor-First National cabal, they would be doing a favor for not only themselves and their fellow artists but the public as well, as their press release announcing the formation of United Artists pointed out: "We . . . think that this step is positively and absolutely necessary to protect the great motion picture public from threatening combinations and trusts that would force upon them mediocre productions and machine-made entertainment."

"The great motion picture public" would benefit, to be sure, but so would they, particularly if the merger rumor were true. (It was.) United Artists was to be their own distribution company for films they were to produce through their own production companies. UA was to distribute at rates closer to the actual cost of distribution than the arbitrary 30 or 40 percent of the majors, thus making profits to the producers (themselves) more nearly reflective of their box-office power, and they were to share in distribution profits, too. They were to have their autonomy and not just a piece of the action but the Action itself.

There was a very large wrinkle, one unique in motion-picture history, perhaps the one that made them appear lunatics to many in the industry: Their films would be not only self-produced and self-distributed but self-financed as well. Each partner agreed to deliver three pictures a year, giving the small distribution company a release schedule of one picture per month. It didn't work out that way.

Not that things started badly. They started with a commercial and artistic maturity, even mastery, that surely justified every hope—public or private, pious or profane—the founders had had for their fledgling enterprise. The first UA release in 1919, Fairbanks in *His Majesty, the American,* was a solid hit, and the second, Griffith's *Broken Blossoms,* a financial success still ranked as one of Griffith's masterpieces. The problem wasn't quality or commercial appeal; it was when? How often?

The three-pictures-per-year quota was never to be met. Pickford in 1919 was still tied to First National and was further slowed down by divorce proceedings from her first husband, Owen Moore, and the worldwide circus occasioned by her second marriage to Fairbanks. Chaplin was still living out his $1 million contract at First National, and not until 1923 was he to deliver to UA a picture, *A Woman of Paris*, which he directed but did not star in. His first starring vehicle for the company was *The Gold Rush* in late 1925, six years and seventeen pictures late. Griffith, too, was tied to other contracts and was suffering financial strain he would never conquer as the result of the overhead on his Mamaroneck studio.

Survival at UA therefore required attracting other producing artists into the venture. The lures of autonomy, customized release, reduced distribution fees, and sometimes even partnership status did not often offset the quid pro quo: self-financing. Few stars then or later had the cash or desire so to put themselves on the line. It was the reason William S. Hart had bailed out before the beginning, and the idea held little appeal for John Barrymore or any of the other talents they pursued in spite of the impressive artistic and financial example the four were providing for the artistic community. Self-employment, in fact, was yielding some of the biggest hits and most prestigious work of their careers.

Griffith made for UA release not only *Broken Blossoms* but also *Way Down East*, *Orphans of the Storm*, *Isn't Life Wonderful*, and others. Fairbanks contributed *The Mark of Zorro*, *The Three Musketeers*, *Robin Hood*, *The Thief of Baghdad*, *The Black Pirate*, *The Iron Mask*, and *The Taming of the Shrew*, which he coproduced and costarred in with Pickford. She, during UA's first decade, produced and starred in *Pollyanna*, *Little Lord Fauntleroy*, *Tess of the Storm Country*, *Rosita*, *Dorothy Vernon of Haddon Hall*, *Little Annie Rooney*, *Sparrows*, and *Coquette*, for which she won an Academy Award. Chaplin's pictures included *The Circus*, *City Lights*, and later *Modern Times* and *The Great Dictator*. This array of pictures is simply an unprecedented body of work produced by filmmakers at the peak of their powers, artistic, commercial, or both. It just wasn't enough.

The artists had never actually run the "asylum." They made (or didn't make) their pictures and hired businessmen to run the company and sell the product. By the mid-twenties, however, it was clear that if

UA was to survive, they needed more than administrators and sales-men. They needed an executive who could command respect on Wall Street and with the bankers, who could reorganize the company's cap-ital structure, and, most important, attract talent: a movieman, some-one who understood not only the numbers but audiences, movies, and the people who made them. In Joseph M. Schenck they found a movieman of the first rank.

Schenck and his brother, Nick, were Russian immigrants who had early deserted the pharmacy business for entertainment and the Pal-isades Amusement Park in New Jersey. They entered movies by way of the giant Loew's theater chain, which created Metro-Goldwyn-Mayer in 1924 to ensure a steady flow of product. Nick Schenck stayed on to become chairman (hence Louis B. Mayer's boss), while Joe Schenck began producing pictures in 1917.

Seven years later Joe Schenck agreed to come to United Artists, and he brought with him not only his production experience and busi-ness acumen but his wife, Norma Talmadge, then an important star; his brother-in-law, Buster Keaton; and Rudolph Valentino, too. After re-organizing the financial structure of the company and persuading the banks to supply production financing for new pictures, he lured Gloria Swanson, then the biggest female star in the world, not excepting Miss Pickford, and Samuel Goldwyn, whose own company had ousted him in 1922. Swanson was to produce few pictures for the company (*Sadie Thompson* among them), but Goldwyn supplied an even fifty, including *Stella Dallas, Arrowsmith, Dodsworth, Dead End,* and *Wuthering Heights.*

Schenck also brought into UA Howard Hughes (*Scarface* and *Hell's Angels*) and two men who, in very different ways, were to become household words: Walt Disney and Darryl F. Zanuck. In one sense, then, United Artists under Schenck not only became a major power itself but spun off two other major companies, Disney's and the merger of William Fox's moribund studio with Zanuck's UA unit, born there and dubbed (in 1933) Twentieth Century.

Zanuck's departure in 1935 was a stunning blow because he took Schenck with him as chairman of the newly merged Twentieth Cen-tury-Fox. But their leaving was symptomatic of problems at UA that could only grow. The original bold concept had made great sense at the beginning: distribution as a service organization rather than a profit center per se, enhancing, instead, profits to the partner-producers. The idea remained workable only so long as the partners were producing or, to put it differently, the producers were the partners.

By the mid-thirties Fairbanks's career was finished (as was the mar-riage to Pickford), Pickford herself had officially hung up her curls and retired from the screen, and Chaplin, instead of supplying the agreed-upon three pictures per year, had contributed only four pictures in sixteen years. Griffith's career was finished by 1932, and he had earlier sold his stock back to the others in order to liquidate his mounting personal debts, leaving Pickford, Fairbanks, and Chaplin (with Schenck and Goldwyn, also partners by this time) in complete charge of the company and the profits.

When the partners stopped producing, their views of UA's fiscal landscape took on decidedly different hues: The founders' investment could now grow and return dividends only through distribution of other people's pictures, and the share of revenues generated by now very disunited artists was, except for Chaplin's occasional entry, nil. The bold venturers of 1919 had not conquered the businessmen; they had *become* them, and like the moguls they had formed UA to escape, they preferred the doors to the boardroom and the coffers shut as tightly as possible.

In 1933 and 1934 Darryl Zanuck had contributed twelve pictures to the company, but he was in essence merely an employee of the others in spite of his personally producing what amounted to a full year's release schedule under the original plan. Not unreasonably, he demanded to be made a partner, with the stock and voting privileges (and profits) that would bring. The others refused, driving him to the merger with Fox. Schenck saw in the episode a pattern inevitably ruinous to a company dependent on its ability to attract filmmakers who could ensure a flow of product, and he cast his fate with Zanuck's future, not with UA's past.

Schenck's exit left a management vacuum that was never to be adequately filled under the dissension-ridden owners. It was not merely a question of who was minding the store. Constant replenishment of the store's product would have been difficult to maintain no matter who had succeeded Schenck. The power vacuum exacerbated relations with the always contentious Goldwyn, who wasted no time in announcing he was prepared to take over, either alone or (later) in tandem with England's Alexander Korda, whose London Films was an important supplier of UA product (and a Schenck legacy). Goldwyn maintained, with some justice, that inasmuch as the other partners were nonproductive and he (now that Zanuck was out of the way) was the unchallenged major producer for the company, he should also run it—or even own it. He and Korda mounted a serious attempt to buy the company but failed to raise the necessary capital on Wall Street or in London. Goldwyn's frustration pushed him to sufficiently obstreperous behavior that the others (no doubt happily) bought him out of the company.

Maybe no one could have handled Goldwyn (others had tried and failed), but certainly Mary Pickford was not executive enough to do so or to run the company as Schenck had. She promoted herself from partner to manager and promptly lost Walt Disney to RKO over a minor negotiating point regarding television rights to the Disney cartoons (in 1935!). The public embarrassment of having lost in short order Schenck, Zanuck, Goldwyn, *and* Disney only worsened already strained relations with Chaplin.

Internecine warfare can affect the operation of any company as quickly as, or more quickly than, as profoundly as, or more profoundly than external market forces. The occasional bad year or years can be weathered by "business as usual," but internal strife precludes business as usual by definition. This is perhaps nowhere so true (save the federal government) as in the movie business, which is and always has been conducted in a continuous glare of magnifying publicity far in excess of any real news value. This is even truer today in spite of the movies' eroding role in national life because the press today is both more aware and less "managed."

Any company suffering from more than the standard complement of politics and dissension quickly feels the blows shuddering down the corporate spine and senses the weakening of internal and external confidence. When the infighting results in executive departures, minor earthquakes and aftershocks ensue, signaling instability and uncertainty both to the rank and file on whose morale the company partially depends and to Wall Street, whose curiosity matches (and is not necessarily better informed than) the public's. When the defections are as grand and public as Zanuck's, Disney's, and Goldwyn's, the effects can be devastating, a fate UA was to suffer with even harsher results in the future.

All was not lost yet, however, and attempts were made in the late thirties and early forties to fill the vacuum that Pickford recognized she could not. A succession of financial managers came and went, but what was needed was another Schenck, another movieman. Korda for a time seemed likely to assume that role and contributed some prestigious pictures during his UA association. *The Private Life of Henry VIII, The Private Life of Don Juan* (Fairbanks's last picture), *The Ghost Goes West, Things to Come, Elephant Boy,* and the original *To Be or Not to Be* supplied, in truth, more prestige than profits, and Korda decamped to run MGM in England (a spectacularly ill-timed move, coinciding as it did with the start of World War II). Agreement was reached with producer Walter Wanger, who had made successful pictures for Paramount, Columbia, and MGM (Garbo's *Queen Christina* among them), but Wanger made a few pictures for UA like *Algiers* and *Stagecoach* and moved on. A similar experiment with MGM's Hunt Stromberg resulted in some weak pictures and a dead end.

Finally, though, there was a dazzling candidate, a movieman in the grandest of styles, who had been releasing through UA since the mid-thirties: David O. Selznick. He had given UA *The Garden of Allah*, the original *A Star Is Born*, *Nothing Sacred*, and others, though not *Gone with the Wind*, which, as everyone knows, went to MGM as the price of securing Clark Gable as Rhett Butler (though the picture had been discussed with UA as a Gary Cooper vehicle). Selznick returned to UA after his and MGM's great triumph with still more pictures: *Intermezzo*, *Rebecca*, *Since You Went Away*, and *Spellbound*.

Selznick knew what was wrong at UA, why nothing had worked for Korda or Wanger or Stromberg or the rest, and it was something Pickford and Chaplin (Fairbanks had died in late 1939) of all people should have understood: They had had no autonomy, and Selznick, perhaps the most autonomous of all Hollywood producers, wasn't about to supply UA with pictures *and* run the company unless the two remaining owners stood back to let him do so. This was an ironic and humiliating concession for Pickford and Chaplin to grant, one not cushioned by *Variety*'s trumpeting of "the elimination of any interference on the part of the owners or their representatives."*

But even born-to-the-celluloid moviemen can go awry, and Selznick did. Without having to buy the company, he had achieved what Goldwyn never could: full control. And he dropped it. He never exercised it. His pledge of ten additional pictures and management of the company in return for a one-quarter ownership went unfulfilled. Selznick turned more and more to brokering, buying properties, signing stars and directors (Ingrid Bergman and Alfred Hitchcock among them), and then selling or lending them off to other companies and producers at considerable personal profit to himself.

This had for Chaplin the distinct aroma of conflict of interest or downright fraud and resulted in more bitter quarreling and Selznick's going the way of Schenck and Goldwyn before him.

By the start of World War II the company was falling apart. After *The Great Dictator* Chaplin was to make only one more picture for the

---

*Tino Balio's *United Artists: The Company Built by the Stars* is rich with information on this and other episodes of UA's early history, based on the UA files, which are housed at the University of Wisconsin at Madison.

present company as owner-producer, the disastrous *Monsieur Verdoux*. (*Limelight* was made for the successor regime.) After the revolving door of abortive alliances with Korda, Wanger, Stromberg, and Selznick and the coming of the war, which cut off the vital foreign market for UA releases, the company scrambled to make do, reaching out in desperation for any product that had sprocket holes, anything that could be distributed and exhibited to keep the company alive. There was the occasional distinguished bright spot which seemed to stand in reproachful high relief as a mockery of the mostly second-half-of-the-double-bill stuff UA was now routinely sending out to feed the machine, to keep the exchanges alive, to dent the overhead. But the *Blithe Spirits* and *Henry Vs* and *Red Rivers* and *Champions* were too few and too far between and must have rubbed shoulders uneasily with *Getting Gertie's Garter* (in 1945!) or *A Kiss for Corliss* (in 1949).

The bold venture of ideals and sometime greatness had gone from *Broken Blossoms* and *Orphans of the Storm* to the tawdry exploitation of *The Outlaw*. ("What Are the Two Great Reasons for Jane Russell's Rise to Stardom?" asked billboards leeringly from coast to coast.) UA had gone from *Modern Times* and *The Great Dictator* to *The Admiral Was a Lady* and *Hoppy Serves a Writ*.

The company that had served as safe haven, as asylum for giants had become, through their own offices, bunkhouse to Hopalong Cassidy.

CHAPTER 2

TALENT

The movie business is the only business
in the world where the assets go home at
night.

—Attributed to Dorothy Parker
(circa 1935)

Pickford and Chaplin were no longer speaking to each other by 1950, but they could read the balance sheets and knew it was time to sell, time to get out. The two legendary proud stars, like irreconcilable marriage partners, had tenaciously refused to yield the child neither could handle or relinquish. Perhaps the handwriting on the wall of enmity erected between them now spelled such imminent doom, or maybe because they were exhausted after decades of bickering, they were ready to call it quits—for the right price.

They turned the company's operations over to a group, headed by a former governor of Indiana, who promised to reduce the deficit now growing larger each week, in return for an option to buy UA for $5.4 million, which turned out to be the right price. This offer seemed the long-hoped-for miracle—to everyone, that is, but the former governor who quickly learned, as others before and since have learned—grocery magnates, real estate tycoons, garment industry rajahs—that success in one field does not automatically confer glory or even competence in another. Within months the governor's basically custodial regime had doubled the deficit and ground production to a standstill. Bankruptcy loomed, but in a twist no screenwriter would be shameless enough to invent, at this very moment, the *real* miracle occurred.

Arthur Krim and Robert Benjamin were not furriers, junk dealers, or glove salesmen. They were lawyers, smart and respected ones, and they knew something about the movie business. Both were partners in the distinguished New York law firm of Phillips, Nizer, Benjamin & Krim (the celebrated trial lawyer Louis Nizer was also a partner). Both men knew their ways around the movie business's legal intricacies from their law practice, which involved important motion-picture clients, and they had learned the day-to-day idiosyncrasies of show business as executives. Benjamin, who was forty-one, had been American head of J. Arthur Rank and a director of Universal; Krim, then forty, was a former president of Eagle-Lion.

Invited to examine the situation, the two surveyed the wreckage at UA and delivered to Mary Pickford the startling opinion that the stock, the company, the option held by the incumbent (which no one in his right mind would exercise) were all, well . . . worthless. Bankruptcy wasn't in the air; it was shoulder to the door of company headquarters at 729 Seventh Avenue in midtown Manhattan. There was, in short, nothing to buy, nothing to sell. But . . . There might be something for Pickford and Chaplin to give away for its approximate value—i.e., zero—in hopes of staving off receivership, and that was control of the company.

In fact, it was less than zero, for the challenge and responsibility of saving UA would require incentive. Krim and Benjamin would succeed the ineffectual interim group for a period of ten years, but they wanted Pickford and Chaplin's guarantee that should they turn the company around—it was now losing $100,000 per week—and make a profit in any one of the first three years of their management, they would be rewarded with half ownership of the company—daring terms for an impossible task.

They did it in less than a year.

The remarkable success story of this second phase of United Artists' corporate life was the result of a number of factors, some products of the moment, many unique to Krim and Benjamin, the force of their personalities and leadership.

When these two men took over UA in February 1951, the movie business was entering another of its periodic crisis phases. The moguls who had pioneered and made the rules were mostly gone or going; public taste, changing times, and the federal government had radically altered those rules. Television had not yet become the ubiquitous despoiler of time and taste we know today, but it had ceased to be a novelty and was making its impact felt in rapidly declining movie attendance. Those aging pioneers who had turned storefronts into palaces lived to see the reverse take place, as Bijous and Orpheums and Rialtos everywhere became supermarkets and bowling alleys. Television's importance was to grow in changing audience habits and tastes, but the greater and more mysterious change had been caused by the upheavals of World War II, which altered audiences worldwide in ways which the content and style of American movies neither reflected nor knew how to address. The *Zeitgeist* was different; the machine wasn't.

Eventually the studios might have caught up with audiences and gone on as before if not for what was probably the most devastating blow of all, this administered by the Supreme Court of the United States of America. In 1948 the High Court ruled (in a case primarily involving Paramount and dealing with such venerable distribution abuses as block booking) that movie companies must divorce themselves from their chains of theaters. This antitrust ruling became known as the Consent Decree and broke the backs of the vertically structured majors (all of which were codefendants).

The consequences of the decree were arithmetically simple: If MGM, say, could exhibit its product in its own far-flung Loew's theater chain, it had only to pay the theater overheads and keep the rest of the box-office cash flow, which it then carved up to pay itself distribution fees and to retire the cost of publicity, advertising, and production; what was left over was profit for the shareholders. Interposing somebody else's tap (i.e., the independent exhibitor's) in this money pipeline instantly and dramatically reduced the flow. This meant that marginal pictures (and they all were growing more marginal as television antennas sprouted in the millions) had sharply reduced chances of earning profits or even breaking even. The flow changed from cash to red ink and eventually to the lifeblood of the industry—the talent.

The studios had been supplying their theaters (and those of independent theater owners, who had always been part of the exhibition landscape) with several hundred pictures a year. Most of these pictures were not what nostalgia so lovingly cracks them up to be. The great majority were routine program pictures churned out to meet the demands of distribution machinery geared and peopled to handle that many pictures a year. Grinding out these celluloid sausages was an assembly-line process much criticized today, but it was efficient at the time because everyone involved—from the producer, director, star to the makeup man and gofer—was under contract, on call, told what to do and how and when to do it. Audiences showed up week after reliable week, and it all worked fairly well; the great companies of the twenties were still the great companies in the fifties. Many people had become fabulously rich (Louis B. Mayer was for years the highest-salaried man in America), and along the way some memorable, still-admired pictures got made. But by 1951 the audience for the B picture, the industry's bottom-half-of-the-bill staple, had discovered the same thing (or only slightly worse) available for free on television. In Sam

Goldwyn's memorable phrasing, "Why should people go out and see bad pictures when they can stay at home and see them for nothing?"

The distribution base simply fell out. The independent theater owners who had celebrated such spacious skies thanks to the Supreme Court found they couldn't sell this stuff anymore, and the distribution companies, having lost their captive theaters, couldn't unload the merchandise on the independents. This meant that if the picture couldn't be sold, there was no point in making it or in having all those people under contract not making pictures no one wanted to see anyway, and little by little the system edged toward collapse. It wasn't overnight, and the *Ben Hurs* and *Ten Commandments* could still break records, and 3-D and CinemaScope and stereophonic this and that could cosmetically and temporarily revive attendance. But all those sound stages and prop shops and costume and furniture warehouses, all those people—those makeup and costume and camera and electrical and prop and greens and commissary employees, not to mention the pricey ones, the producers and directors and writers and stars and their staffs and secretaries and assistants—all the famous assets that had made the studio system work in the first place now loomed as liabilities of the most debilitating sort. Maybe the real estate was worth something, but it had to be maintained, and there were taxes to be paid. It was time to streamline, terminate, cut costs, and let the major overhead fend for itself. Even Louis B. Mayer could go (he went). The assets were "included out," as Goldwyn would have said; the party was over.

In this panicky context the only real asset United Artists had was that it had no assets. No studio, anyway, and no expensive real estate to maintain and pay taxes on, no contract rosters draining overhead, and because the company did not own chains of theaters, there was no wrenching adjustment to be made to the Consent Decree.

The intangible and inestimable asset was the personal credibility of the new management, Krim and Benjamin, which allowed them to establish lines of credit to pay the immediate expenses and operate the company. Krim acted quickly to provide the basis for a cash flow by buying up the low-grade but playable Eagle-Lion film library and putting it to work. (For the most part the earlier UA pictures did not constitute a source of films, a library, because the pictures had belonged not to the company but to the producers.) This was a stopgap measure, but an effective one that bought time to formulate and effect a restructuring of the company.

Krim and Benjamin instituted a series of changes and innovations which would give the company a competitive edge over companies far richer and healthier, even within the context of the current crisis. They saw at once that United Artists would have to finance pictures as well as to distribute them in order to attract the newly available talent being cut loose from old, often long-term ties. But the company would finance *only* and not become a production company or a studio, the liabilities of which were all too ubiquitously apparent. To offset the risks inherent in financing production, distribution would need to change from a basically non- or low-profit service to a conventional profit center, but—the company would share picture profits with the producers it financed.

At a time when profits, though declining, were far more common than they are today, the concept was strategically, brilliantly apt and had a historic effect. Hardly anyone had failed to notice in the early 1950s when Lew Wasserman, then agent for James Stewart, made a percentage-of-profits deal for his client at Universal for a hugely popular western called *Winchester '73*. Those profits made Stewart one of the richest men in Hollywood, perhaps in the United States. Every actor, actress, director, or producer who felt cheated of profits rightfully or morally his or hers under the resented studio system—from which the majority had just been pink-slipped—reflected on the inequities of compensation in much the same way Fairbanks, Pickford, Chaplin, and Griffith had back in 1919. It wasn't exactly the same idea, really, but in certain ways it was better because UA, and not the individual producer, would finance the film.

There were wrinkles. Sometimes the profit-sharing producer would become also finance-sharing, deferring his or her salary until profits were realized, become in effect cofinancier to the proportion of the picture's budget which that deferred compensation represented. Deferments also reduced the out-of-pocket budget, making financing easier and abbreviating the time needed for recoupment, thus reducing the interest to be paid on the money that was financing the pictures.

If some balked at deferring their salaries (some did), they were reminded that not only was UA offering competitive distribution rates, shares of profits sometimes as high as 50 percent for the producer to distribute among his partners, co-workers, or employees as he saw fit (giving producers an enormous carrot to dangle before stars and directors if the producers were not themselves the stars or directors—and they often were), but—and this was a critical advantage, uniquely possible to UA because it had none of the conventional studio assets (or burdens)—UA would charge no studio overhead.

Overhead charges in the movie business are not negligible when it comes to calculating profits. If a studio at that time charged a typical 30 percent overhead on a picture costing $1 million to produce, the break-even figure for the picture became $1.3 million (cost of production plus overhead) *plus* the costs of advertising, promotion, distribution, which also were paid back out of rentals (the money returned to the company after the theater owner has taken his share). If it is assumed for clarity's sake that this averages out to a multiple of 2.5 times the actual cost of manufacturing the picture for it to reach break-even and the point at which the producer will be paid (if he has deferred his fee) or begin to share in profits, or both, the $1 million picture with overhead will need to earn rentals of $3.25 million (2.5 times $1.3 million), or $2.5 million if there is no overhead charge.

Put another way, it means that by charging overhead, the studio gets to pocket $750,000 before the filmmaker sees a penny. This is widely (though not wholly accurately) viewed as pure gravy by producers because every studio facility or property used by the production, from sound stages to arc lights to typewriters to thumbtacks, is charged to the picture anyway, so that the overhead charge is, from the producer's point of view, at best an override and at worst legalized larceny. *

Not owning a studio didn't just mean no overhead, however. UA didn't need a studio because it wasn't a production company and because studio space would shortly go begging in California. But the term *studio* has a specialized meaning apart from the general popular understanding, and it is that a studio is a production organization which is signatory to the many union contracts that govern studio operations. UA was not only free of player and other talent contracts but also direct signatory to none of the unions.

Union membership in Hollywood includes virtually everyone even tangentially involved with making films, from story analysts and secretaries to movie stars and directors. Producers, perhaps because they are viewed as "management," are the only real exceptions. (There is a producers' guild, but it is voluntary, and few volunteer.) Even hairstylists and still photographers are unionized, and once a company is a signatory, union rules are as binding as they are in any business. Because UA was not a signatory and didn't have to deal with unions directly, the individual production company or producer for whom UA was supplying financing was free to negotiate independently with the unions for

---

* On the computer-generated cost sheets for a picture he was directing for one of the major companies, Richard Lester found the following entry: "80¢: Paint for director's name on parking space." "How does one calculate 80¢ worth of paint?" Lester inquired. "Is it 13.33¢ per letter? Does Steve Spielberg have to pay $1.20?"

concessions which might make the difference between being able to make the picture for such and such a budget or not.

While no one could evade union rules altogether, a UA producer could avoid the seniority lists by which studios were bound, and as technicians, too, became increasingly free-lance, the broader-based selection of crew (though still governed by the unions) contributed to a greater sense of producer freedom, control, and independence.

And this was the most potent and enduring of lures and legacies Krim and Benjamin were to contribute to producers, United Artists, and, eventually, the industry: independent production in an atmosphere of autonomy and creative freedom. This laissez-faire approach to production—more than the careful distribution, more than the absence of overhead charges, more even than the promise of profits—was the distinctive difference that would make UA first unique, then the pacesetter for the industry.

It wasn't quite the good old days of freewheeling autonomy of the Big Four, but it looked enough like it to attract the talented who had lately felt shackled by the cumbersome and restrictive paraphernalia of studio management. Producers, stars, and directors who would have months before scorned UA suddenly found 729 Seventh Avenue far more appealing than Pickfair had been, for all the famous social graces.

Two strokes of luck intervened early to gain UA the cash to fuel the financing and attract the attention and respect of the motion-picture community. The first was Stanley Kramer's final picture under a UA contract signed in 1948. Kramer, himself once spoken of as a possible UA head, had since moved to Columbia Pictures, where he found little enthusiasm for his "western without action." Kramer made it for UA, and *High Noon* not only became a huge commercial hit but won Gary Cooper a Best Actor Academy Award. Also in 1951, Walter Heller, the Chicago financier who had been instrumental in helping Krim and Benjamin arrange the critical initial UA production financing, helped UA secure the U.S. distribution rights to Sam Spiegel and John Huston's *The African Queen*, which not only made money but did for Humphrey Bogart what *High Noon* did for Cooper. *

Both these pictures were regarded as fresh and original in their time and added luster to a badly tarnished image. They also suggested not at all subliminally that independent production could more than hold its own with the foundering studio system, and all it took was the imagination and courage to get in the game.

* Because of release dates, Bogart's Oscar (1951) preceded Cooper's (1952).

However fresh and courageous UA's laissez-faire production philosophy may have seemed at the time, the company probably had no other
choice because it had none of the reporting, administrative, or supervision systems necessary for direct control. Short of creating and staffing a
multitude of supervisory departments, "a studio," there was no effective
way to gain them. Almost certainly riding herd on the minutiae of
production details was not to the Krim and Benjamin taste or temperament. Whatever liability absence of control might imply now, three
decades later, it was a dazzling lure then and helped characterize UA as
the only creatively enlightened film company.

"Only United Artists has a system of true independent production,"
director Otto Preminger told *Fortune* in 1958. "They recognize that the
independent has his own personality. After they agree on the basic
property and are consulted on the cast, they leave everything to the
producer's discrimination." Almost exactly twenty years later the same
magazine quoted producer Robert Chartoff, who with his partner, Irwin
Winkler, had produced the sensationally successful *Rocky* (among many
others) for UA, as saying, "It's tougher to get a commitment out of
United Artists, but once they're committed, you get more freedom." In
contrast, David Selznick, then producing a movie for Zanuck's Twentieth Century-Fox, complained to his director, Henry King, "The junk
that is being ground out in the big studios today is as bad as it is, and
rolls up such huge losses, because . . . picturemakers do not have the
same freedom . . . that is given to the independent units functioning
. . . particularly for United Artists."

That the independent producer's creative freedom was strictly limited under the UA approach to production was perhaps not perceptible
to people who had so recently survived the studio system, under which
most had been salaried employees. The nature and amount of creative
freedom permissible, desirable, or simply negotiable are subject to evolution and change in Hollywood, as will be seen, but in 1951 the idea
of independence was both a powerful magnet and a practical possibility.

The newly released flood of talent had virtually all been well
schooled by the system they were so happy to denigrate. However re-
sentfully, they had learned their trades in a rigid system of industrial
control, as supervisors (as producers were called), overseen by owners of
legendary power and little inhibition at exercising it—those same early
pioneers, almost all of them still working. As producers, supervisors
knew not only how to read a budget but how to draw one up and what
the consequences of exceeding it were likely to be. They did not know
merely how to make deals for actors or hot literary properties; they
knew how to make deals for motel rooms to house casts and crews on

location or for box lunches, or how many feet of raw stock would or should be necessary for adequate but not excessive coverage of any given scene, how many gallons of gasoline for how many vehicles, when to bend, when to hold the line.

They were present on the sets and locations, in the editing rooms, on the scoring stages: they went to previews; many of them were capable editors or writers and wielded scissors or pens without asking union permission or on-screen credit. They knew what they were doing, which was, in the most literal sense, *producing*.

Even the remotest student of Hollywood today is aware that the term *producer* has become so elastic as to have lost any precise meaning. Most (not all) producers today are former agents who have packaged a combination of elements that will make the financing of a picture, and a fee, possible. The producer may or may not know the difference between a gaffer and a gofer, but he is known as a producer around the Polo Lounge and in the trade papers, and he hires someone else, who is called a line producer or executive producer or associate producer or production consultant or executive in charge of production or whatever other locution can be dreamed up to add to the seemingly endless proliferation of credits cascading on films today, while simultaneously disguising the hard fact that this euphemism du jour has actually done whatever producing got done. Promoters, deal makers, and packagers promote, deal, and package; producers produce.

In 1951 Krim and Benjamin were able to draw upon a pool of thoroughly trained, knowledgeable professionals to whom independence was not synonymous with indulgence, self- or otherwise. The promise of independence was less a relinquishing of power or control than it was an inspired stratagem to attract expertise in a period—more than thirty years ago now—before anyone had ever heard of the auteur theory, before agents and lawyers had replaced producers, and before poetic license had become the intellectual justification for all manner of creative licentiousness.

Krim and Benjamin protected themselves and exercised plenty of creative judgment. The most basic was in saying yes to this project and no to that one, and they were to have perhaps the best run of commercial, and often critically justified, yeses and noes in the postwar industry. Having said yes was merely the beginning, however, as a typical UA contract reserved to itself standard approvals of script, director, cast, production manager, cameraman, budget, playing time, rating, composer, technical personnel, locations, raw stock, aspect ratio, processing laboratory, number of release prints, advertising campaign and budget, and so on. These approvals were subject to trust and negotiation and were sometimes reduced to a minimum of budget, script, and leading cast, or, in the case of Woody Allen (a very *special* case to be discussed later) even less. But they were there in the boiler plate, and it was within such a labyrinth of approvals and implied refusals—each of which had a direct, sometimes crucial bearing on some aspect of the creative process—that creative freedom and independent production existed. And flourished.

Producers had had to live with some parallel or more stringent structure of approvals—or fiats—before, and the freedom that Preminger, Selznick, Chartoff, and Winkler and the vast majority of UA producers over the years testify to in the fifties, sixties, and seventies was attributable to a benign neglect principally during the production process itself. The UA executive staff did not spend hours each day viewing dailies, as is still the ritual at some studios; visits to sets or locations were rare and less watchdog in character and atmosphere than courteously social. There was looser contact between production unit and front office, because UA did not have the departmentalized structure of the studios through which all requisitions needed to be serviced. There was, therefore, little or no sense of the spying common to a studio set or location peopled with home office representatives, and none of the oppressive big brotherism of a purchasing department, through which every expenditure, however minor, must be channeled and justified.

It looked like, felt like, and, in contrast with what had come before, was independence. It quickly attracted producers and companies like Hecht-Hill-Lancaster, the Mirisch Corporation, directors or producers like Preminger, George Stevens, Joseph L. Mankiewicz, and John Huston; stars like John Wayne, Frank Sinatra, and Burt Lancaster. These independents often made original and offbeat pictures like *High Noon, The African Queen, Marty* (which won the Best Picture Academy Award), *The Moon Is Blue, Twelve Angry Men, The Man with the Golden Arm, Sweet Smell of Success, Moulin Rouge,* and *Around the World in Eighty Days,* pictures that came to suggest a free, unconventional attitude at UA, hallmarked by intelligence, polish, and commercial savvy. It is hard to imagine these and other pictures of UA's born again period being made in the studio system of the moguls. (It is also hard to imagine many of them being made today, a different, perhaps sadder scenario.)

By 1956 Krim and Benjamin had been so successful they were able to buy out Pickford and Chaplin and own outright (with associates) the company they had revitalized. They went public a year later and continued to turn out important and commercial pictures: Billy Wilder's

Some Like It Hot, The Apartment, Irma La Douce, Witness for the Prosecu-tion, and *One, Two, Three.* There were pictures like *West Side Story, Elmer Gantry, Judgment at Nuremberg, Tom Jones.* Richard Lester made *A Hard Day's Night, Help!, The Knack;* Norman Jewison made *The Rus-sians Are Coming, The Russians Are Coming, In the Heat of the Night, Fiddler on the Roof.* There were foreign films like *Never on Sunday* and *Last Tango in Paris.* And finally, two of the most successful series of pictures ever made: the James Bond bonanzas, commencing with *Dr. No* and spinning off a dozen more, and the *Pink Panther* series, another installment of which was being prepared by Peter Sellers at the time of his death in 1980.

The multiple pictures from single sources are worth noting, as is the continuity of relationships with producers and directors over long peri-ods of time. This was to give rise to a much vaunted feeling of family, but it is perhaps more to the point that many of these directors and producers did better work for the UA logo than they were to accom-plish elsewhere. Krim and Benjamin knew how to lure them; more im-portant, they knew how to keep them.

Such success tantalized San Francisco's Transamerica Corporation during the merger-happy sixties, and in 1967 a marriage was arranged. Transamerica wanted United Artists not only because it was successful (the 1968 net profits of $20 million were to make handsome dividends) but because it was visible. Transamerica's stock was stable but sluggish, and the notion that a glamour subsidiary's fortunes would invigorate its investor appeal was shared by Krim and Benjamin, who were able to liquidate their UA stock at handsome and well-earned profits for a quarter of a million shares of Transamerica stock each, which effec-tively jumped UA's price-earnings multiple from roughly eight to twenty-five. The Transamerica stock then stood in the mid-twenties.

Krim and Benjamin's desire to cash in after a decade and a half of successful rebuilding was motive enough. Also, Transamerica's stability would provide a cushion for any bumpy roads the entertainment busi-ness might yet travel. There may have been nonmonetary motives as well. Krim had long been an important figure in Democratic party fund raising, both for New York State and on the national level, and was closely allied to the Lyndon Johnson White House. Benjamin, whose public service was of international stature, was not only a founder and chairman of the Corporation for Public Broadcasting but an ambassador to the United Nations as well. Pursuing these outside interests did not mean abandoning UA. On the contrary. Explicit in the Transamerica agreement was that Krim and Benjamin would remain as UA's presi-

dent and chairman and join the Transamerica board of directors as
well, and they did. But having the cushion of a wealthy corporate parent may have seemed a comfortable guarantee of continuity to men
whose interests ranged wide and whose abilities were such that they
could serve both public and private sectors.

Then came 1970. The $20 million profit that had made Trans-
america stockholders so happy in 1968 plunged to an unforeseen $35
million pretax loss, worsened by the write-off of an additional $50 mil-
lion and declaration of a $45 million deficit. This was a staggering blow
to both companies (though perhaps a more exotic vicissitude to the
financial conglomerate in San Francisco than to the cyclically tough-
ened movie executives on Seventh Avenue). Transamerica's no-non-
sense chairman, John Beckett, looked at the figures and found them "a
revelation." The order went out: "All acquisitions cease until we have a
management system in place *that we can understand* [italics added] and
will give us early warnings."

Beckett's candor was refreshing: Transamerica didn't understand the
movie business and didn't claim to. It had hoped to profit from it without being more than what Beckett called "a classic and deliberate holding company . . . we wanted to give them the feeling that we didn't
measure every dollar. I guess by hindsight we carried this too far."

Transamerica's paternalism was not all that different from the philosophy that had dominated United Artists itself in relation to its partner-producers. Beckett, whose cracker-barrel manner belied a steely,
decisive will, was no ingenue when it came to understanding business
reverses. What he wanted even less than an earnings decline for the
stockholders was to be personally surprised and embarrassed, particularly after coolly predicting higher earnings to Wall Street and the investment bankers. Beckett was having problems with other subsidiaries,
too; at the same time the myth of conglomerate stock market invul-
nerability vanished, and Transamerica's stock slid from a year's high of
$27 a share to $11 a share in just over six months, a slide that also
directly affected Krim and Benjamin's large personal holdings. It was a
difference in stock value of roughly $4 million.

The management systems installed by Transamerica did nothing to
endear the San Francisco pyramid to UA—for all their business theory
sophistication, in fact, they seemed naïve to management—but they
also did nothing to impair the company's progress. UA quickly regained
its footing when Eric Pleskow moved from distribution to the presidency of UA in 1973 (Benjamin had become vice-chairman to Krim's
chairman). Pleskow reorganized, adding West Coast talent agent Mike
Medavoy as head of production, slashing overhead, firing roughly one-

sixth of UA's worldwide work force, deflating swollen production in-
ventories. The new team did what new teams can only do: attempt to
attract the talent that can reverse a downward trend or vivify the doldrums.

The picture that turned the company back to its former upward
spiral was, ironically enough, a disaster, *The Missouri Breaks*. After dismal 1970 there had followed a series of lackluster or just routine pictures, without the classy and commercial trademarks on which UA had
seemed to hold the patents. Maybe UA was through, it was rumored. If
investor confidence plagued Beckett, the confidence of the creative
community had been dimmed for UA, a confidence it needed to win
back after the 1970 debacle and industry rumors of a Transamerica
bloodletting. David Picker, the smart and popular president of UA before Pleskow moved over from distribution, became a producer for the
company, producing pictures like *Juggernaut* and *Lenny*, a move which,
like all management changes in all businesses, produced uncertainty
and suggested instability. ("The czar we know is better than the czar we
don't know" is a maxim not confined to the steppes.) *The Missouri
Breaks* came to UA after a bitterly lost competition by Twentieth Century-Fox, which was experiencing *Lucky Lady* problems. A Fox executive, who had a long-standing relationship with a world-class star
and with the *Breaks* producer, intervened at the latter's request to help
secure the star on the assumed understanding that the casting coup and
the picture—a western script that had floated around Hollywood for
some time—would come to Fox. It wasn't even offered to Fox, causing
considerable internal embarrassment and some bitterness, but instead
came directly to UA, bringing with it three powerhouse talents: director Arthur Penn (*The Miracle Worker*, *Bonnie and Clyde*), and stars Marlon Brando and Jack Nicholson. The ho-hum script by Tom McGuane
had become the hottest property in town.

The picture was a disaster. But the making of the deal—Penn,
Brando, and Nicholson formed a very powerful package indeed—
opened doors that had been closed to UA during the doldrums, and
UA's gratitude to the producer (Fox's attitude is not recorded), even
after the picture had vanished without a trace of profit, was so enduring
that he was to be furnished with an office in the UA headquarters for
many years explicitly because of *The Missouri Breaks*. The deal had cost
millions, but in one important sense it had worked: UA could again
attract major talent for major pictures.

Meanwhile, Transamerica shipped in computers, timetables,
minimum basic objectives (MBOs) and projections. Krim, Benjamin,
and Pleskow went ahead making important and successful pictures and

returning welcome dividends to San Francisco. But as early as 1974 Krim, preferring perhaps not to leave his company's heart in the land of the minimum basic objective, suggested that UA be separated from its parent. The suggestion was rejected.

Many who observed Krim during this period believed he had been disheartened by Lyndon Johnson's decision not to run for reelection in 1968 and the consequent diminution of Krim's own possibilities for significant public service in or for Washington, certainly nil under Nixon. Perhaps as these personal motivations faded, UA came back into fresh focus, and the company, which was largely his and Benjamin's creation, seemed like a child prematurely put up for adoption. It is also likely that what Pleskow later referred to as Transamerica's "nitpicking" cramped the style of a man whose own corporate philosophy was the antithesis of the watchdog systems and controls now being imposed on him. The Transamerica stock, which was supposed to have been so "synergistically" reflective of UA's successes, just lay there, unmoving. After the plunge to $11 per share in 1970, it remained no higher than $15 per share even eight years later in 1978. But perhaps most onerous of all was that in devising "a management system . . . we can understand"—one without surprises—Beckett made chairman Krim answerable corporately to the TA group vice-president for leisure services, James Harvey. Effectively Arthur Krim was made second-in-command of a company he had built, owned, and sold for a now paper-thin paper profit.

Still, the hits continued, and the honors with them. In 1975 UA won its eighth Best Picture Academy Award with *One Flew over the Cuckoo's Nest*; in 1976, its ninth, with *Rocky*. In 1977, riding on a higher commercial and quality crest than ever, Krim reapproached Beckett with a plan for spinning off United Artists in order to improve the stock performances of both companies, allowing Transamerica to retain a controlling interest in the stock and a majority position on its board of directors. Beckett again said no, and Krim and Benjamin decided to go public in an unprecedented and surprising manner.

The January 16, 1978, issue of *Fortune* was provocative and shocking to the motion-picture industry. In an article unambiguously titled "United Artists' Script Calls for Divorce," journalist Peter J. Schuyten quoted Arthur Krim as announcing, "You will not find any top officer here who feels that Transamerica has contributed *anything* [Krim's italics] to United Artists." It was a public broadside fired straight at the heart of Jack Beckett, who shot back that "if the people at United Artists don't like it, they can quit and go off on their own."

Which is exactly what they did.

Within days of the article's appearance a *Variety* story, bannered HIGH NOON AT UA, announced Krim's and Benjamin's resignations, quickly followed by those of Pleskow, Medavoy, and Bill Bernstein, head of business affairs. It was unthinkable, unprecedented, unimaginable: Arthur Krim *was* United Artists! But it had happened, and the five men swiftly formed a new company they called Orion (with careful notation to the press that astronomically Orion was a five-star constellation*) and announced their financing and distributing affiliation with Warner Brothers.

Hollywood had been shocked by the hostility broadcast in *Fortune*, but it was stunned into confusion by the exodus. An open letter in the form of a two-page ad appeared on January 24, 1978, in *Variety* and the *Hollywood Reporter*, addressed to John Beckett and signed by sixty-three producers or directors, including Robert Altman, Hal Ashby, Bernardo Bertolucci, Francis Coppola, Blake Edwards, Bob Fosse, Norman Jewison (who was said to be the ad's organizer), Stanley Kubrick, Alan Pakula, Burt Reynolds, John Schlesinger, Martin Scorsese, François Truffaut, and Saul Zaentz among others. It read:

Dear Mr. Beckett:

We, the undersigned, have made films in association with Arthur Krim, Eric Pleskow, Bob Benjamin, Bill Bernstein and Mike Medavoy.

The success of United Artists throughout the years has been based upon the personal relationships of these executive officers of United Artists with us, the film makers.

We seriously question the wisdom of the Transamerica Corporation in losing the talents of these men who have proven their creative and financial leadership in the film industry for many years.

The loss of this leadership will not only be felt by United Artists but by all of us.

It is a curious letter, sentimental, reproachful, and naïve. If it were meant only as a show of support by grateful producers and directors, a simple "Good luck, Orion" would have sufficed. What John Beckett can have thought of having Transamerica's "wisdom" "seriously questioned" by a bunch of filmmakers—"What wisdom? They walked out," he is reported to have remarked—is mysterious. Did they expect Beckett to invite the Orion five back? The quality of reproach suggests more than mere support for the departed executives, however. It suggests that the creative community, or these sixty-three members of it anyway,

*It isn't.

were in some way serving notice that they had been persuaded that
Transamerica's interference and control were indeed insupportable to
men they respected, and such heavy-handed meddling could not be
allowed to continue for the signers, many of whom had deals in place at
UA, deals made by the Krim regime, which was no longer there to
protect them. (There were many filmmakers who were asked to participate in the ad and didn't: Chartoff and Winkler did not appear; neither
did Woody Allen or his producers.) Many in Hollywood became confused about who had started flapping the family laundry in the public
breezes of *Fortune* and concluded that Beckett's "let 'em quit" challenge
had been the final precipitating straw. In the reams of publicity generated by the walkout, only one source, the *New York Times*, referred to
or even seemed aware of Krim's 1977 proposal (as reported by
Schuyten), which was content to have Transamerica in place as both
controlling stockholder and majority position on the board. This might
have raised the not illogical question of just how intolerable was Transamerica. Instead, industry gossip centered on the subject of Mike
Medavoy's Mercedes-Benz company car (also discussed in the *Times*),
which was far more expensive and flashy than the Chevrolet or Ford
prescribed by the TA management guidelines for a senior vice-president
in a subsidiary company, though common to the point of banality in
Hollywood. This story was so widely circulated that many in the industry actually believed that the automobile was the trigger (the "flash
point" the *New York Times* called it) for the extraordinary wave of resignations. As a symbol of Krim's frustrations with what he, Benjamin,
and Pleskow were allowed to accomplish in executive compensation
areas, however, it made the point. Transamerica, not United Artists,
was calling those shots, and the frustration this occasioned was widely
spoken of as the principal factor for the break.

It now seems clear that the *Fortune* piece was an adroit public relations maneuver designed to make United Artists appear the injured
party and to smoke out Beckett, who characteristically shot from the
hip. In reality the move had been in the works for months. Krim's 1977
spin-off proposal was made and turned down in May, and David Mc-
Clintick's account of the internal strife at Columbia Pictures during the
Begelman affair, *Indecent Exposure*, describes meetings between executives of that company with Krim and/or Pleskow in October 1977,
by which time the Krim decision had apparently been reached and the
executives were discreetly testing other waters.

Employees of that time testify to contemporary rumors in the company, sparked by overhead fragments of conversation, by perceptions of
a slowdown in project acquisitions, most of them discounted simply

because of the inconceivability of Krim and Benjamin's abandoning "their" company. One top-line executive who was left behind claimed to recall hearing Medavoy complain to Bernstein that it was tough to turn down desirable projects when there was no point in making deals that would not be brought to fruition, but premonitory signals like this (which may be "improved" by hindsight) went misperceived or uncredited. While Hollywood reeled (or cheered: There were many who pragmatically saw nothing more than the creation of a new, additional picture company, another "store" to which they could pitch their wares), 729 Seventh Avenue was cast into deepest gloom. Bewilderment, dismay, disbelief reigned. "The Great White Father" (there were many who actually called Krim that) had simply walked out without warning, deserting the "family." There was a deep and impenetrable silence within the company, an almost tangible feeling of betrayal that lingered for months, as thousands of employees wondered, tried to figure it out, and waited for Transamerica to fill the most dramatic management gap in recent motion-picture history.

The repercussions of the Orion defection are still being felt in the motion-picture industry partly because of Orion's subsequent history and the events described in the narrative that follows. Additionally, the Orion move was virtually duplicated two years later, when the spectacularly successful Alan Ladd, Jr., management group at Twentieth Century-Fox decamped (also to Warner Brothers) as the Ladd Company. But probably the aftershocks would have been less severe and attracted less attention were it not for the stature of Arthur Krim and Robert Benjamin. The latter's death in 1980 was mourned by the industry and by national and international leaders for whom his public service and personality had been graced with nobility. Adlai Stevenson's characterization of Benjamin as "a citizen's citizen" was used as the descriptive title for a biography published about him by the United Nations. Krim's personal standing in the industry he transformed is clear and unambiguous. "Arthur Krim is the smartest single individual ever to work in the motion-picture industry," says a producer who dealt with him at United Artists. Even allowing for Hollywood hyperbole, the assessment is common. Its weakest variant is "If Lew Wasserman isn't, Arthur Krim is." But again and again common consent has it that in areas of intellect, taste, judgment, business acumen, and the ability to win the respect of his competitors, Krim was without peer.

He was not universally beloved by those he left behind at United Artists. The epithets *imperious, autocratic, arrogant, cold* were often heard in the days that followed the walkout; but these are rarely pejorative terms in Hollywood, and no matter how bitterly, he was never spoken of without respect. Perhaps the most telling appraisal comes from a former Krim associate who stayed on: "Arthur was the brains of UA, but Bob Benjamin was the heart."

They would be, in show business parlance, "a tough act to follow." Some said "an impossible act to follow." And many claim they felt— but would not utter—that the day Arthur Krim walked out of 729 Seventh Avenue was the day United Artists died.

CHAPTER 3

STYLE

We don't go for strangers in Hollywood
unless they wear a sign saying that their
axe has been thoroughly ground elsewhere, and that in any case it's not going
to fall on our necks—in other words, unless they're a celebrity. And they'd better
look out even then.

—F. Scott Fitzgerald,
The Last Tycoon (1941)

Maybe no one could have followed in Arthur Krim's
footsteps. The particular incentives and circumstances would never be
there again. It was not just that he had breathed life back into a moribund company and the industry in which it became preeminent, nor
was it the 108 Academy Awards* and the profits he had accumulated.
It was also the time span itself, the sheer fact of survival over nearly
three decades in an industry in which one-tenth as long is considered
normal executive life expectancy. MGM eventually fired Louis B.
Mayer, after all, and Krim's regime (1951–1978) lasted longer than
Mayer's (1924–1949). Where permanence is unknown, even the modest long run becomes the stuff of legend, and hints of invincibility
gather, like mists around Mount Rushmore.

No matter how difficult it may have seemed for anyone to fill those
shoes, there were imaginative individuals who let it be known they
were willing to try them on for size. Frosty deliberation chilled the air
in the pyramid in San Francisco and the Transamerica apartment overlooking snowy Central Park, as options were weighed, candidates sifted,
and a decision was reached. In a coolly delivered stroke of surprise,
particularly to the press which had made the walkout national news,
hewing man, woman, and syndicate to the Krim-*Fortune* line, Trans-

---

*Including those eventually earned by *Apocalypse Now* and *The Black Stallion*.

america did not attempt directly to recast Krim at all. James Harvey, Transamerica's executive vice-president, to whom Krim had been told to report, became chairman of the board—albeit an absentee one, remaining in San Francisco, where he also looked over such other subsidiaries as Budget and TransInternational Airlines; Andreas ("Andy") Albeck, UA's senior vice-president of operations, was named president and chief executive officer, to run things in and from New York. Benjamin's vice-chairman position was simply dropped. To those rumormongers on both coasts broadcasting, "UA is for sale," those claiming insight into John Beckett's pride replied, not without cynicism, "Not as long as Arthur Krim is alive, it's not."

It was a classical corporate gesture, promotion from within displaying monolithic (or pyramidal) calm, evolutionary progression, an executives-come, executives-go sangfroid. To the attentive it implied Transamerica didn't want (or need) a star to decorate the top of its corporate tree; to the very attentive it removed the Krim-Benjamin layer of insulation between United Artists and Transamerica; to Andy Albeck it gave a special challenge should he seek to be something more than San Francisco's puppet.

Andy Albeck was not show business; that much was clear. He was the intimate of no great producers; he played poker with no major lawyers; he "tennised" with no powerhouse agents; he supped not with writers or thespians. Nor did he move in the other area of American show business, among presidents and jurists. In fact, it was bruited throughout the industry that *no one had ever heard of him.* Although he had been with UA for almost thirty years, for as long as Krim, he was "Andy who?" in a business obsessed by profile.

Albeck's very anonymity, whatever qualifications he might have had—and for all anyone knew "Andy who?" could have been Thalberg and Selznick combined—seemed to prove Krim's claim that Transamerica simply didn't understand the movie business, in which such things mattered. Several years later, when a convicted felon was chosen to head another troubled company, reaction was mild: The appointment had showmanship; the appointee—convicted embezzler and forger or not—was part of the community. They *knew* him ("The czar we know" etc.).

The style of the thing was wrong. Act II had ended with the San Francisco gunslinger firing off his corporate Colt and the honorable and venerated sheriff turning in his badge. Act III cried for some sort of Big Finish in which a *Destry* Stewart or *High Noon* Cooper or even—for godsakes—Hopalong Cassidy would ride into town, cavalry at his dusty heels to ensure the safety of the abandoned homesteaders. Instead, these scriptwriters elevated the deputy, Edgar Buchanan!

But Andy Albeck was not chosen by Transamerica to be flashy or famous or even to be a moviemaker; he was chosen to run "a management system . . . we can understand." As senior vice-president under the previous regime he had often been Krim's and Pleskow's conduit between the two companies and, as ambassador to San Francisco, had become intimately familiar with the parent company's expectations. As president he would supervise and orchestrate the various UA divisions, delegate and reorganize where necessary, and would provide an approximation of internal continuity without grabbing headlines and making investors nervous.

If Albeck was not the Hollywood notion of a movieman, so what? He had experience, after all: He had been in the movie business for four decades, beginning his career as Indonesian sales representative for Columbia Pictures in 1939, moving on to Eagle-Lion (where he worked for Krim), had become a millionaire through his own independent distribution activities in the Far East, had been with Krim's UA regime from the start, and had served that group with faithful, if anonymous, efficiency. His loyalty to his previous superiors was a "good soldier" plus; he was an ameliorist, not a firebrand, and could, it seemed, be counted on to march to the company drum.

Albeck's personal style, in a business where such things are more than usually scrutinized, was not important, or negligibly so, to Transamerica, which did nothing to help him establish credibility with Hollywood or the home office as anything more than San Francisco's man in Arthur Krim's office. He was styled the Prussian from the beginning because of his ramrod-straight posture which suggested military training in the Weimar Republic and his pronounced Teutonic accent, which never quite sorted out the American r's and v's and w's. The posture, in fact, derived from athletics: Albeck had been an Olympic-caliber runner and skier, who at age fifty-seven still pursued his daily 6:00 A.M. Central Park jog in rain, snow, sleet, or sun and dreamed of returning to Japan, where he had grown up, learning several Oriental languages in the process, and where he found the best skiing in the world.

The accent was not German, but Danish, with overtones which might have suggested (but failed to) his (again) not German, but Russian, birth in 1921, to a Danish father engaged in the import-export business and a Russian mother. He was born, to be exact, thirty-seven kilometers out of Vladivostok, as his mother dashed to catch the last American troopship commandeered to transport refugees from the Russian Revolution to Tokyo, where mother and infant son joined the senior Albeck, who was, in one of this narrative's nicer coincidences, employed as the Japanese sales representative for the still-youthful United Artists Corporation.

The press never asked about Albeck's background, and because he was a reluctant, even obstructive, self-publicist, the exotic features of his biography (and whatever they may suggest about his character, his equanimity in the face of upheavals, business or otherwise) went unreported and unremarked not only by the press but also by most of his staff. Verbal caricatures of him (inside and outside UA) usually suggested Otto Preminger impersonating Erich von Stroheim, though he was in reality a gentle and kindly man.

If Albeck's steel backbone and heel-clicking accent were not enough, he suffered from the seeming aloofness that is the frequent camouflage of the profoundly shy. Too stiff to be extroverted, too disciplined to be falsely gregarious, he watched and listened tight-lipped behind outsize horn-rimmed glasses, their thick panes enlarging the apparent size of his eyes, intensifying the false air of the interrogating *Kommandant.*

Albeck was aware of the figure he cut, and he didn't have the personal vanity to manufacture another image. He tried with suits, shirts, and ties to adopt a look more "with it" than he perhaps cared about, but it never quite worked. The polyester content was always too high for the cashmere and mohair crowd from Meledandri and Giorgio's, the shirts insufficiently Sulka, the ties just wide enough to be the next-to-latest thing. All this was trivial to him, to Transamerica, and to their confidence in him as an executive. But it raised eyebrows in the Polo Lounge and the Russian Tea Room. Style may not be all, but in the movie business it counts.

What Albeck lacked in style, he more than made up for in numbers, Transamerica numbers: systems of budget control, cost estimates, profit projections, returns on investment, all the minutiae of what Pleskow termed nitpicking, but which were the standard reporting systems Transamerica now required of all its subsidiaries. Albeck understood them because guardianship of such "housekeeping" (Pleskow again) details had been delegated to him by his previous superiors, and he had, himself, designed many of the systems and forms in use for internal operations analysis.

Albeck's senior vice-presidential duties had included other unglamorous but necessary chores, ranging from the firing of secretaries for executives whose sensibilities were too refined to allow them to do so themselves, to traveling the globe as the company's hatchet man when worldwide overhead was cut back after Pleskow had become president.

As a result, many lower-echelon employees knew him as Krim's and Pleskow's "Nixon," an image problem which the apparent frigidity of his demeanor did little to correct.

None of that mattered to Transamerica, for they knew Albeck, knew his areas of expertise, felt comfortable with him. As for those areas in which he was, as he cheerfully admitted, inexperienced and without special aptitude, they relied on his ability to delegate authority and hoped for the best.

There was a humane consideration, too, in the Albeck appointment, or at least one which could be interpreted as humane and pragmatic at the same time: The company was in a state of dangerously low morale, from the file clerks in the Hong Kong exchange to the most senior vice-presidents at 729 as a result of the Krim departure and the air of foreboding it engendered. Before confidence could sink without a trace, an internal appointment might serve to buoy drowning spirits. Not only that, but a man who had been with the company for thirty years could hardly move into Mary Pickford's old office on the fourteenth floor without having *some* idea of what was going on. He at least knew the cast of characters both in San Francisco and on Seventh Avenue and in the 113 other offices around the world. He would bring no new, arbitrary broom to sweep clean paths that he had, even if only by association, helped pave. Promoting from within would transmit a signal to Wall Street that it was business as usual, that there was no hysteria or grasping for flashy straws to counteract bad publicity or to toady to the impressionable Hollywood crowd, and it would demonstrate to the stockholders Transamerica's faith in the future of its subsidiary as well as its dignity in the face of the defection of a high and mighty clique that had not been all that agreeable to work with in the first place.

At least that's the kind of sense it made to Transamerica, though it made none whatever to anyone in the movie business. The industry quickly assumed that (a) Albeck's elevation merely confirmed what Krim and the others had hinted at: contempt for the very creative process from which Transamerica derived 12 to 15 percent of its annual take; or (b) the company was for sale, a rumor which was illogical, given Beckett's stance with Krim, but persistent and annoying enough that two years later Beckett would take his extraordinary step to squelch it forever: "Transamerica Films."

It is doubtful, in fact, that Beckett thought often enough about the creative community to have contempt for it, though he clearly had no romantic awe of it either. In his mock folksy way he had tolerated what he called Arthur Krim's "grousing" and was now sanguine that he needn't do so anymore. Nor did he have to put up with playing second lead to the star head of one of his subsidiaries, said some.

There were industry realists who viewed the simultaneous martyrdom and apotheosis of Arthur Krim more skeptically than did the press—or the sixty-three letter-publishing filmmakers—reminding each other that no one had been a tougher, more autocratic deal maker than Krim and intuiting that the exodus had been less spontaneous than deliberated and managed with the same sophistication and shrewdness that had been brought to bear in transforming the old UA. There were also the industry pragmatists who didn't care *who* "Andy who?" was as long as he was a buyer. They inverted the old show business gag about making a deal with Hitler if he had a hot script to read that any producer (or director or writer or actor or agent or lawyer or business manager) might make a deal with Hitler if Hitler had a hot enough checkbook. And Andy Albeck's yearly production checkbook held a balance of $100 million. If the company was back to square one, it was a well-padded square in which to be.

Albeck was a priorities man, and his first priority as chief executive was to reassemble a production department. Though UA did not produce pictures, it caused or allowed them to be produced. Production was where decisions were made: what pictures would be financed and distributed by the company; what scripts, books, plays or ideas would be purchased or developed; what approvals would be granted or withheld. It was the most visible division of the company, the best known to press and public, and, in late January 1978, the most devastated by the walkout.

Albeck knew there would be additional defections in other areas after an interval of time had passed to permit the Orion group to avoid charges of company raiding. Ernst Goldschmidt, the cool, tasteful, and intelligent head of foreign distribution, would almost certainly leave; publicity and advertising resignations would follow; and then the financial officers would begin to drift off. Albeck could almost predict the names and their estimated times of departure, as Orion would come more and more to resemble the old UA doing business under an alias a few blocks away in Rockefeller Center. Defections of this sort could be handled one at a time, and promotion from within could, as in his own case, quickly fill resultant gaps and create an impression of continuity. Not so production. It was too visible, too vital, too . . . empty.

Albeck took out his organizational chart and drew a scalpel-fine pencil line through the name Mike Medavoy. Medavoy had been the most junior member of the Krim regime. But he had been well known, popular, and generally respected, Albeck knew. He was certainly active in Hollywood social and business circles, viewed widely as competent and aggressive. He had been an agent, good; he was only thirty-seven, good; he knew how to deal with talent, to talk that Hollywood talk, and was not shy about advertising either: His office walls in Culver City were decorated with framed, inscribed photographs of Jane and Sly and Liza and Rudy and others Albeck didn't always know. He was acknowledged to possess the skill which Albeck knew or sensed was the single most important for a production executive and which Albeck knew he himself lacked: the ability to attract talent and, once it was attracted, to supervise the yeses with a show of benevolent muscle and deliver the noes in a manner that not only didn't offend but made everyone come running back for more. He wasn't, Albeck knew, the most loved man in Hollywood (the power to say no stimulates other emotions), and he was rumored to rely heavily on story department reader reports, rarely bothering with books and manuscripts themselves. His rejection letters liberally quoted these reports without attribution: "I feel your story/ book/ play/ script/ idea is . . . 'quote,'" but that was neither unique nor unfair in the generally accepted Hollywood evaluation process, Albeck supposed. It did, after all, amount to thousands of project submissions each year—he had the figures to prove it—which would be a crushing reading burden even for Evelyn Wood. Besides, Medavoy's right arm, Vice-president Marcia Nasatir, was known to read closely, to supply Medavoy with often cogent and persuasive recommendations on projects in work or submitted to the company. Nasatir's publishing and literary agency background contributed a highbrow tone that gave the department a dimension of "class" in evaluation, despite Medavoy's more casual approach. What's more, Arthur finally made all the decisions anyway, so it may not have mattered if Medavoy read every word or not as long as his advice was good. But Arthur was gone, and Albeck wasn't going to be making decisions in the way Arthur had. Albeck would finally say yes or no, of course, but he needed someone more painstaking than Medavoy, someone whose judgments and opinions he could trust and then could back to the limit. An expert. He had a candidate in mind, in *view*, in fact, right next door at 729.

Marcia Nasatir was not right next door, she was 3,000 miles and several cultural heartbeats away. Many, including Nasatir herself, thought her an ideal replacement for Medavoy, but Albeck feared her literary background was *too* classy, that she wasn't tough enough to handle creative staffs on both coasts and whatever production problems might arise on twenty or twenty-five pictures a year. What if, God forbid, they stumbled over another *Apocalypse*?

When Albeck said no, Nasatir was bitterly convinced she lost the job because of antifeminist bias in the company and in Albeck in particular, a conclusion that genuinely perplexed him when he learned of it later. "My own wife, Lotte, is a stockbroker!" he protested, adding, "Though not *mine*," as if simultaneously to validate his lack of male chauvinism and nepotism. "Besides," he said, "she was too loyal to Mike and the others ever to be happy working for me." As if to prove his point, Nasatir resigned at once—to join Orion.

Danton Rissner, the executive next door, got the job. A dour and sardonic thirty-eight-year-old New Yorker, head of East Coast and European production since 1973, he was someone Albeck knew better, who was not vulnerable to the "highbrow" charge some leveled at Nasatir, though he was known to read quickly and voraciously, and he had shared a suite of offices in the southwest corner of the fourteenth floor of 729 with Albeck for the last several years. They weren't intimates or even friends exactly, but their proximity made Albeck more comfortable with Danny Rissner than he would have been with Nasatir or some candidate from outside the company. Because Rissner had been with UA since 1970, he could maintain a sense of continuity in a department in which he was, now that Nasatir had gone Orionward, the sole executive occupant.

Rissner's number two production job in the company had involved important responsibilities, including supervision of the James Bond pictures produced by Albert ("Cubby") Broccoli and Blake Edwards's successful *Pink Panther* series starring Peter Sellers, both of which were major sources of UA pride and income and which Albeck hoped to perpetuate. For these, Rissner seemed indispensable. Additionally, he had been a talent agent, like Medavoy, knew the agent lingo and *modus operandi*, and was young. Furthermore, his former boss and mentor Ted Ashley, who had hired and trained him at the old Ashley-Famous Agency, remained a close friend and, as current chairman of Warner Brothers, might try to lure him away from UA, leaving Albeck with no one at all.

Rissner accepted the senior vice-presidency, worldwide production, and moved to the West Coast and Medavoy's old office on the MGM lot. He promptly put in for, and got, a Mercedes.

Putting together an entirely new production team was Rissner's immediate task, and the process was not completed until May, three months later. In the meantime, Rissner's own office was occupied by Gabriel Sumner, Krim's advertising and publicity head, who had no previous production experience and who, after three months and to no one's surprise, resigned to join his former colleagues at Orion, back in ad-pub.

With Nasatir gone, Rissner hired Christopher Mankiewicz as first lieutenant on the West Coast. Mankiewicz, son of writer-director Joseph L. Mankiewicz and nephew of *Citizen Kane*'s scriptwriter, Herman Mankiewicz, * was a well-known executive gadfly, having been, as he announced with affable and bombastic pride, "fired by more film companies than any other young executive in the business!" Chris's experience was as solid and broad as he was. He had grown up in and around the industry, had worked on pictures made by his father (*Cleopatra* among them), was well connected, well read, literate in film and theater, had practical experience in Hollywood, New York, and Europe, and should have been the ideal executive. But while he was unfailingly intelligent, witty, and articulate (he wasn't a Mankiewicz for nothing), he was often too witty, too articulate, and his intelligence expressed itself in a manner too uninhibited not to be abrasive to many. It was widely assumed within the company that Rissner (who was his close personal friend) had appointed him over Albeck's objections (or advice; Albeck rarely, if ever, intruded in lower-echelon personnel matters, though he formally vetted them all) and that his fortunes therefore rested with Rissner's own.

Mankiewicz's volubility effectively complemented Rissner's taciturnity. What Rissner might convey with four letters, frequently profane, Mankiewicz could expatiate on for four paragraphs. The former was a pragmatist, a street-smart New Yorker whose cynicism was sometimes genuine, sometimes a sardonic shield; he was a type A worrier and workaholic who tried to conceal both traits behind an air of boredom. His desk was invariably clean of scripts and books because of the speed of his reading and responses. He chain-smoked and glowered and cracked Broadway jokes and swore, and part of his personal legend at UA had it that Arthur Krim, drawn by pungent fumes permeating the fourteenth floor of 729, had personally discovered him smoking something more acrid than his Benson & Hedges as he sat quietly reading a script at his desk and inhaling down to his toes. If this is true, Krim's admonishments went unrecorded, but it added to the bored-iconoclast, street-kid glamour of Rissner's image at UA.

Leavening Rissner's cynical pragmatism and Mankiewicz's bombast

---

* And brother of screenwriter Tom Mankiewicz, cousin of Public Broadcasting's Frank Mankiewicz and of the promising novelist Johanna Mankiewicz Davis, who was tragically killed in a freak Manhattan taxi accident. It is quite some family to live up to.

was the quiet, moody junior vice-president of production on the West Coast, David Field, wooed away from creative development at Alan Ladd's Twentieth Century-Fox, where he felt blocked from further advancement by other Ladd executives. Field had had previous experience in production of *Movies of the Week* for ABC television and was eager to gain more.

They were an odd trio whose physical distance from the New York center of power was only partially patched by telephone lines and memos, both copiously utilized. Once a month, therefore, the two production staffs gathered either in the boardroom on the eleventh floor of 729 or in Rissner's own California office for a monthly production review, to which were always invited Chairman Harvey and the heads of distribution: international, domestic, and ancillary markets.

These meetings were largely informational in character. Status reports were delivered on each picture in whatever stage of development or production, problems would be raised, solutions announced or reached, and so on. Occasionally, if timing willed it, major acquisition decisions would be made in such a committee setting, as happened in early May 1978, the first such meeting I was to attend after being named Sumner's replacement as head of East Coast and European production when he left to rejoin the worlds of ad-pub and Orion.

"Fellas, this book is a piece of *shit!*"

Chris Mankiewicz's considerable bulk rolled behind the statement, imploring the rest of us to agree. He flung his palms outward toward the room, as if the evidence were smeared there to observe. After a moment he dropped one hand into the pile of sweet rolls on the coffee table before him, piled high with danish and dirty coffee cups.

"Everybody knows that, Chris." Rissner sighed. "It's not about whether it's a piece of shit or it's not a piece of shit. It's about whether we want to make a goddamn deal."

"On this unmitigated, irredeemable piece of *shit?*"

Rissner borrowed matches from someone, lit a cigarette, pointedly ignoring the redundancy. "What's the minimum bid we could make, you think?" he said to the room in general. "A million? A million five?" His voice seemed casual, but his manner suggested constraint as he bent and rebent the borrowed book of matches. He looked up at the circle seated in mismatched chairs around the glass and chrome coffee table in his Culver City office. There was the chairman of the board, down from San Francisco for the morning, looking on with a kibitzer's curiosity, his expression acknowledging nothing more than respectful interest; the president of the company, his mouth a tight line, owllike eyes swiveling from one face to another behind his huge spectacles, glinting in the early-morning sunlight like windshields; there were the heads of domestic and ancillary distribution, ignoring Mankiewicz's outburst and Rissner's question by burrowing into their synopses of the book in question, readers' reports they were supposed to have read the previous night or on the plane from New York but clearly hadn't. There was Mankiewicz, exasperated beyond belief that his opinion was having no apparent effect on anyone else; there was David Field, looking thoughtful and tactful; and I—I was *confused*. Who cared what the distribution guys thought? I wondered. Why? When? What did they know?

I knew, so I answered Rissner. "My guess is that the least they'll listen to is a million five and a gross percentage, and that won't make a deal. If we're not prepared to go that high, we shouldn't make an offer at all because the agent will decide he's been insulted and our relationship with the agency is weak enough as it is. This *is* the first major submission from them in months, right?"

"Right." Rissner nodded.

"The first major submission because they're trying to hype what even *they* know is a piece of illiterate *shit!*"

"Chris, *please.*"

Albeck looked simultaneously alarmed and annoyed. Why didn't Mankiewicz shut up? He had clearly been given more than a cue by his superior. Or could the book really be all *that* bad? He asked the question of Rissner.

"Andy, the guy's last two books were huge best sellers. The movie of the first one became one of the top-grossing pictures of all time. The movie of the second one, which was only routine, did forty million dollars. It's not about quality; it's about money and track record."

"Don't talk to me about track record," retorted Mankiewicz. "My old man won four Academy Awards in two years and then went out and made *The Honey Pot*. I know all *about* track record."

Rissner ignored this and turned to me for an opinion. "How would I know?" I waffled. "I turned down the first book. I thought who in Nebraska knows from sharks?"

"But what about the *offer*?"

"Well," I said, grateful for a money discussion to get me off the hook of commenting on a book I didn't like any more than Mankiewicz did, "if you want to make an offer"—I couched it in Rissner's direction with the second-person pronoun—"it should be as preemptive as possible. Otherwise, we look like pikers. What's he want—an auction, what?"

"One offer, all terms, sealed bids. He's submitted the book five places—"

"He *says.*" Mankiewicz now seemed to be talking to himself since no one else was apparently listening, except maybe Harvey, but it was hard to tell.

Rissner ignored him again. "—five places, expects five bids by the close of business today, and top bid takes it. So the offer has to be the best and farthest we're willing to go. If we go."

Andy looked up, puzzled and impatient. "Are we obligated to make an offer?"

"No," said Rissner, anticipating resistance.

He was rescued by the musings of domestic distribution. "Forty million?"

"Domestic or worldwide?" asked ancillary.

"Domestic, I *think.*"

Albeck shot sharply: "That was because of big boobies in wet T-shirts. Does this book have boobies?"

Jim Harvey's placidity seemed suddenly jarred, by the subject matter or Andy's terminology one couldn't tell.

"It has boobies and rapes and S and M, and not one word of it has any resemblance to human behavior as we know it!" Mankiewicz chimed in.

Rissner looked bored. "Yes, Andy. It has boobies. Wet ones."

While Andy mulled this over, frowning, I asked where else the book had been submitted.

"You have to assume to the producers of the first picture and the second picture, if only as courtesy submissions. They would be buying for Universal or Columbia. Then there's us, probably Fox and . . . maybe Paramount. Or Warner's."

"Danny, you're close to Warner's," said Andy. "Can you ask them what they think?"

"Why would I do that?" said Rissner, appalled. "What difference would it make? Who cares if they like it or hate it? The point is, what do *we* do? Do we make an offer or not, and if we do, what's the goddamn offer?"

"I got it," said Albeck, chastised, gloomy, but instructed.

We voted. Andy agreed; Harvey said nothing.

An offer was framed, approved, and made, as Mankiewicz fumed in uncharacteristic silence. The offer came to slightly more than $2 million for the movie rights, based on a floor price which escalated with performance of the book on best seller lists, in book clubs, and so on; a gross percentage of box-office receipts was added to make the offer unbeatable.

It was beaten.

The producers of the movie made from the author's first book secured the rights for something closer, it was believed, to $2.5 million. Losing the book was almost a relief. We had demonstrated we had the money, were willing to spend it, would be again, and it hadn't cost a penny.

Two and a half years later, when the movie based on the book was released and landed with a critical and financial thud, I had lunch with Mankiewicz, who had been long gone from UA.

"I told you it was a piece of shit." He laughed without a trace of a sneer.

"That was never the point, Chris," I said.

"It should have been." He smiled.

The point was that an alarming product shortage was looming, the result partly of the months of preoccupation with restaffing and partly of hesitations in project development in the last months of the previous management's tenure. Though this was always denied (and not long after flared noisily and angrily in the pages of the *New York Times*), it does not stretch imagination or credulity to assume that men who were already looking around for a new home, as McClintick tells us, might have had little heart for the pursuit and development of projects they knew they could not bring to completion. Then, too, there were the only fitful agency submissions—remainders and seconds—as Hollywood watched and waited for this unproved cast of characters to define itself. As Mankiewicz felt moved to tell *Variety*, "It's not the La Brea Tar Pits out here, you know." But it sometimes felt like it.

The Krim legacy to United Artists was rich in contracts, deals, legal relationships; the library of films made or acquired by UA over the years (including the pre-1949 Warner Brothers film library) represented distributable pictures or remake possibilities. There was a generous backlog of literary materials made or unmade, potentially fertile sources for development and production. It was a treasure trove, but a frustratingly inaccessible one, just beyond immediate reach.

UA needed the new James Bond, *For Your Eyes Only*, which Albeck and Rissner and producer Broccoli had decided to convert into *Moonraker* to exploit the space craze created by *Star Wars*. It wouldn't be ready for production until July at the earliest (and in May there wasn't even a budget). Albeck wanted another *Pink Panther*, but In-

spector Clouseau's return was at least a year away, maybe more, what
with seemingly endless volleys of recriminations and hostilities shooting
back and forth between director Blake Edwards and Peter Sellers, each
of whom claimed full credit for the popularity of the series with such
vehement animosity that it was clearly a situation irresolvable with
mere diplomacy. There was in postproduction a new Woody Allen picture about which almost nothing was known except that Krim had approved it, Allen wasn't in it, and it was not a comedy. One couldn't
apply unseemly pressure on Allen; his *Annie Hall* in April garnered the
UA tenth Best Picture Academy Award, which, in the partisan spirit of
the times, became known as Orion's first. (Beckett can only have
viewed this third-year-in-a-row Best Picture Oscar with somewhat
mixed pride.) The next Woody Allen picture would be ready for production only when he said it was, although he hastened to assure it
would be a comedy. There was also to be a follow-up to the hugely
successful *Rocky*, which showed signs of having series potential. This, at
least, was set to go in the summer, and its negotiations had, in fact,
been Albeck's first official accomplishment as president. Incredibly
enough, there had been no remake rights UA could enforce without
the original producers, Chartoff and Winkler, who were retained as
producers exclusive to UA through a deal negotiated by Albeck which
included *Rocky II* (and eventually *Rocky III*).

These and more were mouthwatering plums, waiting to be plucked
or shaken from the contract tree once they were ripe. But it was the
waiting that was creating such frustration, for there was nothing ready
now. A six-month production hiatus in 1978 could create a six-month
distribution gap in late 1979 or 1980, and as it happened, only one
picture went into production in the first six months of calendar year
1978. This hastily conceived "little picture" with Peter Fonda and
Brooke Shields was brought in by Mankiewicz and produced by his boy-
hood chums Fonda and William Hayward. It was a picture of some
charm but predictably marginal commercial appeal.

In contrast with *Wanda Nevada*, Orion's first picture went into production at approximately the same time and was, to UA's keen
awareness, prestigious and classy. *A Little Romance* had a script by Allan
Burns, was produced and directed by George Roy Hill (*The Sting, Butch
Cassidy and the Sundance Kid*), and starred Laurence Olivier. That it
had been rejected by Universal (which thereby lost its long-term relationship with Hill) and was in turnaround, which means the same thing
for projects that *available* or *at liberty* means about persons in euphe-
mism-addicted Hollywood, in no way tarnished its class. The two pictures seemed to point up a painful disparity of quality (both were to be

financial failures); that pain spurred an already practical problem into a more ambitious direction. Painful or not, the problem was product.

Partly to fill 1978's production gap, Rissner was quietly concluding a distribution deal with Lorimar Pictures, the powerful and rich television company (*The Waltons*) which had lately entered feature filmmaking. These pictures—to include a remake of *The Postman Always Rings Twice* with Jack Nicholson and a movie based on Richard Brautigan's *The Hawkline Monster* starring both Clint Eastwood *and* Nicholson—a total of as many as six movies a year, would supplement the four to six annual pictures from MGM that UA was distributing under a ten-year agreement which would expire in 1983. This left room for another ten to fifteen pictures from UA to utilize and occupy the distribution division effectively—and production's $100 million annual budget.

There were two ways to do it. The first was the acquisition of finished films financed by others who had no prearranged distribution commitments. Such pictures are called pickups, and in recent years they have turned handsome profits for many companies. *Porky's* for Twentieth, *Friday the 13th* for Paramount are just two examples. Nor are pickups to be found only in the low-budget lowbrow department: Both *Chariots of Fire* and *Gandhi* (each of which won a Best Picture Academy Award) were pickups by, respectively, Warner Brothers and Columbia. Profits and honors were there to be plucked without the uncertainties of production.

But pickups were no solution at all for UA because of its method of financing them. Pickups were purchased with funds from the yearly production budget but were not chosen by production personnel. Production might not even be consulted, merely informed that domestic distribution, say, had just spent $1 million of production's money to acquire a Japanese sci-fi adventure called *Message from Space* "which can't keep 'em from lining up at the box office. It's a Jap *Star Wars!* It'll clean up." The only thing it cleaned up was the red inkwell. Then there was something called *The Passage*, which featured Malcolm McDowell as a sex-crazed Gestapo agent who ran around in a jockstrap adorned by a swastika.

Even if these pictures had been good or commercial or both, distribution's happy habit of spending production money without its permission—or knowledge—was deeply resented in a company the very last need of which was further internal dissension and disarray. A million dollars may sound trifling in light of the overall budget, but inasmuch as production budgets are finite, it meant that this million could not be spent on something else, something perhaps worthier. When the digits soar even higher, as will be seen, there are any number of filmmakers who see *their* movies in the detritus of someone else's cutting room floor. Feelings can run high in the traditional rivalry between production and distribution, which is a sort of bus and truck version of the art versus business conflict that has run through the business since Edison. As a final humiliating blow picked-up pictures bore the company logo and, to the uninitiated at least, appeared to represent the company's product. *Jap Chew Bacas? Nazi jockstraps?*

Albeck later explained he was giving distribution executives in whom he had marginal faith "enough rope," but production felt itself the division hung out to dry, and the policy was finally changed. Pickups henceforth would be proposed by distribution and ratified by production (which didn't do much better: *Friday the 13th* was lost because of a stingy bid; we captured, however, something thankfully forgotten, called *Roller Boogie*). Pickups were not apparently the UA answer.

The second option was simply to accelerate the production process. This option is workable only in the narrowest of limits. Movies are made to clocks which run on union time and by filmmakers who are fond of asking, "Do you want it fast or good?"—not always a stupid question. This is not to say that the limiting of indulgence could not have a profound effect on movie costs and financing, as new and skilled low-budget filmmakers demonstrate year after year. Even accepting the automatic inflation resulting from making such films in a unionized context, movie costs almost always directly reflect time, and "fast or good" are not necessarily mutually exclusive concepts.

But accelerating the process presupposes something to accelerate. It is almost always a script, and as anyone involved in any creative endeavor knows—from the most homespun little theater to the most exalted grand opera company—there is no such thing as a creative season. It simply doesn't exist in movies, the theater, music, publishing, or any of those human activities which depend on a muse that strikes only when good and ready and not before. In all arts there are fallow periods, in which the mediocre and worse seem the norm, raising again the ancient cry "The theater/ novel/ poem/ symphony/ ballet/ movie is dead!" No doubt we will one day hear it about the video game—but the cruel fact is that the raw material—someone's inspiration—in whatever form, is not subject to contractual legislation or the wishful thinking of frantic studio executives. One is at the mercy of an ineffable, often maddening aesthetic mystery.

Every executive knows and fears this and tries to convince himself that just a bit more rock turning will yield that holiest of movie grails: a hot property. There results a kind of desperate promiscuity in the executives' relationships to talent, what Scott Fitzgerald called a

"shameless economic lechery," sometimes disguised by pretentious artistic come-ons. What it really means is avoiding "How the hell did
we lose Brando and Nicholson and Penn to UA?" (or Eastwood and
Nicholson to Lorimar?) or some other index by which the company in
question is perceived as lower on the pecking order than somebody,
anybody else.

The vague but very real barometer by which agents rank studios in
preference of submissions can become the subject of obsession. If a production team can last long enough, something usually will go right,
perhaps creating a roll of luck, a consistency of success that becomes
self-perpetuating. Twentieth Century-Fox under Alan Ladd, Jr., enjoyed such a happy run when, after two years of dismal flops, suddenly
Silent Movie, The Omen, Julia, and *Star Wars* erased *Lucky Lady* and *At
Long Last Love* from public and stockholder memory. There took place
that curious alchemy by which success seems to be not a result but an
entity in and of itself, a magic quality that can rub off, and agents hurl
material and talent over the transom in the medieval hope that proximity will work its magic on dross. In such a situation no one else has a
chance until this week's alchemist says no.

A company in transition like UA in early 1978 tumbles almost automatically to the bottom of the list because of uncertainty about internal change of personnel and policy unless there is some extraordinary
or charismatic compensating factor—or executive. When MGM hired
David Begelman, the sense of poised dynamism he wore like his cashmere sport coats was so persuasive it seemed to dispel a near decade of
doldrums. Culver City became Deal City almost overnight, but to any
close observer the deals were for the same old seconds and remainders,
and the results, dynamic and confident or not, failed to impress the
paying public and headed directly for the open drain.

Greed is always a point in the marketplace, but in Hollywood it is
seldom *the* point. (Or it is a point so subtly convoluted that naked
dollar signs cannot or will not suffice.) Agents set prices for subjects
and stars and assume that somebody (or nobody) will pay them. Generally they are right, and the more intangible indices of personal relationships or image or what are called auspices come into play, and the
whole complex of shared experiences and attitudes and prejudices that
compose any old boy (or old girl) network become more refined competitive factors than mere money. In Hollywood, well . . . everybody's
got money.

Often in this scramble for hot material, "Fellas, this book is a piece
of *shit!*" becomes lost in the frenzy over "Can we make a deal?" The
producers who *did* make the deal on the book discussed in early May

are, as it happens, two of the most intelligent and successful producers in Hollywood. Maybe they *loved* the book, or maybe they were simply unlucky enough to learn the hard way screenwriter William Goldman's tough but accurate number one observation about Hollywood: "NO-BODY KNOWS ANYTHING" (Goldman's caps).

Square one required desperate or elementary measures, whether anybody knew anything or not. Rissner chose elementary, obsessional variety. The projects already in development or preproduction would be prayed over and supervised on a day-to-day basis, while the production executives mounted an assault on the creative community. The talent mountain wasn't coming to UA; therefore . . . it was love and war, and all was fair.

Rissner asked the production executives to draw up lists: writers, directors, actors, producers, agents, even lawyers. These lists were pooled, sifted, refined, argued over, applauded or hissed, and finally typed up in neat A lists and B lists and C lists by category.

Each staff member had his own relationships within the industry, varying in breadth and depth, though they sometimes overlapped. When the principal executives compared lists, it was a pleasant (though not unpredictable) surprise that among us all, we knew Everybody. Everybody we wanted to know, that is, for there were D and F lists, too.

Many desirable A's were just unavailable, being committed to exclusive contracts elsewhere. Some were already booked so far in the future as to be effectively *hors de combat*. Others we didn't like personally but admired (A tending to B); others we didn't admire but were crazy about (C tending to B). Finally, the executives chose one from column A, one from column B, and so on and went awooing or agunning, the minimum basic objective being at least one phone call per week. Lunch was good; dinner, better; full surrender or marriage, the goal.

Promiscuous courtships are not only fatiguing but hazardous to health. First, they dangerously increase the work load because there is hardly a creative person alive unprepared to rush forward with a passion he's been nursing for years that everyone else already hates the sight of. Secondly, there is often the dicey moment of failed ardor, when the fervently wooed is left standing at the altar, rejected script in hand. This can become particularly discomfiting when, as happened to one of us, the rejected is a former partner or, as happened to another of us, a father or, as happened to all of us, *friends*. Still, we persevered, and slowly these siegelike courtships began to show results: Norman Jewison came to call; so did Herbert Ross, Alan Pakula, Francis Coppola. In fact, of the sixty-three signers of the published letter to John Beckett that had appeared in the trades in January, fully fifty of them were approachable or amenable, and gradually resistance lowered and projects went into work, supplementing those we had inherited.

Frederic Raphael, author of *Darling* and *Two for the Road*, would write an original screenplay; Richard Lester would produce and direct a picture starring Sean Connery; Raquel Welch would appear nude for the first time in a dramatic picture she would also produce ("Yes, Andy, she will show her boobies"); Gordon Willis, perhaps America's best cinematographer, would direct his first picture for us; Bette Midler would romp in a comedy directed by *Rocky*'s John Avildsen; Richard Pryor would outrage us all in a remake of *The Man Who Came to Dinner* (as, one assumes, Sheridan *Black*side); and Norman Jewison, though he didn't want to direct Frederick Forsyth's *The Dogs of War* anymore ("I've been through so many scripts I feel I've already made the movie") would produce it for the young writer-director who had just finished the most recent rewrite.

We felt a corner had been turned, that we had at last advanced to square two. These projects (there were many others) looked good on paper; they gladdened distribution hearts and studded the annual report with glowing names and promises. They were also foolers; Freddy Raphael's script was never made, even though Al Pacino and Diane Keaton were prepared to costar; Richard Lester and Sean Connery's picture was, and failed; Raquel Welch remained unexposed; Gordon Willis made a debut the reception of which probably cured him of directing forever (I personally received a death threat letter from a disappointed viewer when it was released); Bette Midler never made the Avildsen comedy but made another instead and called it a nightmare to the press; Richard Pryor dazedly told me in the middle of a Los Angeles–Honolulu flight that he had never even *heard* of *The Man Who Came to Dinner* despite the deal memos I had personally inspected in the files; and though Norman Jewison did produce *The Dogs of War*, it was several screenplays and years later, with a different young director and script, because the 1978 writer, Michael Cimino, turned Jewison down, finding the script he had written for himself to direct now somehow . . . wanting. Besides, he had something else in mind.

CHAPTER 4

AGENDAS

Someone at MGM—Lillie Messinger, probably—had mentioned the word *motivation* to Mayer, and it became a refrain with him, though I doubt he knew what it meant.

One day he asked me, "What's the motivation?"

"Mr. Mayer," I explained, "we open with, say, a shot of Clark Gable on New Year's Eve, standing at the corner of Fifty-fourth and Broadway. Then we cut to Times Square, full of thousands of people celebrating. Then we cut to a shot of Joan Crawford standing at the corner of Forty-second and Broadway. The question isn't why? The audience has already read the marquee, and it says 'Joan Crawford and Clark Gable in *Love on the Run.*' The audience *knows why.* The question is *how*? How is Clark Gable going to get from the corner of Fifty-fourth and Broadway to the corner of Forty-second and Broadway?"

We didn't hear much about "motivation" after that.

—Joseph L. Mankiewicz, in conversation (1972)

Andy Albeck had never heard of Michael Cimino, but not many had in the late spring of 1978, and there were other, more important names unfamiliar to him as well. To strengthen his awareness of the creatively prominent, he had reserved for his personal use 729's fourteenth-floor screening room to project each Tuesday evening at precisely six a movie currently in release from another company. He invited his wife, Lotte, and upper-echelon UA executives and their

wives, but not as a social gesture: This was business, on-the-job training
to help him (and others) pin names and faces to specific achievements.
It would also reveal what the competition was up to and what audiences
were buying, for the sole criterion for film selection was that each
movie have grossed a minimum of $5 million at the box office. Pictures
that held less interest for the paying public might well be instructive as
negative object lessons, but common sense steered him to movies and
moviemakers currently winning at least moderate public acceptance.
Tonight's movie was something starring people called Cheech and
Chong. Well, the world changed, and movies with it, and there was
less point in grousing about it, as Jack Beckett might say, than in trying
to understand and adapt.

Albeck had never been overawed by movies or movie people and
knew he would never have total recall of the credits of every film he
screened. He didn't want that. He needed clarity, not clutter. He
wasn't much interested in Hollywood lore, and his habits of mind were
too disciplined and organized for the playful enjoyment of trivia, unless
it could be slipped into some practical pigeonhole. For encyclopedic
knowledge he could always buy an encyclopedia, and Rissner and his
staff could fill him in when he needed fuller or more precise information
about someone they were proposing as director or writer or star or producer.

Knowing the names (or pronouncing them correctly: Irwin invariably came out as "Ervin" or "Irving") was really only a matter of efficiency and courtesy. The larger purpose was to sensitize himself to those
qualities the production people liked to talk about. They used words
like *nuance* or *subtext* or *subtlety* or *style,* and while they were mostly
vague and subjective, Albeck felt they could be comprehended, their
meaning felt, given enough exposure and experience, just as putting the
emphasis on a $5 million gross or better would make a commercial
point to the production staff that was not at all vague and subjective.
This conviction reassured and comforted.

Even more reassuring, he reflected, as he waited for Lotte to arrive
from her Rockefeller Center brokerage office for this Tuesday evening's
screening, was that at his elbow, neatly tucked away in the desk console, was his set of black loose-leaf binders enfolding a cache of the only
objective information that could help him evaluate and balance the
other, more subjective part. The black books contained columns of figures earned by each picture released by each major company. They were
exchanged on a monthly courtesy basis by the several chief executive
officers and were privileged and confidential: bottom-line numbers, picture by picture, month by month, dollar by dollar. Occasionally as late

as 2:00 A.M. (Albeck rarely slept more than four hours a night) he would study these numbers to see what secrets they might reveal, what patterns (cast, stories, directors?) he could discover and pass on to the production people to give their work direction. He had no desire to stifle their zeal and enthusiasm—that was why they had been hired—but sometimes they became emotional and argumentative, even among themselves, and their relish for movies and movie lore and movie gossip and movie people was not something Albeck shared or was much interested in. This did not mean he had no fondness for movies, no taste or appreciation; he had preferences and standards and knew good from bad, entertaining from boring, and he mostly liked what the general public liked. When he didn't, he tried earnestly to figure out why they liked what they did. After all, the company was making pictures for them, not for him—*or* for the production staff. These Cheech and Chong people, he suspected, might take some figuring, though from what he had heard he doubted that the analysis would use such words as *nuance* and *style*.

When his late-shift secretary, Linda Hurley, announced Danny Rissner calling from California, Albeck excused himself from his visitor, picked up the receiver, and simultaneously pulled from the desk drawer one of his self-designed, narrow-lined follow-up sheets. He tapped his razor-sharp yellow pencil flat against the white sheet as Rissner began discussing a multiple-picture deal with Michael Cimino. Albeck listened and incised "Cimino Multi-Pic Deal" in tiny, clear printing on the caption line of the follow-up sheet, and on a lower line, the initials D.R., followed by the date. He then sat back, shoulders squared, and listened carefully to Rissner's presentation, waiting until he heard something that required notation in his fine, meticulous hand. He was skeptical about multiple-picture deals in general and questioned why UA should make one with someone of whom he had never heard. Still, he prided himself on being open to argument and listened courteously.

He learned from Rissner that Cimino had been a successful director of television commercials in New York, a "star" in that competitive, lucrative field, had had a number of movie writing assignments and credits, though he had directed only two pictures, one of which Andy surely remembered, because it had been for UA in 1974: a Clint Eastwood vehicle called *Thunderbolt and Lightfoot*. Albeck inscribed the fact, recalled the picture, and, as Rissner continued, leafed quickly through one of the black loose-leaf volumes to the page detailing UA revenues. There he read that *Thunderbolt and Lightfoot* had returned rentals of a solidly profitable level to the company, a respectable, if not spectacular, hit for Eastwood, who was a name Albeck knew very well indeed. He also knew there had been some unpleasantness between Eastwood and UA over the company's handling of the picture, and the actor had sworn he would never work for UA again. He swiftly pulled out a second follow-up sheet as Rissner talked, carefully penciled "Clint Eastwood" at the top, added a date in the upper-right corner, indicating to his secretaries when they should retrieve it from the files for his attention, and smoothly slid it into his out box.

Rissner listed Cimino's writing credits: There was a shared credit on an earlier Eastwood picture for Warner's, *Magnum Force*; a sci-fi picture for Universal called *Silent Running*, credit also shared; some work on *The Rose* without credit; and it was his screenplay for *The Dogs of War* that Jewison was thinking about producing for UA. This rang a dissonant bell for Albeck, though he could not at the moment recall why. Rissner went on to explain that Cimino's most impressive work wouldn't be released for another six months, although Rissner had seen a version of this new picture, Cimino's second, and was sure that in spite of the Vietnam War subject matter, it would be a major picture and make Cimino a major director, possibly an unapproachable one. If UA acted now, Rissner thought he could negotiate something liveable.

Albeck frowned. This time a veritable glockenspiel rang out of tune. Francis Coppola was off in San Francisco—Jim Harvey's very backyard—still futzing around with *his* Vietnam picture and this newcomer was going to preempt him? *Apocalypse First?*

Rissner hastened to add that there were problems with Universal over the new picture's length, but they would get worked out, and he remained adamant that the picture would be *big*, validating his judgment and justifying UA's pursuit of Cimino before that event occurred.

"I get it," said Albeck firmly. "A coup."

"I don't know if it's a coup, Andy," Rissner answered, "but the guy's talented."

Albeck approved exploring a deal, noting the next day as a follow-up date in the upper-right corner of the Cimino sheet and briskly hung up.

Albeck never particularly liked conversations of this sort because no matter how direct and honest his admission of unawareness of this or that name new to him, he seemed to invite impatience or condescension, deliberate or not. Rissner's manner was testy lately, anyway, though he was always prepared and articulate in pressing his points, which seemed to betoken respect. Rissner was casual about nothing in spite of his offhand manner. In striving not to press too hard, however, he sounded more strained and impatient than ever—on long distance anyway. Face-to-face or just next door on the fourteenth floor was always easier and clearer, particularly when a man addicted to verbal and gestural shorthand, as was Rissner, was not merely a telephone speaker-box voice. Just down the hall was better—*easier* anyway.

And perhaps Albeck was reading tension into Rissner's voice when the abruptness was merely a sign of fatigue. He certainly sounded tired, and Albeck knew there was some sort of blood pressure problem. Well, high blood pressure was almost a membership badge for top-level executives. Still, however driven and ambitious, Rissner was almost two decades younger than Albeck himself. At barely thirty-eight Danny was not, in fact, that much older than Albeck's own son.

He quickly rejected the thought of having to replace Rissner for illness or any other reason, now that things were finally settling down and gearing up. Replacing him would inevitably mean going outside the company, possibly even to a "headhunter," because there was no suitable candidate within. Mankiewicz was too outspoken, too flamboyant for Albeck; Field and I both were too new to evaluate; and now that the major predictable resignations had mostly taken place—Goldschmidt to Orion, Sumner to Orion, the odd ad-pub staffers to Orion or to Warner's to service the Orion account—resignation by Rissner for whatever reason would be proclaimed by the press as further evidence of erosion.

His secretary signaled with a buzz that Mrs. Albeck had arrived for the screening. He slipped the Cimino follow-up sheet into the out box, marched smartly to the door, which he opened without altering his ramrod-straight posture, and cheerily greeted his wife, who was short and blond and whose lightly accented exuberance seemed to suggest a happy *Hausfrau* rather than the broker from Gruntal & Company she was. The two walked down the red-carpeted hall, haunted by the framed posters for *Annie Hall* and *Rocky* and *Cuckoo's Nest* and *Around the World in Eighty Days* and *Marty* and *West Side Story* and *In the Heat of the Night* and *Tom Jones* and *The Apartment* and into the screening room, to watch somebody else's hit.

The daily production meeting the following morning was attended by myself, as vice-president of East Coast and European production; Dean Stolber, the thirty-four-year-old vice-president of business affairs, who had been Bill Bernstein's assistant at the end of the Krim regime; Al Fitter, fifty-three-year-old senior vice-president of domestic distribution, who had been with UA since the fifties; Norbert Auerbach, fifty-six, senior vice-president of foreign distribution, who had been with

UA twice, most recently since 1976; and Bart Farber, fifty-one-year-old vice-president of ancillary markets, at UA since 1961.

Albeck presided at the scarred walnut desk, his follow-up sheets neatly terraced before him, perhaps eight inches high, as the rest of us spread in a facing semicircle on mismatched, threadbare chairs.

Once-white mesh curtains filtered light into the darkly paneled office overlooking Seventh Avenue as the stroboscopic lights of the Pussycat Theater winked across the street. It was hard to think Mary Pickford had ever been in the neighborhood.

Production meetings were held daily, usually in the morning, and never took fewer than two hours to conclude. The meetings were designed to encourage discipline in the production staff, and they did. Production tended to be scattershot in approach—or seemed so to a man of Albeck's precise and methodical nature—and his follow-ups, which he used as each meeting's agenda, both sealed cracks and superimposed a structure on their priorities. The daily sessions also provided Albeck with tutorials in movie and deal making, and like a quick, diligent student, he took notes, studied, and analyzed, either then and there or later, at two o'clock in the morning.

The most important purpose these meetings served, however, was to give the distribution staff direct influence over production decisions. Story ideas, treatments, screenplays, casting and director selections all were routinely submitted to them for review and comment. My confusion in early May over what possible relevance distribution's attitude about a submitted manuscript could have was swiftly clarified: They didn't have an attitude; they had approval. The production staff was in effect placed in a position of having to sell to the distribution staff any idea they wanted to develop, any talent they wanted to hire no matter how minor, with Albeck serving as the final arbiter.

His reasoning was simply that the salesmen ought to have a say regarding their merchandise; as a corollary, they could not then blame production for making lousy pictures they couldn't sell if they had helped design them. As a management theory it seemed simple enough and even made a certain kind of sense, but in practice it became the tail wagging the dog up, down, right, left, and in violent circles. The marketing heads had far from identical needs, goals, and expertise. Fifteen or more hours a week spent on the minutiae of production problems in Andy's drab office, plus home or airplane hours reading (or avoiding) scripts and synopses by men who had little experience, inclination, or competence to judge screen material, culminated in a state of tedium *in extremis* for everyone involved, eager as the distribution gentlemen were to dictate what pictures would get made and how.

The production staff, meanwhile, who felt that only they possessed the purity to carry the creative flame, chafed and seethed with frustration and resentment at having to submit each idea or suggestion (*and* the business terms under which it might be effected) to people whose creative judgment they viewed (with exaggeration, to be sure) as ranging from merely marginal to subliterate. Wasn't it enough that these guys were spending production's money for pickups?

Nevertheless, production submitted once a month to the California or New York convocations (production presentations often actually rehearsed), and Stolber and I, because we were in New York, did so daily. After each meeting I would telephone Rissner in California to tell him of progress or defeat. I felt less like a movie executive than a professional Greek messenger.

This particular gathering began in a bawdy air of bewilderment over Messrs. Cheech and Chong. Ribaldry built as those who had been present at the screening scoffed away their failures to understand either the movie or its appeal to the phenomenal audiences rushing to it all over America. Obviously some subteen aberration was taking place that none of us needed take more seriously than, say, the Hula Hoop. Marijuana jokes and locker room snickers proliferated as the movie was mocked, derided, and dismissed, and we grew more and more complacently superior and relaxed. Finally, this derisory crescendo was halted as Albeck blinked behind his fishbowl spectacles and announced crisply, "I would laugh, too, if we had a picture grossing as much."

The laughter ceased. Albeck turned to his follow-up sheets and began efficiently and rapidly reducing the pile, making notations, inscribing new follow-up dates, occasionally incising a diagonal razorlike pencil line across a page to retire it to the dead file. For all his staccato efficiency the meeting droned on.

Finally, one of Stolber's secretaries timidly entered to hand him a note, which necessitated his departure to attend to some legal emergency in his own office down the hall. After a discreet moment Norbert Auerbach announced his essential presence elsewhere, with a courtly show of regret, and casually excused himself, winking and cadging a cigarette from me as he made his exit.

Other follow-up sheets followed. So did other exits, until finally Albeck and I were alone with only the sound of the antique air conditioner wheezing through the dirty curtains. Albeck was not deluded by the excuses of the others (they did have jobs to do), but he proceeded without his quorum because the time had been scheduled for that purpose and would not be wasted. Besides, he was not merely conducting his business, he was learning it, and his continued attempts to understand, if not conquer, production would not be delayed.

We went through a series of matters and problems: the script progress on *Eye of the Needle*, a current best seller we had bought; editing progress on *Apocalypse* and the equally overdue *Black Stallion*; legal uncertainty about whether we did or did not have the right to remake *Red River* and *Mildred Pierce*; what to do about a departed executive's supposed firm commitment to finance a picture to be written and directed by Joan Micklin Silver; other miscellany.

Finally, he referred to his last remaining follow-up sheet and leaned back in his chair, folded his hands in his lap, and focused intently on what he had written there, then on me.

"Do you know a man named Michael Cimino?" he asked.

"I've only heard of him," I answered.

"Did you see a picture called *Thunderbolt and Lightfoot?*"

I wasn't being much help; I admitted I had not.

He shifted the subject. "Tell me your opinion of multiple-picture deals."

I improvised, insecure enough to want to know where he was going with these questions before putting myself on any particular line. "On the one hand" segued flabbily to "on the other."

He interrupted my rambling. "Why should we say to a man that we will make two or three or four pictures with him when we don't even know what the pictures will be? How can Al or Bart or Norbert evaluate that?"

"They can't," I said, seizing what looked like an opportunity. "If you really believe Al and Norbert and Bart should be saying what pictures we make instead of production."

His explosive bark of laughter startled me. "*They* don't make the decisions." He grinned good-naturedly. "And neither does production. *I* do." He paused, still smiling. "Not because I want to but because Transamerica looks to one boss. You and Danny are the production experts and tell me we should make this or that. Al and Norbert are the distribution experts and tell me they can sell this or that. They aren't always right, and you won't be either, but the more data I have to evaluate, and I *love* data"—his hearty laugh broke out again, relishing this self-definition—"the better I can cast the final vote. And," he added, a conspiratorial lift to his eyebrows, "if they like it and can't sell it, they can't blame production, can they?"

"Yes, they can," I contradicted, "because they can say production took some terrific idea and fucked it up."

"No," he said, "because I am the boss here, and the decision will always be the boss's decision to San Francisco. That's the way it is in business.

"It's up to you to persuade Al and Norbert and Bart and me, and if you do . . . fuck it up."—he stumbled over words he was uncomfortable using—"Transamerica will blame me, not you. So please *don't.* . . . Make me look good." He laughed again as if this were a crackling good jest. The big square glasses glinted, and his eyes seemed to shine. It was the first time I had seen him laugh and relax while discussing business, and it was an agreeable surprise, the intimacy somehow flattering. Then his good humor subsided. "I have been with this company for a long time," he said reflectively, "and I remember when one of the big directors—Stevens?" He stared at my forehead as if the name were written there.

"George?" I offered.

"That's the one," he said somberly. "George Stevens came to Arthur one day and said, 'I want to make *The Greatest Story Ever Told,* and Arthur said, 'Go,' and Stevens went, and he took all our money with him and hired every star in Hollywood, and we knew it was going to be fabulous, just fabulous!" (He pronounced it "fabalous.") "And then he started shooting and shooting and *shooting.* It went over budget, over schedule, over everything. And Stevens kept saying, 'Don't worry, it'll be fabulous!' and what it was wasn't *The Greatest Story Ever Told;* it was the longest and most boring story ever told. So who's to blame?"

"Stevens made the picture."

"Right, but he promised to make a *great* picture, and Arthur believed him, and it turned out to be a dog. Who do you think Arthur blamed? Arthur blamed George Stevens!" He laughed again. "That's life. But who do you think the stockholders blamed?"

"Arthur Krim."

"That's business," he said, nodding.

He smiled again and changed the subject.

"Tell me. If a man comes to you and says, 'I want to write and direct a certain story,' and you say, 'OK,' and he writes it, and you say, 'Terrific! Now go direct it,' and he says, 'No, I've changed my mind,' what do you say then?"

"'You're fired,'" I quipped. Albeck didn't laugh.

"But he's already taken your money and quit. And what if he comes back to you with another project and makes the same speech all over again?"

A light suddenly flashed. *"The Dogs of War?"*

He nodded. "The man wrote his screenplay, and Norman Jewison liked it and wanted to go forward, and now this"—he referred to his notes—"this Cimino wants to make a multiple-picture deal to do everything *but* the thing he said he wanted to do in the first place. Is this *right?*"

"That's *show* business," I said, turning his story back on him. "Perhaps he had a change of heart, that's all." I shrugged, knowing nothing practical about the situation.

Albeck mulled this for a moment, then asked, "But what kind of *man* —" He paused, then changed his question. "What would you do now?"

I didn't welcome this question. Rissner had obviously suggested a Cimino deal, and I was technically Rissner's employee; the position placed on me an obligation of support I had no desire to betray. I could hear the ice cracking beneath my feet as I answered, "I don't think I'd rush to him again—unless I needed or wanted him very badly."

Albeck nodded, without responding. He looked around the room as if searching for a thought. Finally, he glanced back in my direction and said, "I think we need to make some changes here. A real *Hollywood* office, that's what I'd like to see. Arthur didn't need one, but I think maybe we could use one. It won't fool anybody, but . . . what do you think?"

"Sounds good to me," I answered, wondering what a Hollywood office was.

He nodded. "Thank you," he said cheerfully. I went back to work.

I don't know whether Rissner wanted Cimino or thought he needed him. Maybe he was just another talented guy to add to the depleted roster. But he got him. Albeck approved a deal, and the lawyers and agents started bickering over deal points, and nobody else thought much about it because there was so much else to do on so many other fronts.

Albeck was busy disposing of the record company, which had long been a contentious and unprofitable albatross, and he managed to do so at a substantial profit, a Mandrakian maneuver that impressed San Francisco and the rest of us. *Rocky II* was approaching production, making Al Fitter happy, because domestic's performance was decidedly mixed. The pickups had been disasters; *Coming Home* had been critically praised but a slow starter, even with Jane Fonda and Jon Voight; *Slow Dancing in the Big City* was stillborn, despite the last-minute re-shoot of the opening to introduce the characters more engagingly; *Who'll Stop the Rain?* was limping along, to the delight of the distribution staff, who openly hated it. Norbert Auerbach's foreign department was eating well as he entertained regally in Cannes, London, Rome, Paris, giving press interviews which emerged with unfortunate, defensive headlines (WE'RE NOT WASHED UP! screamed *Screen International*'s front page). Auerbach's considerable charm was calming the foreign managers, whose anxiety increased in direct proportion to their distance from 729, now run by Albeck, whom they knew only from his hatchet-wielding world tour of 1973. Production was adding and discarding projects; trying and failing to effect a reconciliation between Blake Edwards and Peter Sellers; courting publishers; wining and dining the As, Bs, and Cs; attending previews of pictures inherited from the previous regime and feeling—and being treated—like barbarians in Camelot when offering creative suggestions regarding these holdovers. We felt defensive, consigned to the "tar pits" without honor at home because of the obstructive distribution influence over every production decision.

True, there were bright spots. *Moonraker* was starting production in Paris in July (though there was still no formal budget when Albeck and I met with Cubby Broccoli and his staff at Studios Boulognes in June); Woody Allen's manager-producers, Charles Joffe and Jack Rollins, had added another picture to their slate, which would not, however, be a Woody project; the *Eye of the Needle* script looked workable; the two pictures David Field had brought with him from Fox—*Corky* and *Ladies of the Valley* (rechristened *Windows* and *Foxes*)—were moving forward; the Lorimar distribution deal was concluded by Rissner, accompanied by the first favorable press the company had seen in six months; we were able to get out of doing Blake Edwards's *"10,"* on the ground that we could not accept Mrs. Edwards (Julie Andrews) as costar in a picture boasting only George Segal and the unknown wife of John Derek. *
There were disappointments, too, like the expensive script for Martin Scorsese and Robert De Niro written by Paul Schrader, then rewritten by Mardik Martin which, Scorsese and De Niro or not, was a picture so violent we doubted it could ever be made. Then there was the improbable comedy about a homosexual couple who own a nightclub in St.-Tropez, where one of them stars in the club's drag act. This was being shot in Rome under a deal made by the now-departed Ernst Gold-

---

*Who knew? It was George Segal then, and no one but Edwards and John Derek had ever heard of Bo. The picture went to Orion and became its first solid hit. Orion had been preparing a comedy series called *The Ferret* to star Dudley Moore as a bumbling detective with a more than passing resemblance to Inspector Clouseau. As it happened, Segal balked, *The Ferret* burrowed to oblivion, and Dudley Moore and Mrs. Derek became superstars.

schmidt (though others would later claim credit for it). One of the two leads, who spoke only French, predicted disaster over coffee in the bar at Cinecittà Studios (his earrings dangling into the espresso as his young son looked on in confused wonder) because the other star refused to speak anything but his native Italian, the "maid" was an American black man, and the picture sounded like Berlitz soup before dubbing. Then, tottering on his high heels, he led me to the screening room, where we both laughed our heads off in several languages, regretfully concluding that outside one or two neighborhoods in San Francisco and Greenwich Village, the picture stood no chance whatever in America.

In all this turbulence, with all the phone calls and plane flights and meetings and memos and previews and planning, Michael Cimino was just another contract until he got around to announcing what he wanted to do. In the dog days of midsummer he did. He even had a script, written several years before under an old UA deal everyone but Rissner had forgotten. The script was long, expensive to shoot, and had been written for Robert Redford, who had already turned it down, but Cimino claimed to be passionately, unshakably committed to it. What it was was *The Fountainhead.*

I hadn't read *The Fountainhead* since adolescence, which may be the best time to read it. Ayn Rand's anthem to individualism and artistic integrity has a melodramatic appeal that is as hard for the adolescent mind to resist as it is for the adult mind to take seriously. Rand's high priestess polemics and philosophical heavy breathing lend Wagnerian weight to the goings-on of her hero, architect Howard Roark, whose artistic purity is such that he will dynamite his own housing project rather than allow it to be defiled by changes in design. Roark's "monstrous" (Rand's admiring word) egotism and his love/hate duels with tempestuous, "exquisitely vicious" (Rand again) Dominique Francon shot the book to the top of the best seller lists in the 1940s. Still in print, it has sold more than 5 million copies to date and was made into a film starring Gary Cooper and Patricia Neal in 1948 by King Vidor for Warner Brothers. Because UA had acquired the Warner Brothers pre-1949 library, it owned distribution rights to the old picture as well as all rights to the book itself. *The Fountainhead* could not, therefore, be remade without UA.

Cimino's choice of subject was to seem more and more revealing as time went by, but in mid-1978 it seemed merely an eccentric idea. At least it wasn't a car movie, a space movie, or another *Jaws* rip-off. The script was submitted together with handsome books of avant-garde architecture, both built and unbuilt, illustrating to us the look of what

Cimino's Howard Roark would design. There was a lot of talk about
miniatures, but one had the uncomfortable suspicion, even then, that
the only way to do justice to Roark's unbuilt city of the future was to
build it. The script updated the story and warmed up Rand's inhuman
characters. Well written and dramatic, it would be an expensive picture
with or without models, because it required very major stars to fill up
the outsize characters of Roark and Dominique and make them matter
to an audience for whom the angst of artistic integrity began and ended
with John Travolta's disco technique in *Saturday Night Fever*. The fact
that *The Fountainhead* had failed once—with Gary Cooper at the height
of his career—and that Robert Redford had already turned down the
script did not enhance its value in Albeck's eyes or in the eyes of the
distribution staff, who found the story remote, highbrow (!), and uncommercial.

Rissner had been pushing for this one, and he thought that the first
film's failure was due not to something inherent in the material but to
poor execution. No doubt he was right. It is one of the worst pictures
Vidor ever made. *Beyond the Forest* is worse, and *Duel in the Sun* hardly
better. Still, distribution didn't want it, Albeck uncharacteristically revealed his own negativism (though he might have felt differently had
Redford said yes), and when asked in the New York daily production
meeting for my opinion, I voted with the majority.

I called Rissner and detailed Albeck's and distribution's attitude and
vote. He was calm, the occasional "uh-huh" punctuating my recital.
Finally, he asked, "What did *you* say?" I told him I didn't like the
project and thought we shouldn't make it and had expressed that in the
meeting. "Uh-huh," he said.

In the silence which followed I uneasily began to feel guilty of some
disloyalty I couldn't claim. I had expressed an opinion which I was
being paid to express but which was, as I well knew, opposed to that of
my immediate superior and coincided with the attitude of *his* superior. I
was stumbling over the coils of company politics even if I was doing so
uncynically and out of conviction.

What I didn't understand then, but came to understand well, was
that having made the multiple-picture deal with Cimino and having
expressed enthusiasm for *The Fountainhead*, Rissner had nowhere to go.
He had committed the only thing of value any head of production has
to commit to a filmmaker: his pledge to deliver—a property, a deal,
financing, whatever it may be. Without the ability to deliver, there is
no power in Hollywood. Maybe only two or three people in the movie
business have unlimited, absolute power to commit and deliver without
the approvals of committees and boards and often shadowy higher-ups,

and everyone knows this. But credibility, the appearance of power (sometimes just as good) can be won only with results. When a "head" of production expresses enthusiasms he cannot enforce within his own power structure, his credibility suffers. His "weakness" as perceived by a disgruntled filmmaker rarely remains a secret in the company town Hollywood famously is. And the result is the endless chorus of production executive noes, which obviate the possibility of being shot down from on high. Yeses are therefore both risky and rare.

I had unwittingly helped demonstrate that Danny wasn't in charge, except with the sufferance of distribution and Albeck, and it mattered not at all that my vote was probably academic. I had not only "sabotaged" the boss's project, but foreclosed on reopening the subject for reconsideration.

Rissner could not go back to Cimino and say he had changed his mind; he also could not go back and admit he had been overruled by distribution. Even blaming the turndown on Albeck was dangerous. As long as the movie community was skeptical about "Andy who?" it was to Rissner's advantage to downplay Albeck's role in production decisions. Finally, Rissner was in the embarrassing position of having wooed, won, and been proved impotent.

Now he was breathing quietly at the other end of the long-distance telephone. My uncertainty about my function—Yes-man? Team player? Loyal opposition? What?—and my insensitivity to any of the problems the situation created for Rissner mingled with my stubborn sense of independence to make me resent his obvious and understandable annoyance. If I could not speak my mind openly and honestly without angering a superior, maybe executive life in a large corporation wasn't worth it. Smooth sailing, harmonious relationships seemed important; intellectual subordination and alienating others didn't. I was so busy being self-righteous I didn't have a clue to what Rissner's larger problems were or what they were doing to him. I was quite prepared to pick up my noble marbles and make an exit, doubtless viewing myself as some version of Sydney Carton in *A Tale of Two Coasts*. Before leaving, however, I wanted to relieve myself of my conviction, and so, to the silent telephone in my hand, I reiterated that I thought *The Fountainhead* a lame-brained, uncommercial project that purported to be about artistic integrity but was really a hymn to megalomania, and given the chance, I would vote against it again.

"Uh-huh," Rissner replied. Then, casually: "Have you seen *The Deer Hunter?*"

He knew that I hadn't and that the picture would not be in release for another six months.

"Well, I think you should see the goddamn thing before you start making uninformed judgments about what Mike might or might not do with The goddamn *Fountainhead*," he said, still calm, or sounding it.

"How do I do that?" I asked politely, hoping a show of passivity would bring the conversation to a quick end.

"Call Joann Carelli. She'll set it up."

"Who's Joann Carelli?"

"She's the girlfriend or the ex-girlfriend or the *friend* or somebody— nobody knows or cares, and it doesn't matter. She worked with Mike on *The Deer Hunter*, and she's smart and helpful. She'll be the producer on *The Fountainhead*," he added, stressing, "*if* the goddamn thing can be resuscitated."

After some brooding I tried Carelli at one of her many private numbers Rissner had given me—Beverly Hills, the United Nations Plaza, East Hampton—and left messages with services. It was just as well I did not reach her. In my dark mood I couldn't have cared less about *The Deer Hunter*.

Rissner might have overridden my objections to *The Fountainhead* with Albeck had he tried; I was only a lieutenant after all. It was true I was second-in-the-chain-of-production-command and just down the hall from Albeck, giving me a valuable practical access the others didn't have, but that meant little. Rissner had worked for years with the others and could have swayed them if Albeck had remained obdurate. Perhaps Albeck would have yielded to such a pincers attack, if only for company harmony.

But none of those things happened because something else did.

At precisely 6:00 P.M. on a Friday in July 1978 Albeck came down the hall to my office. I was startled by this because he was known always to leave the building at that hour (except for Tuesday Night at the Movies). Secondly, he did not pay calls on his executives in their own offices, except under unusual, sometimes ominous circumstances. His appearance in mine at this hour signaled something serious and, I saw, as he silently closed the door behind him, confidential as well.

He sat in the chair opposite my desk and asked soberly how soon I could be ready to go to California. He knew I had a house there and needed only a taxi to the airport; he was easing into something. Finally: "I want you to go sit in Danny's office for a few days. I want to see to it that it is business as usual."

"Danny's office?"

"This is only temporary," he said hastily. "Danny will be back very soon. Nothing will change."

"Back? From where?" I asked, mystified.

"The hospital," Albeck explained as if I must have known. "For a triple bypass."

This was startling and unexpected. Danny and I were approximately the same age, and I had no idea his "blood pressure problem" was so serious. I also had no idea what I would do while occupying his office other than feel like an impostor. And why couldn't Mankiewicz or Field "go sit in Danny's office for a few days"?

Albeck rose and headed for the door, tugging his suit coat straight. "Don't worry about it," he said, as if intuiting my apprehensions. "And"—he stressed it again—"it's only temporary." Just before he closed the door behind him, he turned back to observe, "You smoke too much."

I sat and rearranged the disorder on my desk (and smoked), and suddenly a seemingly gratuitous conversation of a few days before came back to me with a clarity of self-interest which would have made Ayn Rand proud. Norbert Auerbach had invited me to lunch in his office on the tenth floor, where foreign distribution was headquartered. Though Auerbach was famous for stylish dining on several continents, he and I had eaten inelegantly from styrofoam trays delivered from a nearby deli. As we munched tuna salad and saltines, Auerbach had complimented me on my behavior and judgments in the production meetings. "And you know," he added, his bearded face crinkling as he bit into a briny pickle, "Andy doesn't like Danny all that much. Think about it. . . . I'm sure you could handle the job."

His eyes twinkled, and it seemed to me he was purring.

The enigmatic smile invited speculation: Was he sincere? Was he testing my loyalty to my superior? Was he stirring up a little intrigue for the sake of intrigue? Or was it possible *he* didn't like Danny and was baiting me to see what would happen?

And why was I listening?

What didn't occur to me until almost two years later was that this appeal to my vanity and ambition—whether sincere or phony—was part of an agenda I couldn't then read. He was declaring himself a kingmaker (princemaker anyway), and by listening, I was tacitly concurring in his self-designed role. What occurred to me now, as I prepared to go to California, was that my vanity and ambition had sat up and saluted whether I wanted to admit it or not. Maybe, I thought as I seized scripts to read on the plane, *maybe* my resignation should be delayed.

CHAPTER 5

OBLIGATORY SCENES

The motive of success is not enough. It produces a short-sighted world which destroys the sources of its own prosperity. The cycles of trade depression which afflict the world warn us that business relations are infected through and through with the disease of short-sighted motives. The robber barons did not conduce to the prosperity of Europe in the Middle Ages, though some of them died prosperously in their beds.

—Alfred North Whitehead,
Adventures of Ideas
(1933)

Dan Rissner's veins were surgically rearranged into healthier, happier patterns, and my stint in his California office was brief and uneventful. It wasn't my first experience staring at a silent telephone, and it wouldn't be my last, but it both unnerved and relieved me. On the one hand, it illustrated sharply that merely sitting in a chair with a title and a checkbook does not automatically attract creative crowds; I had none of the executive longevity and experience Rissner had built up and therefore none (or little) of his credibility. On the other hand, realizing this sobered me of the heady notion that I was auditioning for his job, no matter how subtly or overtly Auerbach may have encouraged me to view it in that uncomfortably Machiavellian light. If Albeck was weighing and evaluating contingencies and regarded me as an understudy, he kept it to himself. The front lines could not only be dangerous but also be silent; it gave me pause and perspective.

The California lull was an opportunity to indulge in camaraderie with colleagues: jokes and gossip with Mankiewicz, more serious discussions with Field. As Rissner silently recuperated at his Malibu beach house, office discipline grew anxious and flabby, and the camaraderie became competitive in the absence of any clearly defined company future.

If Danny returned, fine. If he didn't, what then? (If I was thinking about it, why not they?) Mankiewicz and Field worked well together with Danny; without him they were the oddest of couples. Their rivalry seemed less political than of the sibling variety as each vied for the attention of their superior and whatever potential rewards that favor might bring. In his absence petty grievances and annoyances bubbled more quickly to the surface, and their stylistic and temperamental incompatability took on a sharper edge, not always comfortable to be around.

Because I liked them both, I was not unhappy to step out of what seemed an incipient flare-up when Rissner returned to the office part time, allowing me to return to New York. I arrived back in early August, where New York Bell kept me busier than Pacific Tel and Tel had done. One of the first calls that rang through was from Joann Carelli, one of whose several answering services had at last given her my messages. We arranged to screen *The Deer Hunter* in New York in mid-August.

The week of August 14 suffocated New York in steam bath heat and humidity. Monday was set aside for my first United Artists board of directors' meeting, to be sweated out in the eleventh-floor boardroom. The San Francisco directors* arrived with their graphs, charts, projections, estimates, gray books, black books, yellow pads and pencils, but these seemed less artillery than props. The TA group proved well informed, relaxed, sanguine about the company's future and unruffled by current or past problems. The tone was friendly and supportive. The *numbers* looked good, ergo . . .

Though precise and well organized, they were not obsessed with "housekeeping" or "nitpicking" or, sensitive to the public charges, contrived not to appear so.

---

*The UA board was made up exclusively of Transamerica and UA executives, chaired by Harvey but with Beckett as the *éminence grise* (or *blanche*, to be precise), exercising his folksy control over this assembly of men who were, in fact, his employees. The proceedings were numbers-intensive but California-casual.

Tuesday brought the routine monthly production meeting and another sweltering day in which telephone lists grew ever longer, reproaching us for all the normal business that wasn't getting done; we were too busy talking about it to do it.

Wednesday the sixteenth, in unabated humidity, Carelli arrived.

Her entrance was unportentous. "I'm Joann Carelli," she announced without ceremony, wilting against the doorjamb of my office. Then: "Hi." She looked early to mid-thirties, was medium height, attractive in an open, easy way with swingy shoulder-length brown hair and large functional glasses with a pinkish brown tint to the thick lenses. She was dressed casually in a manner that acknowledged heat and style without surrendering to either.

"Mike-wants-you-to-see-the-movie-so-here-I-am," she laid out in one flat, vaguely New York-accented word. "The movie's down there," she said, pointing at the floor to indicate a lower story, then laughed as she caught me glancing at her shoes. "On seven," she clarified.

David Field, who knew Carelli through Cimino and Rissner, was in New York for the production meeting and camped out in my office during the day in a tandem arrangement we found comfortable, if cramped. He steered the small talk through innocuous shoals while I listened and did busy work as we waited for our screening time. Rissner was right: She didn't seem pretentious, she didn't posture; she seemed down-to-earth, smart, and cooperative, as advertised, and I was relieved that she in no way resembled Dominique Francon.

A few minutes before one o'clock the three of us negotiated the gloomy back stairs to the seventh-floor screening room. Using this small, shabby television facility instead of the fancier fourteenth-floor "executive" screening room was both practical and strategic. It was practical because the movie's more than three-hour length overstrained the booking capacity of fourteen. It was strategic because Cimino wanted the movie screened far from prying board member eyes or casual curiosity seekers, who might slip in unannounced and uninvited on the fourteenth floor, as UA executives often did when they had a moment or two to kill. It was not a question of exclusivity: Cimino himself was screening the film (albeit surreptitiously) in California for friends and opinion makers in a campaign to pressure Universal into releasing it at its unorthodox length. Universal was so far unmoved and adamantly insistent on a two-hour movie, had even, rumor had it, hired a "secret" editor to do the cutting. We knew this but thought little of it at the time; controversies over length were too standard for this one to seem ominous. Still, there were cloak-and-dagger portents for the future that went unread or at best were lightly skimmed. Cimino knew that UA had purchased distribution rights to the EMI film (Universal was not the producer, merely the American distributor) for several important foreign territories, and he was eager to preclude an early look by UA's foreign division and a possible UA-Universal pincers movement that might force him to cut the picture. Worse, they might take it away from him altogether and cut it themselves. Joann's presence was thus not merely friendly; she was there to guard the door. If she was, as many were later to claim, the Dragon Lady, she was a calmly loyal, utterly unprepossessing one.

We entered the tiny screening room, grimy and redolent of decades of acrid cigar smoke, and went through the nerve-masking rituals of screening room etiquette—selecting seats (empty spaces between each of us), poising ashtrays, coffee cups, cigarettes, and lighters for easy grope retrieval in the dark—and after arranging and rearranging everything, we leaned back in our greasy sprung seats, signaled the projectionist to start, and hoped for the best.

Neither David nor I knew much about *The Deer Hunter* save Rissner's enthusiasm, that it concerned Vietnam (in spite of the James Fenimore Cooperish title), and that it had reportedly cost $15 million, twice its original budget. Three hours and four minutes later we knew a great deal more, including that Michael Cimino was going to be a star.

The movie was exciting, and it was impressive. It was absorbing, repellent, romantic, touching, brutal, confusing, stirring, annoying, technically sure, structurally shaky, and *long*. But mostly it was impressive. Visually it was arresting from the startling first images: caldrons of molten steel in blast furnaces prefiguring the napalm to come. The imagery was beautiful and terrible at the same time and slowly, deliberately gave way to a quieter, more somber seduction, as we were drawn into the fictional Pennsylvania mill town and its steelworkers' lives. Strongly played by Robert De Niro, Christopher Walken, John Savage, Meryl Streep, John Cazale, and others, the characters seemed eccentrically real and dimensional and easy to care about, not the stately, self-explaining figures of epic, but recognizable people, full of mixed, often inarticulate emotions and motives.

Cimino's version of Vietnam was hallucinatory and fascinating. The Russian roulette sequences were so appalling and powerful that like later audiences, we were torn between voyeuristic fascination and a compulsion to avert our eyes; the poignance of homecoming seemed honestly felt, for all its *The Best Years of Our Lives* familiarity; and even the first hour's wedding party sequence—daringly attenuated—seemed a tour de force of filmmaking. The continuity here, like much of the rest of the movie, threw one off guard; the documentary glimpses of

behavior and detail seemed neutral and random one by one but became
highly patterned and evocative in assembly. They built a rhythmic
charge that was sweeping and sensuous, achieving momentum, life, and
empathetic response without conventional narrative devices. The absence of literary mechanics seemed to suggest something fresh and original going on, something artfully controlled as it swept from shot to
shot. The sequence hinted at some notion deeper than the sum of the
images or, if not a depth, then at least a deliberate design, unstated but
reinforced by the swirling, romantic visualizations. The technical expertise suggested, made one search for a concomitant thematic depth.

This feeling was confirmed and heightened by the Hemingwayesque
deer hunt following the wedding celebration, focusing on the romantic
isolation of Robert De Niro's Michael (the autobiographical choice of
name seemed curious), then a wider angle again for the hearty com-
radeship of buddies slouching over what might be their last shared beer
in a roadside tavern, as the least likely of them picks out Chopin on the
cigarette-scarred upright.

It seemed like, felt like virtuoso stuff. Even when we weren't quite
sure where we were going or why, the director knew, and we felt in
good hands. One was aware of length through the deliberate rhythms,
rather than longueurs, of a touch of the grandiose without grandilo-
quence, and if the picture seemed structurally lumpish, the melodramatic momentum didn't allow much time to object.

At some point during the screening, however, I developed an
urgent curiosity to see the physical script Cimino had worked on and
from. That first pyrotechnical hour could not have had more than
twenty pages of written dialogue and description—perhaps less—
sharply diverging from the rarely incorrect (though often challenged)
rule of thumb that one script page averages one minute of screen time.
Visual tours de force don't get written, they get filmed, and I was far
from arguing with what I had seen, but I wanted to examine what had
been written as blueprint, as battle plan, what had been put on paper to
persuade the people who put up the money. "INT. NIGHT—THEY
DANCE. . . "?

Even the picture's confusing and ambiguous-to-the-point-of-
obscurity ending, as the surviving characters join awkwardly and without embarrassment (or clear motive) in a falteringly rendered "God
Bless America" was not bleary enough to dim enthusiasm; it was an
ending one was willing to assume meant something beyond its apparent
simplistic jingoism, that after three hours and more of often brilliant
and stirring technique this movie could not possibly end on the limp
strains of a pop anthem. It was, we decided later, a "talk-about" ending

that would encourage controversy and word of mouth, and if it hinted at character depths or thematic profundities that were on the murky side or if it stroked emotions that were confused or facile, so what? The poignance seemed no less genuine for its awkwardness. Or perhaps that was the point. Maybe the (anything but pat) ending hoped to invoke a feeling of loss that was inarticulated because it was finally unutterable, except as an ardently sentimental hymn. This kitchen choir, different from an earlier barroom sing-along but a clear and ironic echo of it, formally rounded off some inner design, reverberating enigmatically. We didn't know what it meant to Cimino—politically or otherwise— but we knew what it felt like was, well . . . poetry.

There wasn't a lot of conversation following the screening. We were too unsettled and flooded with impressions of what we had seen to indulge in small talk that might sound trivial, and it seemed inappropriate to carp about misgivings. Carelli seemed to expect our quiet reactions but proved herself to be pragmatically direct. As we left the screening room for the elevators, she brightly broached the question that had been conspicuous by omission.

"We're dead with *The Fountainhead*," she said knowingly, "right?"

Field and I exchanged glances.

"Look, Joann, *The Deer Hunter* is a terrific movie, just a stunning piece of work, but you have to tell us what it could possibly show about how Michael would treat *The Fountainhead*."

"Yeah, I know," she drawled. "You're right. But Mike has a lot of ideas. You should talk to him." She shrugged and waved as she entered the elevator which took her to street level and out of the building.

Later—too late—after she had gone and Field had returned to his hotel, leaving me alone in my office writing a personal and effusive letter to Cimino, I remembered wanting to read the script of *The Deer Hunter*. It would have been an academic exercise, I supposed, finally unimportant and perhaps even presumptuous. What was important was the movie, I thought, not how it got that way. By the time I revised that attitude and decided that "how it got that way" was a question of the utmost practicality and importance, my interest had been activated by events not remotely academic but dismayingly real, and again it would be too late.

Rissner continued his smooth recuperation, spending a few hours each day in the office, working the rest of the time at home in Malibu. Mankiewicz and Field (and I, if in from New York) and others of the staff would drive out the Pacific Coast Highway separately or together to gossip with him, take care of minor business, convey team spirit, and maintain the feeling that the ties that bind still bound. There was a unity, in fact, a strong sense of shared endeavor Rissner promoted. As a side effect of distribution's intrusion into the creative domain, we were like shipwreck victims, beneficiaries of a solidarity that obviated the possibility of internecine feuds. Rissner's renewed activity and presence restored an equilibrium that pushed daily business forward. But in his occasional absences, without his cooling influence, it was inevitable that the simmering rivalries for his confidence would one day combust, and they did, spontaneously and loudly, like firecrackers, one hot summer night in the Rocky Mountains.

Mankiewicz, Field, and I had converged in Denver to attend a sneak preview of *Comes a Horseman*, an expensive contemporary western, starring Jane Fonda, James Caan, and Jason Robards, which was director Alan Pakula's first picture following *All the President's Men*. *Horseman* was a holdover from the previous management which none of us had seen, inasmuch as Pakula was clasping it tightly to his vest, perhaps because of tension over the several million dollars it had gone over budget or because we seemed interlopers on creative territory granted him by a departed regime.

All attention was diverted from the picture almost immediately on our arrival at the Brown Palace Hotel as we emerged from airport limousines to hear bellows of indignation from Mankiewicz, aimed directly at Field. The exact flash point is forgotten; what was important was that the hostilities were now public. Mankiewicz, always outspoken, was detonating all over the hotel lobby in his anger or outrage or miff or whatever it was, and Field was upset and repelled by the unrestrained vehemence of the echoing volleys. He retreated behind an Ivy League wall of wounded forbearance, which pushed Mankiewicz to a further public explosion to me—but directed at Field—that "*Sammy Glick is out to get us all!*"

That the two were more or less conscious rivals for Rissner's confidence was undeniable and inevitable, if only because of proximity, that they were no less motivated toward upward mobility than any young executives anywhere seems evident from their career histories. Now, in a company unceasingly beleaguered from outside, with a captain still partially sidelined by his health, anxieties and jitters affected us all. Our own ambitions seemed just and meet; everyone else's took on lurid overtones in an atmosphere in which a change of command was possible, though, superstitiously perhaps, never openly discussed. Characterizing Field as Sammy Glick, however threatened Mankiewicz may have felt, was considerable overstatement, if only in the area of style. Field's Princetonian, patrician air was the antithesis of Schulberg's brash antihero, and Mankiewicz knew it.

The Mankiewicz-Rissner relationship could and would withstand a lot of profanely indignant clashes, but Rissner seemed to find Field's voice increasingly reliable, thoughtful, intelligent. Field was deferential without weakness, strong without obduracy. He had been cool and above it all for months (at least in public), but the "Sammy Glick" fusillade demolished his reserve. He stalked off to his hotel room in white-faced anger while Mankiewicz continued to fulminate, enjoying both the release and his own performance.

I was angry with them both because I liked them both and didn't want to be drawn into a battle in which neutrality would be impossible to maintain. Our mutual histories had mingled often in the past; I had even worked with both before UA. Mankiewicz and I had been executives together in the early seventies in a New York production company called Palomar Pictures, which (after Chris exited somewhat stormily) produced his father's last picture, *Sleuth*, with which I had been involved.

Later, when I produced a couple of pictures for Twentieth Century-Fox with my partner at the time Gabriel Katzka, my office was down the hall from Field's in the Fox Executive Building on Pico Boulevard. We got to know each other then and engaged in occasional bull sessions about books and movies.

Now the three of us had converged on Denver in a disarray that would have grimly gratified the industry wags who were calling us "Untied Artists." The façade of polite cooperation was unraveling publicly, as an unsuspecting Rissner sat in Malibu full of stitches and less petty concerns and as Albeck waited patiently but anxiously in New York to hear the results of the preview.

The sneak at the Oriental Theater was not a success, dulling my appetite and pleasure for the UA dinner following the screening, where I was seated with my parents, who lived in Denver and had been invited as a courtesy by the local UA fieldman. I was pleased to see them (and seldom enough did), but the time and setting were strained. They made comments about "beautiful scenery" and "lovely photography," intending encouragement, which amounted to faint and damning praise. Alan Pakula brooded darkly at a table across the room, glancing occasionally at the lukewarm preview cards, while Mankiewicz and Field, who had been seated with me and my parents, were teeth-grittingly polite to each other and us. Icy glances and cryptic remarks from one oh-so-polite colleague to the other ricocheted over the scampi, white wine, and my bewildered parents' heads. The "politer" it got, the ruder it got.

Finally, after midnight, we straggled back to the Brown Palace, and David and I, who were flying on to Chicago in the morning for another *Horseman* preview, agreed to share a nightcap. Mankiewicz, who was returning to California in the morning, said his frosty farewells.

We ordered brandy and sat down to talk.

"You look pissed off," he observed.

"You could say that," I confirmed. "The movie doesn't work, and Pakula doesn't want to hear about it. I don't really want to get up at six in the morning and schlepp to Chicago for more of the same. I couldn't enjoy the one evening I've had with my parents for many months, and I think you and Chris are both behaving like jerks."

"Both?"

"*Both.*"

His splayed fingers went back to rake through his hair, and his eyes closed behind the steel-rimmed glasses before he spoke.

"Maybe you don't see what's going on."

I sighed. "OK, David, what's going on?"

"He's trying to kill me."

"What?" I asked. His voice was so quiet it might have been calculated to force my leaning forward to hear.

"He's trying to kill me. He's trying to force me out of the company."

"I think he thinks *you're* trying to force *him* out. Why else would he call you Sammy Glick?"

"That was a low blow."

"I've already told him that, and he knew it anyway. Forget about it. He sometimes declaims when he only means to talk."

"Well, that kind of talk is going to force me out of the company."

"David, nobody can force you out of this company unless you want to be forced. Are you writing some kind of scenario to justify being forced out or what?"

"Me?" he said, injured. "You don't hear me going around calling Chris Sammy Glick."

"You don't do it that way, David. You do it with long, suffering silences and soulful, forbearing looks. It's all that Ivy League nobility that drives him up the fucking wall. Why don't you just tell him to fuck off and be done with it?"

"What are you trying to do?" he said almost sorrowfully. "Pit us against each other?"

"Nobody *has* to, the way I see it."

"Which is what?" His voice was still a model of whispery control.

"I see two—*three* if I include myself, and I will—three ambitious people not knowing what comes next and getting stupidly political about it."

"This isn't about politics," he protested.

"It's not?" I asked. "Maybe you're more political than you realize, David, and maybe that bugs the shit out of Mankiewicz. It bugs the shit out of *me*."

He nodded slowly, as if I had just ripped off the mask to reveal that I was the true phantom of this somewhat paranoid opera.

"Give me one example," he said in that quiet, disillusioned voice.

"How about the time I called Freddy Raphael—"

"In France," he interrupted quietly.

"He *lives* in France. Where else was I supposed to call him?"

"You called him about my project."

"I called him about UA's project, to say I was glad we had made the deal, welcome aboard, be brilliant. I've known Freddy for years, and I was glad he was working for us, and I wanted to say so."

"You were bird-dogging my project," he said quietly. "I brought that project into the company, and I didn't think you should have called him without my permission. The minute you got off the phone with Freddy, he called me in California because he thought you were bird-dogging, too."

"And Alan Pakula is sitting upstairs with a pack of lousy preview cards thinking that *we're* bird-dogging Mike Medavoy's project. Is everybody nuts around here or what?" I downed the rest of my brandy and signaled for a refill. David bit his tongue and glared behind me at the wall.

"And let me prepare you for another big surprise," I went on, not wisely but loudly. "I don't have to ask your permission to call anybody. I outrank you in this playpen, and I'll do what I think is good for the projects and good for the company."

"You don't care about this company," he said evenly, "any more than I do."

I stared at him without a word. There was a kind of mournful tranquillity to his voice that said, "Listen, hear me out." I did.

"You don't care about this company. It's just a corporation with a lot of suits walking around carrying briefcases. You may care a little about the people in it, but the company itself isn't anything but a listing on the stock exchange. Not even that. It's just an idea in John Beckett's head. None of this is about the company."

"What's it about, David?"

"Making movies."

"Simple as that?"

"Simple as that."

"Then don't complicate it by escalating your differences with Chris into some plot to force you out of the company. Unless," I said, finishing the second brandy, "you have some very good place to go."

Where we went was to Chicago. The picture didn't work there either.

CHAPTER 6

STAR QUALITY

True artists, whatever smiling faces they
may show you, are obsessive, driven people—whether driven by some mania or
driven by some high, noble vision.

— John Gardner,
The Art of Fiction (1984)

Michael Cimino responded promptly and politely to
my letter about *The Deer Hunter* with his invitation for lunch or dinner,
a get-acquainted breaking of ice and bread. We made a date for mid-
September, when I would be in California, where he remained, protecting *The Deer Hunter* from Universal's scissors, threatening to "kidnap"
the negative if Universal edited it without his consent. In the meantime, I left for Europe to pay executive calls on priorities: John
Schlesinger was finishing *Yanks* in London; *Moonraker* was busy in
Paris, where it occupied every sound stage in the city; *La Cage aux
Folles* was wrapping in Rome; *The Tin Drum* was shooting in Germany.
There would be other projects to weigh, reject, or acquire, foreign employees to meet, new filmmakers to woo, others to discourage, while
the desk piled high in New York with memos, readers' reports, and
unread mail and submissions.

The highest priority of all, however, was not in London, Paris,
Rome, or Munich but in New York, the man *Time* magazine would
soon proclaim on its cover "A Comic Genius." Woody Allen had come
to UA in the early seventies in a modest multiple-picture deal made by
the president and production head at the time, David Picker. The deal
had been renewed and extended by Krim and Pleskow for four more
pictures, the first of which was *Annie Hall*. A career that seemed at the
beginning a fluky and limited one, full of New York angst and schtick,
which didn't travel well into mid-America and had almost no foreign
passport, had turned into a prodigiously likable series of pictures:

Bananas, Sleeper, Everything You Wanted to Know About Sex, and *Love and Death.* They were original not only in subject but in their angle of vision and style, evolving from an early awkward jokiness to the seriocomic poignancies and polish of *Annie Hall.* Taking a flyer on Allen had proved to be one of the happiest and smartest gambles in recent movie history.

Woody's career had never lost its New York accent, which was both liability and distinction. To many he seemed to epitomize the city, an attitude he fostered and later parodied in *Manhattan:* "He was as . . . tough and romantic as the city he loved. Behind his black-rimmed glasses was the coiled sexual power of a jungle cat. . . . New York was his town. And it always would be." Within the industry, too, he seemed to typify the one remaining New York company, revitalizing its reputation for originality and filmmaker independence. In the *Fortune* article that precipitated the exodus of January 1978, Woody had described working at UA as some kind of movie-heaven-right-here-on-earth: "They never ever bother me. . . . They would never come to a set without calling, and they never ask, 'Could you show us something?' They see the picture when I'm ready to give it to them."

What he had most recently given them, *Annie Hall,* had won the Best Picture Academy Award, and he himself the Best Director award, events regarded as exceptional, even inside the industry, because they overcame the academy's perceived anti-New York bias and because Woody seemed openly to give nary a hoot about the movie community or its statuettes. * His Los Angeles barbs were famous and much quoted, but they were mostly innocuous skewer gags, not toothless but without venom. Usually they were the anxious gibes of a nervous New Yorker who found California folkways weird and ominously torpid, an attitude curiously fashionable with a large percentage of the California academy membership. Woody's disdain of the awards, or a certain embarrassment over the attendant hoopla, may have been real, however. Immediately after the Oscar ceremonies new advertising posters prominently displaying four Oscar statuettes (Diane Keaton and the screenplay by Woody and Marshall Brickman also won) were prepared for theater show windows and dispatched hastily to the field. The one place they were never displayed—at Woody's personal insistence—was in New

---

* Though the company was shrewdly campaigning for him. Publicity director Lloyd Leipzig is generally credited with placing *Annie Hall* on Los Angeles's Z channel, the cable television system which had a geographical monopoly on academy voter homes, an innovation that brought the movie to the membership mountain during the period in which votes were being cast. If this strategy was not decisive—and many thought it was—it didn't hurt and was later much imitated.

York. The concession revealed much about UA's attitudes toward Woody's eccentricities, but more important, it revealed that for Woody and his faithful New York audience, Oscar was never a necessary validation or seemed too . . . well, Hollywood.

Before the awards *Annie Hall* had not been a blockbuster. No Woody Allen picture ever had been. *Annie Hall* performed well following initial critical response, but the box-office boost of the Oscar publicity sent it through the ceiling or through what was internally regarded as Woody's ceiling. *Annie Hall* eventually reached rentals of close to $20 million, impressive but modest by blockbuster standards on the *Star Wars* or *E.T.* scale. Middle America responded to Woody's New York anxiety, and for the first time a foreign public seemed to get the jokes and rhythms, giving a lift to *Annie Hall's* worldwide receipts and making possible foreign reissues of his earlier films, which had performed indifferently, if at all, abroad. Still, the authentic "breakthrough" was one year and two pictures away, and Woody's importance to United Artists was never economic anyway. It was the identity he gave UA of being as separate as he was from the Hollywood herd, as original, as independent, as special. He was New York's very own mensch auteur, UA's critics' darling.

Except for his first picture, *Take the Money and Run*, made for ABC Films in the sixties, all the movies Allen had directed had been made for United Artists, which regarded itself as his home, and Woody as filmmaker in residence. It was a feeling reciprocated by Woody and his manager-producers, who often invoked the word *family* to characterize their relationship with the company—or its former management. Woody was believed to share a rapport with Arthur Krim that was nothing less than filial in spite of the breezy flipness of "They see the picture when I'm ready to give it to them." Yet it was true. They *did* see the picture when he was ready, not before. Woody's UA deal was unique in the business. Contractually his pictures could be made virtually without approvals if they could be made below a specified budget figure, though that figure had withered to obsolescence because of inflation and the widening range and ambitions of his subject matter. In practice, Woody submitted a script to Arthur Krim, with a copy to Lehman ("Lee") Katz, UA's formidable one-man production- and budget-estimating department, and if Krim liked the script and Katz vetted the budget at a figure Krim agreed to, that was it. There were no readers' reports, no committees, no creative meetings, no casting approvals (unless informal, from Krim), no dailies, nothing but Woody and his script and his budget and Arthur Krim's blessing.

One reason this worked as well as it did was that Woody's pictures

always came in on budget, on schedule, and were what he had said they
would be. For all the originality and iconoclasm and well-aimed satiric
thrusts at the sacred cattle he saw munching away at the cultural landscape,* Woody had an old-fashioned, deeply ingrained sense of honor
about his commitments. His almost quaint piper-to-payer attitude extended beyond what he could or could not do by contract. That document, in fact, allowed for no approvals whatever, even subject matter,
if the agreed-upon budget figure (as noted above, elasticized as costs
spiraled upward in the seventies) was observed. Approval of the script
was not contractual but by gentlemen's agreement, inspired by Woody's
punctiliousness. As he explained to me later, after I had inherited the
yes or no script prerogative Krim had exercised, "I wouldn't want the
company to spend money on something it didn't believe in," and he
meant it in both commercial and thematic senses. When I asked him,
"If I had said no to *Manhattan,* would you willingly have forgone the
picture?," he hesitated for only a moment as he weighed "willingly,"
then responded, "Yes," and I believed him. It was this fundamental
respect for his financiers, his patrons, that won him the right to make
Interiors, his "serious" picture (Ingmar Allen they called him at 729), in
which he did not star and which may be one of the rare instances in
modern American movie history in which an artist has been allowed to
make a picture because of what it might mean to his creative development, success or failure. That it failed commercially does not diminish
the picture or the mutual respect with which it was financed and made.
Nor does it diminish the tremendous debt of faith that Arthur Krim
incurred with Woody in understanding the importance of *Interiors*
to him.

Because of that debt of faith and the longevity of the relationship,
hardly anyone in the industry (certainly few who remained at UA)
thought there was any way to prevent Woody's following Krim to Orion
at the end of his UA contract. Hardly anyone, that is, but Andy Albeck.

If Albeck had one personal passion, one fixed goal that could not be
reflected or satisfied by charts and graphs, it was keeping Woody Allen
at UA. Albeck had seen *Interiors* and privately assumed it would be a
failure. That wasn't the point; the point was deeper and more personal.

Some said it was because of Krim, but Albeck never felt himself in
direct competition with Krim. His restructuring the company and dele-

*My favorite is J. Edgar Hoover, lampooned in *Bananas.* He is played by a large black
woman who explains, gripped by paranoia, that "her" persona is a disguise: "I have
enemies *everywhere!*"

gating authorities Krim had reserved to himself showed that. It was rather that he did not believe in the indispensability of any one man, himself included. He had known Krim and worked for him for thirty years, first at Eagle-Lion and then at UA, and his professional loyalty was, for thirty years, beyond reproach. His personal regard for Krim was likewise unimpeachable, but he was not in awe of the legend. In many ways direct comparisons would be not only invidious but downright silly. Krim had built a company, had demonstrated superior taste, judgment, acumen, had changed the way an industry did business; Albeck's presidency would be one of maintenance and . . . well, a little remodeling here and there. Even Camelot was susceptible to improvement. But direct competition? Albeck's innate modesty forbade it.

He had had ample opportunity over three decades to observe that things might be done, if not better, differently and that luck and timing had played their mysterious but undeniable roles. To question omnipotence or omniscience was not to discredit: more genuine tribute might spring from a questioning realism than from an uncritical worshiping at the shrine. Krim's talents and achievements were uniquely his, Albeck knew, and their record was secure. Albeck's abilities lay in different directions, the achievements were ahead, as were the unknowable workings of his own luck and timing, whatever they might be—not that he intended allowing the company to rely on those notoriously fickle fingers.

But Albeck knew that in hindsight great success often suggested foresight that wasn't there. James Bond? Who could have predicted that *Dr. No* with an obscure English actor would spawn the most successful series of pictures in the company's history? In the industry's, until *Star Wars*. But popular opinion credited some kind of clairvoyance, some kind of box-office divining rod. Maybe. But *Rocky? Cuckoo's Nest?* The first had had to rely on its producers' mortgages, instead of on a prescient UA, to cover the $100,000 it went over budget. The second wasn't financed by UA clairvoyance at all but by *its* producer, Saul Zaentz. But bows were taken when miracles occurred, and no one remembered the failures or dry spells. Such selective memory gave rise to mythmaking and that endless industry prattle about "gut instinct"—whatever that might be. It sounded often like a lazy reliance on luck, on a roll of the dice, a substitute for analysis and clear thinking. If the dice couldn't be rigged or analyzed into control—and there was ample evidence they couldn't—at least the odds could be computed, and the risks minimized.

One way to do that was through internal discipline. Albeck knew production resented the endless meetings and questions, just as the dis-

tribution staff resented the projections of grosses they were now required to estimate and just as advertising and publicity resented
restricting expenditures to a computed proportion of the new distribution estimates. It seemed a circular process to them, and to the producers, too, but if so, it was a tighter circle, a more orderly way of
doing business, of circumscribing failure, of getting an edge on the dice.
Albeck could do all that. He understood operations and outlays and
tight-ship maintenance, but he also understood that they must never
become punitive in character, never piker-small. He had, in truth, no
taste for constrictive control; disciplined direction could ultimately allow as much or more freedom and originality than any careless or blind
trust in "gut instinct."

Still, it was a far from exact science. There were gambles, and there
were gambles, and it would not do to be intimidated by the high rollers
of the past, however legendary their winning streaks. And they hadn't
been their rolls, exactly, not the George Stevens go-for-broke disasters,
the *Missouri Breaks* fiascos, or the dark-horse *Marty* or *Rocky* jackpots.
There was some mystery at its heart, something that eluded analysis or
system. He guessed it was—for want of a more summary word—artistry,
some capacity that could be invoked only by letting it alone, by letting
it happen, mature under its own mysterious inner laws, and if conditions were right, and faith unabused, a miracle might occur. Not
through luck, but through attentive, careful nurturing.

The way Arthur had nurtured Woody, by letting him alone—not to
run wild or amok, not to go crazy or high-hat, but to make his movies
almost in private, those movies that could trigger laughter and tears at
the same time. If a sign of intelligence was the ability to hold conflicting ideas at once, how much greater the ability of the artist who could
simultaneously inspire conflicting emotions? And Woody could do that,
had done that, would do it again, Albeck believed, and he wanted to
see it happen again—enjoy it again—under his own stewardship. He
knew if UA lost Woody, everyone would say, "Albeck lost him. He isn't
Arthur. He wasn't and isn't and never will be." While all that was true,
it would be a shame to hear it again in that indignant way the press and
Hollywood had of recognizing the already perfectly obvious. It would be
a shame, and hurtful, too, but it would be a bigger shame to lose someone who could make you laugh and cry at the same time.

Albeck was a realist and a delegator and had a company to run.
Rissner was on the West Coast recovering. They decided to turn the
Keeping of Woody over to me, an assignment for which I felt lu-
dicrously ill equipped, the more so as I knew or sensed its importance to

Albeck. I wasn't Jewish; I wasn't a New Yorker. I was a white bread Gentile, born and reared where the buffalo and precious little else roam, maladroit at hip Manhattan dialogue at Broadway delis or Elaine's, and hadn't the slightest delusion that I could supply whatever mystical glue bonded Woody and Arthur Krim. I had been around the theater and movie business for a decade, but never close to Woody's kind of private, personal filmmaking, his repertory company structure, repeatedly using the same performers like Diane Keaton and Tony Roberts or technical artists like Gordon Willis and designer Mel Bourne. And regardless of the fact that I was a relatively unabashed fan, channeling his career through UA's corridors and coffers seemed to me the most quixotic of tasks.

Woody's manager-producers, Charles H. Joffe and Jack Rollins, weren't making it any easier. They claimed complete ignorance about Woody's future plans. They had no idea what they might be; they had no influence over him. He firmly refused to discuss the future until it arrived with delivery of the third picture of the three remaining. But, they added—hammer to coffin nail—"You know, Arthur is like a *father* to Woody. . . ."

Joffe, who bounced amiably from coast to coast in his management of Woody's and other clients' careers, was a voluble, aggressive, likable man, who was frankly gleeful at the manipulative leverage the situation offered. No one at UA was naïve enough to be unaware of this, nor was Charlie concealing his fun. If scratching Charlie's back was the game, UA was willing to scratch if there was even a chance of getting scratched back. Rollins and Joffe couldn't be totally without influence over Woody, we thought, nor were they without other valuable clients and relationships. They were to produce the Raquel Welch bare-it-all movie; a novel called *Mother's Day* was purchased for them but predictably bore too much resemblance to *Kramer vs. Kramer* to get made; another novel, *The House of God,* a satire about medical residents in a large, insanely bureaucratic urban hospital, was bought, developed, and eventually produced, though never released. * These were not flattering bones thrown to Rollins and Joffe; the projects approved seemed to have enough inherent potential to justify development. There were others they submitted that were turned down, not always wisely; *Arthur* was one. † Still, the subtext was clear. Joffe and Rollins knew it, and so did UA: It was mutual manipulation among consenting adults.

---

*Theatrically, that is. It was released on cable television in 1984. *Variety*'s review agreed that it was, in fact, "unreleasable."
†Repeating the pattern of "*10*" and going to Orion, where it became a major box-office hit.

Rollins was in many ways the antithesis of Joffe's ebullient aggressiveness. His tall, dark, mournful reserve and Joffe's fair, short bounce gave them a Mutt 'n' Jeff aspect, a contrapuntal quality that sometimes suggested a vaudeville team called Manic 'n' Depressive. Rollins, though the less manipulative—or because of that—was the more discouraging of the pair. He told me gently, his heavy-lidded eyes dark with sympathetic regret, his voice a painful whisper, that he saw it a foregone conclusion that Woody would leave UA for Orion. We sat in a small front booth in the Russian Tea Room, a few doors from his office, and as a summer dusk gathered heavily outside, he reminisced nostalgically, stirring his scented tea. There were stories about the early management days, about young Woody, about how Rollins put Harry Belafonte in a bolero shirt and witnessed the birth of a star, about gag writers from the old *Your Show of Shows*—maybe I could help out one or two with the odd rewrite job?—and it all boiled down to a sentimental but sincere rumination on gratitude and loyalty and respecting them and the personal histories they sprang from. I sank into a deeper depression; among the arguments resistant to rebuttal, he was strewing his dark monologue with some of the toughest.

Rollins and Joffe were, of course, close to the men at Orion, and we knew it. What we didn't know was that they felt, or later claimed to feel, profoundly offended by Albeck right from the beginning, not merely because he wasn't Arthur Krim (that, too) but because, as Joffe tirelessly repeated, they had dropped a zillion-dollar plum cake in Albeck's lap, and Albeck failed even to nibble. (So did everybody else in the movie business, including Orion, but that wasn't part of the story.) Among the performers Rollins and Joffe represented was a new and unknown comic who was trying out his act at the Comedy Store on Hollywood's Sunset Strip in early 1978. Charlie had invited a UA table, including Albeck, who was in town and who . . . *didn't laugh.* He just didn't get it. He could see that Robin Williams was something, but *what?* The world would soon know what, thanks to television, but to Joffe it was bitterly clear that UA, or Albeck anyway, didn't know talent when it was exploding in front of those windowpane eyeglasses of his, and this blindness weighed heavily against us all. Or so he gravely and often maintained. Albeck shrugged an honest "I didn't understand it," a response Charlie found insufficiently contrite and lacking in class, style, and funny bone, so different, he pointed out so often, from the distinguished, paternal (and presumably hipper) previous tenant of Albeck's office.

I was no more distinguished than Albeck—or more paternal or hip—but I could laugh at most jokes and listen to Charlie's loquacious enthusiasms with interest or patience. In mid-July I had read and approved the script of "Woody Allen No. 3," which would be called *Manhattan*, and Charlie sensed that my enthusiasm for the script was genuine enough to permit me direct access . . . enough rope. After a summer of urging he invited me on a hot September evening to Michael's Pub on Third Avenue, where Woody and his friends played Dixieland jazz on Monday nights. It was hard to imagine how a smoky, overcrowded jazz club could provide much atmosphere or opportunity to establish rapport; but it was the only opening I had, and I took it.

I also took along with me a list of the allusions peppering the *Manhattan* script because I was fearful that some of them were too esoteric for a general audience, one that was now soundly rejecting *Interiors* in spite of positive critical reviews. *Manhattan* seemed richer and more emotionally complex to me than *Annie Hall* had, and I judged that the richness was a by-product of the "serious" movie. *Manhattan* was, as Woody had promised, a comedy, but a poignant one with few "jokes," and the ones there were, were dependent on some degree of audience literacy. "When it comes to relationships with women, I'm the winner of the August Strindberg Award," for example, seemed unlikely to roll them in the aisles of Des Moines. The full list I tucked into my breast pocket had been cribbed from my single reading of *Manhattan*, while one of Woody's assistants waited outside my office door to make sure no copies were made of the screenplay. The list read: "Strindberg, Mahler, Jung, Dinesen, Fitzgerald (Scott *and* Zelda), Kafka, Cézanne, Flaubert, Mozart, Nabokov, Whitman, Coward, Böll, Brecht, O'Neill." Not a laugh riot in the bunch for an audience that Paramount discovered to its horror, just as it was releasing *Mommie Dearest*, didn't really know exactly who Joan Crawford *was*. I resolved somehow to discuss these with Woody, as well as the scenes of neo-Nazis on the march in New Jersey, which seemed to me strident and depressive. *

Michael's Pub was bouncing. Charlie had reserved a down-front table, and we sat drinking vodka and chain-smoking cigarettes while Woody and the band swerved and syncopated through the Dixieland songbook. Woody focused his attention someplace down the barrel of his clarinet, his tennis shoes twisted around each other as he perched on his stool, slightly in advance of his sidemen on the raised platform. This concentration of energy on the music seemed an attempt to efface

---

* These Skokie-like scenes never appeared in the final movie, though an allusion to them remains in the ERA party scene at the Museum of Modern Art, in which Bella Abzug plays herself.

both the room and his own star celebrity, as if he were just another New York jazzman, hoping to be heard above the din of clinking ice cubes.

The room and bar beyond were straining Fire Department limits, the air conditioning was inoperative or seemed so, the smoke thick enough to close down an urban airport; but Woody and the others (including Marshall Brickman, his Oscar-winning screenwriting partner) just kept spinning out exuberant licks, seemingly oblivious of heat, smoke, noise, and the adoring crowd.

Finally, the break came, and Woody scrambled down to join us at the table. Charlie made introductions as the rest of the room gaped enviously. Woody was nervous and courteous and blinked and nodded and said "uh-huh" a lot, and I realized that this was neither the time nor the place to discuss a lot of esoterica. I had read somewhere that Woody had the look of "a neurotic Jewish rabbit," but what his eyes revealed that night was more, I think, sympathy, even pity for us both, that we were going through social motions with no immediate goal or apparent meaning other than his courtesy and my professional assignment, which was, by common consent, not to be broached. It was pleasant, but it was strained. So was he. So was I.

Woody was finally reprieved by the intrusion of a tourist, a German woman who leaned across me over the table and thrust into his face a copy of *Der Spiegel,* containing a good review of his book *Without Feathers.* He was gracious and modest and thanked her profusely when she ordered him, in a far more Teutonic accent than Albeck's, to keep the magazine. He nodded obediently and used this break in conversation as a sensible opportunity to get back to the bandstand and resume playing.

The band two-stepped into something breezy and buoyant as Charlie and I fought our way through the tables and curious eyes, past the bar where singles crunched together, listening to music from a combo they couldn't see, and out onto the sidewalk, where still more fans stood waiting behind a velvet rope in hot evening air heavy with the smell of melting asphalt.

I spotted in the line a young couple I knew. We exchanged greetings as Charlie waved good-bye and chased a cab up Third Avenue. The couple, he a pharmacist and health food entrepreneur, she a dental technician with a morbid fear of never getting married, were from Brooklyn and struck me as being as representative of the general public as anyone I was likely to meet that night. I stood in line with them and read off my list of names. The only one they didn't know immediately was Heinrich Böll probably because I didn't pronounce it correctly. I put the list back in my pocket without explaining and saved it for the files, feeling ridiculous.

Eventually we got back inside, as far as the bar, where we could hear Woody playing and see nothing but waves of smoke and the other sardines packed in around us. At one point my Brooklyn friends asked if I knew Woody, and I responded—gamely, I thought—"Not yet."

Six days later the Polo Lounge of the Beverly Hills Hotel was quieter, cooler, and easier on my nerves than Michael's Pub had been. On Sundays ordinary civilians can book tables commandeered the rest of the week by the high-profile movie crowd that jams the booths from dawn till well after midnight, wheeling, dealing, moving, shaking. Sunday, September 17, 1978, was relaxed, the room only half-full, the atmosphere sun-dappled and leisurely, moving restricted to lazy leafing through the menu and shaking to the bar, where Bloody Mary, mimosa, or Perrier brought a tingle to the California autumn.

I arrived shortly before one o'clock; the tie I wore with my jeans and blazer was in deference not to the occasion or my host but to the sometimes imperious maître d'. I wasn't known at the Polo Lounge, but Cimino was; the mention of his name (and perhaps my respectable tie) got me seated without the usual "when the rest of your party arrives." I was tired from the New York flight the night before and grateful for the calm of sitting quietly, watching equally unhurried guests brunching under the leaves on the patio outside.

The Polo Lounge attracts a conspicuously Guccied and Cartiered crowd, drawn by the pleasant ambience stretching from the small bar across the restaurant booths and tables to the bowered terrace beyond. Many are attracted by the hotel itself, grandly, pinkly situated in the heart of Beverly Hills since they were known as *the* Beverly hills, just up one of which was the home shared by Pickford and Fairbanks when they founded UA, before they built Pickfair, which is also a semiprecious stone's throw distant.

Cimino's choice of the Polo Lounge seemed agreeable, if curiously establishment (the younger crowd sometimes calls it the Polio Lounge), but he lived nearby, I knew, in those fragrant Doug and Mary hills. An establishment venue seemed in character for a man who drove a Rolls-Royce Corniche and whose New York address was the United Nations Plaza. Cimino may be a maverick, I thought, but clearly not a rebel. No Napa Valley vineyards or Third Avenue jazz joints for this part of the New Hollywood. *Luxe*, not funk, was to be the style. Well, more power to him. I had read his prepared bio a few days earlier as homework for this lunch. He was still in his thirties, it read, and his credentials included a Master of Fine Arts degree from Yale in art and architecture (thus, *The Fountainhead*), then an interlude in New York, where he made highly successful television commercials in what is, frame for frame, the most expensive moviemaking in the world. Maybe Yale and Madison Avenue in their different ways bred a healthy respect for the goods.

My host arrived in the middle of these musings, Joann Carelli at his side, pointing me out to him as he scanned the room. He looked almost workaday casual: jeans; open shirt; leather jacket. I was surprised that he was short, no taller than Woody Allen, I guessed, but thickly constructed, the kind of stocky build that goes easily to excess if not controlled. Cimino looked solid. His head was pleasant and smiling, very round, haloed by a broad mane of dark hair, and disproportionately large for his body, an impression exaggerated by the fact that the open shirt revealed throat and gold chain but no apparent neck. This and his small, regular features made the circle of his head seem broader and flatter than it was. It was an agreeable face, though, a copper-tanned, intelligent face, with eyes that tilted downward at their outer edges, giving his smile a gentle gravity. Dominating all was the nose, wide and large, with a suggestion that it had once connected with an even wider, larger fist. It was altogether a head that recalled an antique bust: a young, slightly pampered Roman senator perhaps.

As he approached the table, it was clear that the casual western gear possessed the elegance of fit and detail stitched by a tailor's needle, and I guessed that the gleaming leather boots were worn not for cowboy comfort but because they added to his height. His hello was quiet, controlled, and warm as Joann made introductions; I liked him at once and wished I hadn't worn a tie.

We ordered. There was no lull, no awkward pause, no tentative search for common ground. We launched immediately into *The Deer Hunter*, I enthusiastically adulatory, he graciously appreciative, each of us conveying smoothly to the other that we appreciated the same things in the movie. He answered my questions readily and with calm authority.

Yes, the picture had gone double budget. Costs had gone up even as they were shooting, and there were ruinous delays and hazards that could never have been foreseen and budgeted. It was not hard to understand. I told him we had conducted an experiment with *The Spy Who Loved Me,* the James Bond movie made in 1976 for $12 million. We had rebudgeted the picture in 1978 dollars and found that *Spy* could not be made now for less than $19 million, the $7 million variance caused simply by inflation and the rising cost of labor.

Yes, the location problems in Southeast Asia had been backbreaking and demoralizing, life-endangering and full of inscrutable Asian hidden expenses. That, too, brought easy commiseration. I had learned just days before in Paris that *Moonraker* was being accused of destroying the French film industry by overpaying for services, an accusation righteously hurled by the same agents and union leaders who had so vociferously negotiated those disastrous fees. (A few months later, when *Moonraker* moved to Rio, hundreds of thousands of dollars in equipment would be dry-docked for four expensive weeks in Rio's harbor until appropriate palms could be greased and customs officials satisfied that all legalities—or "customs" of some sort anyway—had been observed.)

Yes, there had been a lot of overshooting on *The Deer Hunter*, to ensure getting the necessary footage, because all the processing was done in America to protect the negative from mishaps (civilian or political) and dailies could not be seen until after production photography had been completed. Something of the sort had happened on *Apocalypse Now*, I had been told, as film exposed in the Philippines was processed in Rome for later assembly in San Francisco. It was crazy and excessive and, in the context of big international moviemaking, somehow normal, by definition. That was the way things were done.

Yes, he was proud of the movie.

Yes, he knew how good it was.

Cimino—"Michael" by now—spoke softly with a self-assurance that radiated reliability. He was calm reason itself, even when discussing Universal's intransigence over the length of his movie. His calm inspired confidence in his judgment: He was going to protect Universal from a grievous error, that was all, and however that benevolent act had to be performed, it would be performed. Calmly. Rationally.

The message was clear enough. Cimino was an artist with an obligation to his work that transcended any other obligation. His tone implied confidence, not arrogance, and if there was a ruthlessness, it stemmed not from recklessness but from conviction. He knew how the picture played because he had constructed it to play that way. He knew that cutting it would have less effect on the content per se than on the movie's internal rhythms (which made the damage harder to reckon but easier to inflict), making it seem not shorter but longer, because less satisfying, and that this paradox would become clear when it was seen with audiences, even to poor, benighted Universal and EMI.

My sympathy was easy to elicit. First, I had a hunch he was right (he was, and Universal recognized it, too: A shorter *Deer Hunter* was tested and didn't work). Secondly, nothing is so easy to listen or agree to as condemnation of one's competition. Besides, he made his case well, as he had made his movie well. I liked it and I liked him, and I wanted the feeling to be reciprocated. I wanted him to make a movie for UA that would be as fine and powerful as *The Deer Hunter*. I just didn't want it to be based on anything by Ayn Rand.

Some shrewdness on his part had kept him away from *The Fountainhead*, and he brought it up now only to indicate a graceful resignation that it was not going to happen—not right now anyway. His manner remained warm but then seemed when we were not discussing *The Deer Hunter* to half conceal some melancholy, some form of postpartum blues, I guessed, or maybe regret over *The Fountainhead* that he couldn't quite mask. It seemed clear that he was not gifted—or not interested—in the trivialities of small talk. Joann filled in the interstices with helpful detail about filming in Thailand, the kind of production gossip that was funny only after the fact but that suggested a sharp grasp of production detail. She made wry observations about the Sunday Polo Lounge crowd, almost all going back home to Pasadena now as the patio outside grew blue with afternoon shadows. Her easy banter lightened the tone, lifted Michael's air of solemnity. He asked me about Rissner's health with polite interest, and I noted, not for the first time, that while charm was not his most evident quality, it was one he could display with the understated smile that connects, the quick, expressive gestures of his surprisingly small and delicate hands.

Finally, as the dining room drained of sun and patrons and we were preparing to leave, Joann handed me an envelope from her shoulder bag. It was another project, Michael explained, an official submission. He hoped I would like it. No . . . he hoped I would *love* it, as he did, as he had for several years now. It was a passion of his, he said fervently. It was called *The Johnson County War*, but he thought he could come up with a better title.

CHAPTER 7

DEALING

"The deal, that's all this business is about," a Studio producer told me . . . over lunch in the commissary. "Who's available, when can you get him, start date, stop date, percentages—the deal, it's the only thing that matters. Listen, if Paul Newman comes in and says he wants to play Gertrude Lawrence in *Star!*, you do it, that's the nature of the business."

—John Gregory Dunne,
The Studio (1969)

The script that became known four months later as *Heaven's Gate* had already been slipped unofficially to Danton Rissner in late August by Cimino's agent, Stan Kamen of the powerful William Morris Agency in Beverly Hills. The unofficial nature of the submission circumvented the provisions of the recently concluded two-picture writing-producing-directing deal Kamen and Rissner had made for developing future Cimino projects at relatively low fees. *The Johnson County War* was not a development deal but a "package," ready to begin preproduction immediately, and Kamen was asking for a "go" commitment with "pay or play" provisions for all elements involved, all of whom he represented. This meant that a yes response would obligate the company to outright purchase of the screenplay and payment of all presently negotiated fees, whether the picture was made or not: in this case $1.7 million, including script at $250,000, Cimino at $500,000 for directing, Carelli $100,000 for producing, and Kris Kristofferson at $850,000 as the star.

The advance word on *The Deer Hunter* was by now buzzing quickly through Hollywood, and it was unlikely that a major studio executive anywhere had not seen the picture. This was sizzle, rather than substance, because the picture would not be publicly shown for months, but the Hollywood heat was rising now. Kamen asserted that protocol dictated his submitting the project to Universal as distributors of *The Deer Hunter*, to Twentieth Century-Fox, which had had a prior interest in the project, and to Warner Brothers, which had long professed interest in Cimino and for which he had coscripted (with John Milius) *Magnum Force*, the *Dirty Harry* movie that had led to *Thunderbolt and Lightfoot* four years earlier.

Leaving the submission unofficial was also a way of denying that UA had ever turned the script down should the company dislike it— "UA couldn't have turned it down; it was never *offered* to them!"— but UA did like it. Rissner did anyway, but, for reasons that seemed clearer within a month's time, did not push it through the company with the same energy he had devoted to *The Fountainhead*. Other internal enthusiasm was lukewarm. Before my return from Europe the story department's Steve Bussard prepared a memo dated August 28, 1978, addressed to David Field, who had distributed the script to the West Coast production and story personnel for their weekend reading on the twenty-fourth. Bussard's memo cited "too many characters . . . [and] not enough time to develop any of them fully." He was disturbed by the "downbeat" ending in which all protagonists were killed and added that "if it is a project we want to do because of Mike Cimino's involvement, we should approach it with expectations of a major rewrite. If it were not for Cimino, I would pass."

Bussard's opinion was not weighty within the company, but the downbeat quality he cited was inherent in the material. The script was set in Wyoming in the early 1890s and told the story of a little-known incident in American history called the Johnson County War by those historians who note it at all. The closing decades of the nineteenth century saw waves of emigration to America from Europe, into both urban centers and rural areas. Homesteading was populating the interior, and animosities erupted often between homesteaders and prior landed interests—cattle ranchers occupying vast tracts of western land, much of it public domain. In Johnson County, Wyoming, this familiar cowboy versus settler conflict took a memorable turn when the cattlemen, organized as the Wyoming Stock Growers' Association (most western states and territories had such groups), coolly hired mercenaries to kill Johnson County settlers suspected of cattle rustling, a lively activity which had been impossible to stem with spotty court convictions and fleet-footed defendants.

Though range wars were common enough movie material, what distinguished this script was its claim that the episode was legally sanctioned by the governor of Wyoming, the U.S. Congress, and President

Benjamin Harrison. In this context the mercenaries were special deputies, hired to enforce law and order, to suppress "anarchy" by whatever means. They were to be paid per kill, like bounty hunters. They were not vigilantes but executioners, and it all amounted to a modest episode of legalized genocide with strong class and racial overtones.

Cimino's screenplay told this story, centering on three fictionalized characters whose lives he lifted from contemporary accounts of Johnson County. Through them he imposed a love triangle on the vivid and violent massacre and battle which ended the script. It later became clear that Cimino had hewed very loosely to pure history in developing the script; but no one knew that at the time, and it would, in truth, have been irrelevant to evaluation of the potential of the drama as Cimino told it.

West Coast story meetings had already been held with Cimino and Carelli before the three of us met at the Polo Lounge in September. When I read the script, I found myself in agreement with Bussard's comments, though, to be fair, I was perhaps less enamored of the western genre than he, having grown up in Idaho just across the state line from the events described in *The Johnson County War* and having spent most of my life trying to get East—or *out* anyway. I had never cared for westerns or understood their appeal, though I had just coproduced one myself (a comedy) for Twentieth Century-Fox earlier in the year. But there was more than "western" to *The Johnson County War* script; there was a solemnity of tone and a sense of "statement," and it swept along with the kinds of violence and extremities of action that had made *The Deer Hunter* so powerful and that we knew Cimino could handle. It was historical revisionism of a kind popular in the sixties and seventies, "setting the record straight," with moralistic appeal to all who shared liberal or even radical notions about civil rights, American involvement in Vietnam, the entire grab bag of causes that self-righteously animated a generation of which we all were, or felt we were, a part. *The Johnson County War* seemed to correct a sentimental and simplistic image of America's open embrace of those tired, poor, huddled masses of patriotic legend; in a way it seemed a sort of counterpart to *The Godfather*, which had transformed an equally familiar genre in dealing with the immigrant classes in urban settings. As Coppola's movie had become more than a gangster picture, so Cimino's script seemed more than a western. That its portrait of America was sensationalist, ruthless, and bloodthirsty did not seem excessive or "political," considering Cimino's assertion of the factual basis to his screenplay and considering *The Deer Hunter*, which seemed apolitical to us as well. If anything, the robber baron juggernaut lent a feeling of moral force to

the doom encircling the characters marked for slaughter on the association's death list. Besides, one might have asked, and *did* ask, how political could a picture be written and directed by a man who drove a
Rolls-Royce and lived in Beverly Hills and at the United Nations Plaza?

Even though the project was not submitted for development,
changes had been discussed and could be made, but not before UA
needed to declare itself or lose the picture to another company. Cimino
would write (or rewrite) and direct, Carelli would produce, Kris
Kristofferson would play the leading male role, and Christopher
Walken, who had gone unnoticed in *Annie Hall* but was movingly
effective in *The Deer Hunter* (and for whom Hollywood gossip was predicting an Academy Award nomination) wanted to play the second
male role, though he was not officially part of the proposal. No one had
been cast in the pivotal female role of the immigrant madam and pros-
titute in love with (and loved by) both the Kristofferson and Walken
characters, but the conversations loosely tossed out Jane Fonda or Diane Keaton as possibilities, and as most of the tossing was being done
either by Cimino or Kamen (who represented both actresses), that issue
was put on a practical back burner. UA weighed the difficulties of such
strong downbeat material and waited quietly for Fox, Universal, and
Warner Brothers to make their reactions known to Kamen.

I read the script the night of September 17, not realizing until later
that this was not the same script on which Bussard had based his memo
of August 28, though my reactions coincided with his. I participated in
conversations the following day concerning what might be done to relieve its depressing quality, the massacre at the end being dramatically
inevitable (and historically accurate, one assumed), and how casting
might be approached to sweeten what Albeck liked to call the marquee.

Kristofferson, at $850,000 and 10 percent of the profits, seemed a
good choice, and Walken, at a tenth as much, seemed a coup.
Kristofferson had long been a pop music force and was then emerging as
an important film actor, though he had announced an intention to
"retire" from movies. He had made a number of them, including *Alice
Doesn't Live Here Anymore,* in which he had been overshadowed by
Ellen Burstyn's Oscar-winning performance, and though he had recently made a strong impression opposite Barbra Streisand in her hugely
successful remake of *A Star Is Born,* it was still viewed as Streisand's
triumph with Kristofferson along for the ride. UA was perhaps the ideal
company to approach with a Kristofferson package, however, as distributor of EMI's *Convoy,* which Field and I had shepherded that summer through previews in Chicago. We both thought the picture weak
and unimportant (it was an $11 million truck-chase movie directed by

Sam Peckinpah, starring Kristofferson and Ali McGraw), but as Albeck's black books told him, it had been a surprise, performing well in spite of contemptuous reviews. Kristofferson seemed the reason for the picture's success and his less than $1 million fee would make it possible for Cimino to make *The Johnson County War* for the $7.5 million he was projecting as the picture's cost. There might have been more desirable star names but none that would not have distended the budget.

Meanwhile, as we vacillated, the Morris office continued to inform us that Universal was getting close to a deal, that Fox had passed, and it subtly implied that Kamen's vacation was the only impediment to the conclusion of a deal with Warner Brothers.* *But,* we were told in dark yet helpful hints, Warner's was unwilling to accept Christopher Walken in the second role and Walken's participation was creatively vital to Cimino. UA had no such qualms. Kristofferson and the female star—Fonda or Keaton—would carry the picture anyway, and if Warner's proved right about Walken's lack of box-office appeal after *The Deer Hunter* had been released, his fee was still supportable within the budget, and the important female star could supply the missing marquee clout. On the other hand, if *we* were right that Walken might win an Academy Award, that could push him into the star category, and since he was a fine actor, creatively acceptable, we were willing to approve him in advance. Indeed, almost any better-known actor would have increased the budget, a situation we were eager to avoid.

The Johnson County War was one of several projects discussed that week in the September California production meeting. Far more urgent to UA than its potential ("Color it red—not for politics, for violence!" Mankiewicz protested), was *Apocalypse Now,* which was in a state of mysterious limbo in San Francisco. Costs were mounting, and the picture, now a full year overdue, remained frustratingly out of reach. Coppola's chumminess with Jim Harvey did nothing to alleviate growing suspicions of high-handed irresponsibility. Rissner had seen at least one provisional cut of the picture, and large numbers of the press had seen an even earlier one the previous summer, when Coppola had invited an audience to view his "work in progress."† This ploy boomeranged smartly; the wisecrack "Apocalypse Never" circulated quickly. Gossip that the picture was unreleasable was common in Hollywood and New York. Albeck was urging a reconnaissance mission to San Francisco and

*Warner's had, in fact, already negotiated a deal for Charles Okun, who was to be the movie's production manager at Warner's and subsequently was for UA.
†A device he repeated with *One from the Heart* in 1981, with similarly unhappy results.

insisted we see the cut of the moment and, while we were at it, find out whatever had happened to The Black Stallion, also languishing a year behind schedule at Zoetrope.

Part of the anxiety over Apocalypse was that the last war epic the company had released in 1977 had lost money. A Bridge Too Far, with a cast including Robert Redford, Ryan O'Neal, Sean Connery, Michael Caine, Gene Hackman, and others, had been picked up for domestic distribution from Joseph E. Levine and, in spite of the powerful marquee, had performed below expectations. Levine, who had gambled greatly with his own money on the picture, was protected from financial failure by the guarantees he was able to secure for distribution rights to the picture around the world, territory by territory. He later accused UA of handling the picture poorly in the United States, but his ire came to nothing except souring the company on war pictures in general.

Another concern was that because Coppola was San Francisco-based there was a special focus on the picture symbolized by the telescope Coppola had placed in Jim Harvey's twenty-fifth-story office in the Transamerica pyramid, which pointed down from its tripod toward Coppola's North Beach office building and bore a small metal plaque reading "To Jim Harvey, from Francis Coppola, so you can keep an eye on me." Harvey's eye was, in fact, calmly, alertly open.

Harvey claimed that the first intimations of trouble on Apocalypse came when a disgruntled crew member, fleeing the Philippines, stopped off in San Francisco to pay him a "social" call and informed him in great distress that the picture was "disastrously out of control." Harvey passed this information on to Arthur Krim, who expressed, he said, mild surprise and seemed to Harvey altogether casual about a situation which now, two years later, appeared only to have worsened and which Albeck was not about to tolerate, knowing its importance as a management index in the white pyramid on Montgomery Street.

But there was a problem further to whatever was—or was not—going on: public relations. Apocalypse was not technically a UA production (which may have precluded anything but the laissez-faire stance the company took toward it). UA had a direct investment of $7.5 million for the U.S. distribution rights and had lent Zoetrope additional money to complete the project, which had widely exceeded its original budget of $12 million. The total cost was now approaching $30 million, with no clear end in sight, and the only way to secure the picture was to keep financing its lengthy postproduction. To have closed Coppola down would have been an automatic write-off of the $30 million or so already expended. If the picture failed, UA would be in the uncomfortable position of enforcing the provisions of its loans to Coppola, attaching the assets not only of Zoetrope but of the man himself.

It was asserted frequently in the press that whatever artistic shenanigans Coppola was up to were legitimate because he was financing the picture himself. This was true only to the extent that the millions UA was pumping into it were collateralized by the picture, its foreign sales, and the various Coppola assets, which were, it was feared, considerably short of $20 million. The situation called up the startling specter of UA's legal department's evicting Coppola, his wife, and their children from their home on Pacific Heights, repossessing the Napa Valley vineyard, the office building, the magazine, the automobiles and whatever personal property was attachable. The headline possibilities were numerous and chilling: LAWYERS THROW "GODFATHER" DIRECTOR INTO STREETS!, UA FORCES OSCAR WINNER INTO BANKRUPTCY! or even APOCALYPSE AT LAST!

UA had no interest in evicting Coppola or repossessing his cars. The reaction this might cause in the creative community might even be salutary at a time of mounting costs and insouciance about budgets, but press reaction could only be disastrous for the company. The same journalists who were almost daily taking potshots at Francis could be counted on to rush to his defense should a corporation (a financial institution at that) enforce its legal prerogatives and foreclose on its options, even in defense of stockholders, many of whom presumably did not own vineyards and Victorian mansions and vintage automobiles. Coppola attracted press attention but rarely scorn. Press people needled and scoffed when they could, but they *liked* him. He was colorful copy and had delivered the goods before. Part of their free swinging over *Apocalypse* was participatory; they somehow goaded him into snatching victory from the grinning jaws of defeat and wanted to be in on the act. They would demonstrate this a year later, when the picture was finally finished and released. Triumph would prove all the sweeter when members of the press could scoff at the scoffers, forgetting that it was they who had scoffed in the first place. Coppola is a superb media manipulator, but even if he were not, their affection and respect had always been close to the surface and, in most eyes, earned. Coppola *is* the Godfather: to his own films, to George Lucas, Philip Kaufman, Carroll Ballard, the whole Mill Valley Mafia, as it is called. Corporations foreclose on such figures at their peril or at peril to their public images, and Albeck and Harvey wanted not merely to stop the cash flow pumping northward but also to prevent Coppola and Zoetrope from self-destructing and forcing UA to take measures that would do little good in protecting the stockholders' investment anyway and none at all if the cost was to be alienation of the world's creative community.

While *Apocalypse's* fate hung shrouded in San Francisco fog, Albeck's continuing analysis of the movie business had led him to break down the product needs of the company into categories. So many comedies in the $3 to $5 million range, so many dramas at $6 to $8 million, so many "little" pictures at $2 million or under were to be made each year and should therefore guide the development process. Chief among his categories was the "locomotive," and two of these—big blockbusters at budgets of $10 million or more—should power the lineup annually. These locomotives would be the driving energy for the sales force and would—in international, anyway, where practices very much like block booking were still common ("If you don't take *Wanda Nevada,* you can't have James Bond")—carry the weaker, smaller pictures. Albeck ordered monthly charts indicating what picture, of what type and what budgetary range would be available for what release period during what upcoming year. Eventually these would be prepared as far as three years in advance and, though constantly changing and flexible, would provide a useful production and development calendar.

He knew that his potential blockbusters for the summer of 1979 were *Moonraker* and *Rocky II. Apocalypse* would fall into this category if it were ever finished. The locomotives for 1981 would be *For Your Eyes Only* and, maybe, *Rocky III* if *Rocky II* worked, but 1980 had a "locomotive gap."

At $7.5 million *The Johnson County War* was no locomotive, only a medium-high budget "action adventure" possibility. Part of Rissner's soft-pedaling the project internally was apprehension over how the distribution men would regard a picture of substantial budget in a genre long out of favor, one which struck violently at some knee-jerk notions about the American past. Production believed it had detected earlier that summer a conservative bias in domestic distribution, which was supported in some measure by current box-office figures on two pictures that were decidedly unconservative. *Coming Home* was a prestigious and highly praised picture but a slow starter; *Who'll Stop the Rain?,* based on Robert Stone's National Book Award winning *Dog Soldiers,* was a clear failure. The picture was openly and loudly detested by Al Fitter, head of domestic distribution, not only because it was a flop at the box office but also for its drug culture subject matter. (At least one of the producers of the picture later claimed that Fitter's aversion to the movie caused him to book it in such a way as to sabotage it commercially. Such charges are often brewed from sour grapes and are seldom, if ever, provable. But it was true that Fitter hated the movie and axiomatic that the salesman's attitude toward his product has its effect. This premise underlay Albeck's whole approach in involving distribution in production decisions.)

Early in the summer of 1978 UA had been offered a witty and literate screenplay written by playwright Judith Ross entitled *Rich Kids*, which was to be produced for $2.5 million by Robert Altman and to be directed by Robert Young, with Altman acting as backstop for Young, whose experience was mainly in documentaries. Distribution had seen nothing in the script to warrant production. Its story of teenage romance in Manhattan necessarily precluded stars, but Fitter and company had yielded to passionate production entreaties that the script was too good not to make. The low budget and involvement of Altman made the picture viable, we argued. Approval was granted, though Albeck was visibly unmoved by Altman's participation, for *Buffalo Bill and the Indians* and *Thieves Like Us* for UA showed up dismally in the black binders.

Somehow it slowly dawned on Fitter that what he had read in the script had not quite registered; what seemed to be a tale of affluent puppy love was, in fact, a story of teenage needs, affection, self-determination and . . . sexuality. *Expressed*. Off camera and discreetly, written with delicacy and wit, but—no doubt about it—"Those kids actually *do* it!" And aren't harmed by it. And the whole thing is a comedy. And the sexual episode brings everything to a blithely happy conclusion.

Fitter was horrified. He saw the national membership of the parent-teacher associations storming 729 to tear it apart brick by brick. We countered that we weren't making it for the PTA or for his neighbors in Old Greenwich, Connecticut, either. As it turned out, we weren't making it for much of anyone. The picture never found an audience,* justifying Fitter's original position and leading to some sour grapes on production's vine. In Fitter's defense the script was "tastefully" enough written, with enough oblique skill, that it was just possible to skim over the pivotal piece of action, but it led to production's forever after treating Fitter as though he were subliterate, and it contributed strongly to distrust between the two divisions of the company. When Fitter's pre-*Blue Lagoon* horror led him to attempt to kill the *Rich Kids* deal, which had already been confirmed with ICM's Sam Cohn, perhaps the most

---

*Or the audience it was made for—teenagers—couldn't get in because of the R rating, "restricted for those under 17."

powerful agent in New York, Albeck, realizing the consequences of reneging, overrode distribution and agreed to make the picture.

An unnoticed aspect of this incident was that Albeck—who had understood *Rich Kids* very well but kept his qualms to himself (the moral ones anyway)—revealed for the first time that he was quietly reading scripts. There had been a hint of this in the quick clarity of his reaction to *The Fountainhead,* but it was now apparent that for six months he had been reading submissions and felt confident enough of his ability to do so to reveal some opinions. It also demonstrated that his delegation of authority was neither avoidance of personal responsibility nor lip service; in the months and years that followed, he continued to read scripts and to avoid second-guessing his creative staff, even when he disagreed, and he sometimes did.

Rich Kids was made. The actual coupling was softened and became so ambiguous that perhaps no alert viewer could say for certain that anything but a pajama party had transpired, but the picture was, I think, consequently weakened, and the incident made us approach distribution cautiously with a picture as explicitly against the American grain (or that handful of it in Old Greenwich, Connecticut) as *The Johnson County War,* to which Fitter's reaction was a surprising "Yeah, Andy. I can make a buck with this. I *like* it."

So did foreign distribution. Norbert Auerbach, who was to distribute *The Deer Hunter* in Germany and France, had by this time seen it and understood the kind of filmmaking *Johnson County* would represent. He estimated he could do "easily $5 million, maybe more" in the foreign market, where action pictures continued to be strong. Both Auerbach and Fitter thought Kristofferson had some box-office appeal based on *Convoy* and *A Star Is Born.* Only Bart Farber balked. He found the violence and language impossibly problematic for him in selling the picture to television. This was his standard aria and did not therefore register strongly.

Still, Rissner was not pushing; production had no united passion, as we had had with *Rich Kids,* for example, and because *Johnson County War* was that outmoded thing a "western," it was tabled for further consideration. What Albeck wanted was a "locomotive" for 1980, and whether we made this picture or not would not satisfy that need. Not a western for $7.5 million.

My former partner, producer Gabriel Katzka, called me Sunday night, September 24, from New York. I had stayed over in California, as had Albeck, for meetings with the Lorimar production group now that Rissner had concluded the important deal for distribution of their self-financed pictures. Katzka chatted briefly, told the latest New York jokes (an art in which he has few peers and for which I have no memory), then settled to the purpose of his call. "Want to be a hero?" he asked slyly.

He told me that Phil Kellogg, the distinguished agent who had retired from the Morris office to become producer for his former client David Lean, had let Katzka know that Lean and Dino de Laurentiis had come to an irrevocable parting of the ways on their projected remake of *Mutiny on the Bounty*, a mammoth two-picture undertaking originally announced by Warner Brothers but since taken over by the flamboyant Italian producer. De Laurentiis had recently moved his operations from Rome to Beverly Hills, where he produced *King Kong* among other pictures, and had spent considerable money on the *Bounty* project, which would require many millions to complete, possibly as many as $20 million or even $30 million. He was building a $2 million seaworthy replica of the *Bounty*, had built a hotel on Bora-Bora to house the crew in anticipation of production in the South Pacific (his remake of *Hurricane* for Paramount also was to use these facilities), and was evidently moving forward lavishly. Something had happened. Kellogg, true to his gentleman-of-the-old-school reputation, would not specify *what*, beyond dark hints and the absolute assurance that should Lean ever speak to De Laurentiis again, it would be through lawyers. Lean was simply withdrawing the project, which Kellogg claimed that Lean, not De Laurentiis, controlled. He was also withdrawing himself. "Would UA be interested?" Katzka asked, exactly as if he didn't know.

Though David Lean had not made a film since *Ryan's Daughter* in the late sixties, he was still the commercial movie world's preeminent director. No one else had accumulated such an unbroken string of commercially successful, critically admired films, starting with the directing credit he shared with Noel Coward on the latter's *In Which We Serve* in 1942. Lean, who was a film editor at that time, told me once that Coward (who had written the script and was starring in the picture, as well as scoring and, for the first time, directing), simply turned to him and said, "David, I'm much too old a dog to learn these particular new tricks," and in that flash of generosity Lean became a director. Their association was to continue as Lean directed the film version of Coward's *Blithe Spirit* and, later, *Brief Encounter*. Dickens followed: *Great Expectations* and *Oliver Twist*. Then there were *Breaking the Sound Barrier* and *Summertime*. But Lean's great reputation came from his American (or American-financed) period, with three enormous sucesses in a row: *The Bridge on the River Kwai*, *Lawrence of Arabia*, and *Doctor Zhivago*. Now Lean was preparing to return with what might be his last work (or works). This was locomotive power with impeccable, gilt-edged credentials.

I had read the first of Robert Bolt's two projected screenplays for the Bounty project, which was called *The Lawbreakers* and told the story of the mutiny. The companion picture, to be called *The Long Arm*, was as yet unwritten but was to deal with the mutiny's aftermath, legal and personal. What I had read was a beautifully crafted piece of classical movie writing, which presented Captain Bligh as a young, insecure sea captain with his first command. He was, as written by Bolt, in his thirties and had none of the scenery-masticating villainy of Charles Laughton's portrayal in the 1935 version. Fletcher Christian, originally played by Clark Gable at his youthful MGM zenith (and later by Marlon Brando at some kind of mid-life nadir), was written as a twenty-four-year-old unschooled sailor, full of life, lust, and future. His mutiny in this script was not against Bligh or British maritime law but against a martial life he could not return to after the spiritual and carnal seductions of the South Seas. The script had great eroticism, and the human motives of the antagonists were clear and sympathetic. Bligh's enforcement of the structured, moral world of which he was both embodiment and guardian was powerful and pitiable at the same time, as were Fletcher Christian's dreams and drives. I knew that this was what Albeck had been waiting for and that he would see it instantly.

It was by no means a sure thing. The high costs—shooting at sea was dangerous for schedules and budgets—and the difficulties of marketing not one but two related pictures—concurrently? consecutively?—were problems which may have discouraged Warner's. My enthusiasm needed to be carefully, precisely, logically presented.

Albeck had scheduled a meeting to go over internal business at eight o'clock the next morning in his suite at the Beverly Wilshire. I knew I wouldn't be late.

David Field was. He had gotten caught in the Wilshire Boulevard traffic between his Westwood apartment and the hotel on what was a fine, clear California day that grew muggy and thick as it progressed. Rissner and Mankiewicz were not coming, Albeck explained, and began the meeting without waiting for Field, in deference to the other participant, the surprise guest, as it were: Dino de Laurentiis.

De Laurentiis's presence had not been scheduled on Friday, and I was not happy to see him there. It occurred to me that my *Bounty* coup might be undercut by the compact producer in his impeccable silk tailoring and that whatever personal glory I had been spinning webs to ensnare might be swept away in a flourishing gesture of that fine Italian hand.

Andy asked us to make ourselves comfortable. I took an overstuffed armchair, and Dino sat pert and erect on a hard-backed side chair. We exchanged pleasantries about *The Great Train Robbery*, his picture starring Sean Connery and Donald Sutherland, which we would be distributing at Christmas in the United States and Canada and which I had visited as it concluded its studio work at Pinewood Studios outside London, fewer than three weeks before. Dino promised delivery of a final cut of the picture within a month and turned the conversation to UA's planned promotion. Albeck deftly turned aside any commitments for expenditures until his "boys" (distribution) had seen it and estimated its grosses.

Dismay lifted Italian eyebrows. "How can you estimate grosses without knowing what you will spend for marketing?" De Laurentiis asked. He swiftly began spinning success around the picture like linguine around a fork. Albeck was patient, even entertained by this quicksilver display of charm, which illuminated Dino's reputation. Nevertheless, he cheerfully resisted naming figures, stressing his reliance on the as yet unknown distribution projections.

De Laurentiis, not pleased but smooth, moved adroitly and smiling to new projects in which we might be interested, including *Flash Gordon* and *Shark Boy of Bora Bora*. Field had arrived by now, and we all listened politely, professing the usual noncommittal willingness to be in business whenever, wherever, however.

Albeck, I thought, threw De Laurentiis a bit off course, although the charm and salesmanship flowed unabated. De Laurentiis's method was always to assert that he was inches away from a deal with Paramount, Universal, whatever, but ink had not yet touched paper, and—smile, shrug—who knew? Albeck wasn't playing the game; he responded with a literalness that unintentionally called bluffs (if that's what they were) and seemed to be unaware of the performance virtues of De Laurentiis's presentation, which were considerable. His phenomenal deal-making success was readily understandable: the presentation was so charming that one assumed so skillful a stylist could not fail to deliver movies equally entertaining and convincing.

After a few more pleasantries he rose to leave, and as we all stood shaking hands, he mentioned, exactly as if it were an afterthought, "By the way, I've decided to drop *Mutiny on the Bounty* with David Lean. It's just too big for me." He shrugged nonchalantly. "Perhaps it is something you'd be . . . well, I suppose not," he said, quickly retracting the thought, smiling brightly, an Italian pixie in the world's most perfectly tailored suit.

Andy didn't bite. He, too, shrugged, perhaps unaware of the project or Lean's involvement in it. I must have made some face or gesture, for David looked at me oddly and then asked, "What's too big, Dino?"

The hands flew upward in a "who can tell?" gesture. "Not for me if I do nothing but work for David Lean," he backpedaled. "But I have *Flash Gordon, Shark Boy from Bora Bora,* my new movie from the author of *Serpico*—"

"Peter Maas?" asked David.

"That's right." De Laurentiis nodded. "And David Lean wants all my time. He is the King Kong of directors and I am just one man. I am a producer, not what's her name?"

"Jessica Lange?" David intuited, quickly going on to "What about Kellogg?" He shot me a look, knowing I was friendly with Phil.

"Oh, Kellogg . . ." Dino shrugged dismissively. We could see King Kong's paw tightening around Gentleman Phil, squeezing, squeezing. . . .

"It's a great picture," he continued. "A *great* picture. The boat is a great boat. The hotel is . . . you should think about it." He beamed. We shook hands all around once more, and he left. I wanted to applaud the performance and kill the performer.

I had no idea what direction to take because I had no idea of the nature of the conflict between Lean and De Laurentiis. Katzka had said Kellogg refused to discuss it, and that was that. I also had no idea (and do not know today) what the legal realities were, but I suspected that Lean and Kellogg owned a script and that De Laurentiis owned a boat and a hotel. If so, he was trying to unload some very expensive props for a picture in which he no longer had any participation. On the other hand, if he was legally involved, he was making some quick moves before Lean could make his. Either way it was interesting, and either way nothing improper was being done. De Laurentiis was, in fact, promoting the picture's potential to possible financiers, whatever his current position.

But my worst 8:00 A.M. fears had been confirmed: I had been scooped, and in a way that would make recovery difficult. Dino, an internationally known high roller, had said he was walking away from something too big even for him. Whatever conflict underlay the split, it was now tainted by dispute and could not be introduced on the elevated plane of David Lean's stature. Andy now knew too much and too little. As I was furiously trying to figure out an immediate salvage approach, he poured some cold room service coffee, asked us to sit down, and changed the subject and our lives.

"Danny's doctor says," he began, his voice unchanged from the measured conversational tone he had used with De Laurentiis, "that unless he quits his job, he will die, and because we don't want Danny to die, I have accepted his resignation this weekend and am naming the two of you coheads of production. David will stay here in California, and Steven will remain in New York with me; but I want Steven to spend a minimum of one week each month in California because this is where the action is." He looked up blandly, but with a glint of self-satisfaction that he had correctly delivered the only slightly passé catchphrase.

He went on in the vacuum of our silence to detail new, equal salary levels and benefits (we each would get a Mercedes), alluded to his certitude that Mankiewicz would not care to stay on without Rissner, urged our restaffing as quickly as possible, and detailed his vision of how such a tandem operation—almost unheard-of in the business—was to operate.

"We will make no pictures without your joint approval. However, I don't expect you to agree on everything. If you did, one of you would clearly be superfluous. In the event of disagreement I may be used as a final court of appeal, but I expect the two of you to work closely together, solving your own problems. You will have equal authority and equal responsibility and equal credit or blame for what you or your staffs do. I hope also you will have equal success—for yourselves and for the company. Danny and Jim Harvey and I all think you will. Do you find this acceptable?"

We did. Mutely.

"Any questions?"

There weren't. Or there were too many to sort out and pose at such an unexpected moment. Neither of us had had an inkling that Rissner was resigning, and if we had, I doubt that either of us would have anticipated this separate but equal division of the top job. I suspect now we were simultaneously both disappointed not to have been singled out and relieved to have the other to turn to. We understood instantly and were to spend marathon conversations discussing the possibilities and perils of rivalry and the sensible wisdom of working in the harmony Albeck said he expected.

It was several hours before we could discuss it. There was a swift movement to business as usual, additional internal miscellany to dispose of, followed by lunch in the swank Bella Fontana Room of the Beverly

Wilshire with the Lorimar executives, who did not know of Rissner's resignation because no announcement was to be made for a couple of weeks. When we finally returned to Culver City and the Thalberg Building, Rissner was waiting for us, a Cheshire cat.

He was sitting calmly on the white, nubby sofa in his office, both of which he had inherited from Mike Medavoy only eight months before, his feet propped on the glass coffee table before him.

"Get ready to have your lives changed," he said. "You'll start living on airplanes and telephones more than you do now, and say good-bye to any hopes for a personal life because there won't be time for that. Don't let the job kill you, and don't try to kill each other. Albeck is a good man who needs your help and wants you to succeed. You need each other's help, in my opinion, and if you don't get in each other's goddamn way, you'll do OK."

He was not retiring, he said, to a sick bed or the beach but was going to Warner Brothers as an independent producer for his old friend and mentor Ted Ashley. He asked us to keep this confidential until it could be announced properly. Then he returned calmly to old business. "What do you guys want to do about Cimino?" he asked.

David and I turned to each other. Neither Cimino nor David Lean had been uppermost in our minds since Albeck made his announcement.

David asked, "What do you think, Danny?"

Rissner exploded. "No! What do *you* think? That's what these jobs mean. You don't get to ask that question anymore except of each other, and nobody else in town has *that!*"

He was being old-soldier tough, and he meant it. We were being thrown into the deep end and told to swim. Treading water, we told him that we thought the project was worth doing and that we wanted to be in business with Cimino.

Rissner nodded, then said somberly, "As my last official act, let me give you some advice. Make the goddamn deal. If you don't, I *will*. With Ted. I'll produce the picture myself for Warner's."

The rhythms of the past few days became clearer. We quickly asked Albeck and Lee Katz to join us. Katz had been given the script and budget to vet several days before. He arrived in his usual stately good humor and colorful Turnbull & Asser shirt, tie, and blazer. He told us the projected budget of $7.5 million was a fantasy, that he would estimate something much closer to $10 million. * He believed the picture far too complicated to be completed on the schedule Cimino had set

* Though the budget presented to UA was $7.5 million, production manager Charlie Okun's detailed budget at this time was $6.925 million and was never seen by UA.

forth, and even if it could be—"most unlikely," Katz maintained—the current budget was still $300,000 understated because of small errors in minor accounts and nonreflected union increases.

This was disturbing to us and to Albeck, but in view of the day and his professed desire to see harmonious pedaling on our bicycle built for two, perhaps he would have approved almost anything we seemed united on. It is not beyond the realm of possibility that had this decision been confronted on any other day, this book would not have been written.

We agreed on a proposal to Kamen. We would make the deal he was asking but insist on a budget corrected to the $7.8 million Katz felt obliged to insist on, which would give us a contractual out should his worst fears prove realistic and which would demonstrate to Cimino and Carelli that we were looking at the numbers from the first.

David and I crossed the reception area to the office he would soon vacate, and I on one phone, he on another, placed a call to Stan Kamen at the Morris office. Because *The Johnson County War* would be a West Coast project and David would be in charge, I told him he should have the honor of making the actual proposal.

Kamen was on another line. "It's important," David told his secretary. Kamen called back immediately.

David read him UA's terms for the picture, essentially what Kamen had asked, including preapproval of Christopher Walken, contingent on his deal's fitting the budget, raised that figure to Katz's still-leery $7.8 million, and aside from an excited slip of the tongue that offered Kristofferson 10 percent of the gross instead of 10 percent of the profits—a slip that Kamen caught and graciously corrected—the deal was accepted. David and I made triumphant eye contact. We were now running production at United Artists with Danny's blessing and Andy's and Transamerica's, and our first official act, a fairly routine one at that, had been to make the deal that would destroy the company.

CHAPTER 8

PROPERTY

The immense profits which have been universally realized in the Western cattle business for the past, and which will be increased in the future . . . may seem incredible to many of my readers, who, no doubt have considered the stories of the fortunes realized as myths. Yet it is true that many men who started only a few years ago with comparatively few cattle are now wealthy, and, in some cases, millionaires. . . . Formerly these pastures cost nothing, and at present only a trifle. . . . Land in less than ten years will be a considerable factor in the profits of the cattle business, as the value of pastures will constantly increase.

—Walter, Baron von Richtofen,
Cattle-Raising on the Plains of North America (1885)

After the excitement of acquiring a property has subsided, the legal department goes to work. The lawyers dictate and document. They telephone and caucus and strike out and amend and keep meticulous notes on sheets torn from yellow legal pads, recording names, dates, hours, minutes, who called whom, offers, counteroffers, proposals, counterproposals, compromises, resolutions, and doodles, all of it date- or time-stamped, carefully clipped together and filed for later retrieval. They exchange deal memos and contracts and try to avoid breaking precedents because doing so cracks open the boiler plate and makes even more work, almost all of it gray, preventive drudgery, some of it necessary, little of it interesting.

One standard procedure *can* be interesting, however: to research the property itself in whatever form (book, play, script, etc.) it exists. This is done to discover if there exist other, similar works that might form the basis for eventual plagiarism suits (practically every successful movie inspires one); to determine in the case of nonfiction whether living persons or descendants of no-longer-living persons might be defamed or slandered or in some other way find screen portrayal sufficiently objectionable to bring suit (descendants of Clyde Barrows and Bonnie Parker sued Warner Brothers, claiming that *Bonnie and Clyde* cast aspersions on their forebears); to unearth previous parties, if any, who may have been involved in or with the material and still retain some claim against it in legal or monetary form; and so on.

UA's legal staff knew, for instance, that *The Johnson County War* had once been in development at Twentieth Century-Fox and therefore expected to find documentation and accrued charges (plus interest) attesting to that, and they did. What the legal department did not know—or had forgotten, as had seemingly everybody else—was that there were additional accrued charges (plus interest) which UA would have to retire in order to obtain clear title to the script, and these were owed to United Artists itself, where the project had also been under development.

The Johnson County War was one of Cimino's earliest scripts, dating back to 1971, before *The Fountainhead* and before Cimino had any Hollywood credits or credibility. He showed the script to publicist-turned-producer David Foster, who with his partner, Mitchell Brower, had produced Robert Altman's *McCabe and Mrs. Miller*. Foster liked the script and made a development deal on it at Twentieth Century-Fox, which put the project in turnaround in August 1972 because it seemed "bloody and nihilistic" to the production head, Jere Henshaw. "It looked to us like a pretty downbeat story at a pretty heavy cost," he later told Rex McGee, writing for *American Film*. Foster must have realized the script would go nowhere at Fox, for he submitted it to UA in March of that year, months before Fox had officially passed. The violence in the script displeased UA's reader (identified anonymously as "HBx"), who recorded on March 17, 1972, "The vogue for bloody violence and killing seems to continue strong *vide* two of the season's top pictures: *Straw Dogs* and *Clockwork Orange*. But . . . this one is mayhem/murder. . . . Vogue schmogue, I say no." So did production head David Picker, and the script made the rounds of the other companies, meeting similar turndowns.

The script's failure to attract backing may have been less because of blood and violence (however reprehensible, often big box office) than because of the project's unknown, uncredited young director. Foster claimed that "people liked the script, but no one was willing to take

that shot to let Mike direct. I believed in the script and I believed in
Mike as a writer and director, but after a certain amount of rejection,
you finally reach a point. You wonder how much more of this shit you
can stand."* Finally having stood long enough or deep enough, Foster
stepped out, and Cimino was on his own.

Foster and Cimino were not the only people interested in the movie
potential of the history of Johnson County, nor were they the first. In
October 1959 *Variety* announced that producer Robert Radnitz and actor Alan Ladd were preparing a picture for Ladd's independent production company to be called *The Johnson County War*. Radnitz, long
associated with "socially conscious" pictures (*Sounder* is the best
known), may have responded to the same issues of law and justice that
were to interest UA almost twenty years later, and it is possible that
Ladd saw some similarity to his earlier *Shane*, which had also concerned
homesteading and cattle barons and was set in Wyoming in the same
period (1889).† Nothing came of their plans, but only two months
after UA had said no to Foster and Cimino in 1972, another script,
written by Gerald Wilson, bearing the same title and dealing with the
same historical events, was submitted by British director Michael Winner, and this, too, was turned down. The script was described by UA
reader Brenda Beckett (daughter of Transamerica's chairman) as "overly
earnest, ponderous, and ultimately tedious." Nevertheless, it attracted
the attention of Steve McQueen, then at the height of his popularity,
who announced in January 1973 that he would star in the Wilson script
and had "hired" Michael Winner to direct.

McQueen had originally learned of the subject through David Foster, who gave him Cimino's early draft around the time Foster produced
The Getaway with McQueen and Ali McGraw, who was to become
Mrs. McQueen in a highly publicized romance during the making of
that picture. The actor shied away from the Foster package because of a
wariness about Cimino as a first-time director, but by the end of 1973 a
number of things had changed to make a Cimino reapproach of Mc-
Queen and McGraw sensible. First, the announced McQueen-Winner
version never got financed. Secondly, there was the 1973 management
change at United Artists when David Picker departed as president and

American Film, the official magazine of the American Film Institute, bowdlerized this
remark, which is quoted from the original manuscript. American film is rarely as gen-
teel as *American Film* seems to think.
†Jack Shaefer, who wrote the book *Shane*, almost certainly had Johnson County in
mind. But his Wyoming is a landscape for myth, and the conflict is simplified and
reduced to one cattle baron, one hired killer, and one brave resister—the mysterious
Shane.

Eric Pleskow moved up. Most important, however, in the interval
Cimino had made *Thunderbolt and Lightfoot* on a snappy forty-seven-day
schedule, which looked good to UA, and the film was to please both
audiences and critics* in the summer of 1974, just about the time Universal released on television a made for TV movie called *The Invasion of
Johnson County*, starring Bill Bixby in a script by Nicholas E. Baehr,
directed by Jerry Jameson. No matter. That Cimino had been an acceptable director to Clint Eastwood suggested that he might attract
other stars (presumably more important than Bixby; possibly even Eastwood again), who might commercialize his now un-Fostered western
property, and UA accordingly made a deal in late 1973 on the same
project it had turned down a year and a half before. Casting was critical. The deal memo which Bill Bernstein, senior vice-president of business affairs, sent to the William Morris Agency confirming Cimino's
deal on November 26, 1973, states specifically that "we will immediately confer on the offer to be submitted to McQueen and McGraw."
Elsewhere the memo notes that "it is specifically agreed that our deal
with Cimino is conditioned on his ability to engage, on terms acceptable to UA, either McQueen, Redford, Newman or Eastwood as the
male star *and* [italics in the original] either McGraw, Fonda or Welch as
the female star."

Cimino moved into an office in UA's Hollywood headquarters in
the Samuel Goldwyn Studios on North Formosa and Santa Monica and
began preparing the picture while waiting for word from the McQueens.
A budget had been prepared in November, and Cimino was doing
script revisions, on which the deal was likewise conditioned. By December 14 the budget ran to slightly more than $2.5 million, exclusive
of the two stars, and was revised downward by slightly more than
$300,000 to around $2.2 million by February 1974. By this time it was
clear that McQueen was going to make *Papillon* instead of Cimino's
picture, and Cimino submitted the script to Robert Redford's agents,
alluding to a May 1 start date in that year.

One year later, in February 1975, the project still had no cast, and
desperation was beginning to set in. Although the original deal memo
had specified the only stars acceptable to UA, Cimino wrote Danton
Rissner (then still in charge of East Coast and European production) a
casting memo on February 18, 1975, suggesting an omnibus cast of the
type used successfully by UA in *Around the World in Eighty Days* nine-

---

*Jay Cocks, for instance, in *Time's* June 10, 1974, issue noted Cimino's "scrupulously
controlled style" and found the picture "one of the most ebullient and eccentric diversions around."

teen years before and currently being revived for such disaster pictures as *The Towering Inferno* and *Earthquake* (and not much later by *A Bridge Too Far*). Cimino termed his casting "extremely optimistic" but added "not impossible." It is an interesting list, for it suggests that even then Cimino had a sense of his material as "epic" in scope and importance, even if history regarded it as not much more than a footnote. The list was "optimistic" but far from shy. It was, in fact, portentous.

John Wayne was suggested for the part eventually played by Kristofferson, Jeff Bridges for the Walken role, and as the female lead, Jane Fonda. The minor characters, some of whom were mere walk-ons, others of whom would be dropped from subsequent versions of the script, included as mercenaries Henry Fonda, Burt Lancaster, James Stewart, Rod Steiger, Burt Reynolds, and James Caan. As immigrants, Cimino suggested Ingrid Bergman, Gene Hackman, George Kennedy, Richard Widmark, Jon Voight and Kirk Douglas, reserving the role of a U.S. marshal for Joel McGrea, that of the governor of Wyoming for Randolph Scott, and that of a U.S. cavalry captain for William Holden. The mayor of the town was a role for Arthur Kennedy, and that of alcoholic William ("Billy") Irvine, friend and former Harvard classmate of the John Wayne character (a startling academic image), for Jack Lemmon. The Lemmon role remained important in subsequent drafts and eventually was played by English actor John Hurt.

What political reactions John Wayne might have had to the script boggle the brain, but nothing ever came of this plan. Instead, the project acquired a new title, *Paydirt*, and the association of Joe Wizan, who had produced the successful Robert Redford western *Jeremiah Johnson*. By December 1975 *Paydirt*'s budget, exclusive of stars, had risen to $3.6 million, a jump of $1.3 million, or more than half the February 1974 budget of $2.2 million. The project continued to resist casting acceptable to UA and was finally dropped. Cimino went on to *The Deer Hunter*, the UA management went on to Orion, and *Paydirt* went onto the shelf.

"One uses history in a very free way," Cimino told *American Film*, in a remark that would come back to haunt him. Certainly Johnson County and Wyoming history in the 1890s had offered plenty of play and color for historians, novelists, and filmmakers for many years. Long before *Shane*, Owen Wister set *The Virginian* partly in Johnson County; long after, Oakley Hall would do the same in *The Bad Lands*. * Films as

---

* Hall's book was submitted to UA (and rejected) in early January 1978. It later became the subject of some legal skirmishing—as would several never-produced scripts by other writers—during production of *Heaven's Gate*. No lawsuits ever resulted. People only sue hits.

various as *The Wild Bunch, Butch Cassidy and the Sundance Kid,* and *Little Big Man* all drew on Wyoming history, indicating the liveliness of time and place.

Almost all contemporary records of this history, however, were related by participants—partisans with reputations or property to protect. Some were nearly illiterate, cowboys relating memoirs of the range, their artlessness diminishing their relevance not at all; others were full of frontier rhetoric, flourishing axes for the grinding. The romance of the Old West was then the romance of a living, contemporary phenomenon, and newspaper reporters then (as now) were not immune to colorful tales, tall or otherwise, which might spice up the Sunday edition. Accounts, therefore, differ wildly, and because there was no clear victor in the Johnson County War, there is no victor's version to wipe the historical slate clean of ambiguity.

The dramatic appeal of the general background, which has attracted novelists from Owen Wister to Thomas Berger and filmmakers from the earliest one-reel directors to Peckinpah and Cimino, is evident from even a brief review.

Wyoming had been a territory since 1868, and by 1873 the pattern of territorial common law was set by the establishment of the Wyoming Stock Growers' Association, formed by cattle ranchers to regulate the business and each other. Cheyenne, home of the association, was known popularly as the Holy City of the Cow—not in jest and not for nothing. The association valued its cattle holdings in 1885 as worth $100 million in dollars of the day.

Most of the big cattle ranchers in the Wyoming Territory (a far vaster area than the present state) were foreigners, corporations formed mainly in England and Scotland by owners who were mostly, but not always, absentee. They were attracted by propaganda such as that from Baron von Richtofen which heads this chapter, as were moneyed easterners, who read books like the enticingly titled *Beef Bonanza; or, How to Get Rich on the Plains.* They came and got rich (or richer) and lived it up at places like the luxurious and elegant Cheyenne Club, where the baronets and black sheep aristocracy palled around with the Harvard and Princeton boys who had heeded Horace Greeley's call. The Cheyenne Club was association headquarters, where members styled themselves a "society of gentlemen" within earshot of the coyote's howl.

Shareholders back in the old country knew or cared little about operation of their cattle. Their return on investment was as high as 35 percent in a very good year; 15 percent in a humdrum one. Their investment was worked by cowboys who were employees of these foreign corporations. They summered on horseback and wintered on the bunkhouse-and-board largess of the cattle barons, while the cattle roamed on the millions of acres of unfenced public land that in effect subsidized the cattle companies. Overhead was mainly a matter of turn-'em-loose-to-graze-and-fatten, round-'em-up-to-ship-and-sell, until several disastrous Wyoming winters in the mid-eighties proved painful setbacks for the business, for the cowboys, and for the cattle.

One somewhat florid but moving account is worth relating:

*The poor range cattle. What of them? . . . They were wandering over the country in droves; now and then on some hill where the wind had blown off the snow they would find, maybe, a mouthful of grass. They were crowded in all the river and creek bottoms eating off the willow, sage brush and grease wood. Under banks, and in all protected places, the poor things crowded to get a little protection from the bitter wind, which chilled their poor emaciated [*SIC*] forms to the bones and froze lots of them to death in their sheltered places. They were compelled to keep moving in order to keep from freezing, and their feet were cut by the frozen snow until their trail could be followed by the blood which flowed from them.*

The voice is that of an association cowboy, soon to be cut loose as the disastrous winter and falling beef prices in the East made themselves felt. He, and others like him, were to turn to what they knew: cattle punching, but on their own.

The association had an immutable rule: Any cowboy who owned his own cattle was blackballed, blacklisted from employment. The not altogether unrealistic fear was that in the free-roving pasturelands, an enterprising cowhand might lasso a calf or two for his own account or claim the odd maverick without informing the ranch house. To discourage further entrepreneurial-minded cowpunchers—and others with a loose sense of personal property—the association framed what was known as the Maverick Law, which held that any beef not bearing a registered association brand was automatically and by definition "a maverick," subject to seizure and auction, with auction proceeds deposited in the association's till back at the Cheyenne Club. A cattle brand in those days had much the same force and effect as a patent or copyright has today, and by the association's definition, any cow bearing a brand not association-registered was considered rustled. Hired detectives roamed the cattle markets and livestock depots, seizing anything that didn't bear the association's M. (They operated very much, in fact, like the Motion Picture Patents Trust operatives in the period recounted above in Chapter 1.)

It is difficult to overstate the power of the cattle barons in Wyoming because they controlled not only the wealth but following statehood in 1890, the State Capitol, legislature, and Congress as well. The first two governors of Wyoming were association members, as were the first two U.S. senators and many other important officials. The State Constitution was drawn up by a convention dominated by the association, and the Republican party was a virtual agency for them, membership of the two organizations overlapping for years to come.

Statehood brought official law to replace the common law of the range, though the wildness of the West would not be tamed until after the turn of the century. The immediate problem was not state law (which the association by and large controlled) or even cattle rustling, but the Homestead Act, which was populating the nation and undoing the cattle business.

When the Land Office opened its doors, hundreds of thousands of homesteaders with the $14 filing fee showed up to claim their 160 free acres of America. Their only requirement was to fulfill their promise to live on and work the land for seven (tax-free) years in order to earn legal title. The great grazing lands of the cattle barons were quickly pockmarked by the homesteaders (many of them former association cowboys), who fenced off their claims, reducing the wide-open spaces to crazy-quilt settlements. In the twenty years after passage of the Homestead Act approximately 430 million acres in the West were occupied by settlers, and half that acreage was placed under cultivation. The threat to the cattle companies was obvious, and they regarded it as land rustling of territory theirs by custom and usage. The United States government didn't see it quite that way, and since land rustling was a charge without legal force, charges of cattle rustling were newly invoked (under the same old association definition) to frighten settlers and drive them off the range before they secured title after seven years.

Cattle rustling wasn't all that hard to substantiate, in fact. North-central Wyoming was infested with genuine outlaws and rustlers. The Wild Bunch, or Hole-in-the-Wall Gang, hung out along the county's Powder River; Butch Cassidy, the Sundance Kid, the Texas Kid, Big Nose Curry, and others built parts of their legends here. Additionally, the millions of cattle freely roaming the public range were a tempting target for settlers who found 160 acres of homestead too small to irrigate profitably and who could, with a lucky rifle shot, bring home the beef for a full winter's provisions if now and then necessary. Daniel J. Boorstin has noted that the problem was widespread enough in Johnson County for the populace to be summed up as "Ranchers, who rustled on the side; and rustlers, who ranched on the side." Maybe the barons

couldn't tame the Wild Bunch, but they could make an example of
Johnson County, and Johnson County knew it.

The settlers organized to form the Northern Wyoming Farmers and
Stockgrowers Association as a challenge to the Cheyenne Club. It was
more than a political move (though it was that, too, dominated by the
Wyoming Democratic party); it was also a response to a series of local
murders committed in the territory over the previous several years,
which were attributed to the Cheyenne association not only by witnesses but by the association itself, eager to establish the price of cattle
or land rustling as a rope or a bullet. The odd, isolated killings (six or
seven were recorded, the victims seen locally as martyrs) were ineffec-
tive in slowing down a now-organized citizenry, and as early as November 1891 Johnson County began heeding newspaper warnings of an
impending invasion and prepared for the predicted assault which arrived in April 1892.

The Johnson Countyite who wrote the cattle passage cited above
was in all likelihood one of the "rancher/rustlers." His name was Oscar
H. ("Jack") Flagg, known suggestively in histories not penned by himself as "Black Jack" Flagg. He was a cowboy turned cattleman, was
blackballed by the association, and eventually earned his place on its
death list. He participated in the Johnson County War and was its first
historian, breaking into print in the *Buffalo Bulletin* with the first of
eleven installments only two weeks after the war had ended.

His account (not published in book form until 1967) is, one suspects, deeply self-serving, but no more so than every other contemporary account. These conflicting and historically ambiguous accounts
inspired Michael Cimino's free use of dramatic license in his retelling,
the September 1978 version of which UA bought.

UA, it should be pointed out, had never heard of the Johnson
County War at the time, any more than had many reviewers and journalists who were to comment knowledgeably on it after Cimino's movie
had called it to their belated attention. This was perhaps an indefensi-
ble oversight. Certainly it was careless. However, United Artists was
not interested in financing a historical documentary, and the script was
being evaluated only for its dramatic and commercial potential. That
this evaluation proved disastrously misguided will be seen, but in September 1978 there was a script which was to undergo subsequent
changes, some of them minor, some significant, and it went roughly
like this:

*Wyoming, 1891. The plains. An isolated settler's cabin sits on frozen ground
as the awesome Rockies rise snowcapped on the horizon. "The air is numb."*

Behind a shelter of hanging laundry, an immigrant speed-butchers a rustled steer with a hatchet. His wife drags the steaming chunks of meat into their cabin as a child plays nearby. Suddenly the immigrant notices boots approach at the edge of the sheets hung to shield him from view. A rifle blast rips through the sheets, turning the immigrant's face as crimson as the hanging steer's hacked carcass. Nate Champion (Walken), enforcer for the Stock Growers' Association, puts down his rifle and walks off without a word as the immigrant's wife and child wail over his dead body, bleeding into the frozen earth.

Following the murder, Champion witnesses a straggling horde of immigrants "three miles long" moving across the winter-blasted plains, pushing their possessions before them in handcarts as they people the land. Immediately after, we see hundreds more, but these are perched wherever there is space on the cars of a railroad train pulling into Casper, Wyoming, seat of the Stock Growers' Association. They clutch their meager belongings.

Also on the immigrant-filled train is James Averill (Kristofferson), on his way back to Johnson County where he is federal marshal, returning from depression-ridden St. Louis, where banks are failing. Times are bad; immigrants are worse; everybody's moving West to outrace the eastern depression or the potato famine or something, many just to take advantage of the Homestead Act's free giveaway. But winter is even tougher than the times, and many are starving, or would starve, were it not for association cattle, roaming the vast Wyoming plains, unfenced public lands.

Averill learns from his Irish immigrant friend Cully, the stationmaster, that there are disturbing rumors around Casper about plans to halt the rustling and the invasion of the land by all these settlers. Tough-looking strangers, the first of the mercenaries, are visible everywhere in Casper, strutting around in their long coats, brandishing their whiskey and Winchesters.

Averill pauses in Casper to visit the luxurious association headquarters and shoot a little pool. While there, he learns from association member William ("Billy") Irvine, his old classmate at Harvard, class of '80, that the association is hiring a band of mercenaries at $5 a day expenses and $50 per kill to execute 125 persons named on a death list, all of whom are in Johnson County under Averill's jurisdiction and protection. At association headquarters Averill has a physical confrontation with Frank Canton, the association's leader, and Averill warns Canton that the association will need a legal warrant for every name on the list. Canton knows (as do we, though Averill does not) that the extermination plan has the approval of authorities up to and including the president of the United States, not only to stop rustling and stem "anarchy" but to depose civil authority (including Averill himself) and take charge of the courts. Legalities will be observed . . . or rewritten.

Averill leaves Casper—Is he followed? He feels it, but cannot be sure—

to return to Sweetwater, where the immigrants are entertaining themselves at
the local saloon with cockfighting and Saturday night brawling. Averill is well
known and respected; he settles an immigrant feud impartially and fairly. He
confides to his friend J.B., owner of the saloon and the hotel above it, where
Averill lives, what he has learned of the invasion plans on his stopover in
Casper.

At dawn he leaves to pay a call on Ella Watson, the immigrant madam
of the Hog Ranch, a bordello on the outskirts of Sweetwater, bringing her the
new Studebaker buckboard and strawberry roan he has brought back from St.
Louis for her birthday. She feeds him, makes love to him. Then, just as
church is letting out for the townspeople, they take a delirious ride through the
mud and huts and tents of Sweetwater in Ella's new rig, scandalizing the
women, thrilling most of the children and men, to whom Ella seems a very
familiar "citizen," to their wives' chagrin.

In Sweetwater they join the settlers in the local pastime, roller-skating in
the tented roller-skating rink, where a sign above the entrance promises "A
Moral and Exhilarating Experience." The dizzying roller-skating is accompanied by music and laughter, underlined by the innocent ignorance of events
to come, still known only to Averill and J.B.

During a romantic interlude that follows, Ella swims naked in the local
stream, and we see that Averill has been followed from Casper, by an association mercenary who hovers threateningly near Ella's idyll, as Averill pon-
ders his dilemma in silence.

Champion, meanwhile, continues his work for the association. Canton,
too, is busy, formally raising his "army."

The Sunday night of Averill's return Champion comes to the Hog Ranch
to visit Ella, learns that Averill is back in town and upstairs, sleeping off a
drunk—not for the first time.

As a favor to Ella, Champion drags the drunken Averill back to the
boardinghouse room over the town saloon so Averill can be roused in the
morning to chair the weekly Monday claims court. Pausing long enough to
register the scores of homeless immigrants sleeping in tiers in the hallways and
in hammocks suspended precariously over the stairway, Champion returns to
the Hog Ranch to pass the night with Ella. Ever the businesswoman, she
makes him pay, but still he timidly suggests she marry him and leave this life
behind. She makes no immediate response, thinking instead of Averill, who
gives her buckboards and strawberry roans but has never proposed.

Early the next morning Averill seeks U.S. Army aid against the association's plans, only to learn that the governor, in support of the cattlemen, has
ordered the cavalry responsible only to him until further notice. The cavalry
captain, to Averill's surprise, has already been furnished with a copy of the
death list, and it is from him that Averill learns Ella's name is on it: a target

*for execution because she is said to take stolen cattle in payment for her
services.*

*Though Averill has long tolerated the triangle existing among himself,
Ella, and Champion (and has known of Champion's employment by the
association), the death sentence against Ella sends him into a fury. He races
to the Hog Ranch, where he finds Ella and Champion together. In a fight
Champion is astonished to learn that Ella's name is on the list, and he reiter-
ates his proposal of marriage to prove his innocence, stunning Averill twice.*

*The fully recruited mercenaries meanwhile advance by rail on Sweet-
water, cutting telegraph lines behind them as they come. Cully, the Irish
stationmaster, watches the train of mercenaries pass through his station, understands what is happening, and, finding the telegraph lines dead, rushes off
to give warning.*

*Claims court, held each Monday morning in the roller-skating rink,
erupts in hysteria as Averill tells the settlers of their danger, reading them their
own names from the death list. He and the situation are without hope. As
representative of law and order he cannot bring himself to recommend violent
action against what may be legal, however morally repellent.*

*Nate and Ella spend the day together, during which it becomes clear she
will accept his offer of marriage in the absence of a competing offer from
Averill. When she returns to the Hog Ranch, she finds it occupied by three of
the association's mercenaries (including the man who followed Averill back
from Casper and watched them as she swam nude in the river). Another,
called Arapahoe Brown, is a former friend of Champion's, now fallen out
with him over salacious remarks Brown has made about Ella. The three
mercenaries have already beaten Ella's girls unconscious, and they now brutally gang-rape her. This violence is interrupted by Averill's arrival. He kills
two of the attackers and their sentry, but the third—his mercenary
"shadow"—escapes. Champion arrives (summoned by John DeCory, the
boy who works for Ella) and is horrified by what he sees; the association's
crimes have now been personalized for him in a way so brutal that he can no
longer ignore and never forgive them.*

*Champion cares for Ella as Averill rushes to the Association's encamp-
ment on the outskirts of town. There he spots the third rapist and instantly
shoots him between the eyes in front of Canton and the others, including a
tipsy-as-usual Billy Irvine. Averill repeats his challenge that the association
must have a signed death warrant for each name on its list.*

*At dawn Cully, the stationmaster, is roused from his camped-out sleep in
the hills by the mercenaries. They mercilessly gun him down in sport, for
target practice and the bounty. If Ella's rape was overture to war, Cully's
murder sounds the first note of the bloody score.*

In Sweetwater itself alarm nears hysteria as opposing town factions debate alternatives in the roller-skating rink. The mayor and Chamber of Commerce urge turning over to the association those settlers named on the hit list, while the immigrants respond with outrage over this betrayal, their defensive fervor exploding. Averill, inflamed by Ella's rape and his realization of the inevitability of mass murder—legal or not—urges the debating factions to stop arguing, take up arms, and resist the invasion with force. All is chaos.

Ella arrives with news of the mercenaries' attack on Champion's cabin, taking place as she speaks. We observe Champion's brave resistance and inevitable death in an avalanche of bullets.

At the same moment the townspeople mount carriage, wagon, and workhorse, grab whatever weapon is at hand, and ride out of town to wage their ragged battle on the mercenaries, who lie in calm wait, led by Canton and the association's Frank Wolcott, former U.S. Army major and personal friend of the president. Among their number, only Irvine appears to have moral qualms, which he dulls with the aid of his ever-present silver whiskey flask.

The battle begins in blind turbulence. The townspeople, fervent but poorly equipped and badly organized, suffer heavy losses. The mercenaries, crisply efficient and professionally outfitted, pick them off one by one as an "accountant" keeps score for the later bounty payments. Averill is wounded, but as night falls, he steals from the battlefield to visit Champion's cabin, where he finds Ella mourning over Champion's bullet-riddled body, reading the farewell note we saw Champion scribbling to them in the last moments before his fatal gunning. Ella sorrowfully agrees to leave with Averill if they survive the battle, and they return again to the field, which is now haunted by the songs of the immigrants, raised tremulously for the dead and dying and as shield against the darkness.

During the night Averill and the men dismantle the remaining wagons and use them to fashion go-devils, mobile wooden shields to be pushed by horses, behind which the men can advance in a circling movement on the mercenaries with gunfire and explosives crudely fashioned into bombs by the local apothecary.

Dawn brings resumption of the fighting and a turn in the bloody tide. The settlers, who still outnumber the more efficient mercenaries, may prevail, but victory is denied them by the arrival of the U.S. Cavalry, flags flying. The army captain, with Canton at his side, claims to have official orders to arrest the mercenaries and take them into military custody. Averill observes that the army is in effect rescuing them from their lost battle. The battlefield reeks of blood and death and lost causes, but the battle is over.

Later, back at the Hog Ranch, Averill and Ella prepare in silence to leave Johnson County together. They emerge from the house, and their image freezes, like "a wedding tintype" of the period, and over this fading memento we read:

I can do nothing except act with the state to prevent violence. Every-thing else rests with the state authorities.—Benjamin Harrison, Presi-dent of the United States, 1891.

Some of the creative evolution of Cimino's version of history is evident; some of it isn't. James Averill, Ella Watson, Nate Champion, Frank Canton, Major Wolcott, Billy Irvine, John DeCory, Arapahoe Brown, and a few other minor characters not singled out in the above synopsis existed, were part of Johnson County history, though their actual biographies were often quite different from the uses to which the screenplay put them.

James Averill, for instance, was not a federal marshal; he was the local postmaster and surveyor, who owned a general store and "sold a little whiskey on the side." He didn't go to Harvard, though one source indicates he may have attended Cornell, and it is certain he was liter-ate, for though mild-mannered and well liked by his neighbors, he was a contentious letter writer to local newspapers and to Washington, pro-testing association harassment of, or attempts to overthrow, land claims, including his own. It got him hanged, lynched. And not alone, for they hanged Ella Watson with him.

Ella Watson, who lived on a neighboring claim, was Averill's com-mon-law wife, as well as mistress of the local bordello. (Black Jack Flagg referred to her delicately as a member of the demimonde). It is possible she was legally married to Averill but claimed not to be in order to file her own separate homestead claim. In any event, the charge that she accepted cattle in payment for her favors is very likely true, for her nickname in history was Cattle Kate. She must have been a colorful character. She was born in Kansas, had a career as a dance-hall girl in Denver, and when she was dragged from her cabin to be strung up reportedly protested they couldn't hang her because she wasn't wearing her "new print dress!" They hanged her anyway, from a cottonwood tree, with Averill, one of the few recorded instances in American history of the lynching of a woman. The hanging occurred in the summer of 1889, three years before the Johnson County War, but Averill and Watson became martyrs, symbols of the ruthlessness of the association toward the homesteaders, and their relationship to the war is very direct, if quite different from Cimino's reworking of it.

It is unlikely that Nate Champion ever knew Averill or Watson or that he was an association "enforcer" or killer. But he was an associa-tion cowboy who made the blacklist when he acquired cattle of his own, and he was very probably a rustler as well. Some accounts deny this, while others cite his reputation as the "king of the cattle thieves."

His death occurred almost exactly as written in the script, except that its locale was not at his own cabin but at the K-C Ranch, which was a notorious outlaw hideout, and he *did* keep a diary of the day of siege that ended in his death. The diary was an hour-by-hour account of his last day and was later widely published by local authorities as a means of enlisting sympathy for the Johnson County populace. The diary's tone is unsentimentally controlled for a man facing death and ends with this paragraph:

Well, they have just got through shelling the house again like hail. I hear them splitting wood. I guess they are going to fire the house tonight. I think I will make a break when night comes if I live. Shooting again. I think they will fire the house this time. It's not night yet. The house is all fired. Good-bye boys, if I never see you again.

NATHAN D. CHAMPION

The brutality inflicted in his slaying must have been substantial, for the county coroner, John C. Watkins, M.D., dropped dead of apoplexy on viewing the body. The two were buried the same day.

Frank Canton was not the head of the association but its chief hireling. He was a onetime sheriff of Johnson County, turned out by the voters, whom he seems never to have forgiven for the indignity. He later became a deputy U.S. marshal and association employee, was positively identified by witnesses as one of the men who lynched Averill and Watson, and was accused in the murders of several other settlers as well. Eyewitnesses failed to bring him to justice or trial, and he was to play the chief organizing role in the Johnson County invasion.

Major Wolcott *was* an association member and is perhaps the most interesting of the villains, for history suggests it was he who instigated the war. He was manager of the VR Ranch, owned by the Scottish Tolland Company, the representative of which was an Englishman named John Clay. Wolcott had sometime earlier borrowed $80,000 with Clay's help from the latter's British associates and in the summer of 1891 found himself unable to repay the loan. Some sources claim that the former Civil War Union officer suggested the invasion of Johnson County in return for forgiveness of the debt, and Clay's safe presence in England at the time of the invasion seems to support the claim. * Wolcott survived the war to make his final appearance in history as, ironically, a cattle rustler.

* Clay was president of the association at the time and perhaps thought the proceedings, for a foreigner anyway, required more discretion than valor.

Of all the characters Cimino borrowed from life, none was to be changed so much or used to such good effect as William Irvine. The real Irvine was not an easterner and probably never knew Averill, but he was a powerful association member, who had served as both president and treasurer of the organization and was part of the Wyoming constitutional congress and a power in Republican politics. In the September 1978 draft, Irvine was merely a foil for Averill, an association member who could supply necessary exposition about the coming invasion. As will be seen, however, in the final drafts he was used to enunciate the thematic substance of the piece, which was not yet fully developed. His name was not chosen at random from the list of "Invaders," as they called themselves, but because it carried with it, by chance, overtones of western riches and power, just as Averill's name tended obliquely to suggest old money from the East.

Other characters are of less importance but of some interest. John DeCory, who worked for Ella Watson, witnessed her lynching and was mysteriously never heard from or of again. Arapahoe Brown was, in life, the ingenious settler who suggested fashioning the go-devils—movable forts they were called by Black Jack Flagg—from miscellaneous wagon parts at the battle scene.

Other script details changed for reasons of economy or euphony. "Sweetwater" was really more prosaically named Buffalo, though the Sweetwater River flowed nearby; Cheyenne, not Casper, was the seat of the association, though a certain unity was derived by the substitution because Casper was the end of the railroad line, and it was from there that the Invaders detrained for the trek north to Johnson County.

In the wealth and welter of detail, however, there was one free use of history that was to loom more important than all the others put together, and that was the fact that the Johnson County War never happened. It was aborted before it started. History *calls* it a war, and it is indisputable that the Invaders' intentions were murderous; but only two men were killed (Nate Champion and his sidekick, Nick Ray or Rae) in a digressionary move on the march toward Buffalo, giving the townspeople time to mount a counteroffensive and stop the Invaders dead in their tracks about sixteen miles south of their goal. The Invaders holed up at the TA Ranch, barricaded themselves for three days, and were, as in the screenplay, "rescued" by the cavalry, thoughtfully dispatched by President Harrison at the request of U.S. Senator from Wyoming (and association member) Francis E. Warren.

As a result of the murders of Champion and Ray, all the Invaders (who counted among their number several federal marshals, many state officials, and the well-known lawman-turned-outlaw Tom Horn) were charged with first-degree murder but were never tried. Legal maneuvers resulted in a change of venue from Johnson County to Cheyenne; but the high cost of boarding the defendants at Fort Russell resulted in their being released on bail, and eventually the charges were dropped. Their defense attorney, interestingly enough, was one Willis Van Devanter, who was also campaign chairman for the Republican party of Wyoming.

Cimino's inclusion of a battle scene at the end of the script and picture was seen as a necessary, even cathartic climax to the conflict and was exactly the kind of big-finish stuff at which he had shown himself so effective in *The Deer Hunter.* It is unnecessary to rush to citation of Shakespeare and Holinshed's *Chronicles* to justify this dramatic license, but the climactic interpolation was to be a major focus of press and critical reaction to the picture.

In 1978 UA was more worried about the characters than about the ending. Through them Cimino hoped to weld not only a romantic triangle but also a sort of three-tier class cake that represented a rough American social system of the period: the Harvard-educated eastern aristocrat; the American-bred laborer; the immigrant entrepreneur. They were the foreground and would be the audience's primary focus regardless of the uses to which Cimino put the background.

Internal story department and production staff memos reveal little unanimity as to what changes should be made, and there were the usual jumbled suggestions attendant on any group indulgence in a subjective exercise. The scattershot suggestions finally focused on three major areas of concern: Who is Averill as a man and as thematic emblem, how can the grim ending be redeemed, and how can we remove the onus of the picture's being a western?

Cimino said he was responsive to these questions and eager to work on their solutions. He had ideas that seemed sensible, and he would, for the first time, be rewriting not to attract casting (except for Ella) or financing but to accommodate the special qualities and limitations of his already secured actors. His energy and enthusiasm were singular, as was his spirit of cooperation.

After years of dreaming *The Johnson County War,* he was preparing to realize it, and though the production staff did not regard the screenplay as in any way final, Cimino was authorized to make a location trip almost immediately after agreement to the deal. He was to find the picture's "look," which became the most distinctive element in the movie, which UA was to encourage and support and rue.

He went where "I feel connected with the road, the mountains," he told Jean Vallely, who was interviewing him for an *Esquire* piece she was doing about *The Deer Hunter.* "They are healing," he said. "I come here before I tell a story. It is my center, my special place." Vallely sensed that "the mountains and the land [were] his cathedral."

The place was Kalispell, Montana, near Glacier National Park, and it was to be the principal location for his film and the center of his world for the next year and a half.

"This is a lonely country," he told Vallely that fall. "That's why the road is so attractive. Maybe, just maybe, we'll find something at the end."

He did. It wasn't solitude, and it wasn't a cathedral. It was 156 acres of Montana land, which he would buy and improve, the rental and improvements to which he would attempt to charge back to United Artists and the movie known as *Heaven's Gate.*

CHAPTER 9

NERVOUS SYSTEMS

> No experience (even the solitary dialogue
> with the self) is without a political dimen-
> sion, and to ignore this is to tell a
> falsehood. But awareness of that dimen-
> sion varies greatly from person to person
> and no doubt from one civilization to an-
> other. I would guess that ours, democ-
> racy-haunted, equality-haunted, was espe-
> cially sensitive to the political (i.e., the
> power games) in personal relationships.
>
> —Mary McCarthy,
> "The Lasting Power of
> the Political Novel,"
> *New York Times Book Review*
> (January 1, 1984)

Andy Albeck wasn't fooled. He knew that whatever else *The Johnson County War* might be or become, it was a western. It read like one, it would look like one, and it would be perceived as one, like *Comes a Horseman*, now dying in theaters all over America, starring the same Jane Fonda they were talking about for Cimino's picture. It was a worry, and for that reason he was eager to learn more about the David Lean scheme, which was also worrisome, perhaps downright crazy, but not one filmmaker noted in Albeck's black books tallied so consistent a return on investment as Lean.

At three o'clock on the afternoon of September 26, 1978, the day after the deal for *The Johnson County War* had been made with Stan Kamen, the man Kamen had replaced at the Morris agency, Phil Kellogg, came to call, and he brought David Lean with him. Lean wore confidence-inspiring smiles, a blazer sweater, natty white trousers that matched the shade of his hair, and the tan he had acquired in the South Seas while making test shots of possible locations for *Bounty*. Kellogg introduced David Field and me to Lean, and when we all were comfortably seated in Field's office, Phil outlined for us the status of the project. In his polite, well-prepared way he brought us discreetly up-to-date, then agreed that there might indeed be legal problems to resolve between the production and Mr. de Laurentiis if one wished to use the boat and certain other production materials prepared at his expense but that Lean and the project were as available as available could be.

The questions and answers were kept polite and low-key, a technique at which Field excelled, and his acuity and deference clearly captivated Lean. The budget question was raised, and Lean startled us both by announcing in his silvery voice that he could not imagine the two pictures together costing $20 million. "I should imagine more in the area of nineteen," he offered, all sincerity and crisp British inflections. My first thought was either he was trying to outhustle De Laurentiis or he was seriously out of touch with the inflation that had taken place over the decade since *Ryan's Daughter.* On the other hand, if he was right, and he could make two full-length period feature films—on water yet—for under $20 million, there was something seriously wrong with *Moonraker,* which already had reached that figure and was climbing, not to mention *Apocalypse,* flirting seriously with $30 million. No budget had ever been prepared on the *Bounty* project since the second script wasn't yet finished, and because a commitment to David Lean was unthinkable without one, we agreed to send Lee Katz, whom Lean knew from early days, to accompany Lean and his production manager as soon as practicable to Fiji, New Zealand, and other South Pacific areas. There they would explore and estimate budgets, see if it was possible to make the pictures for $20 million or $30 million—or at all. (Katz chuckled good-naturedly.) Specific discussions of a deal would have to wait for hard information, but Albeck agreed we could invest the necessary time, money, and manpower to see if this waterborne locomotive would float.

Bounty was long-range. Short-range and urgent was the fact that UA was again scrambling to reassemble a production staff. The announcement of Rissner's resignation—"motivated by problems of health," according to the release issued Friday, September 29—came as a surprise to almost all the UA staff and as a shock to Chris Mankiewicz, whose intuition had uncharacteristically failed him, as, he believed, had his friend Rissner in not giving him advance warning. Albeck had been right: Mankiewicz resigned in medium-high dudgeon, sardonically observing as he packed his papers away in the paint fumes of his office, "This might have waited until I finished the goddamned decorating!"

It was the second round of musical chairs at UA in nine months, and virtually no one in Hollywood believed Rissner was resigning for reasons of health, in spite of his avowal to the *Hollywood Reporter* that "surgery brought the decision on . . . that my life was more important than the job." As to his future plans, he scotched the inevitable rumors with "I am not going to Warner Bros. or Orion—most definitely not. * Where I am going," he added engagingly, "is to Italy—to see a beautiful girl." And he did.

Variety's Dale Pollock dug more deeply or dialed longer than the *Hollywood Reporter* and recorded Mankiewicz's parting shot at Albeck: "There are grave problems at UA with top-level management. I think it will be an extremely uphill battle for David Field and Steve Bach to accomplish what I know they want to accomplish." Chairman Harvey retorted quickly from San Francisco that Transamerica was "one hundred percent satisfied" with management. "We're very enthusiastic about the appointment . . . and we will give them complete support." What else was he going to say? Transamerica *was* management.

Mankiewicz's *Variety* blast was no surprise, considering the anger and hurt he felt, but his gracious nod to his former colleagues and what "they want to accomplish" was. Still, his remarks did nothing to assuage the community's leeriness of UA's topmost executive echelon, and as Mankiewicz went back to independent production and Steve Bussard was allowed quietly to resign, Field and I found ourselves not running the show but being the show. There was no one else.

We moved quickly to fill Chris's half-decorated office and the one Field would vacate in moving up. Andy had made it a condition of our "partnership" that we hire in unison, and we had little difficulty in arriving at our first decision: to bring a woman into the company. Two candidates headed the list, and we were to get them both, though a year and a half apart. Claire Townsend was announced as a UA vice-president for production four days after our own announcements were made. She had been creative affairs vice-president at Fox, where David had worked with her directly, and I, indirectly. She was a twenty-six-year-old magna cum laude graduate of Princeton (alma mater to Field and Harvey as well), intelligent, pretty, and charming enough to have moved swiftly in Hollywood, socially and professionally. Her contacts ranged from the UCLA and USC filmmakers looking for first breaks to established producers like Frank Yablans and Martin Ransohoff, for whom she had worked before joining Fox. Her swift pace aroused envy, and her more spiteful detractors referred to her as Blond Ambition,

---

* He meant as an executive. This was true, for, as he had told us, he went to Warner's as an independent producer.

though she was more than a pretty face. She had worked for Ralph Nader before coming to Hollywood and had published a book before she was graduated from Princeton called *Old Age: The Last Segregation.* * In the year that saw coinage of the media term *baby mogul*, Claire was talented, industrious, and growing up fast.

She was joined at month's end by thirty-four-year-old Gerald Paonessa. Jerry had come to us originally as a producer with his writer, James Kirkwood, whose *A Chorus Line* was by then well on its way to rewriting Broadway history. Jerry had impressed us with his intelligence and clarity of mind. His background suggested a broad-based agility which would be useful to us, for he had gone from advertising to the theater, where he had been associated with playwright David Rabe (who had been his roommate at Villanova) at Joseph Papp's New York Shakespeare Festival, on *Sticks and Bones* and *Streamers*. Most recently he had had exposure to the music business and movies, working for Neil Diamond, then gearing up *The Jazz Singer*.

Claire and Jerry had two qualities that were important to us, apart from their backgrounds and brains: Each had a sense of humor and of decency. These seemed essential to us if we were to prevent the staff from becoming political or fragmented, bringing on yet another chorus of change-partners-and-dance, a restructuring that might include structuring ourselves out, voluntarily or not. Pitting executives against each other in corporate combat was not Albeck's style, and it wouldn't be ours if we could help it. The technique we evolved to aid us in the orchestration of people who could work together was simple and worked. We had everybody interview everybody. If the attitudes and personalities were different, fine, even desirable. But if the chemistry didn't work, we continued looking. We doubtless passed over gifted executives in the process (and were threatened with at least one lawsuit), but months of internal uncertainty, press and community skepticism, and internal jockeying for favor or power had taken their tolls. If we weren't exactly United Artists, we could at least be united executives, and maybe the overdiscussed, underrealized notion of teamwork could buy us enough time to build some momentum and movies.

And have some fun doing it. I doubt if the Harvard Business School addresses itself overmuch to the subject of fun, but I know of no more effective antidote to the depersonalizing aspects of corporate life than a sense of humor. This does not mean we were laugh riots, that the production meetings turned into vaudeville shows, each of us taking a turn

* She came by writing honestly; her father, also employed by Fox, was Robert Townsend, author of the *Up the Organization* books.

on bended knee to warble a chorus of "Mammy." It meant that working twelve, fourteen, sixteen hours a day, often six and seven days a week, frequently on airplanes or in strange cities, hotel rooms, theater lobbies, or primitive locations required laughter and the time to talk to each other. We talked about things that mattered, like making movies and encouraging talent and important grosses, and occasionally allowed humor to deflect the oppression of the endless flow of paper: the charts and projections and memos and printouts that may have been necessary to our conduct of business but were finally numbing and threatened to inundate us—sorcerer's apprentices all—in tidal waves of ink. The harder we worked, the more paper we generated. If champagne flowed for the czars and moguls, ink flowed for us.

By the end of the year the production staff was complete with the addition to the New York office of Richard Parks, a successful literary agent who had been courted by movie companies for several years without succumbing. Parks had been involved in setting up *Paper Moon*, *The Towering Inferno*, *The Other Side of the Mountain*, and other pictures in his eight years with New York's Curtis Brown agency and had been involved in *The Streets of San Francisco* television show, perhaps a good omen. Parks was the only UA executive with an agency background, and he brought with it a reputation for taste, acumen, and honesty. With his addition in December, staffing was complete, and we felt we had moved another inch toward some workable stability.

The stability seemed real because we liked one another. Jerry and Claire and Richard worked well together and with us. We were friends as well as colleagues, with as few hidden motives and secret agendas as one can hope to encounter in any walk of life. We were inexperienced in varying degrees but were equally full of ideals and enthusiasm and not naïve enough to be unwary of pitfalls.

Red flags rose early: November 1978.

We had scheduled Richard Lester's *Cuba* to star Sean Connery for a December start in Spain, Cuba itself not being "available." David came to me shortly after the changeover, visually discomfited by the task, and told me he hated the script, which had been months in development, and wanted to kill the picture. He knew I was close to Lester, had produced a picture he directed, had brought the project to UA, and wanted to see it made before Paramount made its similar *Havana*. He also knew, as did I, that the *Cuba* script wasn't yet "right" but that expensive preproduction work had to begin immediately in Spain to accommodate Connery's complicated schedule, or we would lose star, director, and script in one of the few star packages we had been able to attract since the January exodus.

Connery was pay or play. So was Lester. The twin considerations of abandoning the project (and money) and the personal chagrin I would feel as a result of not being able to deliver to Lester (Rissner? *The Fountainhead?*) and my hopes for the picture made David's position difficult. I respected his candor even as it unnerved me.

We flew to London on Thanksgiving weekend, met with Lester, discussed without panic the misgivings over the script, which was undergoing daily revisions by Charles Wood. We listened to Lester's patient and gentlemanly assurances that it would be right by the time production started. No one can "guarantee" anything about any script; but we both knew Lester to be a man of his word, and insofar as his word could have force in the situation, I was prepared to take the gamble and hope. Field was not.

We met with Andy, who seemed unshaken that we had reached an impasse so early in our relationship. He listened closely to the arguments on both sides and chose to go forward. Pay-or-play agreements and already firm commitments would amount to somewhere more than $1 million. Connery could guarantee that much alone in a television sale. Domestic distribution strongly wanted a Connery action picture. Foreign was high on the subject, the star, the director. Finally, because Lester was, with Woody Allen and Norman Jewison, the most budget-reliable of directors, the project made sense. * We went forward. I was relieved; David was disturbed and brooding.

On the flight from London to New York Field handed me a package. He had searched London for a copy of Tino Balio's history of the company until 1951, called *United Artists: The Company Built by the Stars,* and had somehow found one. He gave it to me on the plane without comment, but that evening, in a relaxed mood over drinks in my New York apartment, he asked for a pen and inscribed on the flyleaf "Good Times—Bad Times—We can do it."

It was a peace offering, important after London and Cuba because the incident could have instigated resentment and rivalry before the partnership got started.

Wanting to contribute something of my own, I thanked him for the thought and said, "We might make it at that. The problem is to find a balance between killing each other and deferring too much to each other. Apart from that we like what we do, we care about what we do, we like most of the people we do it with, and—I think—for the most part, they like us."

---

* It made sense, but the picture didn't make money.

He studied me somberly before responding. "Yes," he said, "but do they respect us?"

"Jesus, David, I don't know. We have to *do* something first."

Early darkness had already fallen by five-thirty the following afternoon, when we met Irwin Winkler outside a fashionable co-op on East Fifty-seventh Street. The weather was raw and windy, and Winkler wore what looked like a down-filled jacket, a cap to protect his head, tinted aviator glasses, and his deep California tennis tan. He was a New Yorker who still retained the city in his speech and liked coming back to stay in swanky splendor at the Sherry-Netherland Hotel.

As we approached, he was regarding the modern gray structure, unimpressed. It was a new building, aloofly austere, arrogantly arbitrary in the planes and thrusts of steel-colored sheathing that disguised the same old grids and girders.

Irwin led us inside the pretentiously scaled lobby, where we teetered along a wooden gangway raised several inches off a floor flooded by some plumbing defect. Rope handrails led us to the elevator past the desk of a bored guard whose cap said "Security."

As the elevator started its climb, I mentioned the name of a famous millionaire I knew lived here. "In the penthouse," I explained. "He grows tomatoes or something on the roof."

Irwin, who lived in opulence he frankly relished in Beverly Hills, cast a dubious look at the anonymous walls of the elevator. "To beat the rent?" he asked, rejecting it all.

He was not wearing his happy face, the face that looked back at you from a front-page photograph in the *New York Daily News*, framed and hung on the wall in his office in Culver City. The news photo showed Irwin and his partner, Bob Chartoff, in ecstatic triumph the night they won their Oscars for producing *Rocky*. Chartoff and Winkler had been exclusive to the company under Krim and were again under the new post-*Rocky* deal negotiated by Albeck, which gave them astronomical fees, precedential percentages, and their own office building across Washington Boulevard from MGM. They were rich, tough, and smart.

Their producing careers had joined years before, and they had produced a long string of undistinguished pictures together before striking gold with *Rocky*. Many said they were lucky, and luck had surely played a role. But their producing career had always had pretensions to more than the mostly program pictures they made early on, pictures like *The Split*, *The Strawberry Statement*, *The Mechanic*, and *Busting*. Their forays into more original pictures had been mostly disastrous—*Leo the Last*, *Valentino* with Rudolph Nureyev, *Nickelodeon*—but they were pictures that attempted more than they could achieve and signaled ambitions beyond the Hollywood norm. Their most recent attempt at prestige filmmaking had been *New York, New York,* another costly failure but, again, an attempt at something different, something better.

The irony that their current power and wealth and academy certification had come from a simple, even simpleminded Cinderella-with-boxing-gloves picture, in which no one, except themselves (including the management of United Artists at the time), had had any faith, had made them proud and difficult to argue with. Sooner or later Rocky Balboa's boxing glove—in which *they alone* had had faith—would settle any argument. In their minds at least. Their confidence was such that they were about to bring their Philadelphia hero back in what was a virtual remake of the first picture, which they (and UA) had the chutzpah to call *Rocky II.* (The second picture did even bigger business than the first, increasing Chartoff-Winkler's weight at the bank and at UA, which saw and enforced the wisdom of yet another hugely successful variation on a backward but foolproof box-office theme.)

Perhaps because of some diffidence about the simplicities of the *Rocky* pictures, which could never satisfy their ambitions for success with higher-brow quality stuff, C&W now wanted to add another champion to their stable, one who couldn't have been farther from Cinderella if he tried. Field and I were rising in that elevator high above Fifty-seventh Street to visit *New York, New York*'s director and star, Martin Scorsese and Robert De Niro, with that project in mind, a movie based on the life of middleweight boxing champion Jake LaMotta.

The prospects were gloomy. Field and I were edgy about the meeting because we admired both star and director (who had had a recent success with *Taxi Driver,* a film of extraordinary violence and copious bloodletting), and as fortunate as we felt to have inherited the *Raging Bull* deal from the previous management, we were convinced the script was unmakable. It was brutally depressing and depressingly brutal; the production would be extremely difficult, calling for De Niro at mid-point to gain sixty pounds, necessitating a four-month production shutdown; and although Scorsese and De Niro had agreed to work for reduced fees in order to get the picture made at a reasonable cost, their agent was beginning to suggest that after two writers and several years of discussion and development it was all going on too long to justify low dollars for people who were in almost universal demand in the industry.

Confidence that these problems could be sorted out was at a very shaky level as the elevator doors opened and we crossed the hall to Scorsese's apartment. A television set was droning the evening news, and friends of the director were scattered about in various small rooms, the walls of which were decorated with old movie posters. Except for the views of surrounding steel towers, it looked less like an East Side luxury co-op than a bunch of Spartan dorm rooms at NYU.

We had been warned by Irwin that we couldn't smoke because of Scorsese's asthma, adding to our nervousness. We shifted from foot to foot until the compact director—quiet, serious-looking—emerged from somewhere, trailing behind him a dark, wiry, silent presence in jeans and bare feet who turned out to be Robert De Niro. Irwin called him Bobby.

Winkler made introductions and began running the meeting as if the picture were the *fait accompli* David and I feared it would never become. Scorsese asked someone to turn down the television and someone did and someone else came in with what looked like a milk shake or health drink from the kitchen blender. De Niro remained silent and watchful. David and I listened politely to Irwin. He was good. He was authoritative and confident without being pushy, and he was clearly a producer, not just a promoter willing to give a hot director and actor their heads. Whatever relationship the three had established on *New York, New York* seemed to have resulted in a businesslike candor. It was our own candor that was lacking, I thought, as Irwin finally wound down.

"We have a serious problem here, Irwin," I began, "because we would like to be able to make this movie, but no one in this room should be under the impression that we think we can with the present script."

"Nobody thinks the script is perfect," said Irwin calmly.

"It's not that it's not perfect; it's that it's not makable."

"You're overstating," replied Irwin.

"There's first of all a tremendous obscenity problem—"

"You mean language?"

"Not just language, though, yes, language is a worry. There must be more *fucks* in this script than have actually taken place in the history of Hollywood. But let that go. This picture as written is an X, and I don't think we can afford that."

"UA has released X pictures before," Irwin pointed out stiffly.

"That's true. *Midnight Cowboy* was an X before family newspapers refused to carry advertising for X pictures, and *Last Tango in Paris* was an X, and Transamerica took its name off."

"What makes you so sure this is an X?"

"When I read in a script 'CLOSE UP on Jake LaMotta's erection as he pours ice water over it prior to the fight,' then I think we're in the land of X."

"But LaMotta used to *do* that before a big fight—get himself all worked up and then douse it—to rechannel the hormones or some goddamn thing."

"Look," interrupted David, raising both palms outward in a conciliatory hold-it gesture. "It isn't about the language or things the writers wrote that you probably won't shoot anyway. If you do shoot them, we'll have to ask you to remove them because you are contractually obligated to deliver a picture with no worse than an R. It's the whole script."

"The whole script? It's not helpful unless you guys are specific," challenged Irwin. "What are your *specific* problems?"

"It's not easy." David sighed. "We have a real question whether this story can ever be made as a movie any audience will want to see, whatever the rating."

Scorsese had been quietly attentive from the first. So had De Niro, who watched closely, silently, slumped into an enveloping easy chair. Now Scorsese put aside whatever milky concoction he was drinking and asked, "Why?"

"It's this *man*," David began quietly. "I don't know who wants to see a movie that begins with a man so angry, so . . . choked with rage, that because his pregnant wife burns the steak, he slugs her to the kitchen floor and then kicks her in the abdomen until she aborts. Violence may be part of this man's life, demons of rage may be fucking up his head, but why should anyone stick around for the second reel?"

"We all agree that's too strong," said Irwin.

Scorsese nodded. "We're not happy with this script either," he said, a tilt to his head including the silent De Niro.

"We'll find a writer who can lick it," Irwin said with even confidence.

"It's not finally about the writer," said David. "Not even with a tough, realistic script that can still elicit some audience empathy. Not unless we understand the rage. The problem is will anyone want to see *any* movie about such Neanderthal behavior? Can any writer make him more than what he seems to be in the scripts we've seen?"

Scorsese's brows knitted. "Which is what?"

David regarded him with a faint smile. "A cockroach."

The silence was paralyzing. I thought it a vivid and apt word but a curious way to win respect, if that's what he was trying to do. But it was a goad, and it worked.

"He is not a cockroach," came the quiet reply from the deep easy chair. De Niro's voice was calm and even and resolute. "He is *not* a cockroach."

Six months later a new script was submitted, and UA agreed to make it. It was still brutal and violent and profane. It was still a serious commercial gamble. But the darkness Jake LaMotta inhabited was that not of an insect but of a man lost in the mysteries and pain of his own violent nature.

The script was unaccompanied by any request for writer payment, and no credit arbitration was ever requested from the writers' guild. The picture would bear the names of the first two writers and no others. But the title page that covered the draft of *Raging Bull* that made Jake LaMotta human said, in small type, tucked modestly in the lower-right-hand corner "RdN." "MS" didn't even claim that.

At six-thirty the following evening we arrived at "21" in considerably lighter moods for the party hosted by Lord Delfont and Universal Pictures for that evening's invitational screening of the latest movie of "RdN," *The Deer Hunter*. There was a comprehensive glitterati turnout. Francis Coppola was there, looking nervous; Michael Cimino was there, looking nervous; the rest of the New York celebrity crowd was there, looking famous and relaxed. Many had already seen the movie, all had heard about it, and almost all knew that Universal was as nervous as Cimino was trying not to look.

Flamboyant producer Allan Carr, an unlikely but effective ally, had told Universal so loudly, so often that it had "a great masterpiece" at three hours and a flop at two that the studio at last gave up the footage battle and agreed to release the picture at its full three hours and four minutes for one week in December in New York and Los Angeles to qualify for the Academy Award nominations. If it were wrong about the picture, if the critics were to react negatively, if there *were* no Academy Award nominations, this one-week "limited engagement" and the subsequent February national release would go down the drain with a $15 million gurgle. Or more. It was a gutsy and risky release plan, and awareness of that heightened the anticipation of the evening.

The air at "21" was full of smoke and chatter from people of power and influence. This was not a screening room in which Michael and Joann could soften up the viewers with tales of production hardship. This was the heavy artillery, the smart crowd, the opinion makers of the media capital, the shrewd, tough fraternity of the famous. It was, in short, the most important audience of Michael Cimino's life, for he knew that in just over three hours, they would accept him or reject him. Not only that, but Francis was there.

As the Coronet Theater filled up after "21," those who had already seen the picture were busy watching the audience for clues to their expectations, but clues were hard to read on faces famous for being relentlessly blasé. David and I spoke briefly to Cimino and Carelli, wishing them well, and took our seats just before the movie began. We were seated directly behind Lillian Hellman, who, sadly, nearly blind, could not see the movie, which was described to her by her companion when the dialogue wasn't enough to explain the action on screen, which was most of the time. It reminded me of my urge to read that screenplay, still perplexed about how it must have looked to EMI when it agreed to go forward, puzzled about how it must have read to De Niro.

For three hours we sat there, trying to perceive the outlines of another, yet unmade movie through the lights and shadows of this one.

When it ended, reactions were not hard to guess. They were impossible to avoid. There were those who railed instantly, calling it fascist, racist, reading into it support of detested American policy in Vietnam. There were those arguing angrily in the lobby about "patriotism" and on the stairs about "populist attitudes" or waiting for taxis and limousines, claiming the portrayal of the Vietcong was "vicious," "a lie." But mostly there were the silent ones, the ones who looked wide-eyed, shaken, moved. They walked softly and unhearing through ricocheting arguments, and I wondered whose good idea it had been to have the party before, not after, the screening.

The Deer Hunter had reached the audience, to touch or enrage it. The word of mouth was loud and heated and more appreciative than not and would continue for many months. The attention, the arguments, the big money began to swirl, as the people did in the lobby of the Coronet. And right at the center of the swirl and the heat and the overexcited babble was Michael Cimino, serenely calm.

Controversy continued, and not just around the movie, though there was plenty of that. The critical reviews were mostly enthusiastic. Vincent Canby in the *New York Times* found it "a big, awkward, crazily ambitious motion picture that comes as close to being a popular epic as any movie about this country since 'The Godfather.' Its vision is that of an original, major new filmmaker." Archer Winsten in the *New York Post* thought it "so real you [could] feel it in your bones." David Denby told *New York* magazine readers that it was "an epic" with "qualities that we almost never see any more—range and power and breadth of experience," and *Time*'s Jack Kroll asserted it "place[d] director Michael Cimino right at the center of film culture." In California, Stephen Farber pronounced it in *New West* "the greatest anti-war movie since *La Grande Illusion.*"

Few reviewers failed to note weaknesses they were to pounce on in hindsight. * Pauline Kael was the most prescient. She called it "a small-minded film with greatness in it . . . , an astonishing piece of work . . . with an enraptured view of common life—poetry of the commonplace." Still, she found it "enraging, because, despite its ambitiousness and scale, it has no more moral intelligence than the Eastwood action pictures." She fueled detractors' fires by calling it "Beau Geste-goes-to-Vietnam" but seemed to sense with regret a movie that lurked there unfulfilled. "There is never a moment," she concluded, "when we feel, Oh, my God, I know that man, I am that man."

Interest in *The Deer Hunter* was not confined to the review pages. *Time* headed a cultural story "Viet Nam Comes Home," aping *Newsweek*'s earlier and snappier "Vietnam Marches Home." Neither *The Deer Hunter* nor *Coming Home,* which also figured in these stories, was *about* the war, and neither claimed to be; but there was a widespread perception that their popular acceptance was an index of American willingness to face up to whatever had happened in Southeast Asia. The issues were still highly emotional, as could be judged by the titles of the stories: Jean Vallely's *Esquire* piece, called "Michael Cimino's Battle to Make a Great Movie," was captioned "The director of *The Deer Hunter* had the guts to make a movie about Vietnam—and the guts to get it right"; Tom Buckley's excoriation in *Harper's,* titled "Hollywood's War," was subtitled "*The Deer Hunter* invents cruelties to sell Vietnam."

Vallely was a Cimino friend (her brother had been cruelly injured in Vietnam) and remained one, perhaps the only one at the time of the press holocaust two years later. Buckley was not, but he had served lengthy tours of duty in Vietnam for the *New York Times,* and he was the first and most vocal Cimino debunker in the press. *Harper's* is not read with the regularity or avidity of *Daily Variety* or the *Hollywood Reporter* by movie people, but Buckley's piece was read by its subject—

---

*Following the events described in this book, there was considerable revisionism about *The Deer Hunter,* initiated by Mr. Canby. John Simon, writing in *Vanity Fair,* found Canby's second thoughts tardy. "Intelligently scrutinized," he wrote, "*The Deer Hunter* was immediately recognizable as scarcely better than *Heaven's Gate.*" The curious suggestion that Canby ought to have known this two years before the fact of the latter movie was not pursued.

and by other members of the press—and was to have profound effects on their relationships during the making of Cimino's next film.

As a *Times* journalist Buckley had read in his own newspaper's Sunday drama section for December 10, 1978 (days before the one-week New York and Los Angeles engagements of *The Deer Hunter*), a long interview by Leticia Kent called "Ready for Vietnam? A Talk with Michael Cimino."

The interview began with Cimino's chatty assertion that Francis Coppola had dropped by his suite at the Sherry-Netherland Hotel to say, "You beat me, baby," in reference to *The Deer Hunter*'s reaching the theaters months before *Apocalypse*. Cimino, Kent learned, was "35, a self-described workaholic," who went on to detail for her his background: the nearly completed doctorate at Yale and the documentary filmmaking following his flight from academia. As for the movie, "it's a very personal film," he claimed, noting he had been "attached to a Green Beret medical unit." Having established these credentials, he went on to defuse any reaction against *The Deer Hunter* on historical grounds, citing the "surreal" nature of the film: "If you attack the film on its facts, then you're fighting a phantom, because literal accuracy was never intended." That he did not hear his own warning flag flapping in the breeze as he unfurled it seems curious, but Buckley heard it. Perhaps Cimino was preoccupied by something else he was up to in his first big celebrity interview with the *Times*.

The film, he explained, was shot partly in Thailand, "which is more like Vietnam than the Philippines, *where Francis shot 'Apocalypse Now* [italics added],'" and he went on with some high-minded talk about the characters, who "are portraits of people whom I knew. During the years of controversy over the war, the people who fought the war, whose lives were immediately affected and damaged and changed by the war, they were disparaged and isolated by the press. But they were common people who had an uncommon amount of courage."

He spoke of the war itself neutrally: "Vietnam is not the only war in the history of the world where there have been terrible atrocities. There have been and there probably will be far worse. *Vietnam was not the apocalypse* [italics added]." And finally: "My film has nothing to [do] with whether the war should or should not have been. This film addresses itself to the question of the ordinary people of this country who journeyed from their homes *to the heart of darkness* [italics added] and back."

What seems at first a standard publicity interview to flog a movie is, in fact, a bit of surprisingly naïve meanspiritedness. The four separate sideswipes at Coppola (including the opening remark and the italicized words) are gratuitous at best. Not only did Cimino "beat" Coppola into release, but he shot his movie in locations with more verisimilitude than Coppola did (even though the movie is not meant to be "realistic" but "surreal") about a nonapocalyptic war. Apocalyptic or not, Cimino wasted no syllables in preempting the "heart of darkness," the title of Joseph Conrad's story on which, it was well known, the script of *Apocalypse* had been based. Perhaps Coppola, in glancing over the allusive interview, may have paused at Cimino's comment farther down that "in every friendship there's the potential for destructiveness as well as for nourishment."

Buckley didn't notice (or didn't bother to comment on) the potshots at Coppola. He had more substantive issues to raise. Cimino wasn't thirty-five but a few months short of forty; he had never served in Vietnam or even in the regular army but had enlisted in the army reserve in 1962, served the standard six months, five of them at Fort Dix, New Jersey, and one in Fort Sam Houston, Texas. Buckley concluded: "Cimino may have seen a couple of [Green Berets] in a chow line or even been in a class with them, but he never wore the Green Beret himself." Yale records revealed that Cimino had indeed earned an M.F.A. at New Haven, but he had done no work toward a doctorate, and he had become known in New York as a maker not of documentaries but of sophisticated television commercials.

The imputations of dishonesty here are neither novel nor grave by Hollywood standards. Cimino never actually *said* he was a Green Beret or had served in Vietnam, whatever the implications of—or inferences from—such remarks as "in many ways, for a large film [*The Deer Hunter*] is extremely personal. A lot of it is based on personal experience. A lot of detail is very autobiographical. . . . I told you I was attached to a Green Beret medical unit."*

If he overstressed his Yale background, he did so far less than David Begelman, who, while at Columbia Pictures, stretched an air force training program in New Haven into a degree from Yale Law School without, in fact, having earned any college degree anywhere. And if presidential candidates and first ladies can shave years from their birthdates, why not an ambitious movie director?

Cimino's Yale background was real enough. Maybe he didn't have any hours toward a doctorate, but he *was* awarded an M.F.A. in painting (not in art and architecture, as he told Kent) in 1963 and had received a B.F.A. degree from Yale, also in painting, in 1961.

---

*Quoted from the original tapes and transcripts of the Leticia Kent interviews, conducted on November 26 and 28, 1978.

Yale appears to have loomed with unusual prominence in his creative development, for he spoke often of a burgeoning interest in the dramatic arts that was awakened there, in acting, and even in ballet.

Certainly drama and ballet were concerns far removed from those he earlier evidenced at Michigan State University in East Lansing, Michigan, which he entered in 1956 after graduation from Westbury High School, on Long Island, New York. At Michigan State he majored in graphic arts, was a member of a weight-lifting club and of a group that welcomed incoming students, and was described in the 1959 *Red Cedar Log* yearbook as having tastes that included blondes, Thelonious Monk, Chico Hamilton, Mort Sahl, Ludwig Mies van der Rohe, Frank Lloyd Wright, and "drinking, preferably vodka."

He was graduated from Michigan State in only three years, with honors. In his final year he became first art director, then managing editor of the *Spartan*, the school's humor magazine. It is here that one can see what are perhaps the first public manifestations of the Cimino visual sensibility, and they are impressive. He thoroughly restyled the *Spartan*'s derivative *Punch* look, designing a number of its strikingly handsome covers himself. The Cimino-designed covers are bold and strong, with a sure sense of space and design. They compare favorably to professional work honored in, say, any of the *Modern Publicity* annuals of the late fifties and are far better than the routine work turned out on Madison Avenue. The impact and quality of his work no doubt contributed to his winning the Harry Suffrin Advertising Award at MSU and perhaps to his acceptance at Yale.

It is easy to suppose that the transition from art director to managing editor of the *Spartan*—from giving a look to running the show—prefigured later developments. His desire to emphasize or inflate his Yale background (while minimizing or obscuring his earlier education, as he continues to do) was ordinary Hollywood (or Madison Avenue) image building, cynical perhaps, though far from sinister, as Buckley had reason to know. Buckley's *Times'* career had included occasional brushes with Hollywood, in addition to his tours of duty covering Vietnam, and he was in late 1978 on the *Times'* cultural desk, a not at all neutral observer. He noted in *Harper's*:

People often abandon uncongenial identities when they go to Hollywood. Former corporate minions, shady lawyers, talent agents, rock-music magnates, packagers and promoters, flimflam artists and racket guys, usurers, accountants with four sets of books, pimps and prostitutes of both sexes, all transformed into poets of the cinema, recline on one elbow on chaises on the marble margins of their swimming pools, crowned by themselves with laurel.

This is not the objective voice of the unbiased journalist but the tightly controlled contempt of the moral guardian, and in that vein he continued:

The Deer Hunter *doesn't hold the mirror up to nature. It holds it up to Cimino. In his narcissistic fantasy, the leading character is also called Michael, but the director's soft, round face becomes the impassive, unyielding bearded countenance of Robert De Niro, who plays the role, or John Milius, who may have inspired it. . . .* *

Cimino's ignorance of what the war was about, symbolically and actually, as reflected in The Deer Hunter, *is incomplete and perverse to the point of being megalomaniacal. He had no technical adviser and no one who even served in Vietnam on his production staff. It is as though he believed that the power of his genius could radically alter the outlines of a real event in which millions of Americans took part and that is still fresh in the memory of the nation. . . .* The Deer Hunter *does not examine cruelty, it exploits it.*

There was more, a lot more. Buckley's indignation extended as well to the critics, whose raves he boxed off from the body of the article in an ironic counterpoint which can only have suggested to those critics quoted that they had been somehow, well . . . "taken."

It was overkill, but overkill from a respected journalist whose outraged sincerity was difficult to doubt or ignore. Nor was he alone. Gloria Emerson, who had also covered the war for the *Times* and whose *Winners and Losers* had won the National Book Award, told *Time* that "Cimino has cheapened and degraded and diminished the war as no one else" and then wrote her own denunciation of the man and the movie for the *Nation* in a piece she called "Oscars for Our Sins."

With a few casual, self-serving misstatements about himself and his background and the emotional sources of his aesthetic vision, Cimino simply torpedoed his credibility with the press. He did so again as time went by, mostly by wary avoidance which read like arrogant dismissal, sometimes with an obsequious and sanctimonious platitudinizing designed to refute the same arrogance he was busy otherwise conveying. Nobody really cared how old Michael Cimino was; but people cared about his personal integrity, and they found it wanting.

*If Buckley is right about this, Cimino in the *Times* interview may have been tweaking Milius as well as Coppola. Cimino shared writing credit with Milius on *Magnum Force,* and the latter had written the "Heart of Darkness"-inspired original script for *Apocalypse.*

•   •   •

None of this had the slightest effect on the business *The Deer Hunter* was doing or the string of nine Academy Award nominations it garnered. In the bustle and glow of success the *Harper's* and *Nation* articles created no stir.

Buckley's imputations that Cimino was a liar, a narcissist, a megalomaniac were irrelevant to the bright halo of success Cimino wore with a certain public display of becoming modesty and calm.

Still, there were those who worried that Buckley's unsettling charges and Cimino's rewriting of history, both personal and (arguably) political, might have implications for the future. Others counted the box office and with shrugs noted that it was "just the press." Still others missed the article altogether.

I was one. I didn't read it until months later, when for some reason I asked David Field about Cimino's age. He answered cryptically, "Read *Harper's*." My secretary got it from the library, and as I read, I wondered with what trepidations David, now dealing with Michael on a daily basis, must have read it. And I wondered, too, why David had never mentioned the article until my casual question, a mystery I never solved. But it would probably have made no difference if he had because by the time Buckley's article appeared with all its bristling implications, the cameras were ready to turn on UA's very own Michael Cimino epic.

CHAPTER 10

THE FIRST SHOWDOWN

One cannot help but feel that in these first months, as Griffith formed his professional manner, he was creating the elements of future failure as well as future success. His secretiveness would grow, and his inability to develop, among his coworkers, critics whom he could freely trust would result in a dangerous isolation and, in time, it would seem to even so sympathetic a friend as Lillian Gish that there was no one near him "who loved him enough to be able to say 'no' to him."

Or perhaps one might more accurately say that he let no such person penetrate his reserve.

—Richard Schickel,
D. W. Griffith: An American Life (1984)

Albeck noted that 1978 hadn't been such a bad year after all. In fact, he could report back to San Francisco the best year in the company's history. Net earnings had risen to a record $28,830,000, up $2.2 million from the previous year—not bad for a company that had been through a major management upheaval three weeks into the new year and a continuing spate of minor ones ever since.

Theatrical film rentals were down in 1978 to around $295 million from $318.5 million the year before, but 1977 had been a record year in which Rocky Balboa made his first knockout appearance and James Bond his tenth. Both would be back in 1979, and so would Woody Allen, the *funny* Woody. Albeck knew that Orion was taking bows for *Annie Hall*, *The Revenge of the Pink Panther*, and *The Spy Who Loved Me* and deserved to do so. He wished it would also take a little credit for embarrassments ("dogs" he called them) like *Uncle Joe Shannon* and *Slow Dancing in the Big City*, but it was no consolation that Orion was having enough troubles of its own at the box office.

Even though theater revenues were down (an item to study more closely), TV sales were up; music royalties were up; direct costs, interest, and overhead all had remained roughly the same; and the bottom line for the film division was almost exactly only $1 million down from the previous record year of $403,048,000, off only a fraction of a percentage point in spite of $23.5 million less in earnings.

Disposing of the record company and putting a halt to its steady drain on other divisions' earnings had been an important and overdue step, and that loss was reduced to $582,000, compared to more than $4 million the year before.

The UA contribution of $28 million net would look good to the stockholders of Transamerica, whose dividends were going up this year, reflecting a 23 percent jump in net income on earnings of more than $3.5 billion. Albeck was glad to contribute the roughly 13 percent to TA's nearly $210 million net earnings. He expected no round of applause. No legerdemain had been involved—just straightforward maintenance and management, tightening up here, speeding up there, as the humming revolving door of departing executives slowed to the occasional quiet whir.

He looked around his office on the fourteenth floor, almost one year to the day after he had moved in. Gone was the drab, musty carpeting. In its place was a decorative border of handsome parquet, surrounding a thick wool rug of some beigey color with an interior deep brown border of its own. The scarred walnut desk had been banished to the warehouse in New Jersey; a sleek oak and granite cube, or series of cubes, which Albeck diffidently joked about as his Hollywood desk (though it was more austerely elegant than flashy), stood before the new window treatments, as the decorators had called them, though they were only very wide venetian blinds set on end that tended to rattle against each other when the air conditioner was on. The guest furniture, all glass and brass and buttery leather, would be arriving soon. Albeck glanced with concern at the eight-foot *Ficus benjamina* in the corner. Its graceful droop would have looked luxuriant were it not for the small brown leaves that rained silently on the new pale rug day after day.

The plant service could take care of the *Ficus*. Albeck had his own garden to cultivate, and it was not the one in New Jersey where he grew Christmas trees, either, but the one here on the polished granite top of his desk, on which rested a neat sheaf of clipped pages headlined

"Johnson County War." He took out a sharp pencil and drew a surgical line through the words, inscribing over them a new title and the date: "Heaven's Gate, January 26, 1979." He noted the two most recent entries penciled in his fine, swift hand: "Ella" and "Christmas." After each he had written a question mark.

Things had moved swiftly on *The Johnson County War* from the start. One week after the deal had been agreed to—though there were still no signed papers four months later, as the lawyers wrangled over what seemed routine legal niceties—money had been advanced for the first of several location scouting trips. Cimino had selected his "cathedral," Glacier National Park in Montana, as his principal shooting site, an area of spectacular physical splendor, if a little remote. He had declared Wyoming "overexposed," not scenic enough to convey the "poetry of America" he wanted to capture. Albeck wondered if what Cimino wanted to capture wasn't changing day by day, changing and growing.

The Deer Hunter had opened and was out of the way. The first euphoric flushes of the national reviews were being set in cool type for the February general release ads, and Cimino had turned back to his UA project for considerable rewriting that answered some of UA's objections and some of his own. About the time he was being hailed as a major new director, he called David Field with a Christmas message.

"I think I've found a way to clarify the characters *and* take the onus off the picture's being a western," he told Field, who reported back to the rest of us. The new version of the screenplay was distributed to sales and production, which responded favorably to it and even more to the title *Heaven's Gate* as an evocative and poetic improvement over the flat-footed historical one and the double-edged but flashy *Paydirt*, which seemed very western indeed.

Instead of beginning in Wyoming in the 1890s, the new script opened at Harvard on Commencement Day, 1870. Averill's graduation was thus backdated ten years from earlier versions, perhaps to acknowledge Kristofferson's apparent age on screen (presumably John Wayne would have been graduated even earlier). The prologue, as it became known through an eventually turbulent history, introduced Averill and his close friend and "Class of '70" valedictorian, William ("Billy") Irvine. The commencement exercises were dramatized, complete with rousing brass band, followed by dancing on the green of the graduates and their girls. The episode culminated in a traditional rush on the great tree in the center of the green, where a symbolic wreath of flowers is poised, "guarded" by the underclassmen. The graduating class rushes the tree, cheered on by adoring girl friends, and Averill, triumphant, full of youth and ideals, retrieves the floral trophy.

The prologue was only nine pages, but it introduced and spelled out thematic material that had been only murkily suggested before. Averill and Irvine had always been written as easterners, but showing them twenty years before the main action of the picture seemed to clarify their bond and its break in the picture's final conflict. Clearly, however, they had taken divergent paths once West, Irvine maintaining "I'm a victim of my class," Averill pursuing instead his youthful ideals.

Cimino also invented in the prologue a new character called the Reverend Doctor, a Harvard dean or chaplain, who introduced Irvine as class speaker and charged the commencement audience with "a high ideal, the education of a nation."

This oblique but central ideal was to serve as Averill's implicit motivation throughout and give resonance to his character. Cimino then and later compared Averill to the contemporary sons of privilege, the Kennedys, Rockefellers, and Vanderbilts who chose the Peace Corps or government as the arenas in which, as Cimino told Rex McGee, they, like Averill, could "fight the good fight." The seeds for the ultimate rupture with Irvine were also laid in the latter's facetious commencement address, in which he finds "the education of a nation" an amusing notion in a world that is, "on the whole, well arranged," class structure and all.

The music and dance and aristocratic beauties would add color, and elegant contrast to the immigrant life of the Plains. The strains of "The Blue Danube" would romantically underline it all, and the roughhouse sequence around the tree would end on "an uneasy balance between fear and great expectation."

The prologue dictated a "bookend," Cimino said, a balancing epilogue, scarcely a page in length, which would follow the screenplay's single greatest change. In the new version of the script, we would see Averill and Ella just after the massacre, preparing to leave Johnson County forever, as before. But on emerging from Ella's Hog Ranch cabin, they would be ambushed by Canton: Ella shot to death, Averill surviving to kill Canton.

The epilogue—"Narragansett Bay, Rhode Island, Summer 1900"—reveals a large yacht anchored off Newport. On it is Averill, having resumed the life of privilege and ease he abandoned three decades before. A beautiful woman is on the yacht, luxuriant and languorous. Perhaps she is the same girl Averill danced with so many years ago on the Harvard Green; we are not to know. He goes on deck, thinks of Ella as "her" music creeps in on the sound track, and silently begins to weep. The End. This script bore as legend: "What one loves about life are the things that fade."

Instantly *Heaven's Gate* seemed more than *The Johnson County War.* Opening and closing with tonalities so different from those in the body of the picture had an analogy in the contrast between *The Deer Hunter's* snowcapped mountain ranges and the hellish fires of Vietnam and seemed to do exactly what Cimino hoped: We simply stopped thinking of the picture as a western. The new scenes would cost money, to be sure, but were worth some reasonable cost if the changes in texture lifted it out of a dubious genre and clarified Averill, deepened the sense of his broken idealism, and provided a bittersweet coda to the violence of the final action. Ella's death now seemed not nihilistic but mournful, underlining the impermanence of "what one loves in life." Not incidentally it gave Averill the satisfying action of killing the chief villain.

There were other changes. Averill's Hamlet-like reticence in announcing the impending invasion had always seemed wrong. In the new version he tells Ella after she has bathed in the river, just following the roller-skating scene, which to quick observers now became a frontier echo of "The Blue Danube" waltzing of the prologue. (It also suggested that Cimino was "designing" the screenplay from considerations of form as much as, or more than, narrative or dramatic concerns.) Averill tells Ella about the mercenaries and asks her to go away with him. This in turn altered the emotional content of Champion's proposal scene later that night. Ella lies to Champion now, claiming Averill, too, has proposed, though this is not strictly true. The lie seems to suggest not her guile but her hidden yearning for respectability, and her subsequent acceptance of Champion's proposal becomes poignant and softer, not merely opportunistic. *He* at least asked.

The important action of going to the mercenary camp after Ella's rape was given to Champion instead of Averill. It had never made much sense that Averill would know where they were or would be allowed entry. Champion would, but the major reason for the change was less logic than to give Champion a moment of decisive action that proves his mettle and demonstrates his split with the mercenaries, thus providing them with a clearer motivation for murdering him at his cabin before they embark on the central business of the massacre.

The other important action change relieved Averill of the grandstanding rallying of the townspeople and gave this role to Ella. She arrives at the roller-skating rink cum grange hall (now called Heaven's Gate, still advertising "A Moral and Exhilarating Experience") to announce the murder of Champion, which she herself has narrowly escaped, and triggers the necessary frenzy for the climax. In this version

Averill has quit (or been fired from) his post as marshal in a violent quarrel with the mayor, who has ordered him to turn death-listed citizens over to the association. Averill refuses and removes his badge, washing his hands (for the moment) of the mounting chaos and his contempt for the settlement burghers. His revived idealism and feelings for the immigrants and Ella pull him back into the fray.

Shifting these two important action scenes to Ella and Champion strengthened both characters. That they simultaneously removed sympathetic moral action from Averill, pushing him ever eastward toward Elsinore, seemed balanced by the prologue and epilogue he had been given. In any case, it was assumed that the contemplative character Kristofferson would play was sufficiently dominant (and on screen for most of the picture anyway) that he would act as moral presence rather than conventional cowboy catalyst, the observer through whose eyes and waning idealism we would see and interpret the action. The deeper effects of these changes would not be apparent until the film was seen for the first time almost two years later. Their budget effect was more immediate.

Lehman Katz sat in his office on West Washington Boulevard in Culver City, surrounded by colorful posters of the annual azalea expositions held each spring on the Côte d'Azur. Their brilliant colors were echoed in the vivid stripings of the Turnbull & Asser shirts he collected and wore with equally vivid, often clashing silk ties from the same firm. The only indication to the casual eye that he had been in the movie business at all, let alone for four decades, was an unobtrusive black-and-white snapshot of himself together with Woody Allen, which rested modestly on a side table bearing stereo components, softly dispensing Mozart or Brahms.

Lee's rainbow attire (always solidly anchored by gray or blue slacks and blazer) was not the only colorful thing about him. He sailed with the dignity and grace some large yachts and men possess as easily through the halls of UA as through the corridors of Pinewood, Cinecittà, Churubusco, Bavaria, or the corridors of Versailles, the Ritz Hotel (any of them, anywhere), not to mention the Villa Narcissa, the elegant and beautiful Italianate residence he shared with his longtime lady friend, at the end of a long road bearing her name, which led to the top of a spectacularly well-situated peak on the Palos Verdes Peninsula. Lee's friend—almost never misaddressed as Mrs. Katz—had inherited a large chunk of Southern California when widowed some years before and was active in art and social circles from Los Angeles to Paris, the Loire Valley, and Venice (the Italian one) and points between.

They were a sophisticated, cultivated couple who could be formal but never fusty.

Lee's charm and humor were innate, or as innate as any such supple personality traits can be. What wasn't innate resulted from his having been everywhere and seen everything, particularly in the movie world. He had written pictures, produced them, "production managed" them, and for fifteen years now had been the dean of executive production managers, a prodigiously versatile one-man band who could guesstimate a budget to within 10 percent on a single reading and could work final figures out to one-tenth of 1 percent with a pencil. As UA's budgetary watchdog, overseeing filming activities typically flung worldwide, doing work often requiring whole departments at other companies, he did not always endear himself to filmmakers with his accuracy, but he was rarely off the money. Most of those who felt the sting of his accurate predictions came to respect him. Even Coppola's ire at Katz's reorganization of *Apocalypse*'s production chaos did not prevent Coppola from trying to hire Lee away from UA to perform his wizardry at Zoetrope. Lee, who loved to dine elegantly and tell gentlemanly tales out of school over cognac about working on, say, *Gold Diggers of 1933* or to discuss the problems of keeping Venice (the Italian one) from sinking without trace into the *laguna*, was nearing retirement age, and though he had no wish to retire, he preferred a more leisurely pace than that he had observed at Coppola's company.

When his retirement birthday arrived, I asked him to stay on, justifying my request to Albeck by saying I thought Katz knew more about production realities (or surrealities) than anyone else active in it. I did then, and I do now. A skeptical Albeck allowed me to keep him, though the two men were as different in style and personality as the cypresses surrounding the pool at the Villa Narcissa were from the baby spruce trees on Andy's farm in New Jersey.

There had been some unpleasantness between them involving Lee's company car (a BMW), and a shade of bitterness remained in their relationship, heightened perhaps by Lee's fifteen years of experience with Arthur Krim. Nevertheless, their relations were always cordial, always polite. But Katz had one habit, almost a professional signature, which irked Albeck and which Katz, seated at his desk among the colorful French posters on February 28, 1979, knew was going to irk him again, and shortly.

On his desk lay a budget for a picture whose budgets he had been vetting since 1973. He had met with his newly hired second-in-production-management command, Derek Kavanagh, who had been doing some preliminary budget checking on his own, and Katz reflected that if he had not seen everything before, surely he had now. He would express this, as usual, in that measured, erudite, courtly, *qualified* style that made Andy Albeck compress his lips in annoyed silence until they disappeared.

Katz qualified everything ("To cover his ass," his critics said) because he understood as few people do that a budget is only an estimate to complete. Its use as a political tool is something else again, and he understood that, too, but that was not his province. An estimate can be inflated, even padded outrageously, or understated with resultant rude surprises. Most budgets are honest attempts to say, "The picture will cost this much," and any evaluation of an honest estimate—or even a "creative" one—can be only on an if basis: if it doesn't rain; if the leading lady doesn't get a headache; if the ruling military junta isn't overthrown; if the director isn't kidding himself; *if* . . . Safeguards are taken to prevent the more unpleasant ifs, and insurance companies make handsome fees in insuring against their nevertheless frequent enough occurrences to make insurance a costly budget item on every picture made. There is simply no way to eliminate them entirely, and vetting a budget is to estimate an estimate. Agreeing to it is another matter, and the portly, elegant "dean" had the eagle eye—and the experienced overview of the terrain—to spot a suspicious quiver a mile away.

The production budget on the desk before him for *Heaven's Gate* was loaded with minor ifs, but the big one was if the director could or would complete the shooting of the picture in the sixty-nine days he had asked for. Katz doubted the one and doubted the other.

The budget memo he addressed to Dean Stolber in New York's business affairs office would be shown to the Cimino-Carelli team as a matter of courtesy and a matter of course. Not wishing to alienate them and thereby incur production's wrath, he began dictating to his secretary, Emily Koropatnicki, couching his skepticism in formal language.

"Dear Dean," his memo began. "A budget dated 23 February 1979 contemplates"—*Albeck will fall silent, bristling at the very words*, he thought—"contemplates 69 shooting days"—to begin only four and a half weeks from now and with no leading lady yet cast—"and totals $9,479,831 of which the prologue and epilogue which 'frame' the story are to cost $836,569." He paused.

He didn't think highly of the dramatic value of these framing "bookends," but such judgments were beyond his purview. Still, a discreetly phrased nudge might send a message to the production staff should they care to receive it. "Costs of prologue and epilogue have been separately set out in individual accounts so that you may judge whether they may be disproportionate to their script value and an alternate, more reasonably priced frame worth seeking." *That should do it,* he thought. *Subtle but clear.*

He then commented on the budget, department by department—sets, costumes, props, vehicles, livestock, greens, and so on—emphasizing the understated costs—shortfalls he called them—that leaped off the page at him in view of the elements that simply didn't gibe, as his experience told him they should. There was too much exterior work and too few interior scenes for weather cover. There were too few extras for so many horses or too many horses for so few extras. Too many miles' travel time to and from locations, too few daylight hours so far north . . .

All of it was guesswork, refined by experience, instinct, professional "smell."

Music: The standard $75,000 entered was short by half; he could feel it. The proportions were skewing away from everything standard. All in all, he thought, a hopelessly understated budget, but how to say so without accusing someone of hypocrisy or downright incompetence? What worried him was it didn't look like incompetence.

"A major concern would be Mr. Cimino's ability to shoot so complicated a script in the time allotted," he dictated as Emily swiftly inscribed the squiggles and strokes of her shorthand. "The schedule could be 12 to 15 days too few with a shortfall of as much as $700,000 thereby to be foreseen." This one factor—time—which would condition everything, seemed less a "major concern" than a major miscalculation, one that would have its unknowable impact on every other account in the budget.

"In sum, this budget may be short," he dictated, "in an area just above a million dollars." He had guessed $10 million, back in September. *Plus* epilogue and prologue.

And that did not even include the latest brainstorm. Sales wanted to know if it could schedule the picture for release at Christmas 1979, inevitably meaning an accelerated postproduction schedule, and acceleration of lab work always meant money.

"Our judgment," he added, less royally than including Kavanagh in the process, "is that expediting operations to achieve the [Christmas] date would increase post production costs by approximately $350,000/$400,000. Best regards . . ."

Katz let his mind wander back to 1973, as Emily exited silently to begin typing. He thought he remembered $2.5 million. Plus stars.

Later that day, too late for inclusion in the budget memo to Stolber, Derek Kavanagh handed Katz a revised analysis of the postproduction schedule. Derek believed it understated by "$445,000 rounded up to the nearest thousand."

That makes it easily twelve million dollars, given this and that, thought Katz, who decided to convey this information verbally and privately to Field, Stolber, and Albeck.

He briefly considered another amendment to his memo. Derek had notified him on February 21 that a period locomotive Cimino wanted to use (budgeted for $15,000) would be available only if routed cir-cuitously through five western states to reach the location because the track gauge the locomotive required was no longer in general use. Its cost would be ten times as much, $150,000. *Why pass that on?* Katz thought. *No one would spend a hundred fifty thousand dollars for a prop. Daft,* he said to himself. Then he added, *Loco,* smiling at his pun. *Why the budget doesn't even allow that for a leading lady!*

"Who the hell is Isabelle Huppert?"

Al Fitter's voice barked a half laugh of disbelief as he mouthed the name he had never heard before. He was sitting on one of the new creamy leather guest chairs in Albeck's office, a coffee cup balanced on one knee, a smoldering ashtray on the other.

Old Greenwich, Connecticut, was not ringing with the name, Field knew, when he telephoned me the previous evening from California to alert me that Cimino wanted to cast Isabelle Huppert as Ella Watson. We discussed it quickly. It seemed an aberrant and fleeting notion, and we resolved to humor him but withhold our approval, the right we had under contracts not yet signed. We were so certain we could handle this silliness we briefly considered not even raising the issue with Al-beck and the others. That finally seemed evasive. Our relationship with Cimino was too new, and his industry status rising too rapidly, not to mention the possible conflict in open forum, I in the room with the others in the daily production meeting, Field on the speakerphone 3,000 miles away.

"Who the hell is Isabelle Huppert?" Fitter repeated, straining to keep his tone polite, the weight of his pendulous stomach drawing him forward in his chair. Albeck's face braced behind his owllike glasses as his glance traveled across granite from Fitter's paunch and puzzlement to me for a response.

As the East Coast and European half of the team I was presumed to know such things. Unfortunately I knew Huppert only by reputation and had never seen her on the screen. Were she a combination of Bardot and Bernhardt, however, it is unlikely my reaction (or Field's) would have been much different. She was a minor French actress with a flat, peasantlike face that was agreeable in stills without being notably pretty. Her performance in *Violette Nozière* had excited attention at Cannes, where she won the Best Actress award, but had not been widely seen outside France, and to the American moviegoer she was unknown.

Albeck pushed forward grimly. "What happened to Jane Fonda and Diane Keaton?"

"Unavailable," Field and I answered in unison, his speakerphone voice cutting out as mine rose in the room. The answer was technically correct but sidestepped an issue we were not eager to scrutinize: Neither Fonda nor Keaton had liked the script (or even read it, for all we knew), and anyway, neither would have consented to second billing after Kristofferson, who had been contractually guaranteed first billing by Cimino. Both these circumstances gave us pause, but not enough: a script disliked or unread by the very stars we needed to strengthen the box office and a contract with an actor which precluded a strong female star because of its billing clause. The second problem was potentially easier, renegotiation being a way of life in Hollywood. As Auerbach's producer-father once said (and Auerbach was fond of quoting his father), "We have to have a contract. What other basis will we have for renegotiation?"

Reactions to the script—or lack of interest in even reading it— seemed negligibly important, subjective responses. When had Jane Fonda and Diane Keaton (or their representatives) become critics anyway? The question seemed logical enough; most rationalizations do.

But not only Fonda and Keaton were unavailable or uninterested. Every acceptable Hollywood actress we had carefully listed under A was equally so, and we were increasingly hard pressed to suggest alternatives agreeable to both Cimino and ourselves. He knew this and rightly rejected the B and C trial balloons as hardly satisfying the company's need for a major name. That he was right was small consolation, for having exhausted the ranks of the As and excluded the lesser names, we made ourselves vulnerable to suggestions of unknown or little-known actresses who might be "right for the part." Like Isabelle Huppert.

The idea seemed so eccentric we wasted little time in debating Huppert's appropriateness for the role. We were more concerned with our ability to finesse Cimino in the delicate game of mutual approval, but we voiced our assurances to Albeck and the others that we could do so. For once we were grateful for distribution's protests (modified only by Auerbach's "helpful in the French markets" nod).

Field, now dealing daily with Cimino in California, correctly warned that we would need to give him a fair hearing if only to preserve the appearance of tolerant appraisal, but we both were certain that persuasion and conviction—sensible, correct, and as unbendable as Andy Albeck's spine—would prevail.

The meeting continued with a discussion of whether we should or should not renegotiate the Scorsese-De Niro deal on *Raging Bull* and what we would *do* with Francis Coppola's real estate if *Apocalypse Now* should fail.

"First of all, and most important," I began, "no one has ever heard of her."

We were assembled several days later in Field's office in California: Field, myself, Cimino, and Carelli. Michael sat listening to our recitation of objections to his chosen actress. His responses, as always before, were measured and polite and as temperate as the February morning.

"With all the attention this film will generate, everyone in the world will have heard of her by the time we go into release."

"But, Michael, when we made this deal, we agreed to Kristofferson because we shared your feeling that he could become a major star—"

"And we still think so," one of us interrupted.

"—but the distribution people don't think he's a star and the exhibitors don't think he's a star and the critics don't think he's a star and the actresses we've gone after don't think he's a star. It was always understood that we would try to beef up the marquee with a commercially important woman, and we're only asking you to make this one concession—which helps you, too, as a major profit participant—to make this picture strong enough to earn back the ten or twelve million dollars we'll have to spend."

"Nine eight," Joann inserted.

"*Ten or twelve.* And for that we don't need Isabelle Huppert."

"One wants to be perfectly open," Michael answered evenly. "Tell me whom you have in mind who is available, affordable, and can play the part."

"There's got to be somebody we've overlooked. As of this moment we have no marquee other than Kristofferson."

"You've got Walken."

"If you recall, Michael, the reason you made the deal here instead of at Warner Brothers was that Warner's wouldn't accept Walken and we would."

"They would now," he said calmly. "They'll take the picture off your hands, and they know that Chris is going to win the Academy Award for *The Deer Hunter.*"

"Tell Warner Brothers thank you very much and that Chris Walken's Academy Award won't make Isabelle Huppert a star."

After a pause Cimino asked, "Second of all?"

"What?"

"I've listened to 'first of all.' What's 'second of all'?"

"Second of all, she has a face like a potato," I said.

Cimino remained unemotional. "I find her attractive."

"Well, you're the one because no one else does."

Field winced. Carelli smiled to herself.

"How can you say that when you haven't even seen her on film?" Cimino challenged quietly.

"We told you we would and we will, but we can't conceal our concerns. There's no way we can get this past the distribution guys and Albeck even if we wanted to, and we don't."

There was a longer pause. I had done too much talking on what was Field's project, and I probably wouldn't even have been involved in the conversation were it not for Albeck's October order that I spend one week a month in California. That and the mounting production estimates from Lee Katz. Finally, Michael broke the silence.

"I'll go to New York and talk to Andy myself."

"That doesn't work, Michael," I said, not wanting him away from the work at hand and certainly not in New York. "We don't even know if she speaks *English,* for Christ's sake!"

"She speaks English."

"How do you know?"

"I've spoken with her."

A dreadful premonition took shape. He had spoken with her? About what? Certainly about the movie and the role of Ella, given his irrepressible energy. How far had he gone? Had he offered the role? Made a deal? They had the same agent; anything was possible.

Cimino, with his *Deer Hunter* accolades, lately was not speaking idly. His readiness to go to New York and persuade Albeck sounded like a not very veiled threat to go over our heads and deal directly with the ultimate authority in the company. This would demonstrate that he was unwilling to bother with us any longer, that we were trivializing UA's reputation with an already skeptical creative community. We heard his tone grow cooler than the morning, and he heard that we heard it. It was something new in our conversations with him, and it would not be the last time we would hear that chill.

But there was another, less self-serving reason we didn't want Cimino going to Albeck. If he had, indeed, already offered the part to Huppert, Albeck might feel morally obliged to honor that commit-

ment, contractual violation (of unsigned contracts) or no. We had seen
this happen more than once in the early months of Andy's presidency.
Seemingly everyone in the movie business had been "promised" this or
that by Krim or Medavoy or Pleskow or Bernstein. Many of these
claims were hustles of dubious merit, but some were real, and some
were undesirable to the new regime. Albeck's policy was firm: A UA
commitment, moral or otherwise, by this regime or the former, was to
be honored even if doing so was anathema to him for some business
reason. At least one entire picture got made for just such a reason (Joan
Micklin Silver's *Chilly Scenes of Winter*, also known as *Head over Heels*);
it was a failure.

Whether Albeck's annoyance with Cimino if he *had* gone ahead
and hired Huppert would have outweighed his sense of honor in this
situation, we couldn't predict, but we didn't want to take the chance.
Nor did we wish to raise, or face, the possibility that such a thing had
happened. The better solution seemed to dissuade Cimino in a peace-
able manner and go on to find another leading lady. We were confident
of Cimino's reasonableness and undaunted by the absence of a single
clue as to who that leading lady might be.

"Do you mean, Michael, that you've spoken to Huppert about the
role of Ella?"

"Just generally."

That could mean anything or nothing.

"Didn't she find it odd that a French actress would be approached
about playing a nineteenth-century Wyoming madam with an Anglo-
Saxon name?"

"Why should she? She's an actress. Besides, almost everyone in this
film is an immigrant, and another accent would only add to the richness of the sound track."

"Not if it's an unintelligible one," I said. "Michael, it's not your
most brilliant idea. The answer has to be no."

Silence.

Cimino's round face betrayed nothing. Joann, who had remained
silent, stirred on the nubby white sofa. A sharp nod of her head sig-
nified that for her, at least, a decision had been reached. Before she
could speak, Michael replied, "I can't accept such a decision from executives who have never bothered to see their director's choice on the
screen, who have never met or talked with her. You are rejecting her
only because she doesn't have a name no matter how right she may be
for the part."

"What do you want us to do? We've tried to be open and honest with you about our feelings and our decision, and now you say you can't accept that?"

"First you could see her on film."

"We don't need to. You say she's great. Fine. We accept that. It isn't *about* that. It's about New York and the investment and the logic of that actress in that time and place and the language problem. . . . Put all the rest aside for a minute, and concentrate on that. If we agreed to reconsider her and used her English as the sole criterion, fairly and honestly, would you accept our decision after we had talked with her?"

Carelli's eyes were roaming the ceiling. Cimino asked, "You'll go to Paris?"

"No," I said. "But I went to school there and speak the language. Have her telephone me, and we'll talk for a few minutes. If I can understand her English over the phone, I'll remove my objections, and David can do what he wants. * I still don't think New York will buy it, but we want to be fair. If I can't understand her English, we can speak French for a minute, and I'll get out of the call without embarrassing you or her."

Michael considered, nodded. "When do you want her to call?"

"Whenever. Make it easy on her. But, Michael, it's understood that if the decision is no, it's final?"

He nodded.

Isabelle Huppert telephoned from Paris to my Los Angeles number the next morning. I didn't understand one word of English she spoke, and the only part of her French that I remembered clearly after the conversation was the part about how thrilled she was to be playing the role of Ella.

Field and I met in his office an hour later.

"We have to say no, and we have to mean no. It's going on too long. It's bad for the movie; it's bad for our relationship with Michael. If we capitulate over this issue, it's bad for us in the company, because I don't know how to justify this kind of wrongheadedness, and if we don't say no now and mean it, he'll have us on a goddamn plane to Paris to meet with her!"

David nodded. "Let's call and tell him no. Nobody's going to Paris."

The Concorde landed at Charles de Gaulle at ten-forty on a drizzly Sunday night in late February. David and I were met by Jean Nachbaur,

---

* This was much less generous of me than it sounded. Huppert's agent in Rome, who was by chance my houseguest in Los Angeles at the time, had already informed me that she spoke English only haltingly and with an impenetrable accent.

the friendly head of the Paris office of Les Artistes Associés, as UA is known in France. On the way into town, we made halfhearted small talk, which failed to lift my gloomy resentment at having agreed to make this trip at all.

Field and I had had ample time to reflect on the events of the past few days and had discussed the issues of casting and our relationship with Cimino fully and candidly with Albeck. Andy was anything but peremptory regarding this trip to meet Huppert and hear her read with Christopher Walken (who had flown from New York ahead of us with Cimino and Carelli).* He viewed it as an expensive but desirable demonstration to Cimino that we were prepared to extend ourselves far beyond the usual limits in considering a serious creative request. Still, there was little doubt in my mind or Field's that we left JFK charged with delivering a swift and final no to end, once and for all, l'affaire Huppert.

We had said no to Cimino in California, and we had meant it. Michael pressed all his arguments, which were neither inconsiderable nor unreasonable. Flying to Paris for one last meeting seemed excessive, but I had Moonraker business to conduct there and was eager to see the final print of La Cage aux Folles in its French dubbing. For Field, the trip was more arduous, but at least it was a respite from the often crushing California schedule.

We settled into the Plaza-Athénée and had a drink. We knew this trip was a showdown on both sides (Would UA cave in? Would Cimino take no for an answer?), and each side was undoubtedly investing the issue with a higher degree of urgency and portent than it warranted. The fact was that never before had we seriously challenged Cimino in the creative area. No one had indulged him, but no major difference of opinion had surfaced either. We admired his work and enthusiasm and believed his perfectionism warranted the most thoughtful response we could give. At the same time we did not want to be bulldozed. Our reasoning, we told ourselves, was commercially responsible and politically smart within the company.

Still, there were crosscurrents. The commercial reasoning was easy to state and obvious to any film major at UCLA. Perhaps it was too easy and was too obviously stated and restated by the distribution people, for whom our esteem was low and continuing to deteriorate, as defense against their involvement in just such decisions as this. In some subtle way, in fact, the more crudely expressed and aesthetically indifferent the distribution opposition became, the more necessary it seemed

* The three of them were in Paris on a public relations tour for The Deer Hunter.

to weigh the nuances of Cimino's arguments in terms other than the purely commercial. We needed to shift the focus from their arena to ours. It was as if being pressed to back distribution in a "Who the hell is Isabelle Huppert?" decision—which we had, in fact, formulated ourselves—furthered their ends, not ours. In an internal political sense this could only additionally erode what little real creative autonomy we felt we had in the company to begin with.

Another complication was that we liked Cimino and thought UA needed him, or his current celebrity and heat at any rate. The relationship was too new to be other than cordial and mutually supportive, we thought, and we wanted to keep it that way with standards of behavior as high as those we hoped he would bring to the film. In short, we wanted our very own epic, our very own hit, and we wanted Cimino. What we didn't want was Isabelle Huppert.

We gathered together in Michael and Joann's Hôtel de Crillon suite shortly before midnight. Chris Walken, whom I had known casually for some time, was seated on a stiff-backed French sofa next to what appeared to be a thirteen-year-old red-headed gamine. I revised my opinion. She didn't have a face like a potato after all: She looked like the Pillsbury Doughboy got up in a shapeless cotton shift. Nothing about her quite registered. Her hair, her face, even her freckles were pale. Her features lacked definition and seemed padded with puppy fat. She was tiny, she was lumpish, she made no particular effort to be charming, and whatever hopes I might have secretly harbored that one look at her would thrill me and change my mind and the direction of this dilemma sank like stones. International stardom couldn't have seemed more remote.

We made awkward small talk with Walken, Cimino, and Huppert, while Joann ordered white wine and grapes from room service. As we talked, it became apparent that Huppert's English was indeed better than it had sounded over the telephone. Cimino had claimed the call intimidated her, causing her to freeze in a language not her own. Still, her command of English that night was only serviceable, and her accent, while charming, was pronounced and often obscured meaning. It was, moreover, clear that she didn't have a clue to who we were or why we were there.

The room service waiter came and left, and after pouring the wine, Michael quietly handed scripts to Walken and Huppert, suggested a page on which to begin, and after a moment of study they did.

Christopher Walken has always seemed to me an exceptional actor. I first saw him perform off-Broadway in Thomas Babe's *Kid Champion* in the mid-seventies, and I had followed his *Sweet Bird of Youth* and his few movie appearances before *The Deer Hunter*. He had a haunted quality that could turn quickly sullen and dangerous, and his talent and looks might have made him a major actor long since, I thought, were it not for a certain reserve about him, almost a secretiveness that deflected attention. *Maybe it's an actor's trick,* I thought, remembering De Niro and Woody Allen. But Walken's recessiveness was entirely absent that midnight and early morning. He was low-key but playful in his reading, young and even engagingly silly at times. Clearly he was there only to help Huppert feel at ease, and I suspected that Cimino, to whom Walken owed a great deal after *The Deer Hunter*, had coached him into making this reading very warm, very charming.

Cimino sat silently with us and listened, interrupting only now and then to suggest a different mood or a different scene, his direction so quiet as to seem whispered. If he had actually rehearsed the two, he had done a good job with Walken.

Huppert was *une autre histoire*. She read indifferently. Her reading English was less good than her speaking English, stilted and more heavily accented. She seemed to have little idea of the script's content as a whole and none whatever of the character of a frontierswoman in nineteenth-century western America. I had conducted or been present at many such readings in the theater and films, and while the process is notoriously deceptive and unreliable, there was nothing here to make me feel Cimino's decision was justified. She was too young; she was too French; she was too contemporary; she was too uncertain in her reading. She was simply wrong.

Still, as the night wore on and the wine bottles emptied, her charm began to take hold. Her short, stubby child's fingers darted here and there, brushing the hair from her eyes, tapping the script in sudden understanding, toying with the pale green grapes when confused, taking on a quality of grace not initially apparent. She curled her legs under her on the sofa and showed off her figure, *saftig* but good. Her eyes seemed to collect light as the night deepened, and her laugh had the lilt and spontaneity of a particularly happy puppy. The word that came to my mind and would not leave was *adorable*. I began to find her captivating and charming and pretty, and never for one moment did I see her as Ella Watson.

Cimino was too perceptive not to have known that our reactions were negative. Nevertheless, everyone agreed to defer conversation until dinner the following evening.

Field and I returned to our rooms around three o'clock in the morning, fatigued by the flight and unsettled by the results of the reading.

We hadn't wanted her to be perfect, and she wasn't, but everything might have been easier if she had been.

The line between rationally weighing alternatives and rationalizing them is notoriously fine. Field and I were a good team most of the time because most of our perspectives were similar. When they were too similar, we often had the resoluteness that comes easily when talking to oneself. We were both, by background and temperament, given to aesthetic hairsplitting and impressed, I think, by our "sensitivity." Without sensing its pretentiousness, we were convincing ourselves that our superior and subtler understanding of the creative process had some moral force that would not only sway Cimino but render distribution's position—whatever it might be in whatever instance—beside the point. In this way it began to seem preferable and somehow nobler to make the wrong decision for the right reasons than the right decision for the wrong.

It was clear that Huppert had appeal. Certainly she could substantially improve her English in the weeks that remained before shooting began. Cimino could, and no doubt would, want to rewrite the role to fit whatever actress was chosen to play Ella Watson, which could minimize (though never obliterate, I thought) the incongruities of Huppert in that role. Finally, there was always the possibility that Cimino was right, that he saw something in her our vision was not acute enough to see. Kristofferson wanted her (we were told this, though the fact that he, Huppert, and Cimino all shared the same agent may have prompted skepticism); Walken seemed to want her; Cimino strenuously wanted her. While these arguments were germane, they did not add up to that sudden yes of inevitability.

The more urgent argument was that after months of trying we had come up with no one else. We had been through scores of names after the initial turndowns by Fonda and Keaton, and during the months of searching it is possible we unconsciously resigned ourselves to having a minor or new name in the role by default. Surely, however, there were American unknowns who could more easily slip into Ella's frontier muslin and gain the approval of the New York office.

If we crossed the line between rationalizing and rationale that night, neither of us knew it. Certainly we did not do so with regard to Huppert's suitability for the role. If we crossed the line, it was in the area of excessive and vain (in both senses of the word) concern over how our handling, or failure to handle, Cimino would be viewed by the Hollywood community, by our colleagues, and by Albeck. We agreed to sleep on it, each knowing the answer would be no but not knowing what would follow.

• • •

Michael and Joann met us the following evening at le Coupe Choux in the Beaubourg near the Centre Pompidou. The setting seemed right, the atmosphere candlelit and congenial, the tables casual and pretty, the food good and unpretentious. The restaurant is often frequented by Parisian show business people, meaning one could talk, drink, and eat well without a tourist crush—a simple, undistracted dinner among friends.

We ordered some wine and avoided the subject of Huppert. I filled the others in on my day at Studios Boulognes, where Moonraker was finally finishing months of production. We had hoped in June to contain the picture's cost at $20 million, but it had gone beyond $30 million, a figure I was not about to raise here and now, and there was still unpredictable and costly special-effects work remaining at Pinewood, including one very difficult effect which necessitated exposing a single strip of negative forty-eight separate times rather than resorting to lab work and optical printers. A mistake or miscalculation in any one of the forty-eight exposures would have destroyed hundreds of costly hours of effort. Happily it worked.

The conversation ranged over this and over the general necessity of controlling budgets, and certainly the verbal nudges were less than subtle. Whatever urgency I tried to convey about budget concerns was muted by the assumptions everyone, including UA, made regarding Moonraker: James Bond couldn't miss. •

Finally, over espresso, the reason for our visit could no longer be avoided. Gently but firmly we traced the history of this situation, pointing out that we had been negative from the beginning, had said no more than once, had agreed repeatedly to reexamine the question, always with assurances from Michael that he would abide by our decision, and had made the extraordinary gesture of flying halfway around the world to listen to a reading in a hotel room in the middle of the night. The answer was still—unequivocally, finally, and forever—no.

Though Cimino was normally quiet, he fell now into a silence that suggested glaciers and frozen wastes. His round, ruddy face seemed to darken in the glow of the table candles, and his eyes to contract to pinpoints. Ill at ease but determined, we struggled through his silence, detailing our reasons, turning now and then to Joann, who agreed with a matter-of-fact "Right" at almost every turn, a surprise event that seemed to turn Cimino to stone.

• He didn't. Moonraker went on to become the biggest box-office success in the history of that remarkable series. Until the next one.

At last, he spoke, his voice quietly poisonous. He accused us of bad faith; he accused us of cowardice regarding New York; he accused us of insensitivity and lack of aesthetic judgment; he rejected us as corporate executives; in tone and manner he rejected us as human beings. Finally, he announced it would be impossible for him to make the picture for people as insensitive and untalented as ourselves, and he would instruct his representatives to move the picture from UA to Warner Brothers.

We had heard this threat only days before and were to hear it again, but at this moment, if he was bluffing, he was persuasive. Whether he could actually do so we didn't know, but it seemed likely. Warner's had been romancing him for months, and the interim reception of *The Deer Hunter* might have overcome its earlier objections to Walken. Who knew? It might even accept Huppert without argument and prove us not only incapable of keeping a major filmmaker at UA but aesthetically wrong in the bargain. Danny Rissner was now there, and he had claimed back in October that he could make a deal with Ashley. Still, we were being bullied, and I resented it and the position we were being placed in. I shot off my mouth: "For Christ's sake, Michael. Kristofferson and Walken are so much more attractive than she is that the audience will spend the entire film wondering why they're fucking her instead of each other!"

My timing was not good. Instantly David kicked me sharply and painfully under the table. Michael was paralyzed for a moment, then loftily looked away in baleful silence as if he had changed planets. Joann feebly mumbled something she meant to agree with my general point, but the damage was done, and dinner was over.

We separated coldly, Michael having washed his hands of us, Joann uncomfortable about her own candor, David and I roiling with frustration, resentment, and anger. Walking back to the hotel through the wind-whipped chill, I turned to David and asked why he had kicked me so forcefully under the table.

"Don't you get it?" he asked. "He must be infatuated with her."

"What about Joann? I thought they—"

"Not for years. Don't you see? It's the only thing that makes sense."

Whether there was then, or ever, a romantic liaison between Huppert and Cimino we were never to learn or care about. Such things are not unknown, but Cimino was beginning to strike me as far too obsessive a careerist to allow an emotional attachment to jeopardize any aspect of his professional life. In any case, if David's shot in the dark was correct, the situations were not mutually exclusive and even had a little old-time glamour: Stiller and Garbo, Von Sternberg and Dietrich.

We dropped the subject, and as far as I know, it was never brought up again. We had other matters to reflect on that night.

We had blown it. We had blown the picture, the relationship with Cimino (whatever it was), maybe our reputations in Hollywood, both personal and professional, probably any credibility we might have had within the company, possibly even our jobs.

What had we gained? Even if the picture were to stay at UA for legal or other reasons, Cimino would certainly veto vigorously any casting suggestions we were likely to make. And how justify to him a little or unknown American actress after having turned down Huppert, who at least had some critical cachet?

Working with Michael could turn unexpectedly ugly very quickly; he had demonstrated at the dinner table that he was prepared to jettison the relationship with United Artists to get his own way. How were we then to win his confidence or cooperation during the actual making of the picture? Or had we unintentionally rendered the picture unmakable because uncastable? Millions of dollars had already been spent or committed; what of that investment? Finally, one central issue emerged from the anxiety: Did we want the picture badly enough to take Isabelle Huppert with it, with all that that might mean in terms of the relationship with Michael?

Had we been struck down by a runaway taxi on that walk back to the Avenue Montaigne, there might be a United Artists today. Instead, we arrived safely at the hotel, had a nightcap, and placed a transatlantic call to Albeck in New York.

Andy listened stoically to our recitation of the events leading to the call. We didn't spare ourselves. We admitted we had been guilty of naïvely underestimating Cimino's resolve and overestimating our own manipulative skills. Andy's questioning was careful and sensible; at the same time he was relying on an analysis he had to take on faith, having no practical experience in such situations himself. He was as realistic as could be expected; he understood that artists were often demanding and difficult; he was keenly aware of the moneys already invested, and, I think, unshakably determined to prove to Transamerica and Hollywood that the "new" United Artists could deliver pictures as major as anybody else. Still, Isabelle Huppert would mean less to John Beckett than she had to Al Fitter.

Then it came, the master stroke of persuasion and manipulated perspective: Who was the real star of this picture? Not Kristofferson, who couldn't carry it alone; not Fonda or any of the others we couldn't have anyway; not Chris Walken or the secondary actors Michael wanted. The star of this picture—it was so clear—was Michael Cimino. We weren't betting that this or that actor or actress would add a million or two to the box office. We were betting that Cimino would deliver a blockbuster with "Art" written all over it, a return to epic filmmaking and epic returns.

Yes, Cimino was the star, we argued, and if our director wanted Huppert, we had an obligation to back him. Perhaps we were making the wrong decision for the right reason even then. We probably thought so.

Perhaps some less enlightened or more hotheaded production executives at another studio might have told Cimino to go fly a kite and thereby saved their company $40 million and its very existence. But in what was perhaps the most naïve and seminal delusion of all, we believed that now that we knew Cimino's darker, colder side, we could better handle him in the future. There was precious little prescience in Paris that night.

The next morning we capitulated.

Isabelle Huppert would play Ella Watson.

CHAPTER II

AVALANCHE

The spirit of actually making a picture [is]
a spirit not of collaboration but of armed
conflict in which one antagonist has a
contract assuring him nuclear capability.
Some reviewers make a point of trying to
understand whose picture it is by "looking
at the script": to understand whose picture
it is one needs to look not particularly at
the script but at the deal memo.

—Joan Didion,
"In Hollywood," *The White Album* (1979)

Winter came early and hard to Montana. Snow blan-
keted the mountains and hills and ice-encrusted rivers and lakes of
Glacier National Park even in late fall as Cimino sought locations and
inspected property. By Christmas the park roads were impassable for the
heavy equipment necessary for spring construction on *Heaven's Gate*,
and the focus of the project returned to milder Culver City, where
Cimino's staff waited for the thaw by designing the town of Sweetwater
(né Buffalo), the main street of Casper, Ella Watson's Hog Ranch, the
Heaven's Gate roller-skating rink, and hundreds of costumes, drawing
heavily on masses of research, scores of volumes of western history and
photographs to ensure meticulous authenticity of detail. Art director
Tambi Larsen, who had designed everything from Inca temples for Yma
Sumac to cavort upon to plain ranch houses for Paul Newman's *Hud*
(for which Larsen had won his Academy Award), was becoming an
expert in late-nineteenth-century railroad interiors, telephone and telegraph poles, building fronts and cornices, flophouse hallways, bordello
decor. Allen Highfill, the costume designer, poured through catalogs
and photograph books; carefully leafed through fabric samples, crum-
bling with age; inspected and rejected thousands of sweat-stained ready-
made costumes; searched for and failed to find silk top hats, then

searched for and found a man who could make them—in Upper Darby, Pennsylvania.

In New York, casting was under way with Carelli and Cis Corman, the well-known casting director who also performed casting chores on *Raging Bull.* The script was finding the nearly final form it would have by late January, and in this period of quiet but intense activity for the production, UA turned its attentions to the Christmas box office.

Christmas is, with summer, one of the two big seasons in the movie business, and Christmas 1978 had not been outstanding for the company. *Lord of the Rings* led the holiday list, based on the trilogy by J.R.R. Tolkien that had been on and off the UA shelf for a decade. At one time it was intended as a live-action picture from director John Boorman; at another, an elegant Peter Shaffer script of the worldwide best seller was to guide the Hobbits to the screen; at still another, plans bubbled for a multimedia musical extravaganza scored by and starring the Beatles, whose decision not to regroup after their 1970 breakup put an end to that.* Finally, Saul Zaentz, the head of Fantasy Records, who had financed and coproduced *One Flew over the Cuckoo's Nest,* repeated these chores with *Lord of the Rings* and brought the tales of Middle Earth to life with Ralph Bakshi's amalgamation of animation techniques that were sophisticated, admired, and failed to overwhelm audiences as Zaentz and UA had hoped. De Laurentiis's *The Great Train Robbery* was no more than sluggish, and Philip Kaufman's remake of *Invasion of the Body Snatchers* was popular, though not a blockbuster. MGM's contribution to the UA distribution lineup at Christmas was *Brass Target,* which proved to be what Albeck had pronounced it when he first saw it—"a dog"—an assessment which, however accurate, did not improve MGM's humor over its distribution relationship with UA. Holiday cheer was dimmed at 729 as sales blamed production, production blamed sales, and MGM blamed Albeck, who noted philosophically that Warner Brothers' *Man of Steel* was swamping most of the competition and quietly determined that Christmas 1979 needed, more than ever, a locomotive to compete with the *Supermans* and *King Kongs* that were becoming the industry's holiday habit, and the audiences', too.

Both sales and production were nervously aware that Christmas 1979 would be the first highly competitive season for films originated (and sold) by the new regime. Domestic early questioned the possibility

---

* The Beatles' films *A Hard Day's Night, Help!, Yellow Submarine,* and *Let It Be* had all been made for UA. This particular lalapalooza idea (David Picker's) was well ahead of its time and might have been inspired showmanship. The idea of Ringo Starr, say, as Frodo, has an irresistible appeal.

of *Heaven's Gate* as a Christmas release as *The Deer Hunter*'s box-office muscles flexed ever greater during the dead, dull weeks following *Superman*'s Christmas cleanup. The critical reception of *The Deer Hunter* in December had assured it of serious academy attention, and the assumption was current that any Cimino picture would, henceforth, be equally a candidate for awards or nominations. A Christmas 1979 release would handily meet the academy's requirement of one week of play time before the end of the calendar year. Albeck's frequent refrain of "I want my Academy Awards!" was issued jocularly, but few in the company took it lightly. Albeck knew the awards—whatever their "artistic" value might be—meant box office and validation in the eyes of the community, and he intended that United Artists under his leadership should take a secondary role to no one in this area.

Cimino was first approached about the possibility of a Christmas 1979 release for *Heaven's Gate* at about the time the picture acquired its new title, in late January. He was at first dubious that a picture (still unofficially) scheduled to begin shooting on April 2 could be ready in time for Christmas but was cautiously willing to discuss the possibility without committing himself. If *The Deer Hunter* should not win awards (it was a 6 to 5 favorite in Las Vegas to win Best Picture), he would have another chance one year later. Still, there were serious practical pitfalls.

There were two parts to the question: Could a Christmas release be physically effected, and at what cost? Cimino requested a meeting to discuss these questions, a meeting of the greatest possible breadth, one which would have the aura of a summit meeting. David Field dutifully assembled, on February 8, himself, Claire Townsend, Jerry Paonessa, and Derek Kavanagh from production (Lee Katz was in Auckland with David Lean); Leon Brachman, recently appointed West Coast head of business affairs; and Al Fitter from domestic, who brought with him from New York both Hy Smith and Ed Siegenfeld of advertising and publicity. Also sitting in were Skip Nicholson and Jay Cipes, executives from Technicolor, the company which would manufacture the release prints.

Both feasibility and cost were technical questions, requiring determination of a timetable for completion of the various production stages, working backward from a hypothetical release date of December 14. Gary Gerlich, UA's executive for postproduction on the West Coast, had drawn up for Field a preliminary calendar based on Cimino's own shooting schedule. Gerlich's calendar was an interoffice confidential memo which allowed for two weeks' overschedule during production itself. Cimino was not to be told this. UA regarded the two weeks' allowance as a necessary and comfortable cushion for internal discussion purposes, but not one which should be acknowledged and, thereby, become inadvertently formalized. Nevertheless, it was. In the spirit of full disclosure in which the meeting was conducted, a "worst case theory" was proposed, which was meant to say that the December 14 premiere could not take place if the picture were more than two weeks over schedule but which instead implied the acceptability of the two weeks in question. Admitting to the two weeks was supposed to show UA's savvy and its reasonable approach to production. It was also supposed to clarify for Cimino that if he found Gerlich's postproduction schedule tight, he could loosen it up by two weeks merely by finishing production on the schedule that he had himself proposed but that he now knew UA didn't believe in.

What might have been a routine meeting became psychologically decisive. Not only had UA tipped its hand, but it had utilized heads of production, domestic sales, publicity, and advertising, vice-presidents of production management and business affairs, and two additional vice-presidents of production to do so, and it had done the tipping with the two relevant executives from Technicolor as witnesses. The presence of such a comprehensive assembly invested the meeting with its quality of summitry and invested the project with an importance that had not been there before—not only to Cimino, but to most of those present as well. Jerry Paonessa quipped, "It had to be important because all of *us* were, right?"

In spite of the budget's escalation by $2 million since September, in spite of there being as yet no approved schedule and no formal declaration that UA was going to make the picture, this assembly, these rows of attentive faces—six of them vice-presidents, two of them senior vice-presidents—the very composition of the group made clear to both sides UA *was going to make this picture* . . . and was already assuming that it would go two weeks over schedule.

Cimino knew that pay-or-play contracts did not automatically guarantee anything but fees. He knew that *Cuba* was being made at least partly because the company did not want to "eat" its pay-or-play obligations, but *Cuba*, even with Sean Connery, was $8 million, far less than *Heaven's Gate* now promised to cost. The near $2 million of pay or play on *Heaven's Gate* plus the additional $1 million spent on preproduction—with more committed—would not force production if UA decided at the last moment to pull out. In fact, Cimino must have known that his frequent assertions that Warner Brothers or EMI would take the picture could have backfired and inadvertently increased the chances of a UA cancellation if UA got cold feet and thought Warner's or EMI would assume not only the picture but the accumulated UA costs as well. Certainly something of the kind had occurred to UA, and it served as partial rationale for entering into the preproduction commitments for design, construction, and hiring of personnel that had been under way since October.

But the orderly progression of preproduction planning was a judgment call by the production and legal departments and could be reversed or halted. On February 8, however, production and legal were joined by sales, advertising, publicity, postproduction, and printing facilities, all working to coordinate plans for release of a picture that had not even been approved, all committing plans and energies to their self-generated Christmas notion. From that date, from that meeting on, it was to be psychologically more difficult—if not impossible—for the company to brake the momentum it was busily self-inducing. This kind of inertia could only benefit the picture. Changing to Warner's or EMI, after all, at whatever point, would cost valuable time, add new elements (and overheads) to the equation, and could also affect Kristofferson's cooperation or, worse, his availability.

Some within the company were to look back on that February meeting as the moment in which the relationship between Cimino and UA altered irrevocably, attributing to Cimino a conspiratorial maneuvering of the company into a position that had the gravest eventual effects. But eager as Cimino may have been to encourage the company's spinning its wheels on his behalf, he calmly resisted the notion of a Christmas release, resisted being rushed, resisted committing himself to a schedule which he knew could prove unrealistic (and which UA must have seemed all too ready to ignore), resisted responsibility for the possibility of failing to meet hypothetical dates. Still, he was willing to listen to UA's wheels as they spun on, his attitude less conspiratorial than garden-variety shrewd. UA was doing all the talking; Cimino was listening. What he heard was Gary Gerlich's schedule. It set out the following dates:

Start of Production	April 2
Completion of Photography	June 22
First Cut	July 20
Final Cut	September 4

Scoring, titles, opticals, negative cutting, recording, and rerecording were set out in detail and to be completed by October 31. A preview was scheduled for November 2. Changes subsequent to the preview and final printing by Technicolor would take the month of

November. This would mean Technicolor's setting aside the time and facilities early, shutting out other pictures, other companies also looking to Christmas releases. Adhering to this—or some very similar schedule—would make *Heaven's Gate* available for a December 14, 1979, premiere.

Gerlich's schedule assumed that editing would commence at the beginning of production, directly behind shooting, so that an editor's cut would be available a week or so after the end of photography. Four additional weeks were allowed for the director's first cut, with an additional six weeks for fine-tuning the picture, a total of ten editing weeks from editor's cut to director's fine cut. * The laying of sound effects and dialogue tracks would be in work from the end of photography in June, allowing a full three months before the tracks were mixed together in October. Routine, almost all of it, which is not to say predictable, any more than any creative process is, even a highly industrialized one. Gerlich's schedule allowed for the normal complement of ordinary glitches and presented no unreasonable pressures, and none at all on the production period itself, which was Cimino's own, plus the two weeks of cushion.

The composer was to have six weeks in which to prepare the music; the rerecording (in which music, dialogue, and sound effects are joined and perfected) was allowed five weeks, including a week of predub (a rough blending of these elements), all of which were more or less standard time periods. A tight area was previewing, with only one contemplated public preview and three days allowed for any resultant changes.

For all the routine adequacies of this schedule, it had nothing whatever to do with *Heaven's Gate*, and I think no one at the meeting (except possibly sales or Technicolor) thought it did. It was both cynical and naïve.

It was cynical in its attempt to manipulate Cimino's schedule using Christmas as a pretext and naïve in its failure to see where that pretext would lead. UA wanted to accelerate production and postproduction less to achieve a Christmas release than to avoid another protracted *Apocalypse* (or *Deer Hunter*, for that matter) completion period. If Cimino had a definite release date, one that played to his ego with academy statuettes dangling as golden carrots, a prolonged postproduction period might be averted. It was unlikely a film somewhere between two and two and one-half hours' playing time could be prepared on this schedule without exceptional diligence; but Montana was not Southeast

* Or five months, if one dates the editing process from the beginning of production.

Asia, Cimino was more experienced than when he began *The Deer Hunter*, he would not have a "perfectionist" star like Robert De Niro or strange, inscrutable governments making ominous sounds in funny languages. There was reason to believe that this schedule might accelerate production, too, and the fact that UA was manipulating and only half believed in it didn't have to be communicated to Cimino (though it was) if he agreed to live with it because there was always the chance he would stick to the numbers on the calendar.

Cimino was calm, cool, reasonable. He pointed out freshly the difficulties of his shooting schedule (though rejecting Katz's skepticism—and, later, Katz as well), but he admitted that a December date appealed to him, had been lucky for him this year, and there was no reason to reject a proposal which could position the picture well commercially and demonstrate his own cooperation and enthusiasm.

The editing schedule did not unduly worry him and had no precedent in *The Deer Hunter*, on which he had had to wait until the end of photography even for viewing of the dailies shipped back to California for processing. The composing schedule might be tight because he wanted John Williams, then hugely in demand after *Star Wars* and *Jaws*, but that could be handled. One preview was no concern; he didn't dote on previews anyway. All they had done on *The Deer Hunter* was demonstrate to Universal that he had been right and it had been wrong. All in all, though he carefully couched the ifs, he rejected nothing. He also accepted nothing. He would think it over.

A possible Christmas release was duly communicated back to New York. Lee Katz's news was less equivocal. He returned from the South Pacific with a tan and a chuckle. There was no way, he reported, that the *Bounty* pictures could be brought in for less than $30 million, possibly $35. Facilities in New Zealand and Fiji were not what wishful thinking had thought; locations, though spectacular, were spectacularly risky because of the water factor. Albeck listened grimly. There was no way he would commit the company to a $35 million investment, even though *Apocalypse* and *Moonraker* were both nearing that, and even if it was David Lean and two movies, not one.

Albeck and I were in New York during this period and explored several alternatives. A *Bounty* coproduction with Warner's was not workable because of Warner's terms. Warner Vice-Chairman John Calley told me it would be willing to cofinance the pictures (which had originally been developed there), but instead of sharing worldwide revenues from a common pot, Warner's wanted a hemispheric split, it taking Western, leaving UA Eastern. Several other companies were not interested in a coproduction, and we ultimately met with Robert Stigwood, the Australian financier who had produced *Saturday Night Fever* and *Evita* and expressed interest in coventuring. His interest drifted away. Perhaps the yacht he kept at anchor in the East River told him too much about boats and water. We were never to know; he never answered our calls.

There were other projects to explore. Field had proposed a production of Edgar Snow's *Red Star over China*, and meetings were held in New York with British producer David Puttnam and Snow's widow, Lois Snow. Puttnam wanted to make the picture *in* China, where he was convinced he could do it for $4 million. Mrs. Snow expressed her interest in Robert Redford's playing her husband, which would have effectively left nothing in the $4 million budget with which to make the film. There were discussions with Allan Carr and Mike Nichols about their proposed Broadway musical based on UA's *La Cage aux Folles*, to be directed by Nichols, written by Jay Presson Allen, choreographed by Tommy Tune, with songs by Marvin Hamlisch. * The movie version of *Hair* opened to brilliant reviews and disappointing business, "a victim of the ads," said producer Lester Persky, "of changing times," said everyone else. There was travel, too: to Rio, Dakar, Paris, London, San Francisco, Paris again, London again; to Phoenix, Denver, Boston, Atlanta, and Seattle for previews of *Hair, The Last Embrace, The Black Stallion*, and *Apocalypse* at last. The company seemed to be finding its legs on both coasts, and with *Bounty* becalmed, David Field carefully pursued *Heaven's Gate* through the February budget, casting, and other preproduction matters, on which momentum was building, as Cimino continued to ponder the issue of UA's Christmas release and postproduction schedule, while saying nothing.

Having agreed finally to Isabelle Huppert as Ella Watson, UA was pleased to see the secondary casting level filled with good, young actors, all of whom had some marquee recognition value and were widely applauded as exceptional talents. Chief among them was John Hurt, who would play William C. Irvine, Kristofferson's Harvard friend and association member. Hurt had never appeared in an American movie before, let alone a western, and it was felt that his mid-Atlantic accent would lend a certain toniness to the Harvard commencement scenes, in which he would be the class orator. Additionally, his English manner

---

* Carr had bought the English language stage rights to the French play several years before, and his hit Broadway version was, for legal reasons, based on the play, not on the films. In the event, Arthur Laurents directed it, Harvey Fierstein wrote it, Jerry Herman composed it, and Scott Salmon choreographed it.

might underscore the large foreign ownership of association cattle ranches. Hurt had no other pictures scheduled until *The Elephant Man* in England in October and viewed "playing cowboy," as he put it, "a lark." It was a lark that metamorphosed into an albatross.

Jeff Bridges, who had worked for Cimino in *Thunderbolt and Light-foot** and who had been Cimino's 1975 choice for the role now to be played by Christopher Walken, came on as the owner of the Blue Rooster Café, the saloon cum hotel where Kristofferson's Averill lives. This character, originally named J. B. Meredith in the screenplay, was given the name Bridges because the actor discovered an antecedent had lived in the West at the period of the "war," and with a simple name change he had the opportunity to portray his own ancestor.

Brad Dourif, who had been poignantly effective (and Academy Award-nominated) in *One Flew over the Cuckoo's Nest,* was cast as the Sweetwater apothecary, whose chemicals would provide explosives for the settlers' homemade bombs in the climactic battle. His name in the script was Eggleston, and he would be required to speak English with a pronounced Scandinavian accent.

Finally, Sam Waterston was cast in the role of Frank Canton, leader of the mercenary gang, a man whom Waterston, with the addition of a mustache, strikingly resembled, though his likeness to Canton's actual photographs was less important than his reputation as one of the fine pool of New York actors from which Walken also came.

Other, more minor roles were filled with lesser names, such as Geoffrey Lewis, who was cast as a grizzled wolf trapper, and Mickey Rourke, who was to play Walken's sidekick and fellow victim Nick Ray. The casting of the majority of the immigrants, each of whom would be sought for his or her look and ability to speak the language of his or her respective old country, was to take place mostly in Montana, and not until the production was closer to principal photography, still scheduled for April 2. In late March there were still no signed contracts with Cimino and his company (which included Carelli) and no resolution of the release question, which had been hanging unanswered for more than six weeks. Finally, a resolution was proposed.

A letter was hand delivered to United Artists' offices from Cimino's lawyers, Kaplan, Livingston, Goodwin, Berkowitz & Selvin, on March 21, 1979. It was a draft agreement for the final Cimino contract and addressed itself to twelve open points which had been the subject of negotiating delays for months. The letter concluded with an abrupt

*For which he received a Best Supporting Actor Academy Award nomination.

demand: "Mr. Cimino insists upon United Artists' final confirmation of its agreement to the foregoing by no later than the end of the business day Friday, March 23."

Insisting without negotiation is a good way to trigger a meeting, and it did. Eric Weissmann and Jeremy Williams of the Kaplan, Livingston firm met with David Field and Leon Brachman the next day, March 22.

Most of the twelve "foregoing" points were standard negotiating items that were emotionally neutral. They included sequel rights, television versions, publication rights to the screenplay, and so on. One or two additional points seemed to UA unrealistic in the extreme or high-handed, or both, but they were not without precedent in an industry in which deal points can have as much status significance as houses, automobiles, and statuettes. There was one point, however—to which we will return—that seemed to UA to be outrageous, indicating a serious loss of perspective and inflation of ego on Cimino's part, though it was of far less material consequence than the statement prefacing the twelve-item agenda, to which the law firm also insisted on "final confirmation." It was, at last, Cimino's response to the Christmas question:

With regard to the budget, Mr. Cimino informs us that as a result of his discussions with United Artists, the approved cash budget of the picture is $11,588,000. It is agreed, however, that any and all monies in excess of the approved cash budget expended as a result of or in connection with the effort of The Johnson County War Company [Cimino's corporate entity] . . . to complete and deliver the picture in time for a Christmas 1979 release shall not be treated as overbudget expenditures for any purpose unfavorable to Company . . . even if it is finally decided that it is not feasible to complete and deliver the picture in time for such a release.

That wasn't all, but it was enough. First, it was annoying to Field and Brachman to read that Cimino had informed his lawyers of an "approved cash budget" because there wasn't one and would not be until April 20, one month later. The budget number was real enough and pointed up that it had risen another $2 million—albeit with UA's awareness, if not its approval—since Lee Katz's vetting of the February budget, which had itself been up $2 million. What was alarming was that the paragraph quoted here implied waiving budget control of the picture by UA in favor of Cimino. All the usual overbudget provisions, by which a director is penalized in loss of contingent compensation (profit points, delayed or deferred salary, etc.), were to be likewise waived. In effect, this paragraph stated, we will do what we have to do, spend what we have to spend to meet the December date, with no penalties to ourselves for any resultant cost overruns, and no guarantees either. The paragraph concluded: "In that last regard [feasibility] . . . as previously discussed, Company [Cimino] agrees to inform United Artists by no later than July 1, 1979 of whether or not a Christmas 1979 release is feasible."

In other words, it *might* work, but who knows? and we'll let you know a couple of weeks after we finish shooting. The Christmas release date had assumed what Joan Didion calls nuclear capability. Cimino was willing to work toward it, accepting none of the economic consequences of that effort, rejecting all the standard restraint penalties built into motion-picture production boiler plate at all companies, everywhere. Any liabilities that resulted from his attempt to satisfy what was, after all, UA's idea were UA's problem. If that meant overtime and additional manpower to adhere to the production schedule so as not to delay postproduction, no penalties were to be imposed. What no one asked was: How do we differentiate between cost overruns designed to meet the Christmas release and cost overruns stemming from other causes?

Even though this point, not the twelve items enumerated below it, was the vital issue of the letter, perhaps the emotional tenor of the negotiation can be better understood through reference to these minor points, which began—a month after Paris—with Cimino's assertion that he and he alone had the right to "designate" Huppert or any other lead actress he chose and again, had informed his lawyers that this had been agreed to with UA, though it had not. *

Cimino insisted on weekly expenses of $2,000, regardless of place of work; it meant he would receive $2,000 per week for the expense of living in his own Beverly Hills home for a projected six-month period of postproduction in Los Angeles. This $2,000 per week was to become retroactive to the September deal date. The letter failed to note that agreeing to this point would require a budget entry of approximately $130,000 over and above Cimino's $500,000 salary. (Nor was it noted that it would take extravagant genius to spend $2,000 per week on living expenses in Kalispell, Montana.)

The publication rights were to be retained solely by Cimino. Ditto the cutting rights for foreign versions (where censorship can and does still play an important role with some pictures). Ditto the preview rights. Cimino was to have advertising approvals "without limitation,"

---

* Certainly not formally. It is possible that Field implied some such thing inadvertently, though the issue was such a volatile one it seems highly unlikely.

a right not granted, to my knowledge, to anyone at any film company since the days of Pickford and Fairbanks, when they owned theirs.

The two important, emotion-inducing clauses were number ten, in which it was stated, "Mr. Cimino has already informed United Artists that he expects the picture to be no shorter than 2½ hours,"* and number two: "Mr. Cimino's presentation credit shall be in the form 'Michael Cimino's "Heaven's Gate"' (or in such other form as [Cimino] may designate); Mr. Cimino's name in such credit shall be presented in the same size as the title, including all artwork titles, and on a separate line above the title, and shall appear in the form just indicated on theater marquees (United Artists to require such treatment in its agreements with exhibitors)."

Putting aside for the moment the fact that no movie company can "require" theaters to do much of anything now that they no longer own them and that "best efforts" is a frighteningly slippery term and concept, the clause was astonishing to UA, for it amounted to making Cimino's name, for all intents and purposes, part of the title. This was not keeping up with the Hollywood Joneses; this was keeping up with the Kubricks and Leans. Stanley Kubrick had had a similar title treatment on *A Clockwork Orange,* the title of which read—to the not very rib-tickled amusement of Anthony Burgess, who was under the impression he had written the book—*Stanley Kubrick's A Clockwork Orange.* All the recent David Lean pictures had been preceded by the words *David Lean's Film of.*

Kubrick was guilty of usurpation of credit in many industry eyes with this possessory title, but in his defense *Spartacus, Lolita, Paths of Glory, Dr. Strangelove,* and *2001* (among others) were invoked to justify the hubris. Lean, as already noted here, was perhaps the most consistently successful commercial director in history. Michael Cimino had made *two* movies, which had been nominated for, but had not yet received, Academy Awards. Kubrick and Lean between them accounted for thirty-eight wins.† Hubris was one thing; this looked like self-apotheosis.

No one at UA who was aware of the contractual demand was unoffended by it. UA tried to avoid the *ad hominem* arguments that were rising with the gorge and reverted to attacking the impossibly constraining requirement to exhibitors, who might wish to feature on the marquee the name of the star instead of that of the director, and to the additional advertising costs that would be incurred, which may have

*He may have so informed Field, but nobody else had heard about it.
†Kubrick thirteen; Lean twenty-five.

been a moot point because Cimino was asking for advertising approvals "without limitation," which would have given him the right to feature not only his name as part of the title but his picture as part of the art as well. * Finally, the who-the-hell-does-he-think-he-is question could be suppressed no longer and was answered by the dignified and normally soft-spoken Eric Weissmann with "He thinks he's a filmmaker for whom this issue is a deal breaker."

Deal breaker is a very powerful negotiating term. It is sometimes pronounced "or else." Sometimes it is a welcome word: It can provide the escape hatch for getting out of a deal or the pretext for caving in to one. In this case the UA response could have been to call the bluff, if bluff it was. But no one wanted to regard six months' work and by now $2 million actually spent (over and above the guaranteed fees) as having been meaningless preludes to acrimony and a gaping hole in the release schedule. The six months of nursing the project toward production had created a strong identification with it. Then, too, there had been another letter that week, from Michael Cimino to David Field. In it Cimino raised his familiar issue: "[A]nother party has already agreed to proceed . . . and we would not want to jeopardize that situation if there is not an absolutely clear understanding [between UA and the production]."

Was there another company standing by, maybe two? It is possible, though Barry Spikings of EMI was later to tell David Field, as Field reported to us, that he had not been prepared to go forward with *Heaven's Gate*, not immediately following *The Deer Hunter* anyway. Warner Brothers had actively sought the picture six months earlier but was at this time making a deal with Cimino for a different future picture (never made), which it would announce that spring. Still, Cimino's letter claimed the other "party" had agreed in advance to proceed with "a budget of approximately eleven and a half million dollars, in addition to any and all overages that would be incurred during the finishing phase of the picture in order to be ready for Christmas release."† Cimino termed it "a difficult and delicate situation for all concerned," which it certainly would have been if he were, as this letter suggests,

---

* And there would have been precedent, too. In the early seventies UA released a picture starring Robert Blake called *Electra Glide in Blue*. The announcement ad was a full page in the Sunday *New York Times*, consisting of a photograph of the director, one James William Guercio, whose fame turned out to be fleeting.

† The "Christmas release" reference is curious, indeed. Cimino had resisted the concept until this point, which had relevance only to UA's internal release schedule. It is hard to imagine why he would introduce the topic elsewhere or why another company would agree to "overages." Assuming there *was* another company, of course.

negotiating with others even as he was spending UA's money and energies. The letter ended on a courteous note that he was "pleased at the prospect of continuing our relationship with United Artists on this project," to which a variety of replies were suggested.

UA caved in. All of us, for neither Field nor Brachman—nor Stolber nor I—had the authority to capitulate to such a request without Albeck's approval. The discussions between UA and Eric Weissmann were bitter and regretted because there was no way UA could—if only to save face—refrain from conveying its conviction that this was an ego negotiation, supported by neither Cimino's industry nor audience record. Asking for an actor or actress, pressing for an increase in the budget for some legitimate production purpose, even expanding the scope of the picture and the financial commitment to accommodate a director's expanding concept of his picture—all these had some point that presumably benefited the movie. Acceding to this demand could be rationalized only by the kind of reasoning that had led to approval of Isabelle Huppert in Paris, and that is how we supported the argument internally: Field, Brachman, Stolber, and I *wanted Heaven's Gate* . . . even *Michael Cimino's Heaven's Gate*. We got it.

The rest of the twelve outstanding points were eventually resolved in ways not precedentially harmful to UA. Cimino got his $2,000 a week but not in Los Angeles; a way of sharing in publication revenues was found; advertising approvals were granted with limitations onerous to neither side; he won the right to make a movie "between two and three hours in length." But incorrectly and emotionally it was the presentation credit that churned the most debate, the most adrenaline. It aroused then and later much concerned speculation about the kind of man Cimino might be, as if he had invented ego . . . in Hollywood yet.

The legal wrangling wasn't over, however. Hairsplitting, the search for "language" acceptable to both sides, continued. On March 28 Jeremy Williams sent Field an interim draft letter from Kaplan, Livingston, reflecting the conclusions of the March 22 meeting. Field forwarded the letter to the legal department and to the head of business affairs, Dean Stolber, in New York, where so many objections were newly raised that on April 10 Eric Weissmann, Williams's senior in the law firm, wrote Stan Kamen of the William Morris office in weary exasperation that the draft letter, "rather than being tinkered with and put quickly into final form, is the subject of a major contract negotiation." He added, "I should not have to be writing this letter. The point of the 'summit meeting' was to avoid further rounds of negotiation." He concluded with the plea "Can you call David Field?"

Perhaps that note of weariness from Weissmann was physical, for he had been up late the night before, watching the proceedings at the Dorothy Chandler Pavilion of the Music Center in downtown Los Angeles, and because he had, perhaps he knew that Tuesday, April 10, the morning after the night before, was just the right time to ask Stan Kamen to place a personal call to David Field. For on April 9 *The Deer Hunter* won five Academy Awards: Best Sound, Best Editing, Best Supporting Actor (Walken), Best Direction, and Best Picture. Cimino, Oscar raised aloft, saluted the audience ecstatically with "Baby, I love ya!"

There were ironies that night. The Best Director Oscar was presented to Cimino by Francis Coppola, who called him *paisan'* presumably in friendship. The Best Picture Award (which Cimino shared as a coproducer) was presented by the Old Soldier himself, who might once have starred in *Heaven's Gate* but instead had made his own Vietnam movie called *Green Beret*: John Wayne, in his last and saddest public appearance.

Backstage, after the awards, when the winners posed for photographs and gave quotes to the press, there was a minor ruckus which received major coverage. Best Actress winner Jane Fonda (for *Coming Home*) berated Cimino for his "racist, Pentagon version of the war." Cimino appeared confused and bewildered as the flashbulbs popped and reporters scribbled.

Outside the Music Center police had earlier arrested thirteen members of the Vietnam Veterans Against the War who were picketing *The Deer Hunter*, while members of the Hell No We Won't Go Away Committee went up and down the rows of arriving limousines, shoving pamphlets through windows that went up and down electrically, admitting or shutting out the committee's denunciations of the film and its "racist" viewpoint.

Back inside the pavilion, when pressed by reporters, Miss Fonda admitted she hadn't actually *seen The Deer Hunter*, perhaps muting her point but not her fervor. It wouldn't have mattered much anyway because Universal told the *New York Times*'s Aljean Harmetz that the Oscar wins caused *Deer Hunter* box-office receipts to rise $100,000 a day in the New York area alone.

Cimino was in Los Angeles that night to receive his avalanche of awards because of another avalanche that winter: a real one. It closed access roads to construction sites for *Heaven's Gate* in Glacier National Park, halting building and other preproduction work until the roads could be made passable. UA and the insurance company declared a *force majeure* and pushed the start of principal photography back to

April 16. The two-week leeway Gary Gerlich had built into the schedule was eaten up before the picture ever began.

But even the insurance company's "acts of God" had less eventual
effect on *Heaven's Gate* than the inundating detail of legalistically split
hairs in late March. In all that haystack, the needle that was vastly
more important than Cimino's expenses or publication rights or advertising rights or presentation credit or leading lady got overlooked:
". . . any and all monies in excess of the approved cash budget expended . . . to complete and deliver the picture in time for a Christmas
1979 release shall not be treated as overbudget. . . ."

Cimino and his lawyers won that point, that right to release the
brakes on the budget. They won the right not to inform United Artists
whether the object of such an extraordinary provision was even feasible
until July 1. And they won these rights without a recorded fight. In the
voluminous correspondence between the lawyers and the company, this
most important issue of all remained unchallenged and unamended.
The files reveal only that on the March 21 draft agreement, used as the
basis for the March 22 "summit meeting," next to the crucial paragraph
David Field noted one word, a word he could have written only with
the agreement of his colleagues and superiors, and after he had written
it, he underlined it: "*Okay.*"

CHAPTER 12

ACCOMPLICES

"Please be assured that all of us are pulling together in friendship and enthusiasm." The friendly enthusiasts included David Field, me, Joann Carelli, and Michael Cimino, who addressed this calming note to Andy Albeck in writing in early April, by which time all had been forgiven. Hollywood's newly anointed star director, awash with plaudits, was preparing to turn his cameras on the sixteenth. He was working reverently in his "cathedral" and had absolved us of the acrimony and invective spilled over the issues of Isabelle Huppert and

his contract demands. His refound poise was perhaps inspired by his
Directors Guild of America award, his Academy Awards, his New York
Film Critics' Award, and the industry power and prestige they con-
ferred, or perhaps it was the physical grandeur of his setting that calmed
him, the part of Big Sky country that the guidebooks call the Crown of
the Continent.

Kalispell, Montana, in Flathead County, is a small, leafy town of
between 10,000 and 15,000 people, who depend heavily on rustic
rather than jet-set tourism for their livelihoods. Kalispell is the access
town for the 2.5 million acres of Flathead National Forest, and it is the
southern gateway into Glacier National Park, which stretches ma-
jestically northward two or more hours by car to the Canadian border.
There it joins Canada's Waterton Lakes National Park. The two are
known collectively as the Waterton-Glacier International Peace Park,
established in 1932 as the only cross-boundaries international park in
the world, symbolizing friendship between the two countries.

This area of Montana was once the territory of the Blackfoot Indians, who called it the backbone of the world, and it's not hard to see
why. Two ranges of the Rocky Mountains run through it, one pushing
north to Alaska, the other tapering south to New Mexico. Glacier thus
straddles the Continental Divide, where water from winter snows and
200 slowly melting glaciers runs down from above timberline to the
Atlantic and the Pacific, trickling across sheer rock faces, running
through forests of spruce, pine (both white and yellow), larch, and fir,
tumbling in falls and rapids into primitive camping, hunting, fishing
areas, finally flowing icily and crystalline across valleys spangled with
wild flowers like the glacier lily, which elegantly raises its long stem and
yellow blossom up through crusted snows before the thaw is over. Seven
hundred miles of foot trails provide ecologically protected hiking paths
for the million or two visitors each year, who can choose between walking sometimes strenuous trails or driving less energetically along Going-
to-the-Sun Road. Moose, elk, deer, mountain goats, grizzly bears, and
many smaller species of wildlife live here and often intrigue the tourists,
most of whom enter through Kalispell, now in early 1979, filling with
hundreds of wildlife specimens not indigenous to the area and not without their own intrigue.

The Hudson's Bay trappers who founded Kalispell as a fur trading
post would have been as impressed by the Outlaw Inn as the movie
people were. It is the town's largest motel, a well-run modern sprawl
located on busy Highway 93. It has a large restaurant and bar decorated
in the wagon-wheel style (music by the Gunslingers), an indoor swimming pool, saunas and Jacuzzis, a lobby that displays western artifacts

and knickknacks in glass souvenir cases. The inn's logo is the cartoon face of an outlaw, his handlebar mustache sweeping with a breadth suggesting the wings of one of Glacier's bald eagles. Above this magnificent facial brush, pinpoint eyes cross in comical ferocity.

The Outlaw Inn, comfortable and friendly, housed the principal members of the cast and crew of *Heaven's Gate*. On the top floor, the fourth, a series of adjoining rooms were redecorated as offices for the producer and director, in which key decisions would be made and from which call sheets for each day's work would be issued. They were equipped with a portable stereo and indoor plants and were a pleasant refuge in which to work, a calm corner from which Carelli could stay in touch with California, a relaxing haven in which to wind down the day.

Editing facilities were located downstairs from the motel dining room, where the editors, headed by Tom Rolf, were arranging metal racks to hold the cans of film they would wind around colorful plastic spools over the coming months. Production offices were across the parking lot in an annex, where production manager Charlie Okun was to ride herd on eventually millions of physical details and dollars.

From these cheery, quietly busy surroundings Cimino issued daily directions to more than 300 construction workers deployed over two states: building the Heaven's Gate roller rink in Kalispell itself; the town of Sweetwater on a three-foot-high platform erected over a parking lot deep in Glacier National Park on the edge of mirrorlike Two Medicine Lake, which reflected the aptly named and improbably beautiful Painted Teepee mountain peak on the opposite shore; and the main street of Casper, Wyoming, across the state line in Wallace, Idaho, a drably nondescript mining town the previous show business celebrity of which was as the hometown of a local girl who made good by being bad (and beautiful), Lana Turner.

Cimino sat down as his personal thaw began, just before the Oscar ceremonies, and wrote his reassuring, hopeful letter to Albeck in New York, carefully "carboning" Field, Carelli, and me, on whom he showered praise and credit at this penultimate moment before production started—or the plug could be pulled.

"The scope, quality and excitement now surrounding the project," he wrote, "are due in no small measure to both David's and Steven's efforts from the very beginning. And the quality and stature of our cast, which is now remarkable and terribly exciting to contemplate working with, is a tribute also to the energetic and skillful efforts of Joann Carelli, who has worked hand in hand with David and Steve from the very first day. The three of them have been helpful and supportive of me beyond any adequate means of acknowledgement [sic]."

The tone of conciliation seemed sincere enough and without cynicism, signifying perhaps that now that he had received everything he had demanded (or nearly so), he was welcoming the prodigals back as allies to his grand design—allies and accomplices.

The April morning after the Academy Awards the UA staff had made its bleary, weary way to downtown Los Angeles for the monthly production meeting to be held in the directors' boardroom on the twenty-ninth floor of the Occidental Tower. *

There we were to go over production matters with Albeck and Jim Harvey, who had come down from San Francisco with his wife, Charlene, to join us at the Academy Awards and the Governors' Ball that followed. The air in the Beverly Hilton ballroom the previous night had been perhaps excessively festive, and most of us were paying for it in the classic morning-after manner.

The assembly (almost two dozen people, including production and legal personnel, distribution heads Auerbach, Fitter, and Farber, advertising and publicity chiefs, plus President Albeck and Chairman Harvey) was brought up-to-date on current and future projects, but most minds were on Michael Cimino's euphoric victory the night before. Because no budget approval had yet been granted on *Heaven's Gate*—and therefore the project was not officially approved (no matter how many carpenters were hammering away in Montana and Idaho)—Albeck coolly tabled discussion on the picture until Field, Stolber, he, and I could meet with Lee Katz in Field's office following the general meeting.

Lunch was served in the directors' dining room at Occidental, courtesy of Jim Harvey, who was to sit in on the *Heaven's Gate* meeting. Immediately before and after lunch we called our offices and returned phone calls we were told were "urgent." Field returned one so labeled. It was from Stan Kamen at the Morris office.

"The budget contemplates eleven million five hundred and eighty-eight thousand seven hundred and seventy-one dollars, Andy," said Lee Katz. We—Katz, Field, Harvey, Albeck, Dean Stolber, and I—had regrouped after lunch in Field's Culver City office.

"*Contemplates?*" asked Albeck. "How accurate is this budget?"

* Now called the Transamerica Tower; located on Transamerica Plaza.

"I believe it to have been made with a crystal ball," said Katz, chuckling heartily. Albeck didn't laugh. He didn't smile. Nobody did.

"Is this a meaningless budget, then, on which we have already spent several million dollars?"

"It's not meaningless, Andy, it's just full of off-the-cuff estimates and probable shortfalls and round figures like—" he glanced at his notes—"like a hundred thousand dollars for extras. That's a figure that's there merely to fill in the blank. It seems evident to me, and, I trust, to David and Steve as well"—he glanced at each of us, seeking a clue to how frankly his skepticism might be expressed in this forum without embarrassment to us—"that the scope of this project has increased at a gallop over the past few months."

"Scope is what we wanted, Lee," observed Field quietly.

"We didn't want just another western," Albeck agreed. "We wanted an epic, an Academy Award-winning epic."

"Well, you're going to be paying for one," said Katz, his chuckle constricting to a rattle as he observed Albeck's lips compress.

"How much?"

"I beg your pardon?"

"How *much* am I going to be paying?"

Harvey slouched in his chair, toying with a pencil, as Katz responded sans chuckle. "I can't tell you with exactitude, Andy. There is only one meaningful area in this budget that will determine the cost, and that is whether or not Mr. Cimino intends to shoot the script on schedule. If he does, if he *can*, my guess is the budget is still understated by at least a million dollars, probably more. Postproduction is a yawning chasm of unknown magnitude if United Artists persists in pursuing a Christmas release. . . ." His voice trailed off.

"You seem doubtful," Andy said in understatement.

Katz again swiveled glances at Field and me. His eyelids closed under uplifted brows as he shrugged. "With all due respect, I regret to say I consider it madness."

"Madness?" The elevating eyebrows now were Albeck's. Katz had Harvey's attention, too. The pencil was held firmly between the tips of two extended forefingers.

"Andy, I could be wrong. I've been wrong before. But I see no chance whatever that a project of this scope and complexity can possibly be finished and ready for release by Christmas."

Field said quietly, "I think everybody knows that Christmas is a long shot, Lee, but doesn't it seem better to apply that pressure and turn those screws than to let him feel it is open-ended?"

"Open-ended?" asked Andy. "He has a schedule."

"So did Francis," Lee said. Harvey's pencil tapped his upper lip, suppressing a rueful smile.

Katz shrugged hugely. "Maybe I'm naïve," he added, sounding supremely not. "I believe the man has no intention of finishing the picture for Christmas."

"After last night?" I asked, guessing at his intuition.

Katz nodded. "He's won the big awards. Chances against his winning two years in a row are astronomical. If he had not won this year, he might work like a Trojan to win next, but his greater chance will be the following year, and he must know that."

"Naïve?" I said. "Sounds cynical to me."

"Merely skeptical. My analysis is not of Mr. Cimino's motives but of his schedule." He smiled. "I have said from the beginning that my major concern was the number of shooting days, and I must still register profound skepticism that any director—with the possible exception of Jewison or Dick Lester—could or would finish this picture on a sixty-nine-day schedule."

"What is your recommendation?" asked Albeck.

Lee looked uncharacteristically startled. "I have no recommendation," he answered. "That's for David and Steve to make. I don't even know what's in the contracts. I can only examine the budget and tell you I think it's made with a crystal ball and bears little relationship to probable production realities."

"*How much is this picture going to cost me?*" asked Albeck, his lips narrowing to nothingness.

"Don't qualify it to death, Lee," I interjected.

He sighed, his breath rippling down the silk of his handsomely striped tie. "I think you are facing at least fifteen million dollars. At least and at best."

"You said one million additional earlier. That would make it twelve million six," said Albeck. Harvey's eyes seemed to be following a Ping-Pong match, though his pencil remained motionless, poised over his yellow pad.

"I said a million over *if* he makes the picture in the sixty-nine days he's asked for. I don't believe he will or can. I think this budget is at least two weeks light, and with the picture operating at something over a hundred thousand dollars a day, six days a week on location, that means an additional one million two, bringing it to twelve million eight. *Plus* the million dollars in shortfalls I estimate, making it thirteen eight, and I arrive very quickly at fifteen million dollars by including overages I believe will take place in miscellaneous overtime, in the music account, the postproduction account, the prologue and epilogue accounts—which I regard as sheerest fantasy—and on the fact that the director went double budget on his last picture." His eyes looked serenely cool as he closed his notes and his case.

Albeck turned gravely to Field. "Should we be making this picture?"

David splayed his fingers, placed their tips together, and dropped them between his knees as he bent forward in his chair. "If you want to get out of it, Andy, Warner Brothers will take it."

Harvey's eyes narrowed.

"Will they pay me back my money?" Albeck asked.

"On some basis, yes. Maybe out of profits or some gross position. Now? We don't know."

"Can we ask them?"

"Yes, we can," I interjected. "But to ask will demonstrate we're nervous about the picture, which will be instantly communicated back to Cimino, who will interpret asking the question as tantamount to a turnaround. There's real volatility beneath all that calm assurance, and he knows that after last night's awards he's so hot probably anybody in town would take this picture . . . which may be a very good reason not to let it go."

Harvey's pencil was immobile, his eyes attentive.

"At what cost does a company decide it can't afford *not* to let a picture go?" asked Albeck sternly.

"Under our system," I replied, "at a cost beyond which the distribution people feel they can make money. They all have been high on the picture; they've all said they could do business with it, but if they feel we can't recoup a fifteen-million-dollar investment—"

"Plus interest, advertising, and promotion."

"Plus interest, advertising, and promotion," I continued, "by an Academy Award-winning director who has yet to make a failure, then I guess we won't make it. *Shouldn't* make it."

Andy scrutinized his notes. This question had been rehearsed with Auerbach, Fitter, and Farber each time the budget had taken one of its now-familiar escalations from the $7.5 million of September. They had been consistently unified in endorsing the theatrical potential of the picture, and all had asserted often the positive effect *The Deer Hunter* Oscars would have on their abilities to sell *Heaven's Gate.*

Albeck turned to Field. "What is your recommendation?"

David paused, then spoke evenly. "I think we should make the picture, Andy. I believe in the picture, and I believe in Michael."

Albeck noted the fact, then turned to me.

"I agree," I said.

"At which cost shall we agree to make it?"

The "shall" was the clue. He had agreed. Harvey looked on with noncommittal interest.

"If Lee is right," said David, "and he's very rarely wrong, we should not go into this movie with any number in our heads under fifteen, followed by a lot of zeros."

Andy nodded. "Will you take the responsibility for telling Cimino that?"

I interrupted. "I don't think we should tell him anything. We should never have let him know we expected him to go a week or two over schedule, and we shouldn't tell him now that we're prepared to give him more than he's asked for. He says he can make the picture for eleven five or eleven six, and we should hold him to it."

"Isn't that . . . bad faith?" Albeck frowned.

"Why? We're not imposing eleven six on him; it's his figure. Maybe he can do it for that amount. Great. But if not, it gives us some sort of moral position, something to hold him to when he starts to go over. *If*."

"Can't we find some more direct way to avoid that?"

"Short of sending David to Montana to hold his hand—or Joann's—for sixty-nine days, I can't think of one. Can you, Lee?"

Katz sighed. "We seem to be in the ironic and paradoxical position of not really trusting the gentleman with our money and, therefore, insisting that he take more."

"If we don't trust him, we shouldn't be making the picture," said Albeck, turning to David, who in turn nodded to Lee.

"What do Michael and Joann say when you tell them your fears about the budget?"

Lee laughed. "They defend it, of course. And Mr. Cimino seems frankly hostile to my skepticism—or Derek's."

David looked down at his hands, studying them. Albeck's concentration on him was intense. He resisted a quick answer, then finally said, "I trust him, Andy," meeting Albeck's gaze. "And I think Steven's right. It's not as if we were imposing a number on him. Let's take him at his word and tell him we'll be watching every penny."

"Tell him *you'll* be watching every penny." I smiled. "I have no intention of going to Montana."

"The way you had no intention of going to Paris?"

"Touché." I laughed. "But it's your picture."

"No, it's not," said Albeck. Maybe he was thinking of George Stevens, for he added, "it's *Michael Cimino's Heaven's Gate*." He turned to Stolber, whose role in business affairs made him, unlike Katz, a formal part of the chain of approvals. "Can we afford to make it UA's, Dean?"

"I agree we should make the picture . . . if we can get the contracts finalized, but we still have a long way to go, Andy," he said.

Field's head turned sharply to Stolber. "You should know, Dean, that Eric Weissmann wrote Stan Kamen this morning asking Stan to call me today, which he did. The lawyers at Kaplan, Livingston and the Morris office say you're holding up the papers by trying to renegotiate everything that was agreed to in this office back in March."

Stolber's round, youthful face tightened behind his horn-rimmed glasses. As a former actor who had sung and danced on and off-Broadway to finance his way through Harvard and NYU Law School, he was usually good at hiding his feelings, but Field's challenge was too direct for bland pretense and had been made in particularly sensitive company.

"And what did you say back?" he asked, making his voice flat.

"I said I'd ask you why deal points that were agreed to in March are still not documented and why renegotiating is going on that production doesn't know anything about?"

"What exactly am I supposed to be renegotiating?"

"I don't know, Dean. That's part of the point. I'm asking *you*."

The sluggishness of late afternoon vanished, and Albeck's glinting eyeglasses shone with alertness. He knew that production often felt the legal and business affairs departments, both working under Stolber, killed or prevented the making of deals—even offers—as often as they facilitated them. Business affairs' function was supposed to be primarily as a service arm for the other divisions, but it operated consistently as yet another link—often a de facto one—in the chain of approvals standing between production and its goals. Production proposed, and as often as not, we believed, business affairs disposed.

"What is the status of the contracts?" Albeck demanded.

"We are searching for language, Andy," Stolber said in his controlled, deliberately toneless voice. "Things may have been agreed to in this office by David and Leon Brachman, but I wasn't here, and we all know there are things in the Cimino contract I was seriously opposed to—"

"Yes, yes, we know that." Albeck cut him off, hoping to avoid a lengthy legal dissertation. "But we agreed to them. Why are the contracts not ready?"

Stolber looked frustrated, coiled. "My function here is to protect the company, particularly where precedential matters are concerned. They can come back to haunt us with hidden consequences and unforeseen ramifications. We need to be protected from those even if we don't know what they are or might be."

"Dean," I said, "we're less than one week from the start of principal photography. Do you think it's possible you are protecting us right out of this picture?"

Stolber looked badgered. First Field, now me.

"No, I don't think so," he said. "We have enough documentation to protect us in the normal ways. The picture can go forward. We'll find the right language, and the lawyers will circulate the documents."

"When?" asked Albeck, his pencil poised.

"I'll try to have them for you by the end of the week," he said dully, "so you can review them over the weekend. But I'd like to add something, Andy—and Steven and David and Jim. I think caution may be less harmful to a project than the harm that can be done by production executives' siding with agents and lawyers whose interests are very much their own and may be inimical to UA's."

"Disloyal, you mean?" asked David.

"That's a pretty strong word," said Stolber.

"Yes, it is," agreed David with icy calm.

"Come on, you guys," I said, trying to mollify. "Nobody is siding with anybody or against anybody about anything. We'd just like a little faster action in the legal department, that's all."

"I'm not sure that *is* all," said Field. "I think we have an obligation to protect the company, too, and allowing the company's reputation to be cleavered by the legal department or distribution or even"—a glance at me—"the other half of production is very much a matter to take sides over. I think we're losing deals because of business affairs. Deals and credibility."

"Are you talking about company credibility or personal credibility?" asked Stolber calmly.

"What's the difference?" asked Field. His voice had that quiet, dramatically softened tone that caused others to lean into it, that permitted him to say very strong things with impunity because of the gentle, nonconfrontational evenness with which they were uttered. Still, the gravity of his complaint was unmistakable and harsh.

Albeck stepped in. "Let's have a separate meeting in which we can discuss this without bothering Lee and Jim about it."

"Fine, Andy," said Field. "But maybe it's not so bad for Lee and Jim to know that New York is sometimes a lot farther than three thousand miles from California."

What? I thought, not in the mood for cryptic metaphors.

Albeck turned efficiently back to his notes. "Let me be sure I understand. David and Steven are recommending we approve the budget at eleven million five hundred eighty-eight thousand seven hundred seventy-one dollars but assume among ourselves that the investment will be closer to fifteen million dollars?"

We nodded. Albeck noted the fact without turning to Harvey for his reaction, which came only indirectly.

"*The Deer Hunter* is a hell of a movie," he said lightly just as if it were irrelevant. Murmurs of agreement floated superfluously around the room.

Heaven's Gate was finally approved.

That Saturday night, April 14, I was invited to the movies and glad to go. The screening took place in the Magno Screening room on the lobby floor of the MGM Building at Sixth Avenue and Fifty-fifth Street in New York, a building better known as the New York home of the William Morris Agency since MGM's withdrawal from major movie activity in the seventies.

The movie to be screened was small, intimate, in black and white, had been filmed in near secrecy in New York, had undergone some reshooting after principal photography had been completed (retakes were anticipated by the budget, which the director did not exceed), and had finally changed its public name from "Woody Allen No. 3" to *Manhattan.*

I had flown in from California en route to London after the draining meetings on the West Coast and was waiting for Field to join me in New York on Monday, the sixteenth, the day UA's western epic would begin shooting. Whatever David had meant by his remark about the distance between California and New York we would discover in a meeting at 729 with Albeck, but all of us could confirm the distance was enervating enough. Coast and continent hopping take their tolls, but April 14 in New York happened to be one of those spring days songs are written about, the sky a perfect blue, the air balmy, soothing my jet-lagged nerves and smoothing the edges of an often-jangled city.

About seven o'clock in the evening I strolled across the lower end of Central Park, verdant now with budding trees, and then down Sixth Avenue to join the *Manhattan* production team and other friends of the Woody "family" invited to see the picture. Woody himself was not there, but Charlie Joffe and Jack Rollins were, Charlie displaying hyped-up energy and nerves, Jack cool and somber and collected. I waved hello and slid quietly into a seat in the small blue screening room.

If there are two hours in my three years and three days at United Artists that remain in memory as pure, unambiguous pleasure, they are these two. From the first frames of Gordon Willis's elegant black-and-white cityscapes of New York (in which the movie's title appears only as the blinking neon sign of the Manhattan Hotel), through the New Year's Eve fireworks orgy over Central Park (which looks like one continuous shot, but is many, so seamlessly assembled that rockets burst in rhythm to Gershwin's *Rhapsody in Blue*), the blend of jazzy hipness and romantic poignance had me helplessly hooked. It seemed to me then (and does now) Woody's best film. The structure, unlike the sometimes jittery *Annie Hall*, seems loose but is tight, precisely controlled. The jokes underline the action and neither undercut nor dominate it. The comedy of manners—mostly bad—is sharp and generous at once, as the characters collaborate in their own emotional disarray. Finally, there is a rueful sense that the unraveling of relationships in *Manhattan* (or Manhattan) is not, perhaps, inevitable. The defensive, neurotic behavior, the angst—real or self-dramatized—of these overeducated overachievers, who talk trendy lit chat at Elaine's and even Zabar's and who wonder what to do with the tickets for the Rampal concert even as their lives are (yet again) falling apart, their self-obsessions and delusions, their "elegant sense of dread" (John Lahr's nice phrase, though he meant it negatively) all are balanced by the sweet poignance of the movie's last line, delivered by Tracy (Mariel Hemingway, in what is surely one of the most unaffected performances in American movies). "Look," she says, "you have to have a little faith in people."

In many ways, the movie is about faith—or faithlessness, of several kinds—and the simplicity of Tracy's naïve insight acts as a reproach to what has gone before. None of Allen's other pictures seem to me to have skewered contemporary relationships, pretensions, fears, defenses, and self-absorption so neatly, so knowingly, so sweet-naturedly. *Manhattan* is not bittersweet; it is alternately bitter and sweet, tense with this ambivalence, an ambivalence Allen's musical sense serves elegantly and well. The Gershwin score reflects and intensifies it: Jazz gives way to romance, romance to jazz, as the movie segues from urban lyricism to sentiment. That it resolves itself in loss—made bearable by Tracy's beauty and optimism and "faith in people" (underscored by "But Not for Me")—makes *Manhattan*, I think, Woody's most satisfying movie.

Later, when Andrew Sarris in the *Village Voice* called it "the only truly great American movie of the 1970's," I thought that was nice but maybe missed the point. What I found in those two hours seemed something I'd grown too cynical to expect anymore: some kind of enchantment. And proud as I was of UA's parentage, I didn't miss the irony that my sole contribution to the movie had been to read the script, take a few notes, and murmur, "Yes, please."

I left the screening room with a silent nod to Jack and Charlie and walked slowly, glowing in the continuing spell of the movie, down a nearly deserted Sixth Avenue. The skyscraping piles of steel and glass that in daylight seemed so forbidding and faceless now glinted with city lights. I could hear Gershwin playing somewhere—or thought I could—and as I grinned at my own pleasure and at the empty street and at the purple sky, I remembered all the reasons I had always wanted to live in New York and all the reasons I had wanted to be in the movie business.

I stopped at some corner where a pay phone stood in the shadows of dark glass towers, found a dime, and made a call to Field's answering machine in Westwood, wanting to say exultantly, "We have a hit!," thinking it might calm his anxiety about his much larger picture. I told his machine, "Call me," and strolled back to the East Side, humming Gershwin through a rare and perfect New York spring twilight, and Montana seemed very, very far from Manhattan.

Joann Carelli's customary cool had deserted her. She was more than miffed; she was angry. She had been trying to reach David Field by phone in California ever since she had received her copy of the budget memo now on the desk in her office in the Outlaw Inn. Where did that Lee Katz get off, she wondered, calling it a budget made with a crystal ball? Both she and Cimino had felt from their first meetings with Katz that he was unsympathetic to them or to the movie or what Mike was trying to accomplish. Even so, he had come on like Mr. Diplomat or somebody, always smiling and chuckling while challenging the budget and, by implication, themselves. How many Academy Awards did this Lee Katz have anyway? "Crystal ball"! No wonder Mike was now demanding that he never have to deal with Katz ever again.

It was the flat-out arrogance of the man that put her off more than any actual claims he made about the numbers. Sure, he was right that the $100,000 for extras was an "off-the-cuff guess." What else could it be, until the roller-skating rink was finished and they knew how many people it needed to look right and how many of them would need to be bussed in and fed and how little they could be negotiated down to? Or the horses. How could Mike know how many horses and wagons he would need until he actually *saw* them in Sweetwater, up at Two Medicine Lake? And what was so "crystal ball" or "off-the-cuff" about the other figures? They weren't humpty-dumpty guesses; they were down there in black and white: props up from $151,507 to $386,593; set dressing up from $245,475 to $333,768; wardrobe up from $268,339 to $510,354; makeup and hair up from $105,804 to $172,500; set construction up from $410,000 to $1,085,000. And of *course*, some of those figures would change if they added extras and horses and things. What did this Lee Katz expect?

None of it had been a secret after all, Carelli knew. David had been kept up-to-date all along. So had Katz and everybody else at UA. *They want an important movie, right? Well, they'll get an important movie, but not if Mike Cimino has to deal ever again with Mr. Lee ("Crystal Ball") Katz!*

Carelli wished Field would call her back so she could air her annoyance, and she assumed his failure to do so was just because it was the weekend. Maybe Monday was better anyway, after they'd gotten the first day of shooting out of the way. She was edgy, and why not? It was a big moment for her, her first as a full-fledged producer, even if she was an employee of Mike's company. Not that she didn't feel entitled or competent, for she had been involved with *Heaven's Gate* for almost ten years now, ever since she advised Mike back in New York that if he ever expected to break through in Hollywood, he'd have to have a script he wouldn't sell unless he directed it. And, she remembered counseling him, you'll need a star, and who are the stars today? Newman, Redford, Eastwood, McQueen. Make it a western, she had said, and he did. She didn't want credit that didn't belong to her; Mike was the one who had discovered the Johnson County War when he took her advice and started looking for a subject, and he was the one who wrote it and rewrote it and rewrote it. She took a little credit for *The Deer Hunter*, though, remembering how Mike had told her about this terrible script called *The Man Who Came to Play* that that Marion Rosenburg from EMI had given him which was only about Russian roulette and had *nothing* to do with Vietnam at all! Joann had urged him to go back to this Rosenburg and tell her his own story if they were so hot to trot. And he did and they were and nobody was complaining now!

So why shouldn't she be producing *Heaven's Gate*? She'd had a kind of godmotherly influence on Mike's career all along, way back in the sixties in New York, when she and Mike—and production manager Charlie Okun, too—all had been with Madison Pollack and O'Hare (MPO). Joann had used her training in graphic arts at Pratt to get into the commercial-making company, looking so "elegant and with-it" in her stylish miniskirts that some of the editorial staff remember thinking she must have been a client. But she wasn't. She was a rep, showing the commercial reels of MPO's directors to the ad agencies up and down Madison Avenue when Mike arrived, fresh from Yale and Michigan State and a little assistant work he called "sweeping the floor" for Pablo Ferro, one of New York's capital G "Genius" art directors. MPO had assigned Charlie Okun to the fledgling Cimino, Charlie, the production man, the nuts-and-bolts guy who ran the floor, held things together, made it all move forward. Forward to Montana, as it turned out.

Joann and Charlie didn't reminisce much about the old days at MPO or much of anything up in Kalispell. There was an observable tension between them, a kind of rivalry that to some stretched back into the sixties, as if each needed to demonstrate to Mike a superior, deeper loyalty and affection whenever their spheres collided, as the artistic and the practical always do in the movie business. And Mike's loyalty seemed to be reciprocated. Almost fifteen years later here they all were. Charlie had been there through the years of Revlon, Pepsi-Cola, Lustre-Creme, United Airlines, and the Yellow Pages commercials. They hadn't all worked, and they hadn't all pleased the clients either, but Charlie remembered them all as "great filmmaking" because Mike had been "a brilliant kid" even then. Charlie was there, too, for *Thunderbolt and Lightfoot* and *The Deer Hunter.* He was *in The Deer Hunter,* in fact, in a way that pleased him and caused his anxious, darting eyes to melt when he told how De Niro's "*This is this*" scene was based on Charlie's own dialogue, a measure of the self-evident pragmatism that guided his work. This is this; work is work; Mike is Mike. He wouldn't contribute in the same way to the screenplay for *Heaven's Gate,* but that was OK because Mike had elevated him to production manager, instead of the lesser positions he had had on the first two shoots, and had allowed Charlie to hire his wife for the wardrobe crew. He was doggedly proud of his loyalty and grateful for Mike's.

Joann and Charlie both had collaborated from the beginning, in their different, separate ways, and if there was little personal affinity between them, there was the glue of shared experience, the shorthand of longtime colleagues, the common fidelity to Mike that would make this Montana stint easier. Or so they hoped.

They knew the dangers, too. They knew that given the chance, Mike was a perfectionist, obsessive about detail, unremittingly demanding. He had been that way at MPO, and his unwillingness to compromise had made *The Deer Hunter* so good. That was why one particular line from Katz's budget memo irritated Joann (and worried Okun) more than all the rest, more even than the supercilious attitude she thought she read: "The gravest question still seems to remain Mr. Cimino's ability to shoot the picture in the allotted time." Sixty-nine days. *Well,* she thought, *no one works harder than Mike, no one has more dedication to his goals, no one pushes himself or his colleagues farther or more relentlessly to achieve them.* But he was also tough-minded and wanted on the screen what he saw in his head. No matter how. In fact, she thought grimly, he could go "berserko" to get what he wanted. Well, she wasn't going to indulge any iron whims in Montana if she could help it, and she *could,* she felt, but she needed outside help. She worried about Charlie's ability to say no to Mike; she worried that Charlie had the same anxiety about her. If they couldn't count on each other to say no, or if their notions of what should be denied or permitted should differ, Charlie would be no ally at all, merely an employee torn between loyalty to Mike and a perhaps grudging obligation to Joann. So UA had better be prepared to back her up when she said no and Mike didn't want to hear it. More prepared than they had been in Paris when Mike insisted on that humpty-dumpty French girl you couldn't even understand to play Ella. If UA expected her to stay within this budget, she thought, their support would have to be a lot stronger than that. And if they didn't believe this humpty-dumpty budget was real, why did they approve it? And if they didn't believe it, why should she sign it?

Heaven's Gate started shooting on schedule, April 16, a day I spent the best part of arguing unsuccessfully before the Motion Picture Association of America's rating board that *Manhattan* should not be rated R just because the Diane Keaton character is heard to use three times (in a flip, not a sexual, way) what is referred to delicately as the "F" word. I cited to the board an experience I had had as a high school teacher in the sixties in mid-America, where the local librarian kept suspect books in a locked cage. One such book imprisoned in this literary jail was required by a student of mine for a paper he was writing on John Steinbeck, who had recently won the Nobel Prize for literature. *The Grapes of Wrath* finally was paroled, but not without written petitions from the student's parents and teacher, all of whom felt the seventeen-year-old would survive exposure to a little symbolic breast-feeding. I argued fervently that the situations seemed analogous to me, that to deny adolescents the right to see a movie about mores because of a word they were mostly using (at least hearing) dozens of times a day was a pious pity. I also cited the absurdity of the R rating's preventing young Mariel Hemingway from seeing a movie she was in. Most of the board agreed. We lost by one vote the necessary two-thirds majority to overturn the rating and, on the advice of the MPAA board chairman, Richard Heffner, scheduled a second appeal one week later. Heffner said he had been swayed by my argument, and he all but charged the board with overturning the R.

David Field arrived in New York that evening. We were leaving for

London on Wednesday the eighteenth and spent most of Tuesday measuring the distance between New York and California.

Field's melancholy asserted itself thickly. He stated gloomily that he felt isolated from the New York center of decision making; that was not difficult to understand because he was the only senior vice-president in the company not based there. He was convinced that his effectiveness, his credibility in dealing with the Hollywood agents and creative talent were undercut by Hollywood's perception that UA was a company run by New York and by the business affairs department, on which Albeck relied too much and which he restrained too little. The argument was overwrought but not without merit, and Field was careful to measure his tone and words, avoiding the personalization of issues that had threatened to flare a week before in California.

Field was right that legal procedures and business affairs maneuvers were glacially slow in the company, frustrating to both of us, sometimes debilitating. I suffered less because I had the advantage of acting on my frustration by walking into Stolber's office, next door to mine, thrashing something out with him, and getting on with it. Field obviously could not do that. He often had to wait hours for a call-back to discuss some legal or deal point with Stolber, only to spend more hours in discussion. Stolber was nothing if not thorough, and whatever he had learned from *Bye Bye Birdie* when he was in the chorus on Broadway did not include brevity. However, had he been a master of pith, Field would still have had to suffer the frustrations familiar to anyone condemned to doing the majority of his business on the telephone, particularly difficult for one who relied extensively on personal charm and metaphorical (if charismatic) locutions to press his points and achieve his ends.

Additionally, frustration continued unabated with marketing's influence over pictures we were allowed to make or develop. The combination of distribution's meddling and business affairs' muddling made Field feel far more impotent than Mike Medavoy had presumably felt in his similar position for two reasons: One, Medavoy had been the sole head of production, not half of a team; and two, Arthur Krim's voice had rung with almost limitless prestige, the yeses and noes fast, authoritative, and uninhibited by the committee system Albeck still favored.

The meeting had subtexts, but the one that Field had confided to me (which was not known to Albeck and Stolber) was that he had been approached by Ted Ashley at Warner Brothers (at Rissner's suggestion?) to leave UA and join the Burbank studio. Field had said no.

He told me he thought Ashley had wanted "a walking Rolodex," someone who could socialize with the stars, be a friend to the famous, and
he felt uncomfortable in such a role. This information startled me and
made me realize that whatever our differences in attitude or approach, I
didn't want to run production alone. I didn't feel capable, nor, I think,
would I have been invited to do so if Field had resigned. As a result of
this conversation, Field and I resolved to share such confidences with
each other as situations arose, and for a while he did.

Much as we all tried to depersonalize the discussion, there were
overtones of Denver. Field's feeling peripheral to the decision-making
process did not reflect the scrupulous equality Albeck maintained in his
dealings with us or in trying to balance our needs and desires against
distribution's. I had the advantage of access, an important advantage in
a system based on collective judgments, but it was a threat to Field, I
felt, only to the degree that he perceived it as a threat and became
aggressively disgruntled. The burdens of the New York/California gaps
of time, space, and manner were something else again, and Albeck was
responsive and surprising.

He announced he felt it inevitable UA would become a California
company, and sooner was better than later. As he saw it, only the
logistical problems and the fact of 729 Seventh Avenue (which UA
owned) prevented the move. The logistics were even then being studied by Robert Schwartz in administration and Orville Dale in personnel, and as far as 729 went, it was quietly on the slow and depressed
New York real estate market. If the building could be sold for the right
price, and the company moved without damage to the lives of employees who had served loyally and well over many years—some of them for
decades—UA would be bicoastal no more.

Albeck's concern for old-line employees somehow validated his concern for Field's anxieties and defused the central construct of the argument. Making long-range plans to move the company to California was
much more than throwing a bone westward, and Field knew it. Albeck
was also too sensitive not to have sensed that the feelings of unrest, if
not dissension, were close to the surface with Field, Stolber, and me,
and he quietly and paternally instructed us to work out our own modus
vivendi over lunch.

We walked west on Forty-ninth Street to Wally's Steak House,
which was becoming the UA commissary, as Vesuvio's had been for the
previous regime at 729. In a spirit of somewhat wary goodwill, we tried
to recapture the feeling of optimism and cooperation we had forged in
October after Rissner's departure. The three of us then had spent a raw
and windy Sunday afternoon on the porch of Stolber's weekend house

in the sand dunes of Amagansett, fighting the chill coming off the cold Atlantic as we thrashed out business policy and warmed ourselves with martinis and hopes for the future.

Similar sentiments of cooperation, warmth, and lofty objectives were renewed at lunch, and we all meant them when we said them. We left Wally's, and walking back to 729 past the Pussycat Theater's sidewalk shill, Field suddenly stopped and stared at the corner of Forty-ninth and Seventh. There a derelict, one of New York's dispossessed possessed, squatted in the street, greasy pant legs rolled above scabby kneecaps, ropy, long hair obscuring features already dimmed by dirt, bloated by drink. He was tapping out rhythms only he heard, with two wooden slats he used like drumsticks against a metal manhole cover. Taxis honked and swerved around him, and he continued tap-tap-tapping from within the peculiar privacy such people inhabit no matter when or where.

"I've always been afraid I'd end up like that," Field said, his voice sepulchral and barely audible. I followed his gaze back to the man in the street and realized that he was, in all probability, Field's age, possibly even younger than David.

"He's the well-known different drummer," I said with a straight face. "Besides, hoboes are good luck."

"Really?" said Stolber. "Who said that?"

"I did," I answered. "Just now." David didn't laugh.

In time to come we were to see the drummer of Forty-ninth Street again, and when we did, one of us would remember David's curious reaction and say "ex-studio exec" as we moved on, but it was a private joke with a built-in shudder.

The three of us arrived back at 729 and went directly to the four-teenth-floor screening room, where *Manhattan* dispelled the drummer and worked its magic on Field and Stolber for the first time, as it did on me for the second. Tracy's "you have to have a little faith in people" had a peculiarly apt ring.

Field and I flew to London on Wednesday, conducted our business on Thursday, and were back in New York on Friday morning, when we heard the first reports out of Montana. They were confused and confusing, but the alarms they set off rang shrilly. Field left for California to learn on Monday that in the first six days of shooting on *Heaven's Gate* Michael Cimino had fallen five days behind. He had shot almost 60,000 feet of film and had approximately a minute and a half of usable material, which had cost roughly $900,000 to expose. Lee Katz's fabled accuracy for once had faltered, though no one as yet could estimate how much beyond $15 million the picture would go at the present rate. That it would exceed that figure seemed certain. All in all, the distance between California and New York seemed suddenly less critical than that between Culver City and Kalispell.

David Field got on a plane.

CHAPTER 13

ROCKY MOUNTAIN HIGH

Nobody really controls a production now; the director is on his own, even if he's insecure, careless or nuts. There has always been a megalomaniac potential in moviemaking, and in this period of stupor, when values have been so thoroughly undermined that even the finest directors and the ones with the most freedom aren't sure what they want to do, they often become obsessive and grandiloquent—like mad royalty. Perpetually dissatisfied with the footage they're compulsively piling up, they keep shooting—adding rooms to the palace. Megalomania and art become the same thing to them. But the disorder isn't just in their heads, and a lot of people around them are deeply impressed by megalomania.

> —Pauline Kael,
> "Why Are Movies So Bad? or,
> The Numbers,"
> *The New Yorker*, June 23, 1980

If you don't get it right, what's the point?

> —Michael Cimino,
> in an ad for Eastman Kodak (1980)

"What do you mean, he doesn't want to talk to you? What kind of bullshit is that?" I said into the telephone. David Field was at the other end of the line, far away.

"He told Joann he doesn't want to talk to anybody from UA. He's pissed off about Lee's budget memo."

"Well, tough. I told Lee to word it as strongly as possible. Where are you?"

"Kalispell. The Outlaw Inn. In something called the Presidential Suite."

"Sounds pretty grand."

"You can have it."

"No, thanks."

"It's just a room, anyway, with a partition that hides the orange bed from the orange couch. I guess Joann thought it would make me feel important. Or orange. Anyway, she and I are going up to the location in a few minutes; but it's two hours away, and I probably won't be able to reach you until tomorrow."

"What time is it there?"

"Almost five. He's waiting for magic hour, twilight, so the light will be perfect."

"When is that?"

"Seven. Eight. I'm not sure. I think it's whenever he says it is."

"Then everybody's on overtime."

"Everybody's on overtime all the time as far as I can tell."

"Then why aren't they getting anything done? . . . What do you mean, 'two hours away'?"

"Two Medicine Lake. Sweetwater. It's two hours away from here."

"Two *hours?*"

"You heard me."

"You mean these guys are spending four hours of an eight-hour day—on *salary*—traveling to and from location?"

"I guess so. Joann says she warned him about the travel time, but he had to have the location. You know, 'the poetry of America'?"

"Yeah. So you're going to talk to him there?"

"I'm going to try."

"What the hell is he doing anyway?"

"I don't know, Steven. I guess he's trying to get it right."

"Call me back."

Field called me back the next day, April 24, from a phone booth in the Spokane, Washington, airport, between planes on the broken route from Kalispell to Los Angeles. We didn't connect. I was in the Rizzoli screening room on Fifth Avenue, trying again to get *Manhattan's* rating reduced to a GP from the R it still carried. Dean Stolber came along to lend moral support and observe the rating board in action.

The hearing began with general remarks addressed to the board by Chairman Heffner, who had been so warmly encouraging the week before. To my amazement, and that of the board members who began to fidget as he spoke, Heffner intoned darkly from the front of the room that he thought the restrictive R rating wholly appropriate and that a lesser, more permissive rating would be a dereliction of the board's moral responsibility.

I was baffled and angry. Stolber and I confronted Heffner in the anteroom of the theater and asked him why he had done such a complete reversal from the attitude he conveyed the week before. He explained, with arch indignation, that because he had no particular obsession about "the 'F' word" (which then triggered an automatic but reversible R), he thought my arguments made sense, and as an admirer of Woody Allen, he was prepared to recommend board leniency, particularly in light of the reviews, which I had served up copiously during the previous hearing. In the meantime, however, he had actually seen the picture and discovered to his shock and discomfort that it concerned in part a romantic and sexual relationship between a forty-two-year-old man (Woody) and a seventeen-year-old girl, still attending Manhattan's swank Dalton School (Mariel Hemingway). That was it.

The board came in with its vote, exactly reversed from one week before: a two-thirds majority (minus one) voted to retain the R. If the rating hurt business, as we feared, no one will ever know. *Manhattan* was an instant success and became the biggest-grossing picture of Woody's career, cracking open his $20 million ceiling and the borders to mid-America. But if that one necessary vote had been delivered at the first appeal, *Manhattan* would have received its GP without the rating board chairman's ever having seen the picture.

Field called again when he reached Los Angeles, late in the day. "Did you see him?" I asked.

"Yeah."

"What did he say?"

"Nothing. To me anyway. He said quite a lot to some Montana Amazon, but nothing to me."

"What Amazon? What are you talking about?"

"Joann and I got to the location, which is spectacular and poetic and worth the two-hour drive, and everybody is very, very happy—"

"Why wouldn't they be? They're all on double time."

"—and when shooting ended, I walked over to intercept Michael at his trailer, and he walked right by me with this Amazon lady that Joann

said was his masseuse without saying one word. They went into his
trailer and closed the door in my face."

"And?"

"And . . . I sat on a cold rock. It gets cold up there at night,
Steven, and I sat on a cold rock for an hour and a half."

"An hour and a half massage?"

"Why do I have the terrible feeling we paid for it?"

"So what happened?"

"He finally came out of the trailer, looked right through me, got
into a production car, and one of the drivers took him back to Kalispell."

"I hope you realize how outrageous this behavior is, David."

"Doesn't suggest a whole lot of respect, does it?"

Pause.

"David, we are in terrible trouble."

It is not unusual—it may even be routine—for a picture to experience difficulties in the early days of shooting, particularly when the
work is on location. If the picture is a big one and the conditions are in
any way primitive, these problems can grow geometrically or exponen-
tially. They don't have to, but they often do. Cast and crew are
brought together, sometimes from distant parts of the world, many
never having worked together before, some never having met before,
none having worked in the configuration presented by the particular
picture.

Every picture is different from every other picture and has its own
unknowns, its own problems, requiring solutions often unique, often
without precedent for those who are expected to deliver considerable
ingenuity on critically short notice. One of the true glories of the contemporary American movie business is how often and well movie professionals meet such challenges. Accordingly, if experience in the
movie business teaches anything, it is that it doesn't teach *everything*.

Unlike the theater, in which the technical and artistic personnel
have weeks or months to work up to production polish, often rewriting,
restaging, refining their work, a movie begins at once, whenever all
those necessary for the first day of shooting are assembled and the camera is up to speed. The popular notion of the leading man and leading
woman performing a love scene for an audience of technicians and
blasé bystanders immediately after being introduced may be exaggerated—but not much. The first day's shooting on any movie, rehearsal
usually limited to a few minutes' run-through before the cameras turn,
must not be less polished and perfect than shooting on the last day,

when work habits, idiosyncrasies, and other variables are well known, and each has adjusted, happily or not, to each. In today's movie business you get it right right now, or you don't get it right at all.

It was not always so. Hollywood lore is full of anecdotes about Irving Thalberg or some other such mogul's previewing, say, the latest Garbo in Pasadena on a Friday or Saturday night and, finding it wanting, ordering rewrites on Sunday and retakes on Monday, seeing new dailies on Tuesday, ordering the recut on Wednesday, and on Thursday or Friday screening a substantially new version of the picture for another preview on Saturday night, this time in Pacoima.

Something very like that actually happened. Everyone involved was under contract anyway; the equipment, facilities, sets, and costumes were there to be deployed at the mogul's command, and it was a simple enough matter—and cheap enough, too—to reassemble everyone and everything for what might be a minor maneuver or a major assault on a film that didn't play well in previews and looked doubtful for Peoria.

Today—when almost no one is under contract and no one, except the conglomerates, owns much of anything, and all they own is stock—the wrap party at the end of shooting is followed by a general diaspora as people go back home or on to other jobs, and reassembling the ensemble (particularly if location work has been involved and must be faked or returned to) is virtually impossible. In the rare instances in which it may be possible, it is almost always prohibitively expensive, except under very special "repertory" situations like Woody Allen's or, perhaps, Robert Altman's. *

This is not merely a matter of ascertaining that the leading lady is audible or that the mike boom has not given her a shadow for a mustache. Such technical problems can be maddening and time-consuming enough, but they are either noted on the spot or quickly thereafter in dailies. Technical perfection is difficult enough to obtain (and is made harder, not easier, by the increased sophistication of motion-picture hardware), but it is attainable, within technology's limits. The larger, more vital narrative and dramatic questions—pace, rhythm, clarity, empathy, meaning, and so on—all may have seemed neatly solved on paper but are inadequate or in some other way an unpleasant surprise on the screen. If William Goldman's memorable dictum about the movie business—"Nobody knows anything"—is correct, the days of Thalberg's *not* making movies but, as wags of the time had it, remaking them may suggest that nobody ever did—for sure. To put it another

---

* Though Allen, as already noted, builds provision for such second chances into his initial budgets.

way, in one of the industry's favorite lines of self-definition, it's not an exact science. It is, however, an exacting and increasingly sophisticated one, which new techniques and technologies have made more so. They demand increasingly complex finishing processes, which require major periods of time—and therefore major money—for their completion. Sound recording, to take the most obvious example, may have improved to the point of preserving the faintest, most expressive whisper of the leading lady in voluptuously Dolbyized fidelity, but it will also mercilessly preserve the script girl's rustling of a page, a gaffer's footfall, the anxious churning of a producer's queasy stomach.

When Thalberg was king—or czar or mogul or whatever monarch he was—a kind of economy of storytelling and visualization was not only the hallmark of the movie as "art", but often also a point of honor. There is a moment, for instance, in Josef von Sternberg's *The Scarlet Empress* starring Dietrich as Catherine the Great, in which Von Sternberg cuts from the royal bedroom to a throng of thousands outside the palace, all Russia rejoicing in the randy goings-on within. The crowd shot was lifted by Von Sternberg from an early silent film made in Germany by Ernst Lubitsch before he came to Hollywood (*The Patriot* it was called), where he was currently head of production at Paramount, where Dietrich Trilbyed and Von Sternberg Svengalied. Von Sternberg simply cut the borrowed footage in at the appropriate spot, added some bell and crowd sounds, and no one in 1934 could tell the difference. Including Lubitsch, who—no fan of Von Sternberg—cited his own footage as evidence of Von Sternberg's extravagance and profligacy.*

Closer to the present period are the many accounts of Darryl Zanuck's rescuing indifferent films in the editing rooms of Twentieth Century-Fox. Too many knowledgeable observers recount these feats of executive prowess for us to doubt them, but it should be remembered that Zanuck also had the power to insist on rewriting (often by himself) and reshooting in a movie business that does not exist anymore, neither for executives nor for filmmakers.

None of it is possible today, logistically or economically. One of movies' great advantages over the theater—permanence—can also be a curse. Film is both permanent and immutable. What is shot in January will be the same in July; that gesture, that glance, that hip swing—like it or not—will not improve with time or repeated performances because

*Or so Von Sternberg told me. He may have been as imperious and arrogant as Lubitsch thought him, but he was proud of his ingenuity and the economics of his creativity.

there won't be any. What is put on film must be as right as it can be the first time it is put on film.

What one can do, of course, is retakes on the spot. And more retakes. And still more. Retakes use up film quickly, to be sure, but film stock is one of the negligible costs of film production. What retakes really use is time, which, as everyone knows (and no one better than movie people), is money.

It is true, as later press reports informed, that Michael Cimino was building sets and rebuilding them, hiring 100 extras, then 200, then 500, adding horses and wagons and hats, shoes, gloves, dresses, top hats, bridles, boots, roller skates, babushkas, aprons, dusters, buckboards, gun belts, rifles, bullets, cows, calves, bulls, trees, thousands of tons of dirt, hundreds of miles of exposed film, and all this mattered economically. But what mattered most was that what he was adding was takes and retakes and retakes of the retakes. And retakes of those. Michael Cimino was taking—and retaking—*time*. Getting it right.

Field ultimately persuaded Cimino to sit down and talk it over. Cimino claimed he felt wounded and harassed by Lee Katz's attitude and by UA's failure to understand and appreciate the difficulties inherent in the shakedown period of this very complicated movie. He expressed regret at the slowness of the start of production and asserted that the daily pace would shortly quicken, thus putting an end, he hoped, to what he interpreted as an unseemly panic emanating from Culver City.

But week number two drew to a close no better than that of week number one. Another 60,000 feet of film had been shot to capture less than five-eighths of a script page per day, while the schedule promised two pages per day, and after twelve days the production was ten days and fifteen pages behind.

On April 27 Albeck, Stolber, and I conducted a telephone meeting with David Field in California to discuss UA's options.

There were at that moment three. The first was the *Cleopatra* option: Let the production run its course and hope for the best. The second was the *Apocalypse* option: Try to control and contain it and thus minimize the overages. The third was the *Queen Kelly* option, so named for the 1928 Erich von Stroheim-Gloria Swanson disaster, which was never finished because its financier (Miss Swanson's lover and a presidential father-to-be) Joseph P. Kennedy pulled the plug. *

---

* At a cost of 800,000 irretrievable dollars, though some footage from the project can be seen in *Sunset Boulevard*, as Swanson's Norma Desmond unreels her glory days for William Holden's Joe Gillis. The projectionist, of course, was Max, the butler, played by Von Stroheim.

The *Cleopatra* option was unacceptable to everyone. It called up shades of *The Greatest Story Ever Told* to Albeck and was, to his orderly and conscientious mind, a decision that would represent a gross breach of faith with Transamerica and a betrayal of his personal standards and pride in efficiency. Nor was it an acceptable option to Field, who, though he was feeling bullied by Cimino and was in a situation he had never faced before (none of us had), knew that at the very best it was no way to win Cimino's respect and that at the worst a picture allowed to run away from his control could do him no good with San Francisco, or with much of Hollywood either.

I, too, rejected the option. Over the preproduction period, Field and I had so reassuringly and confidently recommended expansion of the project on the grounds of our faith and trust in Michael that to reverse ourselves now would have meant admitting the immensity of our naïveté—to ourselves as well as to Albeck. We had simply been disastrously wrong in encouraging the picture's expansion when we agreed with Cimino, and unconscionably so when we didn't and just "went along," as in the case of Huppert.

The *Apocalypse* option sounded sensible, though in many ways inapplicable. When Lee Katz helped Coppola reorganize the production of *Apocalypse Now*, the picture had been shooting for many months and had suffered disasters both natural and otherwise. *Apocalypse* was a production in disarray and near collapse, but United Artists' financial liability was limited. True, the company continued to finance the picture (and was doing so even as this option was being discussed), but the moneys were collateralized, however insufficient the collateralization might have proved. And now, in late April, Coppola had finally—or almost—finished the picture, which was impressive, if imperfect. Out of chaos triumph, maybe.

But *Heaven's Gate*, as far as Field or Charlie Okun or Joann Carelli or even Lee Katz could tell, was not a picture in disarray. The technicians and department heads all were first-rate acknowledged masters of their several crafts. They were not so much behind schedule as *off* schedule because of the often changing demands or expanding conceits and concepts of the director. No acts of God were disrupting anything; the only disaster, natural or otherwise, was the schedule.

The *Apocalypse* option thus seemed paradoxically too broad and too limited. Acts of God—typhoons, heart attacks—are not arguable. They simply *are*. They do not require causal analysis or nitpicking assignment of blame. One can go about the business of salvage in a way proportionate to the damage.

Making a director work faster than he wants to is like watching a pot boil or paint dry. If saying, "Hurry up, Michael"—or Steven or Francis or John or Billy or Francis or David or Stanley or Warren or Francis or whoever—actually had any effect, *1941, Apocalypse, Honky Tonk Freeway, The Sorcerer, One from the Heart, Ryan's Daughter, The Shining, Reds, Cotton Club,* and many others before, during, and since would have happened differently. They didn't, though, and there was little confidence that such a simple, self-evidently sensible solution would have much force, moral or otherwise, on *Heaven's Gate.*

The *Queen Kelly* option was most difficult to discuss because mere mention of it seemed to curse the project. But it was discussed, in numbers less hard than one would have liked. By the start of production UA had spent $3,026,690.22, which did not include the pay-or-play commitments of almost $2 million, or all the commitments made to a permanent crew numbering 118, a cast of 70, hundreds of extras, rentals of land that had been agreed to (not least with the Blackfoot Indians and the National Park Service), and the hundreds of other commitments large and small that had been made in UA's name. We could do no more than estimate what the cost of pulling the plug would be even if we had the hard information we lacked partly because some of those commitments could probably have been retired at less than full value, though which ones and at what costs we did not know. Secondly, because UA was never a studio and lacked a studio's conventional departmental structures, through which typically every expenditure would require an approved purchase order and would be instantly communicated to an electronic accounting system, costs were mounting simply on the say-so of the producer or the director, and cost reports were chronically tardy in arriving from the location, even though UA had its own accountants in the business office in Kalispell. The most sophisticated computerized systems, for all their speed and efficiency, can also be behind because of the near universal habit of late billing and because of purchases made out of petty cash (not necessarily so petty: Thousands of dollars are not unusual). Moreover, as every executive knows, it is not unheard of for a producer or director to commit to something in the company's name and to withhold that information and the accompanying request for funds until a propitious moment—i.e., when it's too late to do anything but pay the bill or be sued. Finally, cost accounting necessarily lags behind cost incurring, and time, the most critical cost factor of all, requires no purchase order anywhere.

The idea of abandoning the picture was anathema to Albeck, but he was grimly prepared to do it if Field and I were to recommend that extreme action. He might even have done it if Field alone had recommended that course. Neither of us did. Nor did Dean Stolber.

We asked Dean, who had the most daily contact with the numbers, if he could estimate the cost of abandonment. He could only guess but thought the cost would be—that afternoon—somewhere close to $8 million. He based this guess on the $3 million we knew we had spent before shooting started, plus paying out the big pay or plays at another $2 million (though virtually all contracts had become in essence pay or play with the start of production, down to and including the one-day bit players and the horses), perhaps $1.5 already expended on actual production, bringing it to $6.5 million, plus another $1.5 million UA might have to pay for other canceled contracts and commitments. (As it happened, the estimate was low. The costs to date for the week ending the next day totaled just short of $5 million—$4,922,840.40, to be exact—but were not reported officially until May 7. This was nearly half a million dollars more than Stolber's guess and approaching one-half the total approved budget of $11.6 million).

At the time this analysis was made, $10 million was regarded as normal for one of Albeck's high-budget locomotives. *Cuba* with Sean Connery had cost $8 million. *Manhattan* cost only a little more than that. *Rich Kids*, in contrast, cost $2.6 million, *Head over Heels* (or *Chilly Scenes of Winter*) cost $2.2 million. Therefore, $8 million was the cost of a medium-high budget picture (or three or four small ones), and abandonment would mean abandoning also any hope of recouping a single penny of that cost (unless something could have been sold for stock footage), plus the embarrassment of an uninformed press outcry over UA's treatment of a director just installed in the pantheon.

Albeck asked for our recommendations. He got them and accepted them. We all opted for containment, the *Apocalypse* model, though without any very clear idea of how to bring containment about. "Hurry up, Michael," was unlikely to work but was the sole solution that would have the desired effect.

There was, of course, a fourth option, and a fifth, and we were to get to them in time, but for the moment there was a company to run. *Heaven's Gate*, even at $15 or $20 million, represented only a percentage of UA's total production outlays in 1979, and the other 80 or 85 percent deserved attention, too.

UA's other important project (and Field's) was *Raging Bull*, shooting at the same time from the approved "RdN" script and also falling behind schedule, though at a much less exaggerated rate. A new *Pink Panther* (for which I was responsible) was being written by Peter Sellers (with Jim Moloney), hostilities between him and Blake Edwards resolved by UA's buying Edwards out of the picture on the assumption that Sellers, not Edwards, was the star. It was to be directed by Clive Donner and produced by Danny Rissner, even though Sellers had recently announced he would never speak to Rissner again as long as he lived, and he didn't. Sellers was making a Fu Manchu picture for Orion at the same time he was writing *The Romance of the Pink Panther*, in which Inspector Clouseau was to fall helplessly in love with a beautiful Parisienne known to the underworld as "The Frog" ("ze Fruuuuuuug," Sellers's Clouseau pronounced it), who is the mistress-criminal after whom he is unwittingly sleuthing in his love-blinded bumbles and stumbles.

The Dogs of War was going into a new rewrite for Norman Jewison to produce but not to direct; *Eye of the Needle* was looking for a star; and Robert Benton was preparing a thriller, his first picture since the phenomenally successful *Kramer vs. Kramer*, which he was calling alternately *Terror* or *Stab*.

The sluice gates had finally sprung open in submissions, and the volume of work surged. When Field and I were attending to administrative duties or overseeing pictures of which we were in charge, or traveling, or attending corporate meetings, Jerry Paonessa, Claire Townsend, and Richard Parks were finding and developing projects of their own, meeting with scores of filmmakers, writers, agents each week, and making or returning the hundreds of telephone calls that are the typical weekly burden of any active production department.

Claire had brought in a project called *Quest for Fire*, a risky original film about prehistoric man she was unable to persuade the rest of us had commercial possibilities.* As an odd and coincidental consolation she found, and we liked, her *Caveman* project, a cheerful, silly comedy which was virtually a parody version of *Quest for Fire*. Claire was aggressive and smart and got around. She also had some entrée to and affinity for the ever more important younger audiences. Some of her projects worked, some didn't, but they were quick in coming, often original, and she was an increasingly visible presence to the younger Hollywood filmmakers and to other studios, which frequently tried to lure her away.

Paonessa continued to work on his projects with James Kirkwood, David Rabe, and others. He displayed a sensitive story mind and personable manner in pitch meetings, so called because someone (anyone)

* It was later made by Twentieth Century-Fox, and it didn't.

comes in to pitch an idea. Though the latitude Paonessa was allowed was narrow, his abilities were not.

Richard Parks continued to do the same (similarly restricted) in New York as well as to supervise the New York story department and story editor Kathy Van Brunt, who shared a literary agency background with Parks and had some experience in publishing. The latter enabled her to become the purloiner par excellence of unpublished manuscripts in New York. Her success in this controversial activity was the source of smug pride at UA and not incidentally added reams of paper to the weekly work load.

About this time Parks somewhat apologetically handed me an appallingly overlong first-draft screenplay by a new writer who was working in the news department at CBS. "It has something," Parks said, adding, "I don't know *what.*" I read it. It was overlong, clumsy, and often amateurish, but *Iceman*'s depth of feeling for its main character, a prehistoric being retrieved from his icebound grave and brought back to life by modern science, was genuine and moving. I asked Parks to negotiate a minimum deal for the material and sit on it because I had a hunch it was something for Norman Jewison. He did, and it was, and we shall return to it.

True Confessions by John Gregory Dunne (from his novel) and his wife, Joan Didion, was developing, as were discussions that the Didion-Dunnes (as we called them) might script a remake of *Mildred Pierce* for Chartoff and Winkler to produce. A Bette Midler project was on again, off again. A rock 'n' roll picture called *The Idolmaker* was being prepared by a new director named Taylor Hackford. There was a western from Walter Hill, called *The Long Riders*, which turned on the stunt casting of brothers playing brothers: Stacy and James Keach as Frank and Jesse James; the Carradine brothers, David, Keith, and Robert, as the Younger brothers; Randy and Dennis Quaid as the Millers; and the lesser-known Guest brothers playing the Ford boys, one of whom killed Jesse James and wrote a famous book about it. *House of God*, the comedy about medical residency in Boston, was gearing for production in Boston and Philadelphia. *Corky*, the thriller starring Talia Shire which Field had brought with him from Fox, was being made by Gordon Willis under the new title *Windows*. Another Field-Fox project had undergone a title change from *Ladies of the Valley* to *Foxes* and starred Jody Foster before she went to Yale and John Hinckley made her name famous in a sadder, more bizarre way.

There were fifty projects in some stage of development, requiring supervision from the occasional to the constant; submissions ranging from 50 to 100 a week; meetings; calls to be made and answered; books, scripts, budgets, production reports to be read and analyzed; travel; and Cannes.

The Cannes Film Festival, held each May on the Riviera, is the most famous and frenzied of the international festivals and one at which United Artists traditionally cut a very high profile. Over the years UA's foreign distribution and publicity machinery had dominated Cannes's Carlton Hotel, which in turn dominates the event. There the low-lying west wing of the hotel was surmounted by UA's imposing rotating carousel, bearing illuminated billboards selling the current product. The portico of the Carlton was annually preempted by .007, so that no guest, journalist, exhibitor, or limousine could approach the hotel without passing under James Bond and his latest inamorata, this year Lois Chiles from *Moonraker*.

Inside the Carlton, Norbert Auerbach—known around UA as the king of Cannes—had taken up residence in a regal two-bedroom corner suite full of champagne and flowers, overlooking the Mediterranean and the palm-lined Croisette, which is all that separates the Carlton from the beach and the sea. It would be jammed for the next two weeks with gawking tourists, film flacks, journalists, producers, directors, would-bes and has-beens, hustlers of every conceivable stripe, exhibitors and exhibitionists, too—starlets, seeking ever more novel ways of stripping for the gangs of *paparazzi* who prowl the festival (and the beaches) night and day.

Auerbach was a pussycat; everyone said so, and the truth of the remark could be judged by the purrs he bestowed on his loyal staff when things were right. His catbird seat of the moment was a silk-striped French settee, from which he could glance out past his whiskers and the Dom Perignon and the gladiolus in crystal vases toward the beach, where, say, Edie Williams might be removing her clothes in her annual madcap fashion while perched on the roof of a Mercedes limousine, as Leicas and Nikons lecherously snapped away. Auerbach was too blasé to be impressed by Ms. Williams's oft-exposed charms, * although he frankly relished the tacky glamour and publicity and beautiful girls and parties of Cannes. He fairly twinkled at festival time, exuding practiced charm in English, French, German, and Czech, often to a lovely woman on his arm, who often was Mrs. Auerbach or one of the previous Mrs. Auerbachs. His obedient staff waltzed attendance, basking in the glow of his eminence and self-esteem.

* The joke along the Croisette that year (Hy Smith's) was: "Did you hear what happened? Edie Williams got on the hood of a Rolls and put her clothes back *on!*"

No doubt part of this splendid living was Sara and Gerald Murphy's "best revenge," for the "king of Cannes" had once been sacked by the very company for which he now served as a senior vice-president. Not sacked, exactly, as Auerbach was fond of relating. Eric Pleskow had merely told him with Viennese charm that "we'd like to try it without you for a while." The "while" was over; he was back now, and in style. As suited the head of the largest international distribution network in the world, the style was imperial, vaguely Austro-Hungarian in tone. All that was missing, mused Hy Smith, head of worldwide ad-pub, were the Lippizaners, but the green Mercedes limo would have to do, as Auerbach worked out possible agendas and permutations thereto in his purring pussycat fashion.

Into this pomp and circumstance Field and I were unceremoniously plunked into single rooms at the back of the hotel, overlooking the same garage Mankiewicz and I had overlooked the year before. This was my second official trip to Cannes, and Field's first, and we wouldn't have been there at all except that UA had several pictures in and out of competition for the festival's prizes: *Hair, Manhattan, The Tin Drum,* and the interloper UA had tried and failed to keep out of Cannes altogether, *Apocalypse Now.*

UA's legal rights in *Apocalypse* were limited to domestic. Coppola could do whatever he wanted with the picture elsewhere. The American release was scheduled for August, and because the movie was not quite finished, UA wanted to keep it out of Cannes and away from the world press and had no legal right to do so.

Coppola was either so confident he had a blockbuster or so hellbent on going for broke that he insisted on entering his "work in progress," as he called it, even though doing so could boomerang, as had his screening of an earlier version two years before. It was, in a sense, the most public sneak preview in the history of motion pictures. In attendance was virtually the entire world movie press, including many of the most important American critics, and whatever its fate, it would be flashed around the world in minutes.

UA also didn't want *Apocalypse* competing with its other festival entries before an always unpredictable jury, often highly political in its point of view or chaotically scrambled in its makeup. This year's jury promised to be more unpredictable than many, as jury Chairwoman Françoise Sagan announced to the press that she had not set foot in a movie theater in more than a decade, and the great Indian filmmaker Satyajit Ray sent his regrets when he discovered the festival had provided him with a tourist-class air ticket, instead of the first-class he required.

• • •

En route to Cannes Field and I arrived separately at the Dorchester Hotel in London on Saturday, May 6. Sunday morning Field called before we were to meet in his suite with David Puttnam, the British producer with whom we had discussed *Red Star over China* and who had produced *Foxes*. Field sounded agitated and whispery and asked me not to show surprise when I got to his rooms and found he was not traveling alone. Without explaining he hung up. *Why the big mystery?* I thought. *Who could it be? Arthur Krim?*

When I arrived at his suite, Field was wearing the handsome cowboy boots Cimino and Carelli had presented to him as a start-of-production gift. The mysterious stranger was not immediately apparent because the living room was crowded: Puttnam was there; so was his wife, Patsy; so was a youngish director called Hugh Hudson. The latter, who had never directed a feature film, was there to discuss the picture he and Puttnam wanted UA to finance, *Chariots of Fire*. Then, emerging from another room, came a tall blond lily who held herself like (and was) a model. She glowed from within and had the kind of silky hair that shimmers when it swings in the television commercials. Her name was Cathy Shirriff, and she had just finished a bit part in Bob Fosse's *All That Jazz* and had met Field only a few days before in California. She was not only beautiful but funny and charming as well, and as we discussed *Chariots of Fire*, which we liked and correctly predicted we would not be able to sell to distribution, it was clear to everyone in the room that the Dorchester Hotel was up to its Oliver Messel Suite in that old black magic.

The three of us were together often in London and later in Cannes. David's and Cathy's pleasure with each other was apparent to everyone they came in contact with, which included *Hair*'s producer and star, Lester Persky and Treat Williams, Charlie Joffe, Jack Hemingway, his daughter Mariel, Saul Zaentz and his wife, Linda, and the Zoetrope staff present for installation of the tricky sound system for *Apocalypse*.

Also present in Cannes was the Orion group, headed by Arthur Krim, Eric Pleskow, and Mike Medavoy. In keeping with the pledge Field and I had exchanged, he told me Medavoy had asked him to meet with them at the Carlton to discuss his coming to Orion.

"I think they're trying to dismantle the company." He shrugged as we shared a drink after his meeting. "From outside. I think Norbert is trying to do it from inside."

"Is that a non sequitur, or what?"

"Norbert's not your biggest fan, Steven. He had a little talk with me—Cathy was there, you can ask her—about my future and UA's—"

"And he thinks you'd make a better head of production without me than with me?" I interrupted.

"Something like that."

"Something a lot like that," Cathy echoed.

"He made the same speech to me a year ago, about Danny. It's called 'divide and conquer.'"

"It's long division, then, because I think he'd like to see Fitter out of domestic, and I'm not sure he thinks Farber is such great shakes. I'm not too sure how he feels about *Andy*."

"Yes, you are. He's openly patronizing to him. Almost contemptuous. You think Andy doesn't know?"

"I think Andy knows. All the same, Steven, I'd watch out."

What I watched, along with everyone else, was David and Cathy growing more radiant every day. The hundreds of photographers lining the way from the Carlton to the Palais du Festival, where nightly screenings were held, had better-known faces to photograph—Jack Lemmon, Sally Field, Mariel Hemingway, Francis Coppola—but they, too, were drawn to this tall, tanned couple, he in tuxedo and she in an elegant black slink of a gown.

"Why do I keep hearing strains from *Lohengrin?*" Lester Persky sighed wistfully. We all did—or would soon. And in any summer but the summer of *Heaven's Gate* they might have lived happily ever after.

The two weeks at Cannes were interrupted for flights back to New York and California to pursue normal business. I flew back again on May 17 to attend the press conference and screening of *Apocalypse*, an event Coppola was promising would be "audacious." It was.

Francis faced 1,100 reporters and journalists lying in wait in the Palais du Festival, where one could almost see 2,200 nostrils quiver as they sniffed for blood. Francis stared them down for a moment, a big, bearded bear wearing a panama hat. The bear growled. He snarled and gnarled and growled again. The nostrils stopped quivering. They may even have stopped inhaling, and ulcers bloomed in the duodenal walls of the UA executives present in the *grande salle*. Then the bear in the panama hat began to speak.

He told them the press had spent four years indulging in irresponsible and malicious gossipmongering over production problems as taxing as any director had ever faced before. He told them they knew nothing about moviemaking anyway, which may have explained their irresponsibility, their gloating, their cannibalizing of misinformation from each other ever since he began his movie. He told them their opinions were of little or no value, based as they were on ignorance without the mitigating grace of innocence, that whatever slings and arrows they were now preparing to hurl at his weary but indomitable frame would have no effect because he rejected them, their opinions, their very function. Only one thing mattered, only one thing would remain, his movie, the objective quality of which he expected them neither to praise nor to perceive, and it mattered not at all that his entire future, personal and professional, was riding on it. Or words to that effect.

They loved it. They scribbled frantically and vainly to record the exact words of their own dressing down, words uttered in a tone that suggested they came not from behind Francis's bushy beard but from a burning bush. It was a master blast, and the press's enthusiasm was such that had they carried him from the *salle* on their shoulders in a rain of roses, I would not have been the least surprised. Or unstirred.

Coppola is not just a great self-promoter; he is a genuinely articulate and infectiously exciting speaker, at a dinner table or on a dais. His bearing has an imposing authority, and the excitement he communicates about anything—his own work, that of someone he admires, the future he dreams of with the vivid clarity of the true visionary—seems to enter the listener directly. He should have called his next movie *One to the Heart*; from Francis's mouth direct to the adrenal glands. Lionel Trilling once observed the gulf between "sincerity," which many film people have and communicate handily, and "authenticity," which is something of a different order. Coppola communicates authenticity in good times and in times of disaster, and he is familiar with both. This was one of the good times.

Apocalypse became the hot ticket in Cannes. UA needn't have worried about a boomerang effect. The "work in progress" walked off with the festival's top prize, le Palme d'Or, the glory dimmed only slightly by having to share it with UA's German entry, Volker Schlöndorff's *The Tin Drum*. It was the first time in the history of the festival that one company split the prize. UA seemingly couldn't lose, at home or abroad, and the Dom Pérignon flowed as only Dom Pérignon can, at the Carlton.

Francis, however, was uncorking the Chianti. He had taken over a small Italian restaurant halfway up a hill in the workaday western end of Cannes, away from the Croisette and all the tack. It was just Francis and his wife and kids and the people from Zoetrope. Francis's colleague Tom Sternberg led the way through the narrow streets up to the restaurant. There we sat with the bearded director and drank red wine and talked and listened and commiserated and congratulated, and when the celebratory mood finally struck, it did so literally. A Chianti bottle flew from one corner of the little restaurant to another, crashing against a

wall. Someone let out a whoop of release, a signal that the frustrations
and uncertainties of four years' work were over. Another bottle followed the first, then another, then the glasses. The restaurant floor was
a sea of wine and shards of glass, a red sea one expected for a moment
Francis might try to part. He didn't; he joined in the celebration as
glass followed glass.

It seemed a good time to slip away. This was, after all, a family
celebration, and I was not part of the family.

I walked back along the Croisette (perhaps leaving a trail of Chianti
footprints) back to the land of champagne and, it developed, even
more. As I approached the Carlton, someone I knew from Hollywood
grabbed my arm and asked if he could borrow $100 to make a cocaine
hit. I gave it to him, and the next day he gave me a personal check to
cover the debt. I meant to cash the check but never did. It makes a
handy bookmark, a curious memento.

Michael Cimino did not hurry up.

By the end of May it was clear that any idea of a Christmas release
was hopeless, though UA's legal position with regard to penalizing the
production for its skyrocketing overbudget was unclear to the point of
opacity. The budget had never been signed by Cimino or Carelli—
though it was their own document—and the legal department went
into huddles that made more tortuous and convoluted an already tan-
gled contractual relationship between the production and the corporation.

Shooting continued to fall behind at a rate of nearly one day lost for
each day shot. Costs escalated as cast and crew were placed on call and
on overtime in an announced attempt by Cimino to recover lost time
and preserve the Christmas date or something very like it. This exacerbated the situation. Work, in obedience to Parkinson's law, expanded
to fill the available overtime with increasingly painstaking perfectionism, and crew members, who found themselves on call ten, twelve,
eighteen hours a day seven days a week, were catching up not on lost
time but on lost sleep, their reading, their letter writing back home.
That they were being paid their normal rates, plus double time, plus
triple time on Sundays made relaxing at the Outlaw Inn or in the physical splendors of Cimino's "cathedral" an altogether pleasant experience
for many, and for the predictable few, not all the highs were coming
from contemplation of the big sky.

Thousands of feet of film, then tens of thousands, then hundreds of
thousands of feet of film were running through the cameras, recording
and rerecording images until they were as perfect as technique, pa-

tience, and money could make them. There was no chaos; there was its opposite: a calm, determined, relentless pursuit of the perfect.

However devoutly desired a goal perfection may have been, putting an end to what looked like arrogant self-indulgence seemed more to the point. It made no sense to send David Field on yet another fruitless journey to Montana to reason with the determining factor. Nor would it have made sense for Field to move physically to Kalispell and, stopwatch in hand, attempt to pace the production. He did not have the production experience to do so and had other, equally important matters pressing him in California. Lee Katz had retired to the briar patch of banishment to which Cimino had consigned him, reviewing the figures that mounted daily without saying, "I told you so," which was polite but did not hasten the process. Sending someone to supervise, report back, and quicken production was essential. The logical, perhaps the only choice was a UA newcomer, as calmly eager to prove his production expertise as Cimino was calmly adamant about maintaining a pace that was costing in excess of $1 million a week with no clear end in sight.

Derek Kavanagh was shipped to Montana. He unperturbedly examined the daily camera reports, the daily production reports, the daily average footage and page counts and screen time shot, as well as the cash flow charts and the accounts paid and owing, and predicted a clear end: If Cimino continued shooting at the present rate, UA's Christmas 1979 release would not complete shooting before January 3, 1980, a date which did not take into account the annual closing of the roads in that part of Montana in mid-October.

Cimino was shooting a daily average of 10,000 feet of film (slightly under two hours' worth) to cover a daily five-eighths of a script page, resulting in a daily minute and a half or so of usable screen material, and was spending nearly $200,000 a day to do so. Kavanagh pointed out that in spite of all the discussions of "shakedown period" and "catching up on time," these figures had varied hardly at all from the first day of production through May, and now into June, on the twenty-second of which Cimino's original schedule had predicted an end to principal photography.

Andy Albeck was a study in concentration. He seemed not at all to notice the small brown leaves that continued to fall to the plush wool carpet from the *Ficus benjamina* in his office at 729. The object of his intentness was the figure $10 million looming up at him from a cost report lying on his oak and granite desk. *Heaven's Gate* had already spent by June 1 the alarming figure he scrutinized, and the director still

had 107 ⅛ pages of a 133-page script left to shoot. The payroll bill for
the first week of June was neatly typed out: $607,356.76. This amount
included payments to 1 director, 1 star, 68 supporting players, 177 crew
members in Montana, 153 crew members in Idaho, 147 crew members
imported from Los Angeles, and 57 extras. Above and beyond these
costs for more than 600 people were the fringe benefits, housing, food,
and the cost of actually making the picture. * If Kavanagh's report was
correct, Albeck thought, as he quickly jotted figures on a yellow pad,
there remained an additional twenty-nine weeks until January, which,
at the rate of $1.1 million per week, would add $31.9 million to the
$10 million already spent—not including interest in the upper teens;
not including postproduction work, which Kavanagh was now estima-
ting as at least $1.5 million because of the amount of film exposed and
printed daily; not including any of the costs of release prints, advertising, or publicity. In other words, Albeck calculated, he was facing a
possible direct production cost of $43.4 million, almost 600 percent of
what this director had said the picture would cost back in September.
What with interest costs and releasing costs, this $7.5 million western
was going to cost him $50 million! Talent was talent and to be prized,
but this was profligacy, which was to be abhorred and squelched. *Now!*

On June 6 David Field and I arrived in Kalispell together. There
was little, if anything, Field had not said more than once to Cimino
that was likely to be more effective if uttered yet again by two voices,
but it was deemed perhaps stronger evidence that laissez-faire was *not*
the order of the day if two bodies, one of them from New York, were to
confront him in reiterating that news. I had consented readily to the
trip (though I dreaded it) because I felt now we had been guilty of
compounding ruinous advice in recommending the *Apocalypse* option
instead of the more painful but more definitive *Queen Kelly* yank. Un-
questionably $8 million was an enormous investment to abandon, but
$50 million was gargantuan. It was not merely that the figure repre-
sented half of 1979's total production budget but that in consequence,
other pictures would not be made, their financing diverted instead to
Montana; distribution would, as a further consequence, have fewer pictures to distribute in 1980 and 1981; and finally, UA's overall odds at
the box office would be dramatically reduced with fewer dice to roll.
Heaven's Gate could consume the company.

Somehow, after Cannes, the inappropriateness of the *Apocalypse*

---

* Such figures varied constantly. The week ending July 7, 1979, had a payroll of
$765,151.21 for 1,139 employees, for example.

model had become clearer. Francis had responded to pressure not merely as an artist but because his own property as well as his career was at stake. He had had failures before and knew he might again. These anxieties had brought *Apocalypse Now* to completion and Francis to his senses. Not only did Cimino have no property invested, but his profit participation in *Heaven's Gate* seemed inviolate because of the "no penalties" Christmas release clause, which had never been binding on him, but perhaps was on UA, even though it was now meaningless. Cimino had not yet been humbled by critics or audiences; he had no *Finian's Rainbow* or *Rain People* on his résumé, and if his certitude that he was making a picture to rank with *The Birth of a Nation* was an act, it was fooling a lot of people, including Field and me. Cimino's confidence was monumental enough that it had succeeded so far in numbing an entire corporation.

Beyond the budget and schedule was the other, more important question, constantly asked in New York and Culver City. Answering that question was purpose enough for this trip to remote Kalispell. *Is the picture any good?* A lousy picture at $5 million was no bargain; a great one at $50 million might be. As Walter Wanger (who produced *Cleopatra* and should have known better) was fond of saying, "There is nothing as cheap as a hit," a maxim that struck Albeck as arguable.

Being in Flathead County told us little new. We viewed the locations, the stills, the construction, the site for the battle. We were driven to Ella Watson's Hog Ranch, where Cimino was shooting interior scenes between Isabelle Huppert and Chris Walken. The atmosphere was calm, collected, professional. Vilmos Zsigmond's camera crew was methodical and expert; Cimino was quiet, poised, and decisive; the actors were disciplined and prepared.

Even the horses were well behaved. During the shooting I leaned against a temporary corral and talked with Rudy Ugland, the wrangler, with whom I had made a picture only a year before in Colorado and New Mexico. Rudy told me he had never worked on a better-organized production, that Cimino was working from well before dawn, arriving at locations hours from Kalispell before the crew had even left the lobby of the Outlaw Inn, and he was arriving back in Kalispell after most of them had had dinner and gone on to other diversions, about which Rudy also seemed to know a great deal, as crew members usually do.

"But aren't you sick of Montana?" I asked.

He laughed his cowboy laugh. "Hell," he said, "this picture can go on forever as much as I care. My boys and I've never been paid like this. I looooove Montana!"

It was almost eleven o'clock at night before Carelli, Field, and I got back to the Outlaw Inn and hamburgers in the wagon-wheel dining room. Carelli was defensively arguing against Field's suggestion of adding another producer to the picture, claiming that she could handle Cimino if UA would back her up when she said no. Charlie Okun glanced over from the next table. "I mean, you gotta take my *calls*, David," said Joann. Charlie said nothing.

"Like locations, I mean," she continued. "Half the land up here is owned by the government, and the other half by these humpty-dumpty Indians. I negotiate a deal with them, right? They say yes, and two minutes before Mike's ready to shoot, some wacko spirit from the sky or something has told them to double the price. I mean, they're Indians, right? What do they know about Hollywood, right? A *lot!*" she said, and broke into sardonic laughter.

"What locations?" I asked. "The battlefield?"

"Well, the battlefield is something else." Her eyes darted around the half-empty dining room. She sounded vague.

"*What* else?" I asked.

"Well," she said slowly, "the battlefield is expensive because we had to clear the land of rocks and stuff and put in that irrigation system."

"What irrigation system? Nobody mentioned an irrigation system."

"For the grass."

"What grass?"

"Mike wants grass on the battlefield," she said quietly.

"Holy Christ, Joann! He's talking about hundreds of people and horses and wagons and explosives. Who the hell is going to see *grass?*"

She shrugged helplessly. "In the first shot, before the battle, they'll see grass. After the battle they'll see blood."

Before we could press the issue, a young actor whom we had seen at the location playing Ella's bordello boy, John DeCory, stopped by the table to ask about the next day's schedule. She introduced him, smiling at the similarity in names as she said, "David Field meet David *Mansfield.*" We all smiled and nodded absently when Cimino, true to Rudy Ugland's word, entered the dining room late, having just returned from the location. He joined our table, nodded to Charlie at the next, as Joann, perhaps to demonstrate her authority, launched into all the reasons a particular parcel of land, owned by the Indians, should not be used for the picture. However well chosen the arguments, her timing was lousy.

Cimino had worked for approximately eighteen hours that day and was clearly in no mood to deal with such challenges. He abruptly slammed his fist on the table, causing plates to jump and heads to swivel in our direction, none quicker than Charlie Okun's.

"*Goddammit, Joann, that's the location!*" He rose without another word, crossed the dining room to the door leading to the editing rooms directly below, and exited through it, slamming it forcefully behind him. Eyes flicked nervously in the silence.

"See what I mean?" said Joann. "So when is UA going to start backing me up, David?"

We finished our drinks, paid for the hamburgers, and followed Joann down the stairs to the editing rooms.

Cimino was seated at a Kem editing machine, mounted with three modular screens, viewing uncut footage with Penny Shaw, one of the assistant editors. The editing rooms were large, orderly, and immaculately organized. The only object at odds with the look of high-tech efficiency was the hamburger and fries Cimino had ordered from room service, which was ignored and growing cold as he raptly studied the footage whirring through the machine.

Without looking up, he motioned us over, pressed a button to stop the film, murmured something to Penny. She quickly removed the footage he had been viewing, popped new spools of film onto the Kem's horizontal mechanical bed, adroitly threaded the film through the drive mechanism, and stood back. Cimino paused, then, still without a word, pushed a button to start the machine.

The frames flickered rapidly to speed, and we saw for the first time what we were paying for. The screen was no larger than an average-small television screen and nowhere near as brilliant as a theater-projected image would be. Even so, what we saw was thrilling. The footage was perfectly composed, most of it shot at magic hour, when the mountains are slate silhouettes, the forests and grasses blue with shadow, the patches of highest snow and the clouds pink and gold with lingering sun. This was it, "the poetry of America."

There were intricate and difficult camera movements, all executed with fluent precision. The interior lighting had a burnished quality; one could almost smell the oil in the lamps.

The performance footage—out of context and roughly assembled—was equally impressive. Kristofferson was no pop idol, here, no supporting actor; he held the screen, a mature, weary man who has seen unpleasant things and expects to see more. At moments he recalled Gary Cooper; at others, his own song lyric rang in my head: "Freedom's just another name for nothing more to lose."

Huppert, to our amazement, looked incandescent. She was difficult to understand on the system's small speakers, but she glowed in lamplight and had a sweetly seductive quality that had been en-

tirely absent in Paris. Walken looked haunted, dangerous, as if inside
something were smoldering and mysteriously vulnerable at the same
time, contrasting effectively with the stoic weariness of Kristofferson's
Averill.

We watched footage for perhaps thirty minutes and, when it was
over, wanted to speak only of our enthusiasm, intensified no doubt by
the immense relief that there was indeed something on film impressive
enough to justify the time and money that had gone into its manufacture. There would be no confrontation scene that night.

The following day we drove high into Glacier National Park to
observe daytime shooting. The scene was what had once been the beginning of the script, as Nate Champion murders the settler speed-
butchering a steer behind concealing bedsheets. It involved a tracking
shot and the portable crane invented and assembled for the picture by
the key grip Richard Deats, laboring where a conventional crane could
not maneuver. The work was tedious and time-consuming but moved
forward inch by painstaking inch.

Between setups I traded information with the sound crew, some of
whom I had worked with before as a producer, while Field tried to back
Carelli in conversation with Cimino.

Later David and I lunched at a mountain lodge on snack-bar food,
neatly nibbled from our paper plates by the mangy mountain goats that
had wandered down from their rocky mountain perches to cadge food
(for the salt, a ranger explained) from tourists and interlopers like ourselves. As the mountain goats lunched on our leftovers, we talked.

"What did he say?" I asked.

"He said, 'If you want out of the picture you've just seen footage on,
I can take it somewhere else.'"

With this remark Cimino himself introduced option number four.
We were sick of hearing this veiled threat used to deflect legitimate
complaints and questions. Back in New York, in Andy Albeck's office,
we suggested we call his bluff, but not by telling him to take the picture
elsewhere; that would only have called for a production shutdown or
further slowing of production as Cimino took steps to get Warner's
or EMI to take over. Nor did we believe that either company would, for
UA's willingness to relinquish the picture would send shudders of doubt
through the community, which was as yet unaware of the magnitude of
our problem. Additionally, now that we had seen the footage—"It
looks like David Lean decided to make a western," I reported with
confidence and relief to Albeck—we wanted to lose it less than we had
before, even with the problems. The point was to disabuse Cimino of

the notion that he had a choice other than to deal with UA on UA's terms.

I called John Kohn, then head of the Beverly Hills EMI office (and an old friend), and told him flatly that *Heaven's Gate* was not for sale, and would he please ask EMI's Barry Spikings to stop telling Cimino how ready he was to take over a picture he couldn't have? I suspected Spikings of mischief in this area and wanted it stopped. Even if my suspicions were groundless, the message would find its way back to Cimino.

John Kohn called Barry Spikings, who, now safely off the hook, called Michael Cimino to say how much he would love to buy the picture from UA, but UA wouldn't let him.

My bluff had been bluffed, and rather neatly, too. We decided to redouble the bluff. We called Warner Brothers and EMI and told them the picture *was* for sale. (This is a well-known business maneuver sometimes called "put up or shut up.") As we suspected, neither company was interested in taking over a possible $40 million investment that UA seemed ready to dump. Then Field, who handled these conversations on instructions from New York, offered the picture on a partnership basis and had several possible formulas to suggest for sharing the financing and eventual profits, if any, all designed somehow to cap UA's investment.

We informed Cimino we were officially looking for a partner. Spikings could hardly now say he wasn't interested. Warner's could and did. So did Alan Ladd, Jr., at Fox. By June 16, the week of the original date for completion of photography, the production had spent $11,680,515, or its total approved budget. Estimates to complete were flying. The production was still claiming smoother, faster days ahead and was entering its probable final cost at double budget, approximately $22 million. Derek Kavanagh had revised his estimate downward from more than $40 million but remained firm at $35 million, or triple budget.

By mid-July partnership with EMI looked unlikely but possible. David Field flew in the Warner Brothers jet to Kalispell with Barry Spikings, Stan Kamen, and Eric Weissmann (Cimino's agent and lawyer respectively). In Kalispell they would look at the footage, speak with Cimino, weigh the risks and advantages, and EMI would be in or out.

Field told the rest of us later he had gone with a curious and ambiguous line running through his head. He had discussed with Jim Harvey the status of the picture and Derek's fears, and Harvey had replied, Field said, "'Thirty-five million? How bad is that?'" Perhaps EMI would feel the same.

• • •

The weekend of July 15, as Field, Spikings, Kamen, and Weissmann met with Cimino, Derek Kavanagh sat in room 243 of the Outlaw Inn and contemplated his luggage. It had been around, all over the
world on all manner of pictures, and doubtless would be again, attracting new scars as amusing conversation pieces, like the several inflicted
in continent traipsing with Blake Edwards and Peter Sellers when Kavanagh was production managing *The Revenge of the Pink Panther*. There
were other scars, other pictures, and there was other luggage, too, most
of it still in England with Mrs. Kavanagh—Shirley—and the children,
as they waited to hear from Derek that the seemingly endless tangles of
U.S. Immigration red tape—work permits, residence permits, and so
on—had been finally sorted out. Until they were, he would be living
out of assorted baggage anyway, so Kalispell or Los Angeles made little
difference. Still, he knew, taking place even now was a meeting that
would decide the immediate fates of his luggage and himself—and possibly even his family. It seemed a sensible idea to do nothing whatever
until a decision had been reached, though he was privately convinced
he knew what it would be. So he left his luggage right where it was,
there in that very burnt-umber room of the Outlaw Inn, and indulged
in not a little sympathy for David Field. And some for himself, too. He
hated burnt-umber. So did Shirley.

Kavanagh had been right: There would be no partners for UA on
Heaven's Gate. That meant he was stuck for the duration. He would be
Our Man in Kalispell, taking over production responsibility of the picture for UA, but without portfolio and without a formal announcement
to the company of actors and technicians, who would regard him as a
spy, and certainly none to the press.

Field and Kavanagh met with Cimino. Field tactfully pointed out
that with no partner to share the costs, slowing the cash flow was to be
Derek's responsibility. No expenditures would be made without his
knowledge and agreement. Field took pains, Kavanagh remembered, to
clarify that neither Derek's presence nor function was hostile. He was
to stay in Montana as a cautionary colleague, a shadow, a conscience,
and was to supplement Joann and Charlie's efforts to speed up the production and keep down the investment. Never would he act against the
best interests of the quality of the film.

Cimino was calm, even pliable after the turndown from EMI. He
agreed to cooperate with the new conditions and almost warmly, Derek
felt, welcomed him aboard.

Having assured himself that all was as well as it could be now that option four was no option at all, Field got on a plane to New York for the July production meeting. He was tired. He had been tired for a long time now and had even checked himself into Manhattan's Beth Israel Hospital for a weekend in late June with what had looked like simple exhaustion. His vacation was to begin in just a few days. With any luck it would also be a honeymoon. God knew, *Heaven's Gate* wasn't.

When Field left Kalispell, Michael Cimino sat down and dictated a memo. It was addressed to Field but was to be publicly posted in the Outlaw Inn. It read in full: "Derek Kavanagh is not to come to the location site. He is not to enter the editing room. He is not to speak to me at all."

Cimino signed it and sent it.

The time had come for option five.

CHAPTER 14

ROCKY MOUNTAIN LOW

To Hell with *Heaven's Gate*

—Bumper sticker,
   Kalispell, Montana (Summer 1979)

Who do I fuck to get off this picture?

—Anonymous Hollywood starlet
   (circa 1930)

Two things mitigated against the rage or panic that the contempt implicit in Cimino's memo about Kavanagh might have justifiably inspired. The first was that United Artists in the summer of 1979 enjoyed, at home and abroad, the most successful box-office period in its sixty-year history. *Manhattan, Moonraker, Rocky II, Apocalypse Now, La Cage aux Folles,* and *The Black Stallion* formed a sextet of money spinners which cut across the full spectrum of moviegoers. United Artists had never had, and never would have, a single block-busting megahit on the scale of *Star Wars, The Godfather,* or *E.T.,* which would perform in such phenomenal fashion as to make even costly failures fade quickly from stockholder memory. UA's pattern under Krim had been almost annually a series of pictures that performed well, if unspectacularly, to balance the odd and inevitable failures. Go for broke had never been the company's style and would not be with Albeck, whose mix of so many low-budget thises and so many medium-budget thats was a deliberate policy to perpetuate stability, to arrive at a more predictably favorable bottom line than the make-or-break blockbuster sweepstakes.

The wisdom of this policy seemed borne out by the exceptionally good business of these six pictures, and the fact that two of them had been troubled and long overdue (*Apocalypse* and, on a smaller scale,

The Black Stallion) encouraged a certain grim stoicism in the face of Cimino's dismissive attitude toward the company and its executives. This attitude reached its high (or low) with the memo regarding Kavanagh, but had been preceded on July 10 (five days before the abortive meetings in Kalispell with Barry Spikings) by a personal telephone call to me from Cimino, asking me to take over responsibility of the picture from Field because "I can't talk to him anymore." This shifting focus from Cimino's refusing to talk to almost anybody to Field's supposed unreceptiveness sounded like an attempt to confuse issues and play upon a rivalry Cimino saw or imagined in my relationship with my cohead of production. I refused. I had no interest in allowing *Heaven's Gate* to become the object or instigator of internecine warfare in the company, and on a more practical level I simply had not followed the picture on the day-to-day basis that Field had, was unfamiliar with many of the details of the production, and was otherwise occupied with "Woody Allen No. 4," *The Romance of the Pink Panther, For Your Eyes Only, The Dogs of War,* and other pictures under my direct or indirect supervision. Nevertheless, the call was followed by one from Stan Kamen, Cimino's agent, echoing the request. He added that Carelli was also complaining that Field would not return her phone calls. Kamen was beginning to be alarmed for his client's future by what was, following the approaches to Warner Brothers and EMI, becoming the subject of considerable industry gossip, and inasmuch as David seemed to be getting married and going off on vacation anyway, couldn't I humor Michael and be his contact at UA?

It seemed to me we had "humored" Michael quite long enough, and were it not for the second mitigating circumstance, the evident quality of the footage we had been shown in Kalispell, the suggestion of further "humoring" would have met a far more heated and definitive response than it did. I simply said no.

But big box office on other pictures and the high quality of this one did not blind Albeck or any of us to the escalation of the economic gamble. If we return to the more or less standard formula by which a picture must return approximately two and a half to three times its cost at the box office in order to break even, even at $40 million *Heaven's Gate* would have to do at least $100 million in business not to lose money. The $100 million film is precisely the big blockbuster category the company had never in its history enjoyed. No one had ever thought *Heaven's Gate* —at whatever cost or quality—had the mass appeal essential to such a box-office performance, and reckless optimism was not rampant enough to change that assessment. Enough was enough. Besides, option five was under way.

.   .   .

David Brown is a civilized, celebrated, genial man who has been a film executive and producer (with his partner, Richard Zanuck) for many years. He has survived management upheavals, changing trends, forgettable pictures, and enormous success without losing his sense of humor, footing, or courtesy. I knew him only slightly (having tried and failed to lure Zanuck-Brown from Universal to UA), but that did not preclude my imposing on his generosity and experience.

We met for breakfast at the Sherry-Netherland Hotel at nine-fifteen on July 10, the same day Cimino and Kamen asked me to step in for Field. "I have a serious problem," I told Brown as soon as we were seated.

He contracted bushy brows. "I've heard rumors," he murmured. "I'm sorry to hear they have foundation."

"Well, they do. The picture's going to cost at least thirty-five to forty million dollars, and we don't know how to slow it down."

"How does it look? Physically, I mean?"

"Like David Lean decided to make a western," I said, using my now-standard line.

He nodded thoughtfully. "That makes it more difficult."

"I know. I'm offering to buy scrambled eggs in return for advice."

He smiled and waved cheerily to a well-known lawyer in an opposite booth. After a moment he said, "No one can advise you in a situation like this. I've been there, and I know how difficult it is."

"You've been there twice."

He looked at me quizzically.

"One, you were involved in a runaway picture when *Jaws* lost control—or that's the rumor."

"It's true. It was largely because of factors that were simply not controllable. The shark, the weather, the Atlantic Ocean . . . But Dick and I had been hardened to that kind of thing before. *Star!*, *Hello, Dolly!*, *Tora! Tora! Tora!*" He shrugged.

"And secondly," I continued, "on *Jaws 2* you actually fired the director."

His eyes widened, then dropped to study his silverware. "I see, I see. As bad as that?"

"Yes. I think so. I don't know. I've never been involved in a situation like this and have no frame of reference. I don't want to fire him— I want to *kill* him." Brown laughed politely but looked startled. "If we do fire him, I don't know what the consequences are for the picture or with the press or within the company. It's an admission of a very ex-

pensive mistake, perhaps a disastrously expensive one. Do we compound the mistake more by letting him continue or by firing him?"

He waved lightly at someone who entered, then turned back to the
table setting. Finally, he said, "My first—it's not *advice*, really . . . I
can't give you advice, but I can offer my own experiences for whatever
cautionary value they may have. On *Jaws* we believed we had a hit.
Steven Spielberg was working hard and diligently, and it was our judgment—not an easy one to arrive at, mind you, but we had worked with
Steven before—that we would not change course. Only *you* can decide
that on the basis of your opinion of your footage, your relationship with
the director, your director's relationship with his actors—"

"They love him. They might walk out with him."

"I suppose it's not possible"—his eyes flicked anxiously, as if looking
away from the word—"to *abandon*?"

"Well, I could shoot him, and we could declare *force majeure*."

He choked on a small courtesy laugh. "No, of course not," he said
definitively. "That option probably expired the day you started shooting. Abandonment, I mean, not murder." He glanced sideways at me,
not certain I had been joking.

"Still," he continued, "firing a director is the most grievous step you
can take on any movie. We did it on *Jaws 2* for a variety of reasons. It
can be done, but it is a most difficult decision. We are talking about
human lives here. Your picture is not what *Jaws 2* was, the sequel to
one of the most successful pictures ever made, a big commercial movie-
movie. Yours, I understand, is something . . . special, personal. My
goodness!" he said with considerable force. "This man just won the
Academy Award! I do not envy you this decision. Still, if you decide
you must replace him, my counsel is this: I recall when my partner was
faced with the unpleasant executive task of firing Akira Kurosawa from
Tora! Tora! Tora! and trying to replace him with another Japanese director. No one would accept the assignment. No one at all. Crass Hollywood—a Zanuck, at that—had defiled a national shrine, a living
monument, and all Japan turned its back in silence."

"Michael Cimino isn't a national shrine or a living monument."

"No," he said, "but if you must fire him, don't do it, whatever else
you do, until you know who will replace him. If anyone *will*."

A few days later I walked down a dark corridor of the Beverly
Wilshire Hotel and knocked on the door of a Famous Director. It was
an early summer evening, and the Famous Director was finishing work
on his latest movie for another studio. Although he had a house in

Malibu, he was staying in town to be closer to the studio and the labs during the final stages of postproduction, and though weary at the end of the July day, he seemed as friendly and energetic as if he had just bounced out of the bracing Malibu surf.

I hadn't told him why I was coming by, but he guessed when he saw the gloom drawing down my face. He laughed. "What we need is some champagne, I think."

The small refrigerator in his suite was stocked with splits, two of which he opened and poured. Finally, after some good-natured shoptalk, he leaned back, sipping his champagne, and smiled. "You tell me your dreams, I'll tell you mine. *Maybe.*" He laughed again and lit a small cigar.

"My dreams are all nightmares," I said. "You've heard the rumors."

"This town is nothing but rumors. I hear Mary Pickford drinks like a fish. I hear Mae West is a fella. Who listens?"

"I think San Francisco listens. To the ones about money anyway."

He nodded. "How's Andy holding up?"

"With grace under pressure I think they call it, but he's smiling a lot less. He won't crack; this thing isn't *Cleopatra.* It's not going to shut down the company."

"I hope not," he said, suddenly alarmed at the suggestion. "I still want to make . . ." He named some pictures, one of which he eventually made at UA, some of which he didn't; one he made elsewhere. "Tell me more about San Francisco."

"They haven't said anything directly. I think they're so relieved that Francis finally finished *Apocalypse* this is not uppermost in their minds."

"They haven't said *any*thing?"

"Listen, they could be on the phone twenty-four hours a day to Andy for all I know. But David says he told Jim Harvey how high it might go and all Harvey said was "'Thirty-five million—how bad is that?'"

"Thirty-five *million?*" the Famous Director said into the bowl of his champagne glass.

"Give or take. We give, he takes."

"Does it *look* like thirty-five million?"

"It looks like you decided to make a western," I said, adjusting my standard line.

Silence. Sip. Cigar smoke. Another sip.

"Mike's got an eye all right. A good one. How are the performances?"

"They look great in dailies. Dailies are dailies. What can you really tell?"

"You can tell if they're terrible. How's the girl?"

"The producer or the actress?"

He smiled privately. Then: "The actress."

"That's part of what complicates it. We fought him on the girl, thought he was dead wrong. In dailies she's the most appealing thing in the picture. You have no idea how I hate admitting that."

He smiled, nodded, looked through his champagne glass at the room, as if it were a director's finder. "Then if San Francisco isn't jumping up and down and Andy is bearing up and the footage looks good and the girl is fine, what's your problem?"

"I want to fire the son of a bitch. When I said thirty-five million, that's what we *hope*. That's if we can contain things, get some control from this point forward. If we can't do that—and so far we haven't been able to—it could go to forty or fifty or God knows where."

"You need a producer. That's why I always work with [he named his producer]. It's not that I'm so penny-wise. He *makes* me stay on budget."

"We need both a producer *and* a director because I can't fire the producer without having the director walk off, and maybe the cast, too. They seem devoted to him, most of them anyway—though one or two are getting cabin fever, I think—and he's this freaking Academy Award auteur. And don't tell me about [your producer] because you know he wouldn't stand a chance of keeping you on budget if you didn't want to yourself."

He whistled out a long, thin stream of cigar smoke. "Mike's a good director. Hell, his picture was *powerful*. You've got a big problem because this isn't just firing some schmuck from a *Movie of the Week*. It's *his* picture, and an ambitious one. You know and I know fifteen guys out there who would take over anything for the credit and the fee, but you can't hire one of those guys. The Directors Guild just gave Mike its highest award. And the academy. Who're you going to get who can do it and won't make you look like assholes?"

"Why do you think I'm here?"

"What's *in* that champagne?" he said, and burst out laughing. "First, under the guild rules you can't even talk to me about it until you've fired Mike."

"UA isn't a signatory to the guild."

"Well, *I* am! I'm a member, and I would be violating the bylaws of the guild if I even talked to you, which is why we're not having this conversation."*

---

* And why he remains unnamed in these pages.

"Well, if we *were* having this conversation—"

"Hell, I'm probably violating some goddamn bylaw even listening to you, *which is why I'm not listening.*"

"If you *were* listening, and if I had already fired Michael—"

"Which you haven't."

"But if I *had* . . . since you're not listening . . ."

He puffed furiously at his cigar, listening.

"If I were to fire a director from a big movie and I were to go to another director, an important one who had also directed some Academy Award-winning movies, somebody whose reputation was substantial enough to counterbalance the firing of Hollywood's latest genius, what would that director likely say?"

"That hypothetical director, you mean?"

"Yeah. Him."

He turned back to the refrigerator, opened and poured some more champagne as he considered.

"First, he would tell you he is finishing his own movie, because if he's so good, he's probably busy. Then he would say that he has another movie he wants to do—possibly even for UA." He glanced up pointedly, raising his glass in a toast to as yet unmade movies. "Then he would shudder to think of the press outcry, the terrible, terrible climate within the guild. And then he would talk to his wife and wonder why in God's name he was even considering buying this kind of grief. . . . But if he thought there was a chance that letting Mike continue would actually destroy the company, then and only then would he probably consider it. He'd consider Mike's feelings, too, of course."

"Of course. But you forget that in this model I would have already fired him."

"Right. Well." He toyed with another cigar, resisted the temptation, and put it back in its box. "This hypothetical director of yours would probably ask you how much footage had been shot and how much was left to do."

"About a million feet shot. How much remains is anybody's guess. Depends on who shoots it."

"Good God," he protested. "Do you know how long it would take just to review the footage? Nobody could say yes or no without doing that. *Weeks.* Has Mike gone crazy or what?"

"He's shooting ten, twenty, thirty takes and printing every take. *Almost* every take."

"And he'll keep on until he gets it right?" the Famous Director said with a little half-smile.

"Or until he gets fired."

"Don't ask me," he said. "Please don't."

He leaned back in his chair, briefly considered the cigar box once more, then raised his champagne glass to the window, where he could see the lights of the hotel's facing wing swimming in the wine. It was getting late, and he was beginning to seem weary and depressed and annoyed by the conversation he wasn't having.

Finally, he turned back to me and said very calmly, "You're stuck. You can pull the plug. You can hire a hack. You might even get lucky and find a director of talent who will help you. But those are all no-win options. You've got to find some way to control him, for his own sake. He's a good director, and I personally like him . . . I *think*. Doesn't matter. But what if this movie flops? They'll crucify him." He paused, then added as the afterthought it was, "They'll crucify you, too. Or Andy."

The compassion was genuine, for a fellow director, a film company, the industry in general. I had not chosen him idly; he was well known to be financially responsible, a leader in reliable, high-quality, commercial filmmaking. And when he said he didn't want to be asked, he didn't mean just because the question would violate a bylaw.

"Or," I said, taking a last stab, "do you think maybe the hypothetical director and his hypothetical producer would step in to save Mike from himself or to backstop the picture the way Richard Lester did on *Superman?*"

"I don't know," he said. "I . . . just . . . don't . . . know. I don't think Mike's pride would allow him to accept me. I know mine wouldn't. But if you do fire him and"—he sighed heavily—"and you feel you must come back to me— No, dammit!" he said, reaching for a cigar. *"Don't.* Please, *please* don't!"

I debated for several days after that whether the plea meant "Don't ask because I don't want to say yes" or "because I don't want to say no." I doubt if the Famous Director knew, or would have known unless and until confronted with a fact. But he had spoken sensible, experienced truths. Only the hacks would be willing and ready to step in. Firing Cimino would mean weeks of shutdown with the meter running at $1 million a week just holding the production together. The Famous Director had once replaced another Famous Director on a picture years ago, before he himself became Famous, and he knew there was a chance we could get lucky, find someone to salvage both the situation and the picture. But if he didn't want the responsibility for what David Brown had called "the most grievous step you can take on any movie," there was little likelihood I could talk him, or anyone else able enough for the assignment, into taking over.

David and Cathy got married and left for a two-week honeymoon on July 21, 1979. I went to California to sit at Field's desk, which was busier and more hectic than Rissner's had been almost exactly a year before. UA had had another personnel change in June, and though it was a happy one, the California office was feeling tentative because the change appeared to be arbitrary, though it was not. Partly because of the production problems on *Heaven's Gate*, Field had felt the need for a production vice-president who had direct production experience, which neither Claire nor Jerry had. When David's lawyer (and mine) called to tell David that Robert Wunsch might be available, we both reacted with enthusiasm, dimmed only by the knowledge that the company structure would mean replacing either Claire or Jerry, not merely adding Wunsch. Bob was an old friend of David's and an older one of mine, a forty-four-year-old Yale graduate, who had worked as a literary agent for nearly a decade in Hollywood, then had left agenting to coproduce *Slap Shot*, which starred Paul Newman and was directed by George Roy Hill. After being executive producer on a smaller picture called *Defiance* for AIP, he had gone to CBS Television as an executive for *Movies of the Week*. Bob thus supplied many qualities: maturity, experience, agency background, production know-how, and judgment. That he was a friend of both of us might leaven the East-West anxieties of our two-headed production monster.

Claire and David had worked together at Fox, where I had produced a couple of pictures and gotten to know them both. Additionally, we still felt strongly the need for a woman executive on the staff; that left Jerry Paonessa odd man out. Because Jerry had projects in development that he could easily produce for the company, we asked him to become a UA producer, and Bob Wunsch joined the staff on June 1, quickly becoming an efficient and instantly trusted member of the team.

Field left for the Bahamas knowing the Famous Director had been fatally discouraging about option five, and though we continued to violate Directors Guild bylaws, there was waning hope of replacing Cimino with anyone gifted (or available or willing) enough to match the style and quality of the footage we had seen or with stature and strength enough to hold cast, crew, and picture together.

The dissonance of wedding bells and the slowly tolling knell in Montana did not go unremarked, but no one suggested Field postpone his life or one of its chief events, and no one wanted him to either. He had earned a respite from *Heaven's Gate*, and his familiar melancholic style and air of gloomy fatigue had broken like clouds in the sunny elation of Cathy's presence, stilling talk of the great gulf between Seventh Avenue and West Washington Boulevard. We were pulling together as people will in wartime, and neither Albeck nor any of Field's colleagues thought Michael Cimino should dominate an executive's life any more than he should the company's.

Meanwhile, back in Coventry, Kavanagh was gathering important information about where the picture was going, even if he had to collect it while circumventing Cimino's frosty dismissal, Carelli's protective custody of her precarious job, and Charlie Okun's defensive anxiety concerning this blatantly runaway production, over which he had no more control than did Carelli. Carelli blamed Field and UA, Okun blamed Carelli, and Cimino blamed Art and kept on shooting.

Nothing had worsened; that is to say, overages accumulated at their familiar, ruinous rate. Had Cimino shown a token acceleration of pace, a token deceleration of cash flow, a token cooperation with Kavanagh, I could have stayed in California and New York while Field was away. Cimino didn't, and I couldn't. And Stan Kamen kept calling, urging me to become Michael's UA contact. "He'll *listen* to you," Stan had said, and though I had no reason to believe this was so, Cimino's memo on Derek Kavanagh made me ready to be listened to.

No matter what I had said to David Brown, I did not (and do not) own a gun. There is little doubt that had I arrived in Kalispell, six-guns blazing, I might have gotten the picture's publicity campaign off to a colorful start, but this would have further slowed production. Instead, I arrived in Montana with a weapon too large and audible to be a secret for long. I packed no revolver; I packed Dean Stolber.

Stolber was diminutive, but not much smaller than Cimino, and though athletically inclined, he tended to spread and shrink, also like Cimino, who could hardly fail to notice Stolber's presence. As noted, Dean had sung and danced his way through college and law school, and his shrinking rarely extended to his stage presence, which could be considerable. Still, he had both the circumspection of the lawyer he was and the practiced mask of the actor he had been when he wanted to wear it. Dean was not only head of business affairs but ran the legal department at UA, too. He was, therefore, UA's number one inside lawyer, * and Cimino knew it. I was betting that a man who used his

---

* There was a general counsel, Herbert Schottenfeld, but his functions were corporate, rather than related to specific pictures. UA's outside firm remained Phillips, Nizer, Benjamin & Krim.

lawyers as assiduously on his own behalf as Cimino did might compre-
hend the importance of my bringing "mine" from New York to Kalispell. You don't just "drop in" on Kalispell.

There was nothing hidden about this trip. I had told Cimino, Carelli,
Kamen, and Weissmann, Cimino's lawyer, that I was coming. I did so
undeluded that this warning might have an effect on the production's
pace, and it did not. I had taken the further precaution of putting in
writing the serious intent of the visit, modulated only by some perfunctory courtesy phrases that I hoped would set a clear, subdued tone.

This letter, dated July 27, 1979, but written several days before and
studied anxiously by the legal department, attempted to convey calm
reason but also to leave no doubt that while UA's support of Cimino's
aesthetic aims was undimmed, the final straw had been flung on 729's
hump with a resounding thud. "The situation," I wrote, "has become
untenable. You must know that your negative responses to our various
entreaties, requests, suggestions and so on haven't helped, and it is no
longer possible for this situation to continue."

Most pointedly (and practically) the letter, in the form of a telex,
was to be hand delivered by Kavanagh, and it informed Cimino that
"when Derek delivers this letter to you he will also deliver a new schedule for the completion of the picture prepared by United Artists." The
telex pointed out that this new schedule did not include prologue and
epilogue, which both Field and I strongly supported and had no intention of losing, but which Stolber and I insisted on using as poker
chips.

Wednesday, August 1, was a bright summer day, and fluttering trees
lined the pleasant streets of Kalispell, cooling the residential areas they
bowered from the sun's heat. Stolber and I welcomed this bracing break
from New York's humidity and drove through the sun-dappled streets to
Highway 93 and on to the Outlaw Inn. After we had checked in (neither of us in the Presidential Suite), we succeeded in contacting David
Field by phone in the Caribbean. Field was disturbed by our Montana
trip. We clarified that the visit was in no way meant to preempt his
supervision of the picture or undercut his authority over it, but the
continuing snail's pace at $200,000 a day required interim action. Pa-
tiently we explained that neither of us intended to usurp his role (who
would want to?), but we also did not believe we could indulge David's
territorial anxieties and the movie's continuing drain.

As we were leaving my room to meet with Joann and Michael in
their offices, the phone rang. It was Stan Kamen. "*Hit* him," counseled

Stan. "Hit him *fast,* hit him *hard,* and let him know you're doing it for his own good."

"I'm doing it for UA's good, Stan," I replied.

"Why do I think that won't move him?" Kamen said reflectively. "My client is a brilliant director—"

"Aren't they all?" I interrupted.

"No, some are bums. This one is brilliant," he continued evenly, "but my duty is to protect him—even from himself—and you have to understand that the only thing *he* understands is force. Be forceful."

"I intend to try."

Cimino had not yet returned from location when Stolber and I arrived at room 475, but Joann was waiting for us. We chatted tensely for a few minutes as she displayed the offices, wondering what Dean was doing there. Finally, she thrust at us neatly bound books of transparencies, hundreds and hundreds, in black and white and color, for eventual use in the publicity campaign.

Publicity and promotion on *Heaven's Gate* had been a nagging worry to UA because Cimino had forbidden any press to visit the production, and that pleased neither the press nor the publicity department, eager for coverage. At the moment the anxiety was reversed: Publicity was worried that a barred press would sniff out the quotient for a new *Apocalypse* now that the old one had lost its scandal potential by triumphing at Cannes. Negative publicity about the tension and overbudget in Montana would be hard to contain once leaked, and a disgruntled but trigger-happy press could be depended on to take potshots, if not lethal aim, at the box-office target.

Joann flipped through plastic pages containing hundreds of slides, talking rapidly, occasionally pushing her long hair back behind the temples of her tinted aviator glasses. We saw much less than we heard, and what we heard was nervous. She was saved from further agitation by Cimino's arrival.

It was now early evening, and the light fades quickly when the sun descends behind the Rockies. The temperature drops with it, but we played at easy warmth and courtesy smiles. As I expected, Cimino was surprised to see Stobler with me.

"What are you doing here, Dean?" he asked bluntly.

"Dean is here now, Michael," I explained, "because we hope to preclude his getting more deeply involved later."

Cimino blinked. I said, "I hope you've had a chance to examine the new schedule."

"When? I'm directing a movie. Besides, Derek doesn't understand the problems of this production."

"He might understand more if you'd talk to him."

"*No* one understands what we're trying to do here: the enormous problems, the creative challenges, the backbreaking labor—"

"We understand all about the backbreaking part, Michael. Do you understand the *bank*-breaking part?"

"I'm sure I can't live with a schedule made by Derek Kavanagh." He paused, then delivered his zinger. "Maybe you can find some other director who can, but I can't."

"We've already tried that, Michael," I said as neutrally as possible. He sank down slowly in a chair opposite the sofa on which Dean and I now took seats. Joann just stood there for a moment, then sat in a chair off to one side, out of our sight lines and sounding out of breath.

"I think Dean should begin," I said.

Stolber didn't vamp, but he did do a verse. "David and Steve both have told us how wonderful the footage looks, Michael, and we're thrilled. We all wanted a beautiful artistic movie, and we know you do, too. But the communication between UA and the production has been a source of grave concern to Andy and all of us. We went into this picture in good faith, and we frankly wonder if that good faith is being returned. Andy wonders. So do I. So do Steven and David. We are prepared to continue financing the picture, but only to a point, which Derek's schedule can help you meet and which we believe is reasonable and will not damage the quality of the movie." Stolber's mask smiled. Cimino's did not.

"What point?" he asked dully.

"Twenty-five million dollars, all in."

"But we *will* come in at that," Cimino protested, his body lurching forward in his chair to emphasize the obviousness of the point. Joann was silent.

"No, you won't," I said as casually as possible, while Dean carefully pulled notes from his briefcase. "Not even close."

"Your own estimate to complete is twenty-six and a half million dollars, Michael," Dean said, "and we don't believe that figure. The latest cost report made by our people, a week ago, estimates that the final budget won't be twenty-five million dollars; it will be twenty-five million *over*, or thirty-six million dollars. You have spent as of today almost sixteen million dollars, and we are not prepared to give you another twenty. We will spend another nine, which is neither punitive nor niggardly. In fact, it is more than you told Danny Rissner this whole picture was going to cost us. Andy has decided we must seal it off at twenty-five million dollars, and"—he smiled again as he nailed the coffin shut—"we hope you will be the director who brings it in at that figure."

A chasm of silence opened. Joann busied herself by turning on a table lamp. Cimino's eyes caught the light and seemed to contract as he focused raptly on Dean, who paused for a theatrical beat and continued pleasantly. "We also hope you can retain final cut because we know how important that is to you."

"But?" said Cimino, his voice leaden.

"But without going into a lot of recriminations which will solve nothing, there are so many contractual . . . *questions*," the lawyer said carefully.

"What questions?" snapped Cimino. "Aside from the budget."

"Well, there's the length of the picture," said Stolber, yielding the stage to me.

"Michael, while Derek has been here without access to you, he has been doing some homework to help us know where we are. He's been studying the camera reports and the footage counts, and by correlating the running time and the page count, he estimates a final screen time of no less than four hours and sixteen minutes, plus credits. That's longer than *Gone with the Wind.* It's longer than either of *The Godfather* movies. It's longer than just about anything, in fact, except the Russian version of *War and Peace,* and that was financed by an entire *country.* Four hours and sixteen minutes—plus credits—is commercially impossible. It is also a violation of your contract, in which you agreed, after some conversations we all remember and don't need to go into here, to deliver a picture between two and three hours in length. *Including* credits."

His voice sounded recorded, mechanical. "I can't tell you how long the picture will be until I see it. It will be as long as it needs to be, as long as it is."

"No, it won't, Michael. It will be between two and three hours. UA can't effectively market a four-hour movie. No one can. We agreed to finance a movie under three hours, and that's what we intend to get and release. We hope you will be the one to do the final cutting, but only you can determine that: one, by agreeing to the twenty-five-million-dollar final cost and the schedule Derek has prepared to make that possible and two, by agreeing to deliver a three-hour movie."

"How can I agree to any of this without the time to study the schedule and until I've seen the movie assembled?"

"Those are the conditions under which Andy will continue to finance this picture, that's how."

"And if I leave?" His chin tilted.

"Walk, you mean?"

"Yes." It tilted further.

"I think you should discuss that at great length with Eric Weissmann," said Dean quietly and deliberately.

It was not the actor's voice but the lawyer's steel that spoke. We would sue Cimino, and he knew it. For everything he had or ever would have. Silent seconds passed.

"How can I accept a schedule made by someone who has had no input from me and cannot possibly understand what remains to be done?"

"We all know *why* Derek has had no input from you, Michael, but he can read. He knows how to count. He also knows how to make up a schedule and a budget that have some relationship to reality, our grasp on which has lately been tenuous, to say the least or the most. His schedule gives you forty-five more shooting days to complete the picture. The quality of the production won't suffer; we're not asking you to fire one gaffer or one horse. Forty-five days at your present rate of two hundred thousand dollars a day is nine million dollars. Take it or leave it."

"What if I take it and it just isn't makable?"

"It's makable."

"How do *I* know that?"

"First, you read the goddamn thing, then you sit down with Derek and discuss the problems, then you agree to it, and then you keep to it. It's simple. We call it living up to a commitment. We have more than lived up to ours, and we are now asking you to live up to yours."

He remained silent for a moment, while his fingers gripped his kneecaps. Finally, he said, "What about the prologue and the epilogue?"

"They can't be made within the twenty-five million," Dean said carefully.

"But they're essential to the whole picture!"

"No, they're not," I said. "They can be lifted out without a trace."

"But everything they add to the picture . . ." His voice was rising, and he glanced at Joann for support. She said nothing.

"We can't afford what they add," I said. "Not now."

"You're prepared to maim this picture!" he replied.

"I'm prepared to *kill* it, Michael. If it were up to me, I would put you and all of us out of our misery and send everybody home tomorrow morning. But as I seem to be one of the ones who got us into this incredibly expensive mess, I'm trying to do what I can to get us out."

"Does that mean you're taking over from David?"

"Not at all. David will be back tomorrow or the next day."

"Yeahhh . . . where *is* David?" drawled Carelli very slowly, as if just returning from some distant place.

"He's reachable by telephone."

"Not by me he isn't," she said sharply.

"Well, we reached him just before this meeting. He knows about the new schedule, agrees fully with our position and the budget, and he also knows it wouldn't matter if he didn't because Andy is still running the company and Andy considers this nonnegotiable."

"About the prologue and epilogue, too?" asked Cimino.

Dean carefully avoided looking at me. We had been waiting for the issue to resurface. "Michael, no one wanted the prologue and epilogue more than David and I, but how can we go back to New York and plead for something—*anything*—on behalf of someone who won't even agree to the only practical plan anyone has come up with to save this picture? If you can't agree to that . . ."

He heard it. His face, which had grown progressively paler, like a sickly moon, suddenly started to flush, as some energy bubbled up inside.

"I'll speed up production," he blurted out. "But my way. Not Derek's way."

"We already know your way, Michael. Your way is why we're here in Montana."

"Ask Clint!"

What? Stolber and I turned to each other, bewildered, not even sure of what he had said, certainly not of what he was talking about, sure only that his face had grown mottled with excitement.

"Ask Clint!" he repeated. "Clint knows. I *can* work fast. I did it on *Thunderbolt and Lightfoot.*" The normally measured voice came back at us in words so rushed they threatened to strangle on each other. "Clint came to me three days before the production was supposed to end and said, 'I'm going back to Big Sur tonight, so you better figure out a way to get three days' work done in one,' and I did it, I did fifty-six setups in one day—*fifty-six setups*—you can't imagine how hard it was or how fast we worked, but I did it and the picture didn't suffer and Clint went home that night and I don't know how, but we finished the picture. *Fifty-six setups in one day!*"

"Hit him hard," Stan Kamen had counseled. "We're talking about human lives here," David Brown had said. Yes, I thought, feeling cold and feverish at the same time, embarrassed at the vehemence of a desperate, pleading outburst that was too revealing, too intimate, too naked. That's how it sounded, and I thought that the human lives we should be talking about were mine and David's and Andy's and Dean's and all those people who worked for a company being manipulated by designs that were grandiose, by which we had been impressed, for which we had fought and argued and pleaded and persuaded, and that chorus of voices (my own included) now hung in the air like a high, thin, wavering whine.

I looked at the small, glittering, excited eyes and said, "I find it incredibly sad, Michael, that you should try to win our confidence by rubbing our noses in your willingness to do in a moment for Mr. Eastwood what you have refused for three and a half months and sixteen million dollars to do for us."

"I know how it looks," he said, his voice more strained than ever. "I can't plead that I've been faithful to my schedule or budget, and it isn't Joann's fault or Charlie's."

"Nobody suggested that it was."

"I accept full responsibility."

"Who else?"

"But you've seen the work. You know what the footage looks like. I can hurry it up now. I've done it before, and I can do it again. Ask Clint. But I've got to have the prologue and epilogue and final cut. I'm asking, I'm pleading with you, for the good of the picture. . . ."

I stood up. It was time to go, time to get out of there. Dean seemed startled, then rose to join me. He said to Cimino, "David will be back from his honeymoon the end of the week. He'll be coming directly to Kalispell. We can wait until Saturday or Sunday for a response, Michael, but you should understand that these issues are not negotiable. There may be some variations in the schedule that you can work out with Derek, but the ceiling on the budget must remain at twenty-five million dollars. Your right to final cut ends with a running time that exceeds three hours."

We left them alone and walked down the corridor, down the stairs to street level without speaking.

When we reached the lobby exit to the dark parking lot, Dean said, "He's going to agree."

"I know," I answered. "And lucky David gets to try to enforce all this."

"We'll have to take over the picture legally. The overbudget provision in the contract entitles us to do that. We'll sign all the checks, the requisitions, the requests for funds, everything."

"Are we declaring him in breach then?"

"No," said Stolber, and he laughed grimly. "Going over budget doesn't place him in breach, not in the contract anyway. Not unless we take over and *order* him to stick to a schedule and budget and he doesn't do it for reasons not beyond his control. Then we fire him for breach and declare *force majeure.*"*

"Then what happens?"

"I don't know. A lot of lawyers get very rich, I think."

"I'd rather have a picture."

"So would I."

"So would David."

We walked into town and had dinner at a restaurant full of ferns and fresh-faced waitresses. The buffaloburgers came sizzling on metal trays, and the baked potatoes were covered with heaps of sour cream and sprinkled with chives like green confetti. We drank red wine and discussed kids and dogs and never mentioned Michael Cimino or *Heaven's Gate* once.

After dinner something occurred to me for reasons mysterious then and mysterious now. Maybe it was the wine. Or maybe we passed a real estate office on our way back to the Outlaw Inn, or saw a For Sale sign staked out smartly on some resident's lawn. Whatever the reason, I turned to Stolber and asked, "How do you find out who owns a piece of property?"

"I don't know. You call the county clerk or something. Why?"

"It's that location for the battle sequence, that land we cleared and improved. Where we paid for the irrigation system."

"*Irrigation* system?"

"Grass. He wants grass," I said vaguely. "I wonder who owns that land?"

He eyed me closely.

"Maybe it's nothing," I said. "But at the very least we ought to be able to recover some of the costs of the irrigation system after the picture's over. Sell it. Sell the *pipes.* Something. Maybe sell it to the owner of the land. If we know who that is."

"You have a very suspicious mind," he said.

"I'm learning," I said.

A few days later one of the New York lawyers had discovered the name of the owner of the land. Stolber called the owner's lawyer in Beverly Hills, Eric Weissmann, a man of scrupulous probity, who agreed instantly that it was "less than appropriate" for Michael Cimino's

---

*The UA legal department was at this time researching the contracts to establish grounds for breach of obligations and declaration of *force majeure.* Going over budget, "even egregiously so," read the legal opinion, was not enough. UA had to take over the production formally.

own land to be charged back to the picture . . . or any improvements
thereto, or irrigation systems thereon or thereunder. Another location
would be sought for the battle sequence, and was. Cimino's lawyers had
quite enough to do without adding, at the very least, conflict of interest
charges to them.

David Field's honeymoon vacation was darkened and hastened to an
end by our trip to Kalispell and the call we made to him from the
Outlaw Inn. Three days later he himself was back in Kalispell to take
over his role on the picture and the picture, too. I went to Maui for a
vacation of my own.

When Stolber got back to New York, he had dictated over the
telephone to Derek Kavanagh a letter which Derek gave Field on his
arrival at the motel. David took it to his room, revised it, and had it
retyped before he signed it. It was addressed to Michael Cimino, and
David would hand deliver it to him. It explained the accompanying
document, also dictated over the phone by Stolber, which was the official take-over notice. Whether Cimino stayed or left, UA was now
producing *Heaven's Gate*. Legal control of the production was trans-
ferred to United Artists from the Johnson County War Company and
Cimino and Carelli, making Cimino, in effect, just another hired director, serving at the pleasure of the corporation and to its orders.

Field met with Cimino, Carelli, and Derek Kavanagh in Cimino's
room at the inn on Sunday, August 5, and delivered the letter and the
take-over notice.

He also delivered the concession we thought would make it possible
for Cimino to remain on the picture in spite of the take-over. The $25
million had been a useful negotiating figure for Stolber and me in Kalispell, but Kavanagh's certitude that it was unmakable, no matter what
Cimino claimed, meant guaranteeing that the prologue and epilogue
could never be made. We consequently persuaded Albeck that Cimino
should be given the more attainable goal of $27.5 million in Montana.
If he stayed within that figure, he could have his prologue and epilogue—on a budget to be determined and fully vetted by UA—and the
total budget, including prologue, epilogue, and all postproduction work
to release of the picture would be increased to $30 million. Final cut
was his as long as the movie, with prologue and epilogue, was three
hours or less.

Cimino's response was to ask to be fired.

He advised Field to scrap the picture and write off the investment.
Field refused, offering instead to accept Cimino's resignation, which

Cimino said he could not offer because, as Field recorded later, "he was unsure of his legal position."

There was nothing for Cimino to do but agree to agree. He would talk to his actors, soliciting their support in speeding the production, which was to double the previous pace. He would also participate with Kavanagh in preparing—that day—a new schedule and budget to meet the $27.5 million Montana objective. It would be delivered no later than the following morning, and it was, at ten-thirty.

Sunday afternoon Field went back to his room at the inn to use the telephone, make notes for the files about the meeting, and begin a draft of a letter summarizing Cimino's reluctant acquiescence, which would be addressed to Cimino with a copy delivered to a relieved Eric Weissmann in Beverly Hills.

At some point the telephone rang in Field's room, and what UA had hoped to avoid was on the other end of the line. Todd McCarthy was calling from *Daily Variety* in Hollywood, having learned that Field was in Kalispell. It wasn't hard to figure out how. All those technicians and crew members with time on their hands, and letters to write back home, the abortive attempt to find a partner, the mysterious office absences of Field, Stolber, and myself could hardly have failed to raise red flags with the Hollywood trade press, and possibly beyond.

Then, too, there was the John Hurt problem, which McCarthy knew about and intended to publish. Hurt, who had looked forward to such a "lark" in the wide-open spaces, had found the situation and the setting stultifying, barren, enraging. He had gone for the most recent ten-week period with only one and one-half days' work in a town the recreational possibilities of which were considerably less rich than those of London. He waited and fumed and raged and threatened because the seemingly endless production schedule of *Heaven's Gate*, on which he appeared to be doing nothing but waiting around to be shot in the battle sequence, might cause him to be replaced in the title role of *The Elephant Man*, scheduled to begin shooting in England on October 15. He was now telling anyone who would listen, including his Hollywood agent, John Crosby, that he would be in England on October 15, *Heaven's Gate* or no *Heaven's Gate*.

Would Field care to comment? McCarthy wondered. No, Field would not. Would he care to comment on the picture in France that had gone ahead without Isabelle Huppert and the three others that were still waiting for her? No, Field would not. He was in Montana only "to say hello to Michael." Yes, there was "a sizable increase from the original budget," he allowed, but the increases were not "out of line. I know we say it about every picture," he told McCarthy, "but this is a film we are extremely enthusiastic about, now more than ever."

Perhaps this call prompted another activity that afternoon in Kalispell, for Field found time to draft a publicity release announcing UA's take-over of the production. No such story was ever announced or printed, possibly because Stan Kamen strongly protested such an announcement but more probably because taking over the production and simultaneously expressing enthusiasm "now more than ever" might have seemed somehow inconsistent.

Around six o'clock that Sunday evening Joann Carelli came to Field's room, and they reviewed the events of the day, including progress on the revised schedule to be delivered in the morning, which now called for an additional thirty-nine days, adjusted to reflect the six days that had gone by since Kavanagh drafted the earlier forty-five-day version. The new one would, Carelli reported with some relief, allow John Hurt to leave for England and *The Elephant Man* before October 15, when the state of Montana would start shutting down the mountain roads for the winter anyway.

"But," Carelli asked Field while she was there, "what I don't understand—and neither does Mike—is: What happens if he falls behind now?"

"Then he gets his wish, Joann," Field said. "He gets fired."

"Oh," she said. "Oh."

CHAPTER 15

SWITCHBLADES

Today's reader is not interested in analysis but opinion, preferably harsh and unexpected. . . . Needless to say, the more violent and *ad hominem* the style, the more grateful [the] readers will be. Americans like to be told whom to hate.

—Gore Vidal,
"Literary Gangsters,"
Commentary (March 1970)

Michael Cimino did not get fired. He got smart. He hurried up.

This was grimly gratifying to Andy Albeck. April, May, June, and July were gone forever—and millions with them—but August and most of September registered a doubling of the previous production pace and, therefore, an approximate halving of the cash flow estimated by Derek Kavanagh. Derek uncomplainingly remained UA's presence in Montana, calling in reports each evening to Field: so many pages shot; so many minutes of film; so many feet exposed; so many feet printed; so much projected screen time for the finished picture; so much slippage from the new schedule and budget; so much money; so much time. Kavanagh was notably free of vindictive recrimination in these reports. He committed to writing his praise for Charlie Okun, the crew, even Cimino, whose tardy but real cooperation had moved the production forward to become, at a point in late August, two days *ahead* of the new UA schedule, with no loss in quality to the torrents of film feeding into and pouring out of the cameras.

One could see the footage. One could, that is, if one were in Kalispell to do so, but even then it wasn't much, and it wasn't easy. Of the almost 1.5 million feet of film exposed on *Heaven's Gate* (1.3 million feet of which were printed*) and the thousands of rolls of film exposed by still photographers, not one frame, not one color transparency, not one black-and-white glossy found its way back to California or New York before shooting was completed. Even then, months in which they were neither volunteered nor yielded went by. Viewing the material in Kalispell (or later in California) was a grudging "courtesy" accommodation by Cimino, now and then to reassure and calm executive nerves. These courtesy displays of footage were the result of patient entreaty, not so patient badgering, and, finally, correspondence which hammered at this or that legal point to nail down UA's right to see what it had paid millions to manufacture and, in fact, owned.

Part of this withholding was justified by the UA laissez-faire tradition. ("They see the picture when I'm ready to give it to them," Woody Allen had told *Fortune* about the previous regime.) Withholding the stills material was no doubt the result of legitimate concern over what UA's reaction would be when the publicity department finally received the material in August 1980 and discovered that of the 8,047 duplicates approved and delivered by Cimino and Carelli, fully 4,000 were stills of Cimino and his crew.

A larger and deeper reluctance to display footage was designed to ward off premature evaluation and interference, something all directors—perhaps all creative artists—are eager to avoid, and in the case of *Heaven's Gate* it was both protective and practical. Viewing 1.5 million feet of film composed of multiple takes of single shots could have only induced panic or torpor. Fifty-three takes of Kris Kristofferson brandishing a bullwhip at the Sweetwater mayor, for instance, begin to blend together, whatever nuances may exist from take to take, and serve to recall vividly where the money went, dazing the mind, perhaps, more than dazzling the eye.

Central to all this, it seemed, was a tenacious desire for control coupled with a penchant for secrecy. Cimino's initial contractual demands for total control over advertising and publicity ("without limitation") had hinted at this from the start, and there may have been a justifiable logic to it. In years spent on Madison Avenue manufacturing images for shampoos, cosmetics, and soft drinks, the manipulating—and obscuring—of detail were techniques over which he had demonstrable mastery. But withholding material from UA until UA legally demanded it or dictating UA's uses of it seemed merely high-handed or

---

*This is roughly 220 hours of film, or nearly ten days of nonstop viewing, or the equivalent of more than 100 normal-length feature films. It was said to be a record and probably was.

uncooperative. Barring the press from the production was an extreme and highly risky method of controlling what was said and written or not said and written.

Perhaps this was not to be unexpected and was merely sensible in one whose autobiography did not stand up well under scrutiny, and Cimino was neither the first nor the last to erect barriers between himself and the press, even in an industry that courts fame and personal publicity and in which image building is not less well known than on Madison Avenue.

"I have no personal life" was a standard interview line he often used, a statement readily corroborated as fact by colleagues past and present, but it is also a statement that suggested attempts to deflect attention away from scrutiny of a man, redirecting it to a perhaps contrived image. Personal mythmaking requires distancing the subject from the viewer, and Cimino regularly sought an exaggerated privacy not only from the press but also from UA. No one at the company had his private telephone number; all calls, appointments, questions were first screened by Carelli; and it was the object of some amusement that he would come to use aliases when booking airplanes and hotels, as if his fame required traveling incognito. (Maybe it did. "Sam Book" was a favorite *nom de voyage*, borrowed from an analyst with the National Research Group, which performed market research for UA. Another was "Mr. Michael.")

All this may have been a genuine desire for privacy, with which no one could quarrel, but to those who were constantly denied access to the person and the production it may have recalled the charge Nick hurls at Michael in *The Deer Hunter*: "You're a maniac control freak!," to which Michael replies, "I just don't like surprises." There were a few in store, and not only for Cimino.

"It could have been a *lot* worse, Andy," Hy Smith said. He stood nervously before Albeck's desk, glancing from me to the front page of *Daily Variety* for August 10, which lay open on Albeck's desk. The headline read: CIMINO'S "GATE" HEAVEN BOUND, NEARS $30 MIL.

Hy glanced at me, tugged nervously at his bushy black mustache, which looked as if it might have modeled for the Outlaw Inn's logo, as Albeck considered the headline and Todd McCarthy's by-line, then turned to an inside page, where the article continued for a dozen detail-filled column inches.

"I mean, who but Michael and Joann thought the budget of this picture was going to remain a *secret*?" Hy said, addressing the ceiling. "This is show biz. Show and *tell*."

Albeck didn't reply, but yes, it could have been a lot worse. It could have read "$36 Mil," as Derek Kavanagh continued to insist, or "$40 Mil" or even "$50 Mil," as had appeared all too possible only a few weeks earlier. Hy Smith didn't know those figures, and Albeck was not moved to reveal them. One of the most cherished myths of the industry is that there are no secrets in show business, but there *are*, and Albeck knew that one way to keep them secret was not to tell someone whose job was, after all, *telling*.

He looked up. "What does he mean here, 'budgetary quicksand'?" he asked, quoting McCarthy.

"He means he couldn't come up with a hard number," Hy replied breezily, "but he could come up with a cute metaphor."

"'Cute'?" said Albeck. "I don't call 'no end in sight' *cute*," he said, quoting again. Then to me, "Is this correct about Hurt and Huppert?" he asked, glancing at *Variety*'s accurate account of their missed or threatened other pictures.

I nodded.

"Look, Andy," said Hy, sounding strained, "the guy is a *reporter*. We can't blame him for going out and getting a story we've been keeping the lid on for months. If there's anything in that piece that's not true, it's the line from David about how enthusiastic we are, 'now more than ever.'"

"Aren't we?" Albeck asked blandly.

"Of course we are," said Hy. "Those cyanide capsules I distributed to the staff are only . . ." His voice trailed off as Albeck's face remained set, unsmiling.

"We're enthusiastic," I reassured. "Maybe not more than ever but . . ."

"Where else will this story appear?" Albeck asked.

"Only everywhere," said Hy. "They all read *Variety*. Rona reads it. Liz Smith reads it. Gene Shalit reads it. Ronald Reagan reads it. The cat is out of the bag; the lid is *off*."

"And we can't control this?"

"Sure, Andy," said Hy, exasperated. "We have no stills, no production information, no cooperation, no interviews, no nothing, but so what? We'll save it all. I'm going down to my office right now, in fact, to write a Cimino bio. How does this grab you for a beginning?" he asked, his hand tracing the words in the air. "'Born in a manger . . .'"

Like Michael Cimino, Andy Albeck avoided personal publicity, but there was nothing contrived or calculated about it. He shared the widespread layman's skepticism about press methods and motives and doubted, in spite of the pressure he applied on Hy Smith, that they could be managed. He was too modest and reticent a man to court press attention and seemed astonished he could attract it. "Fools' names and fools' faces" was something his grandchildren chanted, and he thought frankly there was truth to the adage, particularly for one who lacked the imperial ease of an Arthur Krim or even the aggressive assertiveness of MGM's Frank Rosenfelt, who was sometimes abrasive and boastful but sounded, well . . . convincing.

Still, Albeck had promised to do interviews after he had been in office one year and had something to talk about, and the three years he had agreed to serve as president were more than half over now in late summer of 1979, when he agreed to his first—and only—major press interview. That agreement had been extracted only after considerable cajoling and mock-desperate pleading by Hy Smith. Some of the desperation was kidding on the square. Ad-pub people, for all the manipulating of news they are imagined to do, are easily intimidated by the press because their jobs often depend on the cold black print they assiduously court but can rarely control, though their own habit of hype sometimes persuades them they do. Because the press is dependent on information for its functioning, an uneasy alliance exists between publicists and reporters, the character of which ranges from backscratching to backstabbing, on both sides.

The Hollywood movie press has, of course, been notorious for its friendliness and malleability since even before the formation of United Artists in 1919. This remains particularly true in the international movie press, as the Cannes Film Festival proves annually, as do the fortunes of certain substantially endowed starlets (financially and otherwise), whose success at press management has handily outstripped that of, say, Ron Ziegler or Jody Powell.

But the changes wrought in American life by the *Washington Post* and "Woodstein" were everywhere evident by 1979, even among the movie press people, who had seen *All the President's Men* (or actually read it) and were preternaturally paranoid about being scooped on important business stories. "See what the boys in the back room will have" took on new meaning for much of the press, particularly the *Los Angeles Times*, which had either ignored or badly underestimated the importance and public interest in the year-old David Begelman forgery and embezzlement scandal at Columbia Pictures. The *Times* had admitted having been "uncertain how to handle" the Begelman story, an uncertainty not shared by the *Washington Post* (again) or the *Wall Street Journal*, both of which covered the story fully and soberly, though this did not make it "big news." David McClintick, who covered it for the

Journal and subsequently wrote the best-selling *Indecent Exposure* about the case, credited Liz Smith, popular columnist for New York's *Daily News* (and, to a lesser extent, Walter Cronkite on CBS), with making the story a media event. The power of the popular press remains formidable.

As Hollywood's (and Begelman's) most important, most widely read hometown newspaper, the *Los Angeles Times* was further compromised by the sympathetic and humane assessment of its sympathetic and humane (and widely respected) arts editor, Charles Champlin, who termed the case "a crimeless crime" with "a culprit who doubles as a victim."

Many in Hollywood thought this view rather *too* compassionate and openly questioned the *Times'* seriousness about Hollywood news. As a consequence, the paper had embarked on a laudable and vigorous pursuit of "hard" news, covering the business, rather than the show. This policy was applauded politely but not without misgivings by professional publicity people like Hy Smith, growing daily more fretful about *Heaven's Gate*, sensing its potential to become a story harmful not only to the picture's public and box-office images but to management as well, for the official UA policy was to "protect" the picture even at management's expense. The *Los Angeles Times* had long been asking to do an in-depth UA business story, and Smith implored Albeck to cooperate before *Heaven's Gate* "hit the fan," as Hy put it. Albeck agreed.

He did so reluctantly and on condition that Field and I sit in on the interview, so he could steer attention to the pictures, publicity for which was the only rationale he had been willing to accept for the interview.

Field and I joined Andy, Hy, and Charles Schreger of the *Times* in the small conference room adjoining Albeck's office in New York, braced for questions about *Heaven's Gate* and Cimino. They never came. The interview was low-key, dignified, polite, unprobing, and dull. There were questions about the corporate relations between Transamerica and United Artists and a few perfunctory questions, a few perfunctory answers about Andy's background. The Orion question was politely posed, and Andy spoke with fond respect of Krim, Pleskow, and the others, engagingly sharing with Schreger the same warmth about them we had heard him express in private. In the only remotely personal moment of the interview, Andy said, "Eric Pleskow is one of my best friends." Schreger took notes; Hy Smith relaxed.

Albeck's sometimes stern and mirthless demeanor when dealing with Smith was not that he lacked a sense of humor or failed to appreciate Hy's. It was rather that he sometimes found Smith's wisecracks and jokes more highly developed than his sense of economy, particularly when it came to promotional budgets. Smith responded smartly with a format for consolidating newspaper ads for all the pictures UA was distributing: UA's, MGM's, and Lorimar's. He framed them inside a bold line and headed the combined ads "Entertainment from United Artists." It was an idea later much imitated (conspicuously by Universal), for the grouped ads gained accumulated impact in reduced space at less cost, while emphasizing the company name.

This pleased Albeck but was not enough. Distribution and advertising costs were rising as fast as or faster than production costs, in an economy saddled with both double-digit inflation and interest rates. The old-time buying of business with massive ad campaigns was becoming not only prohibitively costly but also, to Albeck, the mere trading of dollars for dollars.

He had required distribution and ad-pub to limit their expenditures to a percentage of their own box-office estimates, the same estimates used to evaluate production proposals. When the estimates were low, so were the advertising budgets, although there was some flexibility based on close tracking of box-office performance, and contracts usually contained minimum figures the company was obligated to spend on advertising, often broken down into categories of print, radio, and television buys. It was a downside risk approach that seemed self-defeating to producers with weak or slow pictures, including MGM and Lorimar. But Albeck was not interested in buying box-office gross (if that even worked, and there was considerable evidence that it did not). He was interested in rentals, in profits, in *net*, and not only for UA. Profit participation was one of the backbones of independent production, but the feeling was widespread (not entirely without reason) that "profits are meaningless," because back room chicanery, "creative bookkeeping," and studio overheads pushed profits ever farther from the pockets of the creative "partners," while plushly lining those of the studios.

Albeck insisted on running an honest ship but a tight one. He intended to make profit participation real at UA, but he could not do that by buying business on weak pictures like UA's own *Wanda Nevada* or *Uncle Joe Shannon*, or Lorimar's *Americathon* or *Carny*, or MGM's *Hero at Large* or *The Human Factor*.

It is axiomatic in Hollywood that "there are no bad pictures, only those undersold." Producers blame sales. Disgruntled independents could go elsewhere, but MGM and Lorimar were captive producers, bound by exclusive contracts, and if they were unhappy with UA's results on *Voices* or *International Velvet* (from MGM), or *Fedora* and *The*

Fish That Saved Pittsburgh (from Lorimar), well, so was Albeck. UA's distribution fee of 30 percent was not the license to print money commonly supposed. As is well known, 30 percent of nothing was nothing. Moreover, 30 percent of nothing *minus* high advertising costs was that much less than nothing.

Albeck sighed, then braced his shoulders and his mind.

Maybe these exclusive distribution deals should be retired, he thought. Certainly MGM was unlikely to renew in 1983, when the deal expired. Fine. What was the point of distributing the very pictures that UA had, in many cases, turned down before they were offered to MGM or Lorimar? UA had its own weak pictures to worry about, but at least they were pictures that Albeck, distribution, and production had been able to agree on, so there was some continuity of approach, and he could, if necessary, cut his losses without enduring the wounded howls of bad faith or bad salesmanship from outsiders. Production planning, he thought, should expand to take up the MGM slack after 1982, possibly even earlier in the case of Lorimar. That was another reason for no more *Heaven's Gates*. They gobbled up not only money but also other pictures, pictures that would never get made.

He glanced at the *Ficus benjamina* in the corner of his office, still raining its few remaining dark brown leaves on the beige wool carpet. He jotted a follow-up note to have it replaced. That would be far easier than replacing the MGM or Lorimar product or, he frowned, than replacing a man, as production had tried to do on *Heaven's Gate* and as he himself would soon have to do. Any day now. A major executive at that. He did not relish the termination of a man's career, for in this case it would amount to that. It was a part of business life that grieved him, that recalled the hated epithet "hatchet man," and he had had enough experience trying to do so dispassionately and cleanly in the past to know that it did not get easier, no matter how necessary. And this time it *was* necessary, he concluded regretfully and maybe even tardily. For the good of the company and the man himself. It would end the snickering "Lord Smirnoff" jokes that had started in ad-pub and worked their way through every floor of 729, including the mail room, cruel jokes that Albeck pretended to ignore or not to hear. He spoke instead of the bleeding ulcers, which were real enough, and to which the job and its pressures—and perhaps Albeck, too—contributed.

All men have their weaknesses, he thought, and while business was business, it need not preclude charity. No, he corrected himself quickly, not charity. Not after almost three decades of loyal service. Decency. Compassion. And without embarrassment to the man or the company. He would think of a way.

He fell into a quiet musing, and the compression of his lips would have looked fierce to his visitor were not the eyes so still and inward-looking behind their magnifying lenses. After a moment he looked out and said, with subdued cheeriness, "What do you think of a palm? Or a *Dracaena*? They say they're almost indestructible. Even by *my* . . . 'vibes.'" He smiled.

"Maybe a palm," his visitor said, shrugging.

"That would be fabulous," Albeck said with a sigh. He pronounced it "fabalous."

It was around midnight on August 23 when David Field finally tracked me down in my hotel room somewhere in rainy Cleveland, Ohio. It had been raining off and on all summer in Cleveland, where shooting on *Those Lips, Those Eyes* was three wet weeks behind schedule. I had spent the evening with producers Herb and Steven-Charles Jaffe and director Michael Pressman in nearby Cleveland Heights and Cain Park, the outdoor summer theater in which the original screenplay by David Shaber mainly took place. We debated various ways to regain time and money as the rain drizzled and actors Frank Langella and Thomas Hulce swapped theater stories, waiting for a break in the weather so an important nighttime musical sequence could be shot on Cain Park's outdoor stage, where only rain danced. And danced.

By midnight we had given up, and as I entered my room, tired and wet and wanting a drink, I answered the persistently ringing telephone, never guessing how badly I would need one.

"It's Albeck," Field said from 2,000 miles away, and from the sound of his voice I thought for a moment that Andy had died. Field asked me to sit down and listen, and I did.

The West Coast publicity department had obtained that afternoon an advance copy of the *Los Angeles Times*' "Sunday Calendar" magazine section for August 26, which Field read to me in a shrunken voice. It was the lead cover story, and the headline read SHOOTOUT AT THE UA CORRAL: ARTISTS VS. ACCOUNTANTS. Charles Schreger had struck, not, the gossip went, without help. Rona Barrett had also seen an advance copy of the piece and announced on ABC's *Good Morning, America* that the article was already circulating rapidly through Hollywood and looked to insiders as if it had been "orchestrated" by Orion. Orion denied the charge, she reported, having planted the thought.

In the opening paragraph Eric Pleskow, whom Albeck had called "one of my closest friends," called him "a pencil sharpener." He set a stiletto tone that not only shocked Hollywood but stunned morale within the company he had recently departed, at levels high and low, nowhere more than on the fourteenth floor of 729 Seventh Avenue.

"Quite simply," Schreger breezily editorialized, "UA, a company that was viewed historically as vibrant and innovative, has fallen into the hands of the money men"—the "accountants," presumably, who had taken over when the "artists" departed. The article began on the cover and continued inside, illustrated with a photograph of Albeck, on whom Pleskow and other unnamed "former colleagues" honed their hatchets for two full pages. "Administrator" he was called at best; "an office boy," at worst.

The article was mainly a rehash of the nineteen-month-old story in *Fortune* that culminated in the Orion walkout, liberally spiced by the "name-calling" (even Schreger called it that). The Transamerica-Krim conflict was old, dead stuff, and perhaps it needed pepping up with invective. Transamerica was, of course, villainous as charged; Albeck, by association. His use by the former regime as its "conduit" to Transamerica, his current good relationship with San Francisco, the very neatness of his desk (no "artistic" clutter, no movie star pictures on the walls), even the posters left by the former regime in the corridor (Schreger faked them and got them wrong) were cited to skewer the "accountant," the "administrator."

The perhaps one-third of the article that was not devoted to Transamerica's "nitpicking" and Albeck's "housekeeping" (Pleskow, both times) was devoted to the "shoot-out" Schreger staged. "Two sets of management," he wrote, "are claiming credit for the current good fortune of United Artists." There it was.

UA was pacing the summer box office with *Manhattan*, *Moonraker*, *Rocky II*, *Apocalypse Now*, *La Cage aux Folles*, and *The Black Stallion*. All were made possible, directly or indirectly, by deals inherited from the previous regime. Two, *Apocalypse* and *The Black Stallion*, had actually been started, though not finished, by it, and the *Rocky II* and subsequent *Rocky III* deals were technically Albeck's. Orion's box office to date had fallen below its and industry expectations, with the very notable exception of "*10*," which had ironically been at UA and rejected.

Albeck neither publicly nor privately claimed credit for inherited deals—nor did he assign blame for the *Uncle Joe Shannon*s and *Slow Dancing in the Big City*s that were left behind either. But he did differentiate for Schreger the difference between a deal and a picture, a distinction subject to notorious confusion in Hollywood.

"A contract by itself," he pointed out, "means nothing. In this business, from the point that you have a contract to the point you have a finished picture there probably are 50 different traps, all of which are going to kill the project. It's the ability to take a picture from point A to the point of completion [that] makes a picture." Pleskow was having none of that. "There's no way those films would be there if it were not for us," he announced.

No one had ever disputed that, but the irony that the "accountant" addressed himself to the broad process of filmmaking and the "artist" solely to the importance of the deal was lost on Schreger and the *Times*. Perhaps the snappy headline and the invitation to indulge in insult and invective was a tacit admission by the *Times* that it endorsed the cynical (and ubiquitous) observation that the true art form of Hollywood is the deal. Perhaps Schreger's indifference to what is a crucial movie industry question resulted from his interest in acquiring a studio job (which he soon got and accepted at Columbia Pictures). Perhaps his orientation, too, was for the deal. "Being an agent," he opined in the same article, "someone who negotiates deals for talent, is perhaps the best training" for a chief executive. Perhaps so, if deals are movies and negotiation is the essence of the process, but I knew that Rona Barrett and Hollywood weren't clucking over the implications of the astonishing assertion of the primacy of the deal, and they wouldn't reflect on it or debate it or analyze the vehement vying for acclaim and credit either. They were quoting "pencil sharpener"; they were repeating "office boy"; they were visualizing "the hands of the money men" wrapped around the throats of the "artists." I felt my own throat constrict as Field finished reading the piece in his funereal voice. The sound of Ohio rain continued as the backdrop to a long silence. Finally, I asked him to read it again. He did, and it didn't get any better.

We talked long into the night, and he told me Andy was "devastated," but this came from Hy Smith, who was the only person in the company with whom Albeck discussed the article, ever, and when reporters here and abroad clamored for a response, the only one they got was "no comment." Smith could not explain how the article about United Artists had become a springboard for personal attack by former colleagues. He could not explain because the *Times* had given no inkling of the piece's intent, no opportunity for rebuttal, clarification, or serious philosophical discussion. Smith hadn't known Schreger was talking to Orion; no one knew—except Orion, of course—where "the *mano-a-mano* contest," as Arthur Krim called it, apparently gave even him pause. Krim wrote the *Times* saying that "there is room enough in this industry for both of these companies to succeed and much too early to make judgments about either." But the judgments had been made and printed and discussed in the Polo Lounge and the Russian Tea Room and on network television, and their reverberations were to continue. Until the very end, in fact.

• • •

A small irony of the Schreger piece was that David Field and I and
Heaven's Gate were totally incidental to it. There was a reference to the
movie as a project we were responsible for, one that sounded somehow
"interesting."

Just how "interesting" it was to the *Los Angeles Times* was revealed
with stunning swiftness that also explained Schreger's curious avoidance
of it as an issue. Seven days after the "Shootout" article appeared, the
Times' "Calendar" section gave equal space (cover story, continued inside for two pages) to something entitled "AN UNAUTHORIZED PROG-
RESS REPORT ON 'HEAVEN'S GATE,'" which appeared on the same
Sunday, September 2, in the *Washington Post* and went out on the wire
service the two papers share.

The futility of stonewalling the press had never been so clear or so
forcefully demonstrated, and it was a lowly extra, one of the 1,200 or so
"local hires" on *Heaven's Gate*, who did it.

Les Gapay, a free-lance writer who had previously worked in Washington for the *Wall Street Journal* and the *Congressional Quarterly*, had
taken up a quieter life (he thought) in northwestern Montana. He wandered into the *Heaven's Gate* production office in Kalispell one day to
try to get an interview for what he thought would be "a puff piece."
"We've turned down the *New York Times*!" he was told. So—in what
sounds like a Warner Brothers plot from the thirties—he applied for a
job as an extra, worked on the movie for two months, got $30 a day
plus lunches, and got his story, too.

"Local uproar" was the theme, and if anything, Gapay downplayed
it. Northwestern Montana in 1979 was feeling the effects of unemploy-
ment, inflation, and high interest rates, as was much of the nation, and
the continuing energy crisis threatened a dull, dry tourist summer.
Heaven's Gate changed all that, to the delight of merchants and the
many locals who found work on the picture. There was less merriment
among environmentalists and the National Park Service staff, who
charged that *Heaven's Gate* was also changing the local ecology: moving
heavy equipment and hundreds of people into Glacier National Park;
importing earth and plants not indigenous to the area (and possibly
plant pests as well); causing damage to logging roads and roadside vege-
tation. The difficulties Joann Carelli had told us of in finding locations
for the picture were substantially more than a matter of price, for in late
May Park Superintendent Phillip Iversen withdrew permission for continued filming in the park after permits expired on June 10. Iversen
later told the Associated Press that Cimino was "in the business of
creating illusions and the park is in the business of protecting the natu-

ral features in a national park and the two seem to have a conflict. . . . I can't compromise park values."

On June 10, the day the permits expired, Hollywood's own non-compromiser dug his heels in at a press conference for local papers at the Outlaw Inn. Cimino claimed that he had learned of the withdrawal of permission by reading the AP's wire report in the *Kalispell Daily Inter Lake*, and said, "I should have been the first to be contacted instead of learning it from a worldwide news source." He charged that "Iversen has achieved publicity at my expense to a degree which approaches libel." Iversen replied calmly to the *Daily Inter Lake* that not one but two copies of the notice had been sent to the company: one hand delivered on location at East Glacier on May 29; the other sent by registered mail.

Cimino countered with "the personal and financial distress Iversen has caused me." In a community sensitive in 1979 to "financial distress" the uproar escalated. Local merchants, including the Outlaw Inn and the local Chevrolet dealer, Teamsters' Local No. 448, and various private citizens working on the picture took a two-page ad in the *Inter Lake* to thank and praise Cimino; Cimino took a one-page ad to thank and praise *them*. Citizens wrote letters angrily denouncing the production or angrily denouncing Superintendent Iversen. It was a classic case of environment versus economy, and Cimino demonstrated, in a gesture neatly addressing both issues, "proof of his professed love affair with Montana," as the *Inter Lake* called it, by announcing his local real estate purchase.

The "uproar" was reported as far away as the *Missoula Missoulian* ("MR. IVERSEN AND HIS PARK" MIFFS FILM DIRECTOR ran a banner headline), the *Great Falls Tribune*, the *Whitefish Pilot*, the *Hungry Horse News* (where a full-page ad printed in red proclaimed "Iversen Must Go"), but this was all a teapot tempest until Gapay's article appeared on September 2. He lightly summarized it, concentrating instead on the "uproar" within the production itself.

Extras were fainting; their toes (including Gapay's own) were being crushed; they were being bruised; they were forced to wallow in mud and swelter in heat. They inhaled fuller's earth, dust, and chemical smoke. There weren't enough bathroom facilities. They were treated rudely. On one shooting day sixteen people were injured; on another, work began at seven-thirty in the morning and lunch was not provided until four-thirty in the afternoon. They were shunted off with printed notices reading "Please do not approach the actors or crew members." They overheard an assistant director tell a wagon driver, "If people don't move out of your way, run them over." Crew members railed against the violence in private and warned extras not to take their children to see the movie.

"We don't have anything to say," the production responded officially. Unofficially, Gapay thought (but did not print), "they knew it was going to be a lousy movie while they were working on it."

It was a tale of gory, reckless excess, illustrated with photographs by the author (since no others had been made available), and in all the economic, environmental, muddy, sweaty, bone-cracking, bladder-bursting mayhem, the enterprising "extra" noted that "the biggest spender of all was Cimino, who bought not only a $10,000 Jeep* but also 156 acres of land." (Gapay kept track of that land and noted with some amusement several years later that Cimino's "love affair with Montana" had apparently cooled. In mid-1984 the land was up for sale, but there were "no takers.")

The *Times* and the *Post* bought the Gapay article in mid-August, about the time *Daily Variety* broke its own version of the event, and the two papers agreed to nonexclusive rights, provided publication was simultaneous in Los Angeles and Washington. The story was later sold separately to the *Chicago Tribune* and the *Miami Herald*, which also ran it, as did countless others. Gapay's piece became a source for all those barred journalists and commentators; so did the first truly national coverage in *Time*, dated one day later, September 3, 1979, which announced "The Making of Apocalypse Next" over one full page and a third of the next, complete with photos, quotes, and details of the production it referred to as "History's Most Expensive Minor Footnote."

It was ironic that David Field had been the agency of *Time*'s arrival in Montana, for he himself, had briefly been a journalist, between Princeton and Hollywood, and he claimed disdain and distrust of the media, knowing what context and skill could do—or undo—to remarks made for attribution. Nevertheless, he made one. "I think Michael is making a masterpiece," he told James Willwerth, the *Time* correspondent he had authorized to go to Kalispell. Field's assessment of the film as a "masterpiece" did nothing to quiet the rage of perceived betrayal that issued from Montana when Cimino and Carelli learned their "security" had been breached. (They did not, of course, suspect "the extra" in their midst.) "David said he felt sorry for the guy!" Joann howled to me over the telephone. "Because he used to be a journalist, too! Some humpty-dumpty journalist he feels sorry for! What about *us?*"

Like *Variety*, *Time* could have been a lot worse, and in fact might have been, had Willwerth gone to Montana after rather than before

---

*Carelli bought one, too.

Gapay's far stronger "unauthorized" piece. *Time* ran separate pictures of the director, Kristofferson, and Huppert and wasn't snide and was mostly accurate, but it set a tone for subsequent journalists to follow with its *Apocalypse* allusions (also prominent in *Variety*), the "Minor Footnote" gibe, and Willwerth's quotation of a "production insider" that the atmosphere between Cimino and UA was one of "switchblades and garbage-can covers." This colorful observation was due, no doubt, to Willwerth's visit coinciding with the doubling of pressure and pace that resulted from the take-over, though that event was shielded from him.

Field was quoted in his "masterpiece" speech; Kristofferson explained somewhat mysteriously that "the movie ends where *The Great Gatsby* begins"; and Cimino—"like Napoleon," *Time* described him— fell back on "I have no personal life" and described the problems of production and authenticity, as he was to do again and again in the future. Subduing his ire at press invasion of his domain, he kept things high-toned. "If you make an honest film," he said, "the audience will relate to the people who live and die in that film. . . . You make a movie with as much passion as you can bring to it." He further observed, "You follow an obsession . . . it leads you somewhere."

Fortunately *Heaven's Gate* was leading him into the penultimate throes of its production as this first burst of press attention occurred, with a sequence big enough and dangerous enough to justify clamping a new lid on direct press coverage. The battle sequence that was to end production and the picture was to involve scores of horses, hundreds of wagons and other period vehicles, all principal cast members (except Walken, whose Nate Champion is killed just before the battle's start), hundreds of extras and crew and stunt and special-effects men, and thousands of explosive charges both large and small for the better part of a month. All this was to be captured by half a dozen cameras, some manned, some locked into place with a fixed focus and operated by remote control or simply turned on and left running until the magazines were empty, piling up film and still more film. It was dangerous physically and logistically, and nerves that had been tightly wound for months began to fray and then unravel under the strain. If switchblades were flashing, they were less between Cimino and UA than between Cimino and isolated but determined members of his own production.

There is among those who have worked under Cimino, in fact, an almost unqualified admiration and respect for his perfectionism and dedication. Still, one man's "dedication" is another man's "ruthlessness" as the "To Hell with *Heaven's Gate*" bumper sticker, widely rumored to have been of internal, company origin, may have suggested.

"Cimino had no respect for his actors or his animals," stormed stunt man-wrangler John Scott to Alberta's *Calgary Sun*. Scott had worked for eight months on the picture, supplying both horses and wagons, as he had done for many other pictures in the past. He knew that no sequence involving stunts, explosives, and animals was entirely safe, and the size of this one posed alarming hazards. Presumably the actors and extras understood the perils, and full medical and first-aid crews were present throughout to attend to the inevitable injuries that had ranged, over months now, from cuts and bruises, heat prostration, and Les Gapay's crushed toes to hospitalization of several, including a professional stunt woman. But the horses didn't understand all that or that there were veterinary first-aid people, too. They didn't know that stunt coordinator Buddy Van Horne was thorough and inventive and rigging stunts for maximum safety. The animals would know only a situation that simulated war and that approached it in atmosphere and hazards. The explosions and gunshots, the sound and fury all would be real, as would the billowing clouds of dust from tons of fuller's earth covering the battlefield, possibly obscuring the camera crews or unmanned cameras planted in paths the horses were to charge across at full, furious gallop. No one on the production took it lightly or casually, but John Scott openly rebelled. "We had a big fight over abusing horses. He wanted to use one of mine in the [battle] scene. . . . I refused and the Hollywood horse he used was killed. It was sickening!" he recalled with force.

Other crew members who were as disturbed as Scott by the treatment of animals on the picture remained silent, no doubt fearing for their jobs. That did not stop some of them, however, from filing confidential complaints with the American Humane Association alleging mistreatment of animals. They cited cockfighting in the Sweetwater saloon as Averill arrives in town (forbidden by the Montana state penal code); they alleged that real blood was extracted from living cattle by hypodermic needle, to be used instead of synthetic blood for makeup effects; they charged killing of bled cattle for use as props (a serious violation of National Park Service rules in Glacier because the carcasses attract park grizzlies, known to kill; this was one of the bases on which Superintendent Iversen acted in withdrawing permits and approvals to shoot in the park); they alleged use of trip wire to cause horses to stumble in mid-gallop, a practice long banned in the industry because it often leads to injuries that require destruction of the animals; and finally, they pointed to the killing by buried explosives of the horse cited by Scott, which "blew [the stunt rider] sky high," and when he landed, he landed in the hospital.

UA learned of the reports filed with the AHA only later, perhaps because they had no legal force. One horse owner did press a lawsuit for "severe physical and behavioral trauma and disfigurement" of the animal, which, it was asserted, had had to be treated by a psychiatrist. The case was settled out of court.

In all the chaos and physical peril, the wonder to Derek Kavanagh was that only one horse was killed, and none of the riders or actors or extras. Kavanagh never personally saw evidence of wire tripping and maintained that it wouldn't have mattered if Cimino had respect for the animals or not, because boss wrangler Rudy Ugland *did* and, as Kavanagh reported later, "would have wire-tripped *Cimino* before letting it happen to one of his horses." Still, the reports were made, and they, too, were to reverberate in the future and in the press. "Disgruntled employees filed those reports," said one crew member. "Well, who wouldn't be disgruntled on a twelve-week shoot that lasts for six months?" commented Kavanagh, who remained generous with his praise for the crew, the wranglers, the stunt men, and Cimino, who, as always, pushed no one harder than himself. The problem, thought Kavanagh, was that Cimino could stand that kind of pressure. Not everybody could.

The second glint of flashing switchblades occurred on another sort of battlefield.

Tension between Joann Carelli and Charlie Okun had been observable from the beginning of production to those who were watching. Each needed the other's cooperation and approval, and each resented the need. Joann's position was the more secure simply because she was the producer of record. Charlie, an anxious but conscientious man, stood to lose any conflict in which Carelli or UA opposed him. If company and producer should do so at once, he would not so much be torn by conflicting loyalties as crushed by opposing juggernauts.

Lee Katz, who of all the participants in the drama had been most prescient, had cheerfully accepted physical banishment from Montana, his taste in location jaunts frankly favoring the more luxurious. But he remained very much a daily, even hourly participant in Montana events through both Kavanagh, with whom he shared advice and experience, and, following the August take-over—which effectively removed Joann Carelli as producer of the picture—Charlie Okun. Because Charlie's job now required him to report directly to UA, through Derek in Kalispell or Lee in California. An appearance of ambiguous loyalties could not, therefore, have been more apparent had it been plotted, no matter what degree of loyalty Okun felt for the "brilliant kid" to whom he had shown the Madison Avenue ropes fifteen years before.

Cimino had regarded Katz as some kind of nemesis since *Thunderbolt and Lightfoot*, when there had been a budgetary dispute over a television version of the movie. That Okun and Katz were communicating at all would have been an irritant. That Cimino believed their communications were "clandestine" he found much more than irritating, and he resolved to finish the battle sequence first and to settle this piece of hash second, once and for all.

Cimino finished the battle sequence in late September and on September 29 wrote David Field a "personal and confidential" letter (which he nevertheless sent copies of to Carelli, Kamen, Weissmann, and me). He praised David's "continued support and enthusiasm" and claimed to be "absolutely convinced that we have something quite remarkable here, and despite my own exhaustion my enthusiasm for the film has . . . only increased."

So had his determination to do something about Charlie Okun and Lee Katz. He wrote Field that their communications "have violated all sense of ethics," and "I find this situation of direct and clandestine conversations between Charlie Okun and Lee Katz to be totally offensive to Joann and myself, and also to you because [Katz] acts as your representative" (and was so acting on UA's instructions). He asked Field to "censure" Katz and to prohibit Katz from having "any and all contact with myself and Joann through this next year of finishing, as he is only a divisive influence."

Production ended at last on October 2 in Butte, Montana, where the last scene was shot, Sam Waterston as Frank Canton recruiting mercenaries at a nighttime railroad siding, a scene that had been deleted by UA as "unnecessary" but restored by the writer-director. The company's wrap party was held at the War Bonnet Inn in Butte, where hostilities between Cimino and his friend and production manager broke out openly and Okun, according to the termination notice Cimino sent him on the fifth, asked to be fired.

Okun denied having made any such request and defended himself against Cimino's written charge of "outrageous behavior" and "personal and obscene insults to myself and Vilmos Zsigmond"—as well as "unstable behavior" which merited "a reprimand by [the unions]"—by counterattacking (in writing) Cimino's "viscious [sic] and irrational manner." He accepted the termination and asked that accounting settle his affairs. He did not fail to remind Cimino that he had been "a personal friend of 15 years."

Much later Okun was to say philosophically, "I didn't get fired; I got whipped. You got whipped; we all got whipped." In yet another error of perception on *Heaven's Gate*, I assumed that with the end of principal photography, the whipping had stopped, but then I didn't really focus on Cimino's reference in his letter to David Field about "this next year of finishing." Maybe David did.

CHAPTER 16

HEADHUNTING

Good Times—Bad Times—We can do it.

—David Field (November 1978)

[*Heaven's Gate*] is about a friendship between two people whose cultures are very
different . . . and the analogy it seemed to
me, was this: In 1980, say, a well-en-
dowed Harvard graduate might very well
decide to join the Peace Corps. What if,
after living in the Amazon jungles, that
Harvard graduate discovered that his best
friend was a cannibal chieftain? He might
say to the cannibal, "Friend, I think you're
terrific, but it's about the way you be-
have . . ."

—David Field,
"Michael Cimino's Way West,"
American Film (October 1980)

If any sequence in *Heaven's Gate* had the inherent potential
to exceed budget and schedule, it was the battle sequence, and it did.
The time and money saved by Kavanagh and Cimino in August were
lost in the explosive mayhem of September. When accounts were tallied, cost to the end of production on October 2 (four days late) came to
$27,024,884.29, barely under the $27.5 million figure at which Cimino
would have the right to film prologue and epilogue at a budget of $2.5
million. No such budget had been made, let alone vetted, and the
prologue and epilogue went on immediate "hold," without approvals.
Field sent Cimino a telegram on October 3, reading "CONGRATULA-
TIONS . . . THERE IS A PRESENT FOR YOU WHEN YOU HAVE TIME TO
GO TO WILLY'S WITH ME AND PICK OUT THE LEATHER," but Cimino
had more on his mind than leather goods; his letter to Field on Sep-

tember 29, denouncing Lee Katz and Charlie Okun, had ended with a postscript that "everything is in readiness" for shooting of the prologue.

Everything was *not* in readiness at UA, in spite of Field's strong conviction (and my own) that the Harvard sequence opening the picture and the Newport, Rhode Island, "memory" scene ending it would add dimension and texture to what we obstinately refused to characterize as a western. Fitter in domestic and Auerbach in foreign agreed with us, generally supportive of anything that would make the picture bigger and, therefore, theoretically more salable.

Postproduction would surely bring the picture's cost to $30 million *without* prologue and epilogue, but that was still less than either *Moonraker* or *Apocalypse Now* had cost, and both were generating millions of dollars at box offices here and abroad, as was *The Deer Hunter* in those few but important territories for which UA had distribution. Thus, we unconsciously rationalized $30 million into a somehow "normal" cost for the kind of locomotive Albeck had priced only a year before at $10 million . . . "or more." The rest of the industry seemed to be operating on a similar assumption, unconsciously or empirically, with pictures like *1941*, *The Blues Brothers*, *The Wiz*, *Star Trek*, *Raise the Titanic*, and *Reds*, all with budgets escalating to the same $25 to $30 million range, or even beyond.

This industry-wide spending spree had not yet appeared as the race of the lemmings it eventually proved (and continues) to be, but "everybody's doin' it" was hardly a rationale to present to Andy Albeck in attempting to win approval for the prologue and epilogue. Albeck's obvious relief that shooting on Cimino's swollen epic had finally ended could only have been dissipated by the prospect of resuming production, however briefly, and on nonessential scenes at that, whatever their artistic merit or justification. How could he—"an accountant"— approve them without seeming to *reward* Cimino for failing, yet again, to live up to his commitment? And was it only accountancy? Was there no moral content to a financial commitment, as to any other kind?

Though Field and I knew Albeck was resistant, we both thought he was ultimately persuadable on grounds of audience appeal if a way could be found to control Cimino, something we were abjectly aware of having failed to do at virtually every step of the process. Things looked even dimmer when Harvard flatly refused permission to shoot on campus because of problems encountered earlier in the year when another UA picture, *A Small Circle of Friends*, shot there, disrupting the neighborhood. Cimino announced he would find another location or, failing that, *build* Harvard, possibly in Florida. This alarming suggestion blithely rendered the notion of control hopeless.

Undaunted, Cimino and his staff moved into their offices and cutting rooms in Culver City—except for the ones who went scouting locations for a substitute Harvard—and began editing at approximately the time the picture had originally been scheduled for release.

Every marketing consideration that had made *Heaven's Gate* suitable for Christmas 1979 had escalated in importance with the budget of the picture, and the Christmas season of 1980 was selected as the new and immutable release period. More precisely, *Heaven's Gate* was to premiere on successive nights in November 1980 in New York, Toronto, and Los Angeles, all three cities presenting the movie in seventy millimeter exclusive-run versions on a reserved-seat basis. It then was to open in December in other urban centers, to benefit from the traditional holiday rush, and go into wide general release only in February, presumably trailing behind it the Academy Award nominations it would have qualified for by opening in Los Angeles before the end of 1980.

This plan for finishing and marketing the picture was made with the full cooperation of Cimino and Carelli, on the basis of a postproduction schedule they worked out with chief editor Tom Rolf, which read (in part), "The picture will run 18 reels.* The final cut will be ready on May 18, 1980; the answer print† the week of October 25, 1980."

Setting a specific date for the picture's release was vital to distribution's ability to book the picture effectively and to advertising and publicity's efforts to rework the negative image the picture had acquired in the press. But the most urgent need a specific release date satisfied was that of avoiding a prolonged perfectionism in postproduction or a meandering and attenuated period like that of *Apocalypse*. If United Artists began making commitments to theaters for such and such dates, with Cimino's blessing, cooperation, and assurances of readiness, the public nature of such commitments might drive postproduction forward, locking him into a schedule that was both binding and generously ample.

November 1980 was more than a year away. Interest on nearly $30 million invested would accumulate at a double-digit clip, but a full year was not (*is* not) an inordinate amount of time to finish a film of ambitious or epic proportions. A full year may even be slight when the task involves reducing more than 200 hours of film to 3 hours which are coherent and well paced and possess enough interest to warrant an au-

---

*About three hours.
†An answer print is a fully finished print, approved by the director after all mixing, recording, and lab processes have been completed.

dience's attention. The extravagant wealth of 1.3 million feet of printed film as editing room choices might have daunted a less aesthetically decisive director than Cimino seemed to be; but once again he professed "enthusiasm," and his aura of calm control lulled us into a faith we wanted—and no doubt needed—to cling to: that he knew what he was doing.

Whether he did or did not would be apparent before November, even before May 18 and the final cut, for he promised a fully cut (though not scored, mixed, or finely tuned) version on May 1, thus giving himself a full six months to shape and deliver the no-longer-than-three-hour movie on which his right to final cut depended. The questions of prologue and epilogue might be resuscitated (and might not) when the editing process was well advanced, after the first of the year, say, when Albeck's attitude might have softened or, even better, we might have devised a foolproof means of avoiding a pattern we knew too well. For now, we could get back to business as usual or, with any luck, *un*usual.

A year had passed since Field and I had taken charge of production. The *Los Angeles Times'* demoralizing characterizations of Albeck and UA had a deeper effect than merely arousing our sympathies for a man who had earned our affection and respect; it induced a salutary mood of self-examination.

In addition to fomenting a phony and one-sided shoot-out, the *Times* had (anonymously) quoted Hollywood agents who claimed UA was at "the bottom of the list" for property submissions or "off the list" altogether. These tidings were advanced to demonstrate what happens when the "moneymen" take over from the "artists." The assertion was daily belied by the ever-increasing number of submissions to UA, but to the extent that it revealed agency attitudes, it revealed practically nothing about Albeck and a great deal about Field and me. Production credibility in Hollywood almost never derives from the board or CEO level (Krim is probably an exception), but from the production staff itself. UA's failure to establish or win credibility wasn't Albeck's failure; it was our own. *We* were the visible ones; *we* were the ones in daily contact with the creative community and the worlds of agents and lawyers and managers and movers and shakers and *lists*. The list *we* headed was clearly the wrong one, and we resolved to change all that.

It wouldn't be easy. The pressure was intense on all of us, but weighed most heavily on Field, over whom a pall had fallen since his return from his honeymoon and the take-over trip to Kalispell in early August. It was as if everything around him, including the so recently sunny marriage, were shadowed with gloom. The melancholy hovered, and the personal confidences he shared simultaneously produced sympathy and chills. They reminded us too much of the fragility of ties that bind but seldom bond.

We needed solidarity, our own consensus that could elicit that more difficult consensus from the company, and ultimately the most difficult one of all: an industry consensus of confidence.

Columbus Day weekend of 1979 we got started.

Gay Talese had been (famously) working on *Thy Neighbor's Wife*, his chronicle of American sexual behavior and mores, for years, and no one in publishing or the movie business was unaware of it. Both Field and I badly wanted to read the manuscript, not scheduled for publication until the following spring. It sounded hot: hot subject; hot property; hot movie.

It also sounded hot to the William Morris office, which represented Talese and was guarding the manuscript the way Nixon guarded the Watergate tapes. The agency planned to submit it widely in mid-October, hoping for a fast auction, in which bidders might drive the movie price to a record high. No situation could have been more tantalizing to people who were reputedly off the lists—especially if the book lived up to the hype.

It did. Kathy Van Brunt, UA's New York story editor, was told simply, "Get it," and she did. One full copy of the manuscript, still warm from the Xerox machine. I don't know *how*, and never found out, but her doing so eventually touched off a minicontroversy about "literary espionage," "burgled books and purloined letters."

Field and I read the manuscript overnight and arrived swiftly at the same conclusion: *Thy Neighbor's Wife* would be a hugely commercial book which, because of its multiple nonfiction stories, possessed not one movie but several. One of them, however, demanded telling: the harrowingly intimate story of John and Judith Bullaro, the California insurance salesman and his wife, whose experiments in sexual liberation all but destroyed their lives together. It was a cautionary tale of some contemporary relevance, and commercial, too: a Cecil B. De Mille morality cum prurience play, replete with sex and skin. What it was, was box office.

"Jackpot time," I said to Field.

"I know. What kind of price tag?"

"Big," I answered. "More than ICM got Benchley for *The Island*." He nodded. "That means . . . two and a half million?"

"That's my guess. You ready?"

He nodded. "Let's go talk to Albeck."

We knew that if Kathy Van Brunt had gotten a copy, there were, or soon would be, other copies in other hands, diminishing our surreptitious exclusivity. We also knew the Morris office had not yet framed an official strategy beyond the auction concept, in which it expected the bidding to be heavy. Our only strength was speed.

We explained to Albeck the appeal we thought the book had and told him our guess about the likely price. He flinched at neither, merely blinked, and turned toward the eight-foot palm newly gracing the corner of his office. There were no questions about "boobies"; we had been too graphic for that. "We're talking X rating, Andy."

Albeck turned back to his desk, buzzed, and asked Connie Jones, his early-shift secretary, to round up Fitter, Farber, and Auerbach. All were given the material and were lubriciously enthusiastic, save Farber who was aghast. "X?" he kept saying. "I'm supposed to sell X to NBC?"

"We have to buy it first, Bart," someone reminded him.

"How do we do that?" asked Albeck.

"We can't get this book in an open auction," I said. "Somebody will be willing to pay more in money or points, or Talese will go with somebody he has dinner with at Elaine's."

"Or the Morris office will tip it to a client or someplace they can package it easier," said Field.

So? Albeck's expectant expression asked.

"So we take it off the market with a preemptive bid before anyone else is ready to make an offer."

The only sound was the air conditioner and the leaves of Andy's new palm, shivering softly against each other. Deliberation yielded to determination. We got our consensus.

The following morning I had breakfast at the Plaza with Ron Mardigian, who was to represent *Thy Neighbor's Wife* in Morris's California office. He was in town for strategy meetings on the book, but our breakfast date was coincidental and had been made days before. After he had told his latest craven-executive jokes and I had told my latest venal-agent jokes, I asked about the book.

"Do you mind if we photocopy it first?" He laughed.

"Don't bother. How about 'sight unseen'? Sell it first and photocopy it later. High bid gets reading privileges only."

He laughed. "What'll you give me?"

"For reading, nothing," I said, and decided to gamble. "For the book? A million? Some points?"

Mardigian's dark Armenian eyes widened, then narrowed as he studied mine. "You son of a bitch." He grinned. "You son of a *bitch!*"

Letting Morris know—or guess—that we had read the book was risky, but the surprise and hint of an offer might disarm them. Talese's pages were cards in a poker game, the dealing of which the Morris people wanted strictly to control. They had promised it on a simultaneous basis to every studio in the industry as well as to certain important producers and directors they represented and to others whom they *wanted* to represent. None would relish being scooped by UA, and many would resent it, suspecting the agency of having dealt from the bottom of the deck, depriving them of the jackpot before they got a good look at their hands and a chance to up the ante.

Realizing that we had read the book would activate the photocopying machines, we knew, but it would also throw confusion into the mail room on the Friday before a holiday and consternation into Owen Laster and Martin Bauer, heads of the literary and movie departments at Morris in New York. They could refuse to entertain a preemptive offer, of course, merely by not taking our calls, but what if I had been serious with the million-dollar offer at breakfast? Once they listened to such an offer, they were obligated to report it to their client; we were convinced we could frame the offer in a manner they—and he—could not, would not refuse.

Around noon we called and offered $1 million and points. "That's our *floor* figure," Marty Bauer, who was doing most of the talking, said scornfully.

"OK, make it a million and a half," we said.

Bauer laughed, but it was anxious laughter. "The auction is next Thursday," he said.

"Does that mean you're prepared to turn down a firm offer of one and a half million dollars without conveying it to your client?"

Pause. "We'll call you back."

I turned to Field. "I told you they'd listen. And they'll tell Talese. They have to."

"And they'll advise him not to take it."

"Right." Neither of us could face the obvious question: What if they turned down the limit of $2.5 million Albeck and the others had agreed to? There'd be no going back to Andy, no raising the stakes. We'd have lost a showy hand and, more important, the book.

They called back. They hemmed; they hawed; they stalled and recriminated and turned down the $1.5 million. Dean Stolber had joined us by this time, and after a brief caucus and a final clearance from Albeck we called back. We tap-danced a bit, then hit them with an offer, to expire at the end of the business day, only a few hours away: $2.5 million plus percentages, but—and it was a deal breaking *but*—the book must come with full, unrestricted, totally unconditional releases from Mr. and Mrs. John Bullaro. We wanted to show and tell what Talese had shown and told, without euphemism, evasion, or fictionalization.

"Gay has all those releases," said Bauer after a pause.

"Good," we said. "Then it's a deal."

It was a deal.

High-stakes negotiations can be anxiety- and adrenaline-producing, and Field and I were glad to have the long weekend to recover, he in California, I at Richard Parks's farmhouse in the Berkshires, four peaceful hours' drive from New York. Reading scripts before an open fireplace, watching the Berkshire leaves turn color felt soothing, bucolic. But the long weekend suddenly got short.

Columbus Day noon the phone rang. It was Marty Bauer calling from the Morris office in New York, insisting I come back to New York at once to meet with himself, the Morris lawyers, Talese's lawyers, and Dean Stolber, whom Marty had already tracked down in Amagansett and who was at that moment on the Long Island Expressway back to the city. "We have to finalize the deal today," he stressed, without explaining. "No signed deal memos by the end of the day no *deal.*"

I made the four-hour drive back to New York in just over three. Teams of lawyers, Stolber, Bauer, and I worked into the night in the eeriness of deserted offices in the dark and silent MGM Building. Finally, all the minutiae of schedules of payments, guarantees and representations, wherefores and moreovers were agreed to, and the deal memos signed.

Bauer excused himself and loped into the next room to make "a few calls," a strained smile spreading under his Brillo Afro. Stolber and I glanced at each other in silence, pleased to have signed papers but annoyed and mystified by all the vehement rush.

Bauer came back into the room, nodded to me and then to the phone on his desk, where a button blinked impatiently. "It's Tony Schwartz at the *New York Times,*" Bauer said. "He wants to talk to you."

"For Christ's sake, Marty," I said, annoyed because I had wanted UA to announce the book's purchase in its own fashion. It was too late now. I took the call.

The next morning as I entered 729, Julie, the doorman, rushed to greet me, his smile like sunrise. "Front page of the *New York Times!*" he shouted in his New Jersey accent, and thrust the morning edition at me. There we were in a little box on page one, with a long story inside bearing Tony Schwartz's by-line. I read it in the elevator as it rose slowly to the fourteenth floor, still warmed by the smile on Julie's face and the lift in morale it presaged.

When I showed the *Times'* piece to Stolber, I was struck by something in the eighth of the article's fifteen paragraphs. "Reached yesterday in Los Angeles," Schwartz wrote about Talese. Yesterday in Los Angeles? But he was in New York on Friday night, when the offer was accepted. Of course. Bauer hadn't gone in the other room merely to get Tony Schwartz on the line for a little William Morris publicity. He had gone to call Talese in Los Angeles, where the author had been negotiating with the Bullaros for the "unconditional" releases on which UA had conditioned the purchase. The mysterious rush to sign deal memos was suddenly clear: Talese had surely had releases acceptable to his publisher, but if the Bullaros' signatures on a release acceptable to UA required payment (Bauer later confirmed that it had and that it had been substantial, though no figure was mentioned), why should the author negotiate and pay unless the UA deal was ironclad? But it was. Talese and the Bullaros had their arrangement, and UA had the book.

The importance to UA of *Thy Neighbor's Wife* was more than the book itself, though our belief in it was justified. It stayed on the best seller lists for fully half a year and attracted the interest of dozens of filmmakers. Nor was it the publicity, which was national in scope and uniformly positive for UA, * which *Variety* correctly interpreted as "an all-out effort to remove any feeling that may exist that the company lacked clout." The deeper relevance of the purchase was that UA had bought the book not for a specific producer, director, or production company, as was the UA custom, but for itself. UA was going to become a production company.

Heaven's Gate, even by October 1979, when it ended production and the unthinkable was still unthinkable, had suggested new thinking was in order.

Independent production on a laissez-faire basis—that is, without authentic producers—was breaking down as a reliable method of production. Even those studios still exercising strong production control were plagued by runaway budgets (Universal's *The Wiz* and *The Blues Brothers* come to mind), and UA did not have the structure or staff to enforce

---

*However, Talese believed, perhaps rightly, that the publicity had some negative influence on book reviewers.

its own contractual protections without extreme disruption of routine, as *Heaven's Gate* had shown.

There were still producers who produced, of course, but there were many more who didn't. If the only practical way to control production was to become a production company—instead of the merely financing and distributing company UA had historically been—then UA would become one. A studio. And *Thy Neighbor's Wife* was a first step toward a company that, one year later, was to be restructured into a studio that, if what happens in the remainder of these pages hadn't happened, might exist today.

The rise in morale was visible at 729 and in the Thalberg Building, too. We had no Christmas picture for 1979, but we had two for 1980: *Heaven's Gate* and *Raging Bull*. We had another James Bond in preparation, *For Your Eyes Only*, and *Rocky III*, and *The Romance of the Pink Panther*, and *Eye of the Needle*, and *The Dogs of War*, and Claire's silly, sweet *Caveman*, and *Thy Neighbor's Wife* and, with the ink on Talese's contracts still damp, we signed some more—with Tom Wolfe.

The Right Stuff was submitted by Chartoff-Winkler under their exclusive UA deal. We had already read the manuscript (Kathy Van Brunt had struck again) but had made no effort to buy it for two reasons: One, it was too soon after *Thy Neighbor's Wife* to expect Albeck to go for another heavy purchase, and two, Field and I had plenty of consensus about it as a book and none as a movie.

The book was a dazzler. We hurtled through Wolfe's account of the Mercury astronaut program the way John Glenn hurtled through space. But at reentry time Field saw a movie in it, and I didn't. It seemed to me two books: one, a romantic elegy for a vanished code personified by test pilot Chuck Yeager, the gallantry, bravery, and isolation of one man trying to break the sound barrier; the other was a razor-eyed chronicle of camaraderie, the Mercury astronauts, the "Spam in a can" crew, more distant in kind from Yeager than Yeager was from the Wright brothers. These two elements enriched the book but presented a danger for a movie because Yeager was so romantic, so appealing that one kept gravitating to him and away from the narrative, the obvious "story" part that a movie could tell, which was the space program. You couldn't make a movie out of Yeager, I argued, not in 1980, not about breaking the sound barrier, of all forgotten things, not to mention that David Lean had already done so. The Mercury program had possibilities, I allowed, but only *just*. Space flight had been co-opted, I thought, by Luke Skywalker and Mr. Spock.

Besides, the triumph of the book wasn't the astronauts; it was the writing, that supersonic prose, the prowess not of narrative but of pen. And so on. Practically no one agreed with me, but nobody pushed it. Albeck would never go for the several hundred thousand dollars it would take, not without unity from his production heads. Then Chartoff and Winkler arrived.

When Bob and Irwin wanted something, "push" didn't exactly "come to shove," it sort of *was* shove, and they wanted *The Right Stuff* badly. Field and I presented our separate views of the material to Albeck, and the conflict of opinion seemed to give Field an energy he hadn't displayed in months. He was articulate and persuasive, evangelically fervent in his desire to acquire the book. I understood his case, as he understood mine; we just didn't agree.

Just before we were scheduled to go to London, he from Los Angeles and I from New York, Andy asked for a final decision. Under our veto rules, in which either could kill, but both must agree, I voted no, and that, I assumed, was that.

We arrived at cold, wet Heathrow about the same time and checked wearily into the Dorchester, where messages were waiting asking us to call Irwin Winkler in California. We placed the call, and when Irwin's New York accent came on the line, crackling with transatlantic static, he lavished gratitude on us and our help with *The Right Stuff*. "I know how tough it was for you guys to push this through with Andy," he said, "but it's the smartest deal UA ever made!"

What the hell was he talking about?

"Tom Wolfe is on his way to L.A. to talk about the movie, and we won't forget the help you guys gave us—*especially you*, Steve!" After he hung up, I winced putting down the receiver and gritted my teeth as David came in from the phone in the other room.

"'*Especially you*, Steve'?" I asked. "How much did I pay?"

"Half a million."

"I thought a decision had been made."

"It came up again while you were on the plane. Warner's wanted it. Laddy wanted it. Andy did, too, finally."

"Did he also suggest a screenwriter who can solve the fucking huge problems of this book?"

"Nope."

"Did Bob and Irwin?"

"Nope."

"Did *you?*"

"Nope."

"Well"—I sighed, his candor cooling me off—"let's think of some-body."

We talked. Bob and Irwin talked. Everybody kept coming back to the structure of the book: There was Yeager, and there were the astro-nauts, and the two didn't narratively fit together. Wolfe's journalistic freedom enabled him to cross-reference the two, but doing this in a movie, when there was no narrative conjunction, would seem gra-tuitous or pretentious or just historically confusing. Yeager would have to go. But we couldn't talk five minutes without coming back to him, particularly Wolfe's brilliant picture of Yeager standing straight and cool in the desert, half his face burned away, cradling his smoldering helmet under his arm, "a knight of the right stuff." It was sensational writing, an unforgettable image.

But Yeager wasn't a movie. We threw him out again and concen-trated on the astronauts, and that was worrisome, too, because we had a hunch that Albeck and the salespeople—with seven lead males to cast—were visualizing Eastwood *and* Newman *and* Redford *and* Nichol-son *and* Hoffman *and* McQueen *and*, for all we knew, Woody Allen for comic relief. We didn't encourage such fantasies, but neither did we stress the impossibility of making this a star movie. It was an ensemble piece, and the astronauts were too young to be played by established stars, all of whom had broken the forty barrier. This movie was about egomaniacally competitive jet jocks, who finally became, as Wolfe calls them, "The Brotherhood," *buddies.* And just like that, the screen-writer's name tumbled into place.

"The star of this movie is America," said William Goldman ear-nestly. He leaned across the table at Wally's Steak House to underscore his point to Field and me just before Christmas. Wally's seemed an appropriate locale to discuss Bill's writing *The Right Stuff:* meat and potatoes, no stuff righter.

"*America* is the star of this movie." He rephrased it in case we hadn't gotten it. "That's what makes it commercial. Look at the head-lines or the TV news. Mr. Sulzberger and Mr. Paley aren't dummies. They know what sells is what people care passionately about, and it's not the economy or Amy Carter or Aunt Lillian—it's *America.*"

I had known Bill for a long time and had worked on two movies with him, but even I was getting a little lost.

"The *hostages!*" he explained. "*Iran.*" His voice was tightening with passionate sincerity. "Here we are, the most powerful nation in the world, just the most powerful nation in the *history* of the world, being held for ransom by a religious fanatic we never heard of. The most powerful nation in the world is being humiliated by a *nut!* I care about that." It was obvious; he was radiating concern.

"God knows America makes mistakes and always will, but look at what we've done in the past, look at these guys' courage"—he tapped the proof copy of Wolfe's book lying on the table at his elbow—"the strength of character and bravery and grace that Wolfe captures; it's just *awe*some. That's what this book's about and what America's about—or should be—the way we needed to be after the Russians sent dogs into orbit and all *our* rockets were exploding on the launching pad. After Watergate and Vietnam and Nixon and Carter"—(the passion in his voice made me see *them* exploding on launching pads)—"we need to say and hear something positive about America. America has—or had and can have again—*the right stuff!*"

That did it. I got excited, Bob and Irwin got excited; Andy and the sales guys got excited; even business affairs got excited as it wrote the biggest screenwriting check in the history of the company. Bill's enthusiasm had struck a chord that vibrated and hummed from sea to star-spangled sea.

Field didn't seem excited; he hadn't felt good at lunch that day and had excused himself to go back to the Carlyle without eating. I called him there to cheer him up. "I thought you were wrong, David, but if Bill can get that kind of excitement into that script, we can make a fucking *great* movie!" Somewhere the Mormon Tabernacle Choir was singing.

I wanted to talk about *Answered Prayers*, but Truman Capote seemed interested only in cosmetic surgery.

"I beg your pardon?" I asked, thinking one of us must be losing his grip. Capote's grip was firmly on a slender crystal swizzle stick, which he turned around and around in a champagne glass filled with a sable liquid dark enough to have been Kahlúa and vodka, but which I knew to be Tab because I had watched the waiter pour it from a can.

"*Sur-ger-eee,*" enunciated the most famous and imitable of American literary voices. "They just lift it up and snip off what's *de trop,*" he said, lifting the champagne glass and the swizzle stick, which proved to be hollow, to his lips.

Everyone else at the party, hosted by Lester Persky, who had coproduced *Hair* for UA, was crowded around the buffet, from which my date arrived carrying a plate of dubious-looking hors d'oeuvres shipped in from California. She stood there staring at the small man sipping Tab from a champagne glass, dressed in black tie, crowned by a very elegant Borsalino, its brim pulled down in front. It was silky gray, the color of a particularly sleek Siamese cat.

"Is 'La Côte Basque' typical of *Answered Prayers?*" I began again. "Or—"

"That's yesterday and tomorrow," he said tartly. "This is today. Who's *she?*" he said as my date sat down, then, without waiting for an answer, added, "If journalists were not present, I would tell you I felt *tight.* See?" He lifted his chin toward the light, closing his eyes languidly to let us inspect his firm jawline and the faintly mottled, grayish pink skin stretched tightly over the cheekbones and around the eyes, which seemed closed, but betrayed him by fluttering as he made sure we were paying attention.

"Uh-huh," I said, fascinated. What I saw was tight but not quite symmetrical.

"It isn't vanity," he said, his eyes blinking back open. "Or age. Everyone who can count knows how old I am anyway. It's *morale;* it's being able to confront the silvered glass each day without a shudder. Snow White's stepmother knew the feeling," he added, and began to chuckle as his firm new chinline settled gently onto his cupped palm.

I must have looked dismayed, for he surprised me with "Don't worry about *Answered Prayers.* I'll have something for you long before then."

That was in New York, and late in the year he did have something. It was called *Handcarved Coffins,* and was subtitled "A Nonfiction Account of an American Crime," a return to the genre of *In Cold Blood,* and we added it to the shelf newly occupied by Gay Talese and Tom Wolfe.

Lester Persky, with whom we had been working on a number of projects, brought us the Capote material, which was being published first in *Interview* magazine and was to form the major portion of *Music for Chameleons.*

Field had not wanted to buy *Handcarved Coffins* on much the same ground that I had not wanted to buy *The Right Stuff:* Both pieces had oddly similar adaptation problems. Each had a clear narrative (in Capote's case, pursuit of the perpetrator of a series of grisly murders committed in the American West), and another level which enriched but conflicted with the narrative. In Wolfe's case it was Yeager; in Capote's case it was himself, for in a sharp divergence from the style of *In Cold Blood,* in which the writer's presence and voice were artfully and subtly eliminated, they were very much a part of *Handcarved Coffins* and gave the story a mystical, poetic level through the character and dialogue of the narrator, called T.C. The nonfiction story centered on a detective

Capote called Jake Pepper, who is investigating a string of violently bizarre killings he believes to have been committed by a wealthy rancher called Quinn (all the names were pseudonymous), and though we are encouraged to share his belief (as does T.C.), the investigation is haunted by ambiguity and lack of objective evidence and proof.

A key to the killings is Addie, a spinster schoolteacher with whom Jake falls in love. Like the victims preceding her, she has received anonymously in the mail a beautifully carved miniature coffin made of balsa wood, inside of which is her own photograph.

The drive to the story is Jake's pursuit of Quinn, his overconfidence, his righteousness in his quest, which leads ironically (and ambiguously) to Addie's death. It is a powerful tale, but it is Jake's; in this dark, violent, moving landscape T.C. had no place.

Perhaps because of *The Right Stuff*, Field displayed scant resistance to Capote's nonfiction novel, and we acquired it for Persky. Herbert Mitgang reported in the *New York Times* that we had done so for half a million dollars, but that was untrue.* We paid half what the *Times* reported and received "free" options on two other short pieces in *Music for Chameleons* as well.

Beverly Hills. The Bistro. Lunch. This time the Borsalino was the color of crème brûlée and looked just as smooth. The crystal swizzle stick was replaced by a pink plastic straw, the champagne glass by a tall tumbler, but the drink was still Tab, the jawline and voice as familiar as ever.

Lester Persky chatted amiably, and he and Capote gossiped about goings-on in the Hamptons while I screwed up my courage. I decided to begin indirectly.

"Truman, it's a help from a legal point of view that everyone is pseudonymous in this story, so we don't have to worry about getting sued by Quinn, but it would help us—and the screenwriter—to know where they really lived, where these murders happened, the real locales for Jake and Addie, I mean."

"Oh, somewhere in the West," he said, and stirred his Tab with the straw.

"The West is a big place. It has a lot of different looks and accents."

"Accents?"

"Are we talking Idaho dialogue or Oklahoma dialogue or what?"

---

* Although Capote himself, for whatever reasons, perpetuated the misinformation in interviews. See *Conversations with American Writers* by Charles Ruas (Alfred A. Knopf, 1984), page 4.

"All the dialogue's in the book," he said, glancing away to other tables, other clients.

I glanced at Persky. His eyes rolled quickly in warning.

"The dialogue is brilliant, Truman, brilliant. But we may have to make some changes."

"No, it cannot be a musical!" he said with mock ferocity, and then burst into disarming gales of self-amused giggles.

"'Singin' in the Sagebrush,' you mean?" Persky contributed.

More laughter, dwindling.

"The screenwriter . . ." I began.

"Just who *is* this screenwriter?" he asked, the giggles abruptly silenced. "I have approval, you know. Lester, you told me I have approval."

Persky's eyes shifted to mine, then smoothly to Truman's. "Of course, Truman. Not exactly contractually exactly, but—"

"You told me I have approval, Lester." The voice was as firm as the jawline. Persky's eyes searched for someplace to light.

"Judith Rascoe," I said.

"Who?" asked Capote. Persky frowned, and not without reason. He had never heard me mention the name until this moment because I had never thought of it until this moment. It may have been my earlier mention of Idaho that triggered the thought, for it was Judith Rascoe's home state (and mine). We had grown up in the same town, though we met each other years later in London, when Judy was coaxed from fiction to movies. I had suggested her for the screenplay for Robert Stone's *Dog Soldiers*, which she had written with great skill, though the movie made from it, *Who'll Stop the Rain?*, was a failure. Because it was, I sidestepped it now.

"She's a *real* writer, Truman, and a westerner, who did a wonderful short-story collection a few years ago called *Yours, and Mine*. With a comma."

"Nice," he said cautiously. "Short stories?"

"Wonderful ones. And she did the screenplay for *Out of Africa*."

"Isak Dinesen?" he asked, his eyes narrowing.

I nodded.

"I've written about Dinesen, you know." He sounded wary, testing.

"I remember," I said. "*Observations*."

He began stirring the Tab with his straw again, then slowly smiled. "Well, if she's good enough for Karen, Baroness von Blixen, she's good enough for me! But I'll give her all the help she needs. Every *word* she needs." He nodded helpfully, though it was help that might interfere and that we were eager to avoid.

"I don't think that'll work, Truman."

"Why not?" The voice was sharp and quick, not the famous one at all.

"I think . . . I think . . . you'd *intimidate* her," I said, improvising.

"I'm not *that* brilliant," he protested.

"Oh, yes, you are," said Persky, triggering new gales of laughter.

When they subsided, I broached again the factual basis of the story, the landscape, the weather, the people. Capote was masterfully evasive and slithered through my questions like a quicksilver snake. Finally, a new and horrified thought in my brain, I asked, "But this *is* true, isn't it, Truman? I mean, this 'nonfiction novel' *is* nonfiction, isn't it?"

His smile was Cheshire-sweet. "Wouldn't you like to know?" he purred.

CHAPTER 17

HEAD TO HEAD

Friendship and sentiment and the giving
of one's words are very important. . . .
This is a lonely country, and people die of
loneliness as surely as they die of cancer.
But I also know that in every friendship
there's the potential for destructiveness as
well as nourishment.

—Michael Cimino,
The New York Times
(December 10, 1978)

The year 1979 ended not so much with a consensus as
with a series of well-meant compromises. Aggressive acquisitions put
UA back on the lists or demonstrated we had never been off. One
purchase we had agreed on, one Field had wanted, one I had wanted. It
was not buying for the sake of buying. The appearance of three strong,
original pieces in close sequence after a long, arid parade of repetitive
and derivative material was an unpredictable harvest in a process that
knows no season. Still, we had demonstrated our ability to focus the
cumbersome committee system, and Albeck had demonstrated the flexibility and daring to let us do so.

We started 1980 with new and illogical titles, both of us "senior
vice-president in charge of worldwide production," and a new policy
Albeck had devised of self-determination in project development that
(up to a certain budget figure) eliminated the hated committee system
altogether. We also started the year with a bump, for Claire Townsend
quit, to join Sherry Lansing, newly (and famously) installed as the first
woman president of production at Twentieth Century-Fox . . . or anywhere.

Claire's leaving was painful but not unforeseen. Neither was Albeck's dismissal of his major executive with the bleeding ulcers, which, in its different way, was equally painful.

Albeck had struggled to find a way to protect the man from humiliation and loss of face and had chosen not to take the serious action alone. He assembled the senior vice-presidents in the small conference room adjoining his office and polled us. We were unanimous. The man should go, even though, as Andy pointed out, because of his age, it probably meant the end of his career. Then, because we all took part in a profit-sharing plan Albeck had devised and sold to Transamerica, he instructed us that we should in unison approve of the replacement—whoever he might be—since our profit participations would depend on him, as his would on us.

Albeck's treatment of the former executive was compassionate and generous. The man was continued on salary for a year (or until he took another job), not merely as a reward for past service, but because he could at the end of that year retire without losing one penny of pension, profit, or benefits he would have received if his ulcers had not been slowly bleeding him to death. Albeck also allowed him to make his own announcement of his leaving and gave him carte blanche in doing so.

The executive made his announcement. *Variety* printed that he "turned in his resignation after a dispute with prez Andy Albeck."

Andy's predictable comment was *no* comment.

Literary properties—even best sellers—were all well and good, but they were long-range. We needed pictures. One had come our way in October, in turnaround from Paramount. It was called *Thief*, and was written by Michael Mann, who would also direct it as his first feature film. It was to star James Caan and was ready to go forward in Chicago.

A second turnaround project (from Warner's) came to UA and presented production with the most decisive conflict of its brief history.

The French Lieutenant's Woman by John Fowles had been in development with a variety of producers and directors for more than a decade. I had first read the book's manuscript in 1968 and sent it off to Ben Benjamin, Vanessa Redgrave's agent, because she was then right for the title role as no one had been since.

The book's difficulties were many, for it was not only a contemporary re-creation of a Victorian novel but a treatise on the Victorian novel as viewed from today, with multiple endings for the reader to choose from. John Gardner called it "unended fiction," hard to do in a movie.

The version of *The French Lieutenant's Woman* that was submitted to

UA had a script by Harold Pinter and was to be directed by Karel Reisz. Sarah Woodruff, "the French lieutenant's woman," would be Meryl Streep, who, then not *quite* a star, was nevertheless the perfect choice. Charles Smithson, her Victorian lover, had not been cast.

The script had Pinter's usual precision and economy, though a more romantic feeling than his other work. To achieve Fowles's odd then-and-now parallax view of the story of Sarah and Charles, Pinter invented a film company making a movie of *The French Lieutenant's Woman*. That movie would be the spine of this one, but we would also see, alternating with it (and roughly parallel to it), the "actors"— "Anna" playing Sarah, and "Mike" playing Charles—rehearsing the movie, involved in a location love affair juxtaposed against the Victorian love affair they were filming.

The script suggested that the two stories would enhance each other, Sarah and Charles becoming richer because of Anna and Mike, and the dilemma of Anna and Mike becoming more urgent because as the end of filming approaches, so inevitably does the end of the affair. In this way, Pinter achieved the multiple (not quite un-) ending effect—one ending for Charles and Sarah and another for Anna and Mike—as well as the alternating detachments and immersions so much a part of the experience of the novel.

Field was passionate about the project and about Sarah, who liked to call herself Tragedy. He seemed to relate almost mystically to it and her. I could not overcome a fear that Pinter's elegant and simple device to achieve Fowles's double-tracking effect was dangerous. I feared that instead of one story composed of two complementary, ironically counterpointed sets of characters, we would have two movies, each distancing the viewer from the other and allowing neither sufficient emotional continuity to work. It was the kind of movie one could not know worked without making it, and at $8 million, with a star who wasn't *quite* a star and with no leading man (on whom much would depend), I argued as strongly against it as Field did for it.

Besides, I was pushing Scott Spencer's *Endless Love*, a doomed love affair between contemporary adolescents, which seemed far closer to the marketplace than a doomed etc. between Victorian adults that had been kicking around for more than a decade.

I far from disliked *The French Lieutenant's Woman*, just as Field didn't dislike *Endless Love*, but we both knew that one expensive obsessional-love movie was enough. This was the conflict we had successfully (or luckily) avoided in the past; we had disagreed often enough before and yielded or not, and hard feelings had been few or quickly forgotten. Now, however, we were head to head in direct competition.

We could both lose it but thought we could not both win it, and it made for tensions, to be resolved quickly and unexpectedly.

I met Franco Zeffirelli and his agent, Janet Roberts, at Sardi's for drinks one wintry Friday evening. I didn't know Zeffirelli, but Janet was an old friend who told me he was passionate to make *Endless Love*, and could we meet?

Zeffirelli exuded the same sentimental charm that had made *Romeo and Juliet* and *The Champ* unlikely but real box-office hits. Though he was somewhere in his fifties, his appearance and energy were those of a particularly exuberant young man, not that much older, in fact, than the hero of Scott Spencer's novel. We ordered drinks and began to chat. I was concerned about the screenplay because there was a danger the story would be not romantic but depressing, and I had no special ideas who might write it. Perhaps Zeffirelli did? Perhaps he had some ideas about how to make it tragic and compelling and sentimental all at once? Without depressing the very teenage audience it seemed meant for?

He talked about *Romeo and Juliet*. He talked about *La Dame aux Camélias*. He talked about the beauty of young people in love. He talked about passion and ardor and romance. I had the odd sensation that he was levitating with romantic sensibility, and the table with him.

Finally, charmed but earthbound, I turned to Janet, who adored her client but sensed my restiveness. She peered at me through her smoked glasses and sprang the surprise she knew me well enough to know would delight: "Franco will work out the script details later. The question is the writer. And we know just *who*." She beamed happily. "Judy Rascoe!"

A door opened beneath my feet. One often finds oneself in competition with oneself in the movie business, but I was not about to jeopardize *Handcarved Coffins*, no matter how endless and charming Zeffirelli was. My enthusiasm for *Endless Love* had been less than Field's passion for *The French Lieutenant's Woman*, and my fears about Pinter's adaptation seemed suddenly picky and pedantic. Besides, pressure was mounting, for Stan Kamen, who represented director Karel Reisz, was in New York and pressing for a decision. Sam Cohn of ICM, Meryl Streep's agent, was pressing, too, claiming his client would work for far less money than she could command in the marketplace in order to make the movie, that it was an artist's dream, and distinguished, too, the kind of picture UA had an obligation to make, and so on. Sam knew I had been resistant and had asked for a summit meeting with Albeck and me. He would bring Kamen, and Stolber could sit in, too.

It was quite a sight, perhaps the two most powerful motion-picture agents in America—one East, one West—perched on the buttery leather chairs before Andy Albeck's "Hollywood" desk, doing a non-competitive pitch meeting.

Albeck was chipper, sat back in his usual ramrod posture, and listened with interested courtesy to the pitch.

Sam dripped ashes on the beige carpet, pushed up the sleeves of his crew-neck pullover, and sailed eloquently and passionately into his plea that UA make the picture. Sam is not only an agent but a lawyer, and one of the most articulate, persuasive men in the movie industry. He talked and readjusted the chair and smoked some more and talked some more and ran his hand through already dissheveled hair, pushed again at the sleeves of his pullover, and talked and smoked and "ashed." When he yielded the floor to Kamen, Stan's remarks were brief and modest perhaps because Sam had so eloquently exhausted the subject there was nothing left for him to say.

Andy smiled and nodded politely, his hands folded neatly in his lap. "Thank you, gentlemen," he said, and looked across the room to where I sat on the small sofa. "This is a creative decision. I leave those decisions to my boys. What do you say, Steve?"

I bade *Endless Love* a last farewell and plunged in. "Everyone here knows I've been troubled from the start because I just don't know if Pinter's dual-time structure works or doesn't, and I don't think anyone *can* know without making the picture. It will or it won't. Frankly I'm curious."

"Eight million dollars curious?" Albeck asked, smiling.

"Let me put it this way, Andy. Next year this company will have another James Bond, another Pink Panther, another Rocky, another Woody Allen, plus *Raging Bull* and *Heaven's Gate* and some others that have a chance. I think this company now and then can afford to make a picture simply because it should be made."

Andy smiled. Stolber began staring at the floor, his face pale, as if something alarming had happened to his shoes.

"Gentlemen," Andy said with firm nods, first to Sam, then to Stan. "There you have it."

Sam looked exultant, Stan relieved, and Stolber stricken. As the meeting broke, I went back to my office to call Field. Within seconds Stolber sat white-faced across from my desk, his yellow legal pad clutched to his chest, his entire weight perched on the edge of the chair.

"I can't believe what you did," he said, his voice constricted.

"Did what?" I asked.

"Railroaded Andy that way in front of Sam and Stan. Left him no out, no room at all. You just committed this company to *eight million dollars* because Andy asked you a courtesy question!"

I had never seen Stolber shake before, but he was shaking now, with disbelief and consternation.

"You misread it, Dean. Andy knew I would say yes. He watched me during that meeting. He knows my responses by now; I'm not that hard to read. He would never have asked me the question in that way if he hadn't been prepared to take yes for an answer."

"It was a *courtesy* question."

"The courtesy involved was to make it *not* a chief executive decision but a *production* decision and to make sure Sam and Stan saw that for themselves."

Stolber shook his head and rose. "I want you to know that I am going to Andy to discuss this, and I am going to have to express myself in the strongest terms. I'm sorry."

"Don't be. If you feel that way, you should."

"I'm going to. *Now*," he said, and left.

I called Field. After I had told him the good news, there was a silence so long I thought the line was dead. "Are you there?"

"Yeah, I'm here." He sounded sepulchral.

"What's wrong? Is it Cathy? What's happened?"

"Steven," he said, "why didn't anyone call me?"

"*I'm* calling you."

"*Then*. In the meeting."

"I don't know, David. Andy just turned to me and said what he said, and we agreed to make the picture. I guess he didn't think of it, or the timing was wrong or something. He knew your attitude anyway."

If the long silence that followed was meant to produce guilt, it produced only anger.

"Somebody should have called me," he said again finally.

"*I just did*," I said, and hung up the phone, wanting to throw it fourteen stories to Seventh Avenue below.

Just then Stolber stuck his head around the doorway, and I motioned him in. He relaxed into a chair and smiled.

"I owe you an apology," he said. "Andy says it was just the way you said it was. I guess I didn't catch the cues."

"There weren't any, Dean. You just have to give Andy a little more credit. Don't believe everything you read in the papers."

"Did you tell David?"

I nodded.

"He must have been thrilled," he said happily.

"Yeah," I said. "Thrilled."

Field was not thrilled by much that California winter. The lack of progress in filling Claire's empty office should have indicated more than it did, and his subsequent indifference to *The French Lieutenant's Woman* I wrote off to the pervasive effects of a dissolving marriage and a preoccupation with Cimino and *Heaven's Gate* and the still-unresolved problems of the prologue and epilogue, though Cimino was busily preparing them.

When I returned from a trip to London, where I had met with Reisz and his producer, Leon Clore, to view some videotapes of the actor Reisz was proposing for Charles, Field calmly listened to my enthusiasm for Jeremy Irons sight unseen, said, "Fine," and Irons was approved without question, without discussion.

Field seemed to get his energy back that winter for only one strong battle, and it required energy and persuasion: the struggle to win for Michael Cimino the right to make his prologue and epilogue. Field believed in them, as did I, and it was a battle he cared about making. When he won it, perhaps he felt he had accomplished all he could.

I should not have been surprised to get the phone call I got on March 11, but I was. It was Andy Albeck, calling from California.

"Hell*ooo*," he said with the invariable cheer he used on the telephone. "How *are* ya?" with a little lilt on the verb.

I was in bed with the flu and a temperature of 102.

"When will you feel well enough to come to the Coast?" he asked. "David resigned this morning to go to Twentieth Century-Fox and work for Sherry Lansing. I'd like you to come out here and take over."

I was poleaxed. I had ignored every sign. The melancholy segueing to gloom; *The French Lieutenant's Woman*; Claire's still-empty office— all should have told me this was coming. Naïvely I had assumed that our long-standing pledge to inform each other of sudden career moves would be honored, but it wasn't, and I had allowed the daily distractions to blind me to what seemed in retrospect obvious, maybe even inevitable.

"I'll be there tomorrow, Andy. . . . Did David say *why*?"

"No," said Andy. "But I always assumed one of you would leave or

FINAL CUT

have a heart attack, and the other would take over. So it's you," he
said, and signed off cheerily. "See ya!"

I never did speak to Field about his decision. He flew to San Francisco to explain it personally to Jim Harvey and later said he had
stressed again to Transamerica the impossibility of coherence in a company in which the right hand was separated from the left by 3,000
miles.

He told others in the company he was leaving because I wanted him
to, but that reminded me too much of the company discontent he expressed to me long before, in Denver, when he felt targeted by Chris
Mankiewicz's Sammy Glick outburst. Maybe it was just that now, unlike then, he had someplace to go.

The one thing that had always been clear was that Field wanted to
be in New York, where he perceived the Power to be; I wanted to be in
California, where I perceived the Action to be. We both wanted it
both ways, which couldn't be, and in that sense perhaps he was right:
Two heads were not necessarily better than one.

We gave a going-away party for him a few days later in Bob
Wunsch's office, and when the forced festivities were over, I walked
him to the long, quiet corridor with its chromium-framed blowups of
movie stars and stills, and as he turned to exit down its quiet length, he
gave a mechanical wave of his right hand, its finger splayed in a gesture
that looked half-defensive, half-dismissive. He said, "It's all yours."

CHAPTER 18

STARTING OVER

It's hard to finish a movie.

—Michael Cimino,
"Michael Cimino's Way West,"
American Film (October 1980)

All art is knowing when to stop.

—Toni Morrison,
quoted by Carol Sternhell in
"Bellows' Typewriters and
Other Tics of the Trade,"
New York Times Book Review
(September 2, 1984)

Cimino and Carelli discovered David Field had resigned by reading it in the papers. "I went berserko!" Joann exploded just after I arrived March 12, full of vitamin C and aspirin. "We go from Rissner to Field to Bach, and we have to read about it in this morning's *trades?*"

Joann's concern was anxiety that Field's resignation might disrupt the resuscitated—but not yet approved—prologue and epilogue. Field's support had been there to see; mine had not. I assured her I shared the conviction they were important enough to fight for but reminded her that Albeck's reluctant agreement was conditional on budget approval, now risen to $3 million, thanks to Field's and my persuasion with Albeck, but that no actual budgets had yet been drawn for approval or rejection.

Five days later, March 17, Derek Kavanagh and Michael Cimino flew to England, where Mansfield College at Oxford had granted permission to shoot during Easter recess in early April. A schedule was prepared for thirteen shooting days, and after a meeting on the eighteenth with Cimino, Denis O'Dell (the British production manager), and other English personnel, Kavanagh telephoned me with Cimino on the line to say he estimated the thirteen-day schedule would cost $5.2 million. I jotted down the details as he conveyed them as well as Cimino's vociferous rejection of this estimate. "Usual diatribe against UA & DK," I wrote, as if hearing a very familiar song. Kavanagh pointed out patiently that in addition to the thirteen shooting days, Cimino wanted fourteen days of rehearsal and prelighting, interrupted by Good Friday on April 4. The 300 dancers (and costumes, hats, wigs, shoes, etc.) had suddenly and mysteriously become 770 and . . . a very *old*, familiar song.

"Come home," I said.

"What?" asked Cimino, startled.

"Come home," I repeated. "The figure you were given was three million dollars. There's no point in wasting everybody's time and UA's money on hotels in Oxford for a shoot that is not going to take place."

The second chorus began. "I can get that figure down. Derek's figures are all wrong anyway, and I'm staying here to get them right."

"Fine," I said. "You're on your own. Derek," I continued, "I need to know how much we will pay in abandonment costs because I'm telling Andy we're abandoning the prologue and epilogue. Secondly, please bring the schedule and all your figures back with you so I can justify pulling the plug. How soon can you be in California?"

"Tomorrow maybe. I can tell you the abandonment cost right now," he said. "It's one million one hundred thousand dollars."

"Thanks," I said, and hung up. My assumption was that Cimino would indeed find a way to get his budget down to $3 million, and I communicated that to Andy. If he didn't, the $1.1 million in abandonment costs would grow very little in the meantime.

I had moved into David Field's former office as sole head of worldwide production fewer than thirty-six hours before, and with my office in New York now empty and Claire Townsend's still vacant, I had too much to do—and no inclination whatever—to allow *Heaven's Gate* to control the company or my life in it. I also thought Kalispell had demonstrated that when confronted with limits he believed would be enforced, Cimino was quite capable of adjusting his enthusiasms economically. The next day, March 19, a new budget appeared, detailed down to taxi fares and accounting fees. Including a 5 percent contingency, it came to $2,965,372.

Albeck had given his word: If the budget could be vetted by Katz and Kavanagh at $3 million or less, Cimino could go forward. Enforcement of that limit was vital, even if to do so meant aborting production at midpoint, something I told Cimino I was prepared to do. Still, a disciplined plan was far preferable to abandonment.

United Artists had first approached Anthea Sylbert in September of 1978. A vice-president of production at Warner Brothers, Sylbert was almost uniquely experienced among Hollywood executives in having actual production experience. She had spent many years as a costume designer, first in the theater and later on such films as *Carnal Knowledge* and *The Fortune* for Mike Nichols, *Rosemary's Baby* and *Chinatown* for Roman Polanski, and *Julia* for Fred Zinnemann. Her influence on films she designed often extended beyond wardrobe, and she became widely known as a sensitive but tough-minded collaborator. The petite good looks (the *New York Daily News* called her dashing) were disarming; she could wear a Fortuny gown as if born to it, was as brainy as anyone in Hollywood, but—if pushed—had the lungs and vocabulary of a stevedore.

Her working relationships with some of the most powerful talent in Hollywood (stars as well as directors) were strong, and in 1978 I had urged Field to approach her. She had not been interested. Warner's had assigned her to supervise Robert Towne (they had worked together on *Chinatown* and *Shampoo*), who was then writing a project he would direct and, it was implicitly understood (by Sylbert anyway), she would produce. In the intervening period, however, Warner's made George Roy Hill producer of *Greystoke*, * and Sylbert agreed to meet with me.

Though we didn't know each other, we both had worked on *The Heartbreak Kid* in the early seventies, she as designer, I as a minor executive. I observed her calm, unflappable work on a picture considerably less effortless than it ultimately appeared. Sylbert simply *worked,* avoiding hysteria, tantrums, and nerves. That's what I wanted at UA, and that's what I got.

She came to work on April 7, bringing with her satchelfuls of projects to which Warner's had been indifferent and trailing behind her writers and producers happy to follow her over the Hollywood hills from Burbank to Culver City.

At the same time Wunsch delivered a welcome surprise package, the second *National Lampoon* movie, to follow the phenomenally successful *Animal House. The National Lampoon Picture Show* was to be a movie version of the humor magazine's funny and irreverent movie parodies, sending up everything from *Kramer vs. Kramer* to mad bomber and ballerina movies.

Richard Parks, who had been promoted to vice-president of production at the New Year, was taking more responsibility for production in the East now that I was based in California and was supervising *The Iceman* script he had called to my attention months before. Norman

* The picture was finally directed by Hugh Hudson and produced by Stan Canter and Hudson.

Jewison was concluding production on *The Dogs of War*, and we sent *The Iceman* to him. Jewison responded strongly to the sensitive script by John Drimmer and agreed at once to produce it, reserving also the right to direct.

There were other projects to concentrate on: a novel by Vincent Patrick called *The Pope of Greenwich Village*; a comedy about a mermaid called *Splash* that was so sweetly silly it was irresistible when producer Brian Grazier proposed it. Anthea liked a project in turnaround from Paramount called *Swing Shift* and thought it might be good for Goldie Hawn, so we added that to the list. Pulitzer prizewinning playwright Frank Gilroy came in with something called *The Edge*, an original screenplay he had written for the Ladd Company that was almost a comedy version of *Double Indemnity*. Bob Wunsch became an unexpectedly expert troubleshooter, solving production problems on *Thief* in Chicago and *Caveman* in Mexico, by getting on planes, exercising common sense with tough clarity, and returning to Culver City, matter-of-factly free of a smugness he might well have permitted himself.

For Your Eyes Only was preparing for shooting in Corfu, Cortina, and other European locations; *Rocky III* was on the verge of discovering Mr. T and making him the most offbeat new film "somebody" since Cubby Broccoli cast Richard Kiel as Jaws in the James Bond series; *The Right Stuff* was being written; *Raging Bull* was being edited; and *Thy Neighbor's Wife* was perched high on the best seller lists, resisting heavy-breathing suitors, including Francis Coppola, because Zoetrope, not UA, would control the making of the picture, as it had on *Apocalypse*. Judith Rascoe had, to my chagrin, agreed to write *Endless Love* for Zeffirelli (and Polygram), and Persky and I, with Capote's blessing, decided to wait for her to finish that job before beginning work on *Handcarved Coffins*, which Hal Ashby had agreed to direct.

There was a sense of energy and coherence at UA that came as much from the new alignment of personalities as anything else. We added a vice-president for creative affairs on the West Coast, Craig Zadan, who had dampened his feet in the New York theater, published a book about Stephen Sondheim, and effervesced with ideas as young and lively as himself.

Only one position remained to be filled, and that was an additional vice-presidency on the East Coast. I knew whom I wanted and thought with Anthea's help I could make it work. Albeck was dubious I could lure Marcia Nasatir back to UA and feared there might be some residual resentment that she had not been made head of production at the time of the mass exodus, but he was delighted to let me try.

Nasatir had stayed at Orion for only a matter of months and had since been fighting the frustrations of independent production. By an odd coincidence, Anthea, Marcia, and I all had lived at different times in the same apartment. Loonier bonds than that have led to enduring relationships in Hollywood, and we began our siege.

Nasatir feinted and dodged and listened and argued and resisted and postponed and considered and maybed and hemmed and hawed and negotiated and agreed. We worked out her salary, title, start date, and Andy welcomed her back to UA with a genuine feeling of warmth, respect, and surprise. But the big surprise was for me: She changed her mind; she resigned before she started.

"*I will never speak to you again as long as I live if you do this thing,*" yelled stevedore Sylbert, but Nasatir did it anyway. I went back to Albeck, my countenance covered with albumen and yolk. He refrained from "I told you so" and the search began again.

So did Michael Cimino. The prologue to *Heaven's Gate* began shooting in Oxford on a rigidly controlled schedule of five shooting days and five days of preparation worked out by Cimino, production manager Denis O'Dell, and Derek Kavanagh. At the end of each shooting day Kavanagh was to call from Oxford and confirm that the schedule had been met, the cash flow respected—or not. If not, I was to instruct Kavanagh to shut down and order Cimino back to Culver City. Albeck and I had agreed to this day-by-day policing and made it clear to Cimino that there was no leeway. We would "eat" whatever moneys had been expended at the first sign of overage. Possibly because he understood and believed that, production moved forward flawlessly for the first and only time in the long history of *Heaven's Gate*, and so did Cimino, on budget and on schedule.

There were five basic elements to shoot, which would occupy about twenty minutes of finished film. The first was the picture's opening shot: the sun rising behind a clock tower as Kristofferson runs through an archway toward the camera, which moves with him while he dashes across the courtyard and disappears around a corner. The second was Kristofferson's continued run to catch up with a spirited brass band and the other members of the graduating class as they march through the streets of "Harvard" on into Christopher Wren's elegant Sheldonian Theater. There the commencement exercises (the third element) are held, the speeches made, ideals lifted high (by Joseph Cotten, cast as the Reverend Doctor) and mocked down (by John Hurt, back as William C. Irvine, having in the meantime completed *The Elephant Man*). The several hundred costumed extras serving as audience to these exercises would be seen again in the fourth element, the waltz sequence on the green, followed by the final segment, the graduates' rush on the great tree, Kristofferson's capture of the floral wreath within, the farewell song, and the girls gazing down from the windows above.

Given the style of production Cimino and his cameraman and crew had grown accustomed to, shooting these five elements in five days required rigorous preplanning and discipline. O'Dell, Kavanagh, Zsigmond, and Cimino devised a system utilizing multiple cameras, meticulous prelighting, and camera rehearsals that would alternate the five shooting days with the five days of preparation: a day to prepare, a day to shoot, and so on.

One day each was allotted for the marching band sequence, the graduation ceremonies in the Sheldonian, the dancing on the green, plus one night's shooting for the rush on the tree, and the fracas between the upper- and lowerclassmen. The fifth day was scheduled for shooting at Pinewood Studios, involving front projection of previously shot footage and interiors of the yacht, constructed on a Pinewood sound stage.

There was one major problem: Oxford refused permission to film the opening shot of the picture near Christ Church on a Sunday, the only day the UA schedule permitted. It was a crucial shot to Cimino and, though simple in content, required good weather and precision movement because the camera would have to follow Kristofferson's race across the courtyard on prelaid metal tracks. With ingenuity, secrecy, and some "persuasion" of university guards, the street and shot were prepared after Saturday midnight, earth was poured to cover asphalt, sixty feet of dolly tracks were laid, and Cimino and Zsigmond "stole" the shot at dawn in three takes, wrapped, and cleared the site before authorities were aware it had been used and before the bells rang announcing 8:00 A.M. church services. It had worked.

It *all* worked. Each day conference calls took place between Oxford and Culver City to discuss the planning. Each night Kavanagh, sometimes with O'Dell or with Cimino or with Teddy Joseph, UA's head of production services in the United Kingdom (or all three), called to report that Cimino had adhered to his schedule. For one nervous moment Cimino complained he could not shoot the waltz sequence in the time and manner prescribed and was told, if not, *wrap*. He did it, and he did it on budget, and it remains the single most beautiful sequence in the film.

The only excessive expenditures in England, as it turned out, were the bar bills at Pinewood racked up by Mr. O'Dell and two assistant directors (for others as well as themselves, one assumes.) They totaled (respectively) £218.72 and £550.40, and their combined cigar bill came to £61.55, all of which they charged to the picture, * to the very British embarrassment of Mr. Kavanagh, who issued very un-British bellows of outrage.

Still, not quite all was clockwork harmony. Teddy Joseph, a man of considerable experience and therefore patience, felt moved to express in writing his displeasure with Joann Carelli during one of Derek Kavanagh's brief returns to Los Angeles. He called her "extremely abusive" and added, "I will be delighted when Derek returns to London and can look after this production."

Teddy may have overstated; Joann Carelli was seldom "abusive" (to me anyway), but her presence had long been an unresolved problem. She had made important contributions early in casting and in music, and her strongest influence in that area was still to come. But she remained a shield between Cimino and the company and was widely regarded as uncooperative and contentious. She politely (or not) explained that Michael was in the editing room, at the lab, in the screening room, on a plane, indisposed, unavailable. She fielded virtually all communications between Cimino and UA, except mine, though that would come. Her role in protecting Cimino's privacy began to seem mere obstructionism and created an undercurrent of ill will that swelled and finally overflowed. Teddy Joseph was not the only one to enter his feelings deliberately into the record.

Joann's producing function on the picture had basically been assumed by Derek Kavanagh since the August take-over, but her preparation of the publicity materials and music was important enough to justify her remaining. Besides, I had no desire to give Cimino cause to slow down his editing with time-consuming quarrels over her value to him or the picture. If she was sometimes a shield, she was also sometimes a conduit to Cimino. As long as that was true, Joann would stay.

May 1 had been agreed to as the screening date for Cimino's cut of the movie. The domestic distribution staff, now headed by Gene Goodman, was preparing a November opening in New York, subsequent openings to follow. Blind booking laws, which prohibited the booking of pictures until they had been seen by exhibitors, were then in effect in more than a dozen states and being rapidly enacted elsewhere. A booking print for exhibitor screenings (in which only minor changes in picture continuity could be made before release) was to be delivered on July 1, delayed at Cimino's request to July 14. The May 1 date, then, was less arbitrary than imperative, for should major changes (and time)

---

*The pound then stood at roughly $2.18.

be required, they would seriously jeopardize the booking print and impair UA's ability to book the picture.

Shooting in England had resulted in some slowdown in editing, but William Reynolds, who had won Oscars for *The Sound of Music* and *The Sting*, had been engaged solely to edit prologue and epilogue and had accompanied Cimino to Oxford. His work would be completed before June 14, when he would go on to his next picture, *Rich and Famous*, for director Robert Mulligan at MGM, where David Begelman had resurfaced after his forgery and embezzlement conviction as president, instituting a massive and aggressive program of production. Addition of the prologue and epilogue, then, would not extend the overall editing schedule, though the shooting in England had understandably slowed it.

In consequence, I began pressing Cimino in early May for a new screening date. He was vague, and Carelli buffered most of my pressing. The weekend of May 9 Joann and I were both in East Hampton and talked there. She stressed the delays occasioned by Oxford but assured me—somewhat uneasily, I thought—that a cut would be ready by the end of the month.

I made a quick trip to the Cannes Film Festival in order to discuss progress on *The Romance of the Pink Panther* with Peter Sellers, whose *Being There* was in competition, as was Walter Hill's *The Long Riders* from UA. It was agreed I would meet with Sellers and writer Jim Moloney at Sellers's home in Gstaad in mid-June. I left Cannes early to return to Los Angeles and discover by the end of May that there had been no response from Cimino. I pressed harder. His response was vague. I insisted on seeing something, and the evening of May 29 he ran for me the fully cut prologue. It was thrilling filmmaking and brilliant editing (which remained virtually unchanged at the time of the New York premiere) and had the desired effect of encouraging me to extrapolate from that twenty minutes a full-length movie edited with equal precision and skill.

Cimino guardedly hinted that the movie might be longer than three hours. He had not seen it himself, he said, uninterrupted and from start to finish, and had not timed it precisely.

I flew to New York the next day, uneasy about what sounded like waffling. Tuesday, June 3, I decided to go on record and telexed Cimino to confirm what I had told him in person: "YOU MUST KNOW THAT ANDY IS EXPECTING THE THREE HOUR MOVIE YOU AGREED TO DELIVER WHEN DEAN AND I WERE IN MONTANA. ANY SIGNIFICANT OVERLENGTH WILL HAVE TO BE ADDRESSED IMMEDIATELY. . . . CERTAINLY THE LAWS GOVERNING BLIND BIDDING PRECLUDE ANY BUT

THE MOST MINOR PICTURE CHANGES BEING MADE BETWEEN INITIAL SCREENING AND FINAL DELIVERY."

I again stressed the need for a firm screening date and after another week in which Cimino made no response whatever, Dean Stolber and I called Eric Weissmann to advise him of this fact and alert him to a situation fast becoming critical. I sent another telex: "IN LIGHT OF THE EXTREME TIME PRESSURE WE ALL FACE AND YOUR LACK OF RESPONSE TO MY JUNE 3 TELEX, I MUST NOW FORMALLY ADVISE YOU THAT THE PRESENT CUT OF THE PICTURE, IN WHATEVER FORM AVAILABLE, MUST BE SHOWN TO UNITED ARTISTS' EXECUTIVES AS SOON AS POSSIBLE. . . . THE EARLIEST POSSIBLE DATE FOR THIS SCREENING WOULD BE MONDAY, JUNE 23RD. THIS GIVES YOU SLIGHTLY LESS THAN TWO FULL WEEKS FROM TODAY TO FINALIZE YOUR CUT." This direct order got a response, but not the one I had hoped for. On June 12 Eric Weissmann and Jeremy Williams of the Kaplan, Livingston law firm participated in a meeting with Michael Cimino, Joann Carelli, Dean Stolber, and Bob Wunsch to explain to UA why Cimino could not show the cut on June 23. Cimino blamed lab problems and an English production manager who, he claimed, had "mental difficulties." (It was pointed out that this gentleman resigned *before* production got under way in England to avoid the very breakdown he thought Cimino's pressure would cause him), and (according to Jeremy Williams's notes to the Kaplan, Livingston files) "[Cimino] expressed dismay that UA was not appreciative of the great difficulties under which the production had labored. He also expressed dismay at the adversary style with which UA has been conducting its relationship with him. Specifically, he stressed the great difficulty of working under actual or implied threats." Stolber was unyielding, and Cimino agreed to a screening on June 26 or 27, adding that "he would have a working print for showing to exhibitors by about July 16" (Williams's memo).

Had I been present at the meeting, I doubtless would have expressed some dismay of my own that the picture was now one full year overdue and at least $20 million over budget, but I had other areas of dismay to occupy my mind. I was on a plane to Europe for an emergency meeting to avert what loomed as potential catastrophe, for *The Romance of the Pink Panther* had fallen to pieces.

Peter Sellers was wraithlike. The smile he wore seemed paralyzed in place, and I thought I had never seen so delicate a man. His skull, his fingers, the tightly drawn, almost transparent skin—all seemed frail, infinitely fragile.

I had arrived in Gstaad a few hours before from Geneva, in a tiny chartered plane the vertical climb of which into and over the Alps had unnerved me. I wondered how Sellers, with his weak heart, could survive the same flight as often as I knew he did. He greeted me warily, his smile fixed, and looked apprehensive and tentative, rather than the "difficult" I had been warned to expect.

The Romance of the Pink Panther was to be produced by Danny Rissner, who had only days before sent Sellers his notes on the script Sellers and Moloney had been preparing. Sellers's reaction to the notes had been hysterical, "suicidal." He vowed never again to speak to Rissner and insisted that the picture could be resuscitated only if Sellers's wife, Lynne Frederick, were named executive producer. She had, he said to his agent, Martin Baum, prevented his "jumping overboard" when he read Rissner's comments while yachting in the Aegean (directly after his brilliant work in Being There had been overlooked by the Cannes festival jury). I saw none of the hysteria, merely a spectral presence, a man made of eggshells.

The Sellerses had arranged rooms for me at Gstaad's Palace Hotel three days before its official summer opening. I was eerily uncomfortable as the sole guest in the vast hotel and preferred joining Sellers and his wife, whatever the mood, along with Jim Moloney and Sellers's assistant Michael Jeffery, at the Sellerses' chalet.

The atmosphere was uneasy only until Lynne Frederick came into the room, exuding an aura of calm that somehow enveloped us all like an Alpine fragrance. She was only in her mid-twenties but instantly observable as the mature center around which the household revolved, an emotional anchor that looked like a daffodil.

Sellers was willing to talk—politely, softly—about anything, it became apparent, but the movie. He talked about his recent film Fu Manchu ("a nightmare"), Rissner (ditto), electronics, photography, music. He showed off his state-of-the-art sound system and insisted I listen to sound track music from Fu Manchu and pass judgment on it. I was being tested and apparently passed, for he then toured me through the chalet and displayed quiet pride in the huge blowups of his own professional-quality photographs, one of which I especially admired, a nature photograph of a bird in flight, backlit by a starburst sun. His smile softened and relaxed, and he suggested we go out onto the chalet balcony to view the town below; he brought his camera.

Moloney joined us on the balcony, for there he could smoke, an activity forbidden inside the house. The two of us lingered there, greedily inhaling carcinogens in the tonic Alpine air, and I asked, "When do we talk about the movie?"

"Leave it to Lynne," he said.

We went to dinner in town. Sellers seemed more open, freer in company, and, to my astonishment, after dinner insisted we go for drinks to a local disco, where he and Lynne were apparently well known. It was small, cramped, loud, full of cigarette smoke, and Sellers encouraged Lynne and Michael to dance and later did so himself. He seemed to bloom in the hubbub of the crowd, unaffected, even energized by the smoke, the heat, the din. I studied Lynne, who even when dancing seemed mysteriously alert to the slightest fluctuation in her husband's mood, without seeming oversolicitous. *She has radar,* I thought.

The next day we met for lunch at the chalet. Lynne expertly prepared an enormous salad of tuna with lemon (no oil), shredded carrots, cherry tomatoes, and chopped celery. She explained to me it was part of Sellers's diet, which she supervised scrupulously. We ate at the kitchen table and drank Perrier, chatting amiably about everything but what I had flown thousands of miles to discuss. During our after-lunch cigarette on the balcony I said to Moloney, "It's lovely and all that, but when do we get to the *movie?*"

He shrugged and advised me again to "leave it to Lynne."

We went back inside, where Sellers experimented with the music system. He smiled at the music and looked absent and otherworldly, and finally, as the music ended, Lynne entered from the kitchen, took his hand, and said calmly, "Now, what about this movie, darling?"

"What, darling?" Sellers said. "Oh, yes, the movie . . ."

He moved to sit in an easy chair; Lynne sat beside him on the arm. He started to speak hesitantly, his voice feathery and thin. The litany of recriminations and fears I had been led to expect came gently, almost contritely, and gave way to comments about the screenplay that were intuitive and intelligent, and his voice grew stronger as he spoke. Little by little it took on overtones of Inspector Clouseau, and I couldn't help smiling, then laughing. As I did, he grew livelier, and he and Moloney played with ideas, bouncing gags and situations they wanted to write. The afternoon passed, and finally we realized we sat in half-dark, and Lynne said gently, "Darling, why don't you and Jim just *write* it, so Steve can go back to America?"

He seemed startled by the simplicity of the solution. "May we?" he asked uncertainly.

"Seems a good idea," I answered. I noticed then, as he rose, that not once in the long, talkative afternoon had he let go of Lynne's hand, nor had she moved away. She transfused him simultaneously with calm and energy and the hand he clung to was less a hand than a lifeline.

I arrived back in Los Angeles two days later, June 17, to see a first cut of Taylor Hackford's rock 'n' roll film *The Idolmaker*, a Santa Barbara sneak preview of *Those Lips, Those Eyes*, and dailies on *Cutter and Bone*, being directed by Ivan Passer. Our painful awareness that we did not know the footage on *Heaven's Gate* had altered policy; whenever possible, UA would now monitor films in progress on a daily basis.

The *Heaven's Gate* screening had been arranged for Thursday, June 26, and Albeck, Gene Goodman, and Dean Stolber were flying in from New York to see it with me. Cimino's familiar passion for secrecy had led to his insistence that no one else on the staff be permitted to see it; that suited me because I did not want reaction to the movie dissipated by too many voices, should it be harsh.

At 8:00 A.M. on the twenty-sixth Albeck, Goodman, Stolber, and I left my office in the Thalberg Building and crossed the lot past the guard gate to the MGM Main Theater. As we approached the entrance to the theater, we were startled to see it blocked by an armed guard, who refused to admit us until we had identified ourselves.

"Mr. Cimino's orders," he explained politely, checking us off his list, perhaps wondering what duties we performed in the Cimino organization.

Once we were inside the theater, Cimino nervously greeted us. He seemed shrunken and drawn by the long hours he had spent preparing for this screening. I refrained from mentioning the armed guard, and Andy spoke politely about the importance of the movie. Cimino reiterated his enthusiasm for it, but his voice sounded strained. He said, "The final version will probably be fifteen minutes shorter."

We sat down, spacing ourselves widely in the large screening room, and saw "Michael Cimino's 'Heaven's Gate.'"

All five hours and twenty-five minutes of it.

CHAPTER 19

PICTURE

Then I saw that there was a way to hell,
even from the gates of heaven.

—John Bunyan,
Pilgrim's Progress (1678)

The first image seemed to glow from within.

A pale sun burns behind black branches; then the camera tilts down, following the lines of a clock tower. At the left of the frame, young James Averill, beardless and dressed formally in black suit and tie, bursts through an archway and races across the screen, the camera following until he vanishes around a corner. We hear, then see, the band, brass instruments glinting as "The Battle Hymn of the Republic" blares and they march on through the streets. Averill breathlessly catches up to them. Billy Irvine is marching, too, and they exchange a muffled greeting. The camera follows the marchers into a great hall, which rises in tier after tier of balconies, overflowing with guests of the graduating class of 1870. The color, the movement, the textures are silken, a seamless flow enlivened by trumpeted tempo. Then, stillness as the patriarchal Reverend Doctor gravely impresses high ideals upon the graduates, while they inspect the beautiful girls flirting down from the balconies above, and Billy Irvine disrupts it all with his facetious valediction. And suddenly we are outdoors again and the pale sun has turned golden, as "The Blue Danube" soars and the young couples swirl in dizzying, rapturously romantic waltz around the great tree in the center of the green . . . and then a high-spirited melee around the tree . . . and then a song . . . and candlelight on blushing cheeks and . . .

Wyoming, and the rhythms change, grow statelier and slower. Vistas of mountained majesty peel by, images so beautiful it seems impossible they could give way to panoramas still more dazzling, but they do, and then the train appears, a dark, continent-conquering force, and there are immigrants huddled on top, their faces swollen with fatigue and tight with apprehension, and we are in Casper, where white smoke billows from rooftop chimneys, pluming above the spider webs of telephone and telegraph wires, and wagons and buggies and pedestrians and horses raise curtains of dust that filter the light to a glow, a radiance, as if the sun that shines on Casper holds some special promise. But then there is darkness of a human sort, and blood and a cockfight, with its flashing silver knives edged in scarlet, and butchered steers draining crimson life into the earth, and immigrants pulling, pushing, dragging wagons across the frozen land, and the guns report and again and again, then sudden stillness and the lambent glow of Ella as she bathes in a stream strewn with sparkle, the delirium and gaiety and fiddles as roller skates glide, then a slow waltz and the calm of a lake, shimmering with the dappled image of the moon, then . . .

It was an orgy of brilliant pictorial effects, and no one who sat in that theater would ever again question where the money had gone, for it was there to see: the sweep of movement before the camera, by the camera, spectacular effect following spectacular effect until there couldn't be any more, but there were, and still more after that. But little by little the anxiety of anticipation gave way to satiety, then to a sense of claustrophobia induced by the inundation of image and effect. We became disoriented, victims of sensory overload, deafened by undifferentiated sound tracks: the jingles of bridles; squeaks of boots; thwacks of hatchets in flesh; concatenation of foreign tongues and accents all talking at once, or *more*, all singing at once, keening folkloric ballads, mournful dirges for vanished lives and approaching deaths. And still there was more. The battle, the pandemonium, the chaos, the terrorized animals, the blood, the cataracts of dust and debris and explosives were relentless, and the brain numbed, waiting for the last moaning immigrant to fall in the swirling dust, for the last brutal death to be done, for the last wave of picturesque fuller's earth to blow across the last unblinking lens, and when the last fading image—as exquisite as the first—ran through the projector, I felt bludgeoned by vainglory and excess, surfeited by style, sound, and fury. My own.

"No *way* is this company going to release a movie that's five and a half hours long," said Albeck, minutes later in my office, his mouth a line that could have been drawn with a ruler.

"I couldn't *hear* anything," said Dean Stolber.

"What's your plan?" asked Albeck, turning to me.

My plan? My *plan?* I was still reeling and dazed.

"Do we fire him?" Albeck asked sharply.

I thought for a moment. "We can fire him, sure. But if we do, who cuts the movie?"

"You?" asked Albeck. "The editors?"

"I don't think so, Andy. Nobody knows the footage but Cimino.

This isn't a case of trimming or losing a sequence or two. The battle sequence *alone* is an hour and a half long!"

"Can we find someone else?"

"We can *try*, and then we can deal with Cimino's press conference."

"What press conference?" asked Stolber.

"The one he'll call to denounce us. The one that will say to the press and the world that we think we have a thirty-five-million-dollar disaster on our hands."

"How am I supposed to book this picture?" asked Goodman, sounding in pain.

"There *is* no picture, Gene. There is five and a half hours of staggering self-indulgence, but there is no picture."

"I couldn't *hear* anything," repeated Stolber.

"We told him if he did not deliver a picture at three hours, he would lose his final cut. Has he lost it?"

"As a practical matter, Andy, it doesn't matter. We can *order* him to cut it down, but you heard him: He agrees it's too long—fifteen minutes too long! If he refuses, we fire him, admit disaster, and we're back to 'Who cuts the picture?'"

"What were those antlers on the front of the train?" asked Stolber.

"I don't know," I answered. "He had antlers in the logo of *The Deer Hunter.* Maybe it's his *homage* to himself."

"Can we bring in other editors?" asked Albeck.

"There's a girl coming down from San Francisco who worked for Francis on *Apocalypse* to replace Bill Reynolds. I've already asked Reynolds to stay on, but he says he can't do that to Mulligan and MGM, so I've got a call in to Mulligan."

"Would it do any good to ask Begelman?"

"Begelman wouldn't give UA a tip on a horse."

I remembered something. "There's an editor in New York I worked with on *The Taking of Pelham 1-2-3* called Jerry Greenberg. Maybe he's available; maybe he could make some sense out of the battle sequence. An *hour and a half!*"

"What about all my theaters?" asked Goodman plaintively.

"I'd get on the phone *fast* if I were you," I advised.

"I don't know," he said, trying to cheer himself up. "I didn't think it was *that* bad."

"Yes, it is," I said. "It's intolerable, unbearable."

"Some of it's beautiful," he said wanly.

"All of it's beautiful," I said. "It's just unwatchable."

"What is your plan?" asked Albeck once more.

"I don't know, Andy," I answered wearily.

"This man responds to pressure," Albeck pointed out sternly. "You pressured him in Montana, and it worked."

"It *helped*," I corrected.

"You pressured him in England, and it worked. I have an investment of more than thirty million dollars, costing millions more in interest. There is no way to leave this man alone without pressure and a schedule. We either fire the man today or give him a target date."

I looked around the room and realized I was alone.

"He already has one," I said. "November."

Cimino was not ordered to deliver the picture in November; he volunteered to do so. He maintained that his postproduction schedule was still valid and reluctantly responded to pressure from Reynolds and me that the picture was vastly overlength. MGM and Robert Mulligan parted company over *Rich and Famous* (which became, instead, George Cukor's last film), permitting Reynolds to stay with *Heaven's Gate*. He did so, he later told Dale Pollock of the *Los Angeles Times*, appalled by "the immense waste and self-indulgence," but he was fond of Cimino and determined to find the film within the footage.

Jerry Greenberg flew in from New York, looked at the battle sequence, and took it back to New York with him to cut it down to a coherent narrative, either Greenberg or Cimino flying coast to coast every ten days to check on progress. Because I had worked with Jerry before, I tried to pressure him. "Cut out the goddamn immigrants," I pleaded. "All that singing and wailing. They're so strident and unappealing you start rooting for the mercenaries." He informed me that editors take their directives from directors, not from executives. So much for old times' sake.

Access to Mr. Cimino became impossible. He was under brutal pressure, it was true, was spending fourteen and sixteen hours a day in the editing rooms, and perhaps understandably did not relish spending precious minutes or hours explaining or showing the progress being made. Gradually the picture began to come down in length. Five hours, four and three-quarters, four and a half, four. There could be no precise timing until Greenberg finished the battle sequence in New York. In the meantime, I had to fight to see reels or sequences, but Reynolds's patient, paternal paring away of excess began to reveal what in contrast anyway, began to look like a movie. But it was a movie by which I felt held hostage, to which I had access only by entreaty or show of corporate muscle, and I resolved to change that.

• • •

On July 15 I asked Joann to come to my office. She arrived, sat opposite me on the sofa, and asked "What's up?"

"The jig," I replied. "I'm removing you from the picture, Joann."

"How come?" she asked without surprise.

"Because Michael uses you as a shield—always has—and I need direct access to him now. You know what trouble we're in. I can't have you standing between Michael and the company any longer."

She folded her arms and looked absently out the window to the parking lot that fronted the building. After a moment she turned back and smiled. "Ya know," she said, "I can't tell you what a relief this is."

I had been prepared for anything but that.

"I'm tired of being the fall guy, having the fights, making everybody mad at me because they can't find Michael to get mad at. I've been working on this picture for over two years now. I'm not a rich woman. I'm not even receiving fees now. I'm *relieved.*"

"How will Michael take it?"

"He'll scream a little, but he won't quit, if that's what you mean. . . . But could I ask you a favor?"

"What?"

"Do we have to announce this or anything?"

"What do you mean?"

"Well, I'd like to be able to get work sometime in the future"—she laughed—"and it doesn't help if it's on Rona Barrett that I just got fired from my own movie!"

I gave her my word it would not be announced, and it wasn't.

"So how do we explain my absence?" she asked logically.

"Music," I said. "With a musicians' strike in Hollywood, the scoring was going to be done in Europe anyway."

"Munich." She nodded.

"Go to Munich, Joann. Record the music. Make the album."

"Right!" She nodded, cheered.

"Who *is* this composer, anyway, now that Michael has agreed not to compose the music himself?" I asked, grimacing.

She laughed. "You've heard the music. I gave you a tape."

"It's wonderful. I just never heard of the guy. What happened to John Williams?"

"Too expensive."

"And the Italian?"

"Morricone? He fell asleep." She laughed. "I'm not kidding you. He came to London to meet us and fell asleep in the meeting."

"And where did you find this guy?"

"David Mansfield? You know him," she said. "He plays John De-Cory in the movie."

"That little *kid*?" I asked, and recalled meeting him a year earlier at the Outlaw Inn. He played Ella's helper at the bordello, the fiddle player in the Heaven's Gate roller rink band.

"He's no little kid." She laughed. "He just looks like a little kid. Who do you think arranged all that roller-skating music and found the antique instruments and taught those guys to play them? He used to be with Bob Dylan's band. I discovered him."

"Joann," I said, "go to Munich. Do the music. And don't tell Michael you're off the picture. I will."

Later that day Dean Stolber sent an official telegram to Michael Cimino. It read: "Joann Carelli is hereby removed from her position . . . and henceforth she shall have no further connection, position or capacity with the HEAVEN'S GATE production. . . . All personnel connected with HEAVEN'S GATE, including Michael Cimino, shall report to Mr. Bach."

Cimino did not quit or scream. He went back to work.

The next day, I received good news. Martin Baum, Peter Sellers's agent, was on the line.

"I've just received a cable from Peter," he said, "and I want to read you part of it. 'Script on way to you by courier. No joking, I think it's bloody terrific, and I hope you will.' How about that?"

"I'm thrilled," I said. "I can't wait to read it."

"Wait till you hear how he signs this cable," said Baum, laughing. "'Peter Shakespeare and Jim Bacon.'" I laughed, too.

It was a piece of news too good to hope for and too good to last. When Marty Baum called me a week later, it was to tell me that Peter Sellers was dead: a heart attack in London.

Not long after, I received a package in the mail and a note from Sellers's secretary, Sue Evans. She wrote: "Mr. Sellers wanted you to have this." Carefully rolled in a cardboard tube was a photograph: a bird in flight, backlit by a starburst sun.

"Right now there is nothing in my world or yours as important as my being able to see you for half an hour."

Bill Goldman's voice was cryptic and tight on the line; I could almost hear his jaws clench.

"Come on over," I said, though I had just walked into my New York apartment as the phone was ringing. I hung up, put down the bulging script bag, and turned the air conditioner on high. What could be so important? I wondered, but I liked Bill and liked seeing him, even more now that the script for *The Right Stuff* was so good and so near completion of its final draft.

I started to fix a drink but left the ice cubes rattling in the sink when the buzzer sounded. Bill slumped into the small foyer, his tall frame hunched forward, the Fu Manchu mustache exaggerating the droop of his expression. He took a couple of paces into the living room, quickly surveyed the layout, and thrust an envelope at me.

"What's this?" I asked.

"Either you go into the other room to read it, or I will while you do," he said. "I don't want to watch your face while you read."

I went into another room and read and wished I had taken the time to make that drink, for what I read was a letter from Bill to his agent, explaining why he was quitting *The Right Stuff*. He spoke of anguish and nightmares. I read it again.

When I walked back into the living room, Bill was at the window, staring into the courtyard below.

"Don't jump," I quipped, hoping to lighten the gloom. It didn't work.

"Don't you see?" he said. "I want to say something good and positive about America, and what I'm doing is dreaming about falling to my death—because of Phil."

"Phil" was Philip Kaufman, who had signed on as director of *The Right Stuff* on the basis of Bill's first-draft screenplay. He hadn't been the first choice (George Roy Hill was, but Hill had insisted on producing as well as directing, and Chartoff and Winkler had not unreasonably refused to step aside) or the second either, but he was a *good* choice, everyone agreed, and everybody met and talked and considered carefully and nobody noticed very much—because we all had been over the subject so many times before Phil came on the picture—when he said, "It's a pity to leave out Yeager; after all, isn't he what 'the right stuff' is all about?" We were listening, all right, but not paying attention because what he really said was ". . . isn't he what *The Right Stuff* is all about?"

Bill's problem that afternoon in my apartment when he was abandoning the picture, America, Chartoff-Winkler, United Artists, the Mormon Tabernacle Choir, and me in one five-page letter full of anguished nightmares wasn't Phil Kaufman at all: It was Yeager.

It had come to a head with "a few notes" Phil asked to put together for Bill and the producers as suggestions for second-draft revisions. The "notes" amounted to a thirty-five-page memo which virtually rewrote the screenplay, enthusiasm for which had been a key factor in Phil's wanting to direct the picture in the first place. He said.

But that wasn't the serious part, the nightmare part. According to his memo, Phil wanted to illuminate "the passing of a higher quality"—the right stuff, Yeager. But that (and the lack of narrative cohesion) had been the reason for eliminating Yeager from the beginning. His romantic, righteous, solitary, right-stuffness was too movie hero-apt, too Gary Cooper-easy; this movie had to be divided up among seven guys who weren't Yeager—not at first—but who reclaimed and redefined that "higher quality." Yeager had it, sure, Bill pleaded, but the astronauts would show it being earned, being forged, unless . . . heart-stopping, Empire-State-Building-trip-to-34th-Street-below premonition . . . unless deep down Phil *didn't believe the astronauts had it.*

"All I want to do," Phil amiably insisted, "is add a prologue and a coda about Yeager, the way Wolfe does in the book."

And Bill said, "But Wolfe had four hundred-some-odd pages between the prologue and coda to show our guys, *America,* earning the right stuff, and we've got only two hours of screen time to do that!"

And Phil said, "But I'm only asking you to do what Wolfe did, and you're so nuts about Wolfe. . . ."

And Bill said, "But Yeager is Wolfe's metaphor. You want to make this movie about a *metaphor?*"

It went on like that for weeks.* Phil didn't seem to see the problem, and Bill saw nothing but the problem. He was passionate to say something about the right stuff *now,* not *then,* and deeply feared that Phil's phrase *the passing of a higher quality* (emphasis added) was the antithesis of everything he wanted to do, and he began having nightmares that led to my standing in the middle of my living room with a letter in my hand. If Bill quit, the movie was off because UA had taken sides and wanted to make Bill's script—with or without Kaufman—but if Bill left, there would be no script to make. How—*why*—go forward with a director we had been prepared to fire or with a writer who had fired *us?* Then there was the part Bill didn't know and I couldn't tell him: *Heaven's Gate* didn't look "like David Lean decided to make a western" anymore, and Bill was canceling out one of my insurance policies against its potential failure.

I wanted to throw things, punches, scripts, anything, but Bill talked me out of it without knowing he was doing so. The sun was setting there on East Sixty-second Street when Bill said, "Don't you see?

<hr />

*Goldman recounts his own perspective over this conflict in his book *Adventures in the Screen Trade.*

Whether Phil is right or wrong, whether he even understands that he really admires only Yeager, doesn't matter because that's what *I* believe he believes, and the only stuff I could write for him now would be . . . well, the wrong stuff."

Bill left, and I made that drink. I sat and wondered. How to make an artist do something he doesn't want to do or can't do. There are no threats, no blandishments that have effect because the "art" part comes from within and is more subject to fears that result in nightmares of death than to warnings of guild denunciation or even simple greed. They can be assuaged sometimes only by walking away. When Joan Crawford told F. Scott Fitzgerald in the thirties, "Write hard, Mr. Fitzgerald, write hard," she was saying the only thing that can be said. She was shrewd enough to know that "Write well, better, faster, *deeper*" has no practical bearing on an interior process ultimately unknowable.

"Edit hard, Michael," I was saying, "edit hard," and I knew that "Edit well, better, faster, deeper, *shorter*" would have no more effect than expecting a brilliant comic to be happy without the lifeline of a hand he needed to hold or "forcing" Bill Goldman to do something he felt he could not do: Right "the wrong stuff."

So there would be no *The Romance of the Pink Panther* and no *The Right Stuff* for UA. * But there were a hundred other projects in development, production, or ready to go, and the production staff was vigorous, aggressive, and united. We were watching dailies now and visiting sets and locations, and we had added a new production management executive to supplement Lee Katz and Derek Kavanagh: Dennis Brown who joined us from EMI. Every UA picture now had a production executive (Wunsch, Sylbert, Parks, or myself) *and* Katz, Kavanagh, or Brown riding herd, and results began to show in less slippage—or quicker warnings.

In spite of disappointments like Sellers's death and Goldman's defection and the daily drain of energy everywhere apparent as Cimino continued cutting, we had managed to put into production *For Your Eyes Only, Rocky III, The French Lieutenant's Woman, Thief, Caveman, Eye of the Needle,* and soon, it appeared, *Thy Neighbor's Wife.*

Talese's book was still at the top of the best seller lists. Our progress on it had been relaxed, in spite of (or because of) the dozens of letters from agents, writers, and directors asking to work on the project. The

* *The Right Stuff* was made by Philip Kaufman for the Ladd Company. Sam Shepard played Yeager, who was a consultant on the film and also played a bit part as a patron of Pancho's bar.

decision not to turn the book over to Coppola and Zoetrope was a corporate decision, not an aesthetic judgment. Besides, Francis was preparing his own movie about the sexes, *One from the Heart*. Also, there had been no rush because I had discovered the liberated material was, to some, deeply intimidating.

"I think the book is fabulous, Steve, just fabulous," explained Sidney Lumet that summer over lunch in the Russian Tea Room. "But there's just no way to do this movie without showing"—he searched for the word—"*insertion*, and my God, Steve, I wouldn't know how to direct that. I mean, what do I say to the actors? Is it—is it possible—" He went pale as some revelation struck him. "My God! Is it possible I'm a *prude*?"

William Friedkin wasn't, as *The Exorcist* and *Cruising* had shown. He agreed to write and direct what he warned would be an X-rated movie. Andy's eyes widened, but I reminded him that we had always assumed *Thy Neighbor's Wife* would be an X, as *Last Tango in Paris* had been. The Capote material would soon begin writing, and after Meryl Streep had finished *The French Lieutenant's Woman*, she would make Bob Benton's thriller, his first picture since *Kramer vs. Kramer*; Bette Midler agreed to star in Frank Gilroy's *The Edge* but wanted a new title, a new director (instead of Gilroy), and a new screenplay, which David Newman agreed to write; Faye Dunaway wanted to do a remake of *Sweet Smell of Success*, playing a vicious and powerful gossip columnist, once played by Burt Lancaster; there was a *Black Stallion* sequel; there were more.

There were also pictures ready for release. "Woody Allen No. 4," *Those Lips, Those Eyes*, *The Idolmaker*, and Martin Scorsese's *Raging Bull*.

No picture was put into production during this period of UA's history with more misgivings than *Raging Bull*. It was violent, dark, and profane. The adamance of Chartoff and Winkler and the passion of Scorsese and De Niro had finally overwhelmed trepidation and got it made. The picture had gone overschedule and overbudget, though not egregiously so, and in mid-July UA saw it for the first time.

There were only twelve minutes of boxing footage in the movie, but they were the most vivid and brutal I had ever seen. The black-and-white photography looked like pages torn from the forties, black blacks, white whites, and an infinitude of grays. The unknown supporting actors, Joe Pesci and Cathy Moriarty as Jake LaMotta's brother and wife, were casting miracles, perfectly directed. Scorsese's skill with violence—verbal, physical, aesthetic—had found perhaps its ultimate subject, but the superlative, the not quite predictable revelation was De Niro.

Scorsese intended opening the picture with De Niro as the older LaMotta, swollen by sixty pounds, bloated with the weight of his years, and I had been opposed to it. I thought the transformation from lean street kid to ramshackle debris should be delayed, gradually revealed, that to show the end at the beginning would repel an audience that would need fortitude just to get through the film. Scorsese, I saw as the film began unrolling, had been right. He had feared publicity about De Niro's weight gain would be too widespread and that audiences would sit through the film not seeing, not hearing, waiting only to see the "fat man." He undercut that voyeuristic fascination at the start, replacing it with curiosity not about an actor's stunt but about a man's life.

The passion that got the movie made showed in every frame. I glanced across in the dark of the Magno screening room at Andy Albeck, sitting stiff and straight in his seat, attentive and expressionless as the violence on screen reflected brightly on his spectacle lenses. His reaction was impossible to read. I turned back to the screen, where De Niro was not acting but inhabiting his role, in what seemed to me the most compelling performance I had ever seen on film.

The lights came up slowly in a room full of silence, as if the viewers had lost all power of speech. Nor was there the customary applause. Martin Scorsese leaned against the back wall of the screening room as if cowering from the silence. Then Andy Albeck rose from his seat, marched briskly to him, shook his hand just once, and said quietly, "Mr. Scorsese, you are an Artist." He turned and left and walked back to 729 and to work.

Albeck meant what he said to Scorsese; he had been profoundly moved by *Raging Bull,* but he was dubious about its box-office potential. He believed it too violent and nihilistic for any woman to enjoy in spite of its artistry. Still, it would be a major contender for honors at year's end, and if there were enough of them, maybe major business as well. That the picture would open just days before *Heaven's Gate* seemed somehow fortunate—*if Heaven's Gate* opened.

By October it was down to under four hours and would not get shorter if the picture were to be released in November, as planned and booked. The booking print Cimino had promised for July 1, then 14, then 16 was never made at all, as perfectionism or uncertainty multiplied delays in an expensive process that was growing dangerously protracted. The premiere openings in New York, Toronto, and Los

Angeles were set. Gene Goodman had been able to book other urban areas but not, of course, any with anti-blind-booking legislation. Postponing the picture's release was the merest of possibilities and, after cursory discussion, was rejected. Removing the pressure, we felt, would only compound the delays, encourage the maddening perfectionism (or indecision) from a director who continued adamantly to insist he would meet his schedule and vehemently to protect the picture from UA's interference. This was not difficult to do with four editors working on two coasts on different sections of the picture, sections often torn apart for reevaluation of ten, twenty, thirty, forty, fifty printed takes of individual shots, then reassembled, examined and reexamined for nuance and detail, and often disassembled all over again.

Any attempt to see the picture in toto was regarded not merely as an intrusion into the creative process but as an active threat, for UA still had the power to take the film from Cimino, a power I deeply did not want to exercise. Doing so would have thrown the finishing processes into chaos at best, would have attracted widespread public attention of a sort that could only damage the picture, and would in all likelihood have further prolonged the postproduction period (now pushing the picture's cost over $35 million), without having the at least theoretical advantage of the creator's guidance.

Cimino could forestall the picture's being taken from him, or could protect his final cut, simply by prolonging the postproduction period until the very last moment, when any discussions of final cut would have been academic. This was the situation that obtained by mid-October, when Jerry Greenberg and Cimino finally finished the battle sequence and Cimino pronounced the picture finished. He announced adamant opposition to further cutting (as he had done with The Deer Hunter). To reduce it below three hours and thirty-nine minutes would strip it of pictorial value and the internal rhythms he had built into it from the first day of production. Bill Reynolds, by this time elevated in Cimino's confidence to "executive in charge of postproduction," demurred, but his suggestions, too, were rebuffed. Reynolds privately lamented that he thought many sequences too long, and his was the sole voice urging public previews. Cimino reminded everyone that all public previews had accomplished on The Deer Hunter was to prove to Universal that he had been right all along, so what was the point? Besides, it would take time, and time was the enemy. It was pointed out that there seemed to be plenty of time for endless reexamination of footage or for monomaniacal reworking of technical processes, but those all were justified in the name of Art, while seeing how the picture played before an audience was both pointless, because Cimino knew how it would play, and ignoble because a question of mere Commerce. Besides, there wasn't any time. The man who could take days to shoot a page of dialogue could not now figure out a means of sparing four hours to see how that dialogue played before viewers unadmitted to the pantheon.

All summer long I had seen interim versions of the picture or sequences or individual scenes or single shots until I realized I wasn't seeing or hearing them anymore: I was sitting in dark rooms and allowing them to pass before me. I had lost the capacity to respond to the picture on any but the most mechanical levels.

Every shot, every scene went past eyes that had lost both critical and personal objectivity. Some saintlier observer might have succeeded in suppressing what I seemed to see each time the movie rolled on: the waste, the arrogance, the indulgence that had accompanied its birth pains. The only thing that enabled me to sit through the last few screenings was the music, which I found beautiful and moving, but even that pleasure was mitigated by memory of the contractual battles with Joann Carelli, who—it turned out—owned all of David Mansfield's music and had sold it to the film. Whenever I saw young Mansfield's face on screen, his chin pressing down happily on the antique fiddle he played, I wondered if he knew that Carelli had sold his songs to UA for exactly ten times what the documents showed she had paid him. The music was not lyrical enough, finally, to hide from me the simple, brutal fact that I was burned out on *Heaven's Gate*, and so, I suspected, was Cimino, whose cold but exhausted hauteur suggested that his oft-expressed enthusiasm had long since flickered out. His eyes may have reflected the embers of ambition, but the flame of passion was long gone.

Changes continued. Trims here, snips there, adding back this, altering that. There were protracted battles over the credit roll at the end (eight minutes long), the musical overture at the beginning (seven minutes), the main credits where Cimino, because he didn't like a particular phrase of music playing over Joseph Cotten's credit, just *moved* Joseph Cotten's credit, heedless of Cotten's contractual rights, unleashing floods of legal paper, threats, and recriminations. This seemed not merely cavalier but offensive to most of us, because Cimino was at the same time demoting Charlie Okun in the credits to a position *below* Denis O'Dell, English production manager on the prologue, in spite of Okun's year and more on the picture, as opposed to O'Dell's mere weeks. Cimino was also adding a corporate credit of his own to his three other credits in the already overlong credit sequence. This additional credit was protested legally and instantly by UA. He was ordered to remove "Partisan Productions Presents," put Joseph Cotten's name back where it belonged, and to spell Denis (not "Dennis") O'Dell's name right. He simply refused. Perfection, apparently, had its own curious laws. *

The advertising and publicity departments had grown numb with frustration in dealing with Carelli, who had been recalled to coordinate publicity to prevent Cimino from personally doing so and further delaying the editing. It was at this time that she delivered the thousands of stills (including the 4,000 of Cimino and his crew) but virtually no stills of major action sequences in the picture. No originals, only dupes, were delivered; these included only three approved stills of Isabelle Huppert and six staged stills for inclusion in the trailer and one portrait shot—of Michael Cimino. There was simply no way to publicize the picture with so little material and give any sense of the picture's chief virtue, its physical look. There was, however, a group of extraordinarily beautiful transparencies given to *Life*, which Carelli used to explain where all the originals were, and even they turned out to be dupes.

The production, advertising, publicity, distribution, legal, and postproduction departments seemed gridlocked in wearing battles with *Heaven's Gate*. Production had been dominated by it for two years and had seen pictures canceled or neglected, lives disrupted by it; advertising had buckled with frustration and was forced to accept Cimino's own advertising campaign; publicity had nothing to publicize; distribution was working hard to book a picture it had not seen in theaters which "utterly disgusted" Mr. Cimino, as he wrote into the record; legal was churning paper work about credit violations, horses with psychiatric problems, unsigned contracts and budgets, lawsuits real, pending or threatened; and postproduction belonged to *Heaven's Gate*, inasmuch as Sol Lomita, UA's executive in charge of that department, was assigned personally to take over the mountains of technical and laboratory minutiae involved in the physical preparation of prints.

They had done it. By intention or accident Cimino and Carelli had made the process, the *idea* of *Heaven's Gate* so unpleasant, so punishing for virtually every department of the company, from accounting to photocopying, that every employee affected by it wanted nothing more than to see it released and be done with it. Perhaps Albeck was an exception; the compiler of this chronicle was not.

In order to make that happen, Technicolor began printing reels at the end of October, three hours and thirty-nine minutes worth, still with incorrect titles. Neither I nor anyone else at United Artists saw

---

* The Joseph Cotten credit was ultimately corrected, though not for many months. The other credits remain, misspellings and all.

this version of the picture. Insisting on doing so as it was going into final printing would now have no practical result because no changes could be made without endangering the heavily advertised New York opening. Even pulling the disparate elements from the lab—picture, titles, sound effects tracks, dialogue tracks, music tracks—for an executive screening might, Cimino protested (and Sol Lomita confirmed), endanger the finishing schedule, now perilously tight—unless we decided, three weeks before the opening, to postpone. Cimino's right to final cut had, through delays, become the most academic of issues. Perhaps no decision at this critical moment could have been entirely right, but the one I made was the only one I saw, the only one I wanted to see, with results I could not, did not foresee. I took a fateful leap of faith: The picture would open as scheduled.

Just before the presidential election of 1980, as Cimino's reels were printing, Lois Smith agreed to leave Lord Grade's Marble Arch Productions to fill the vice-presidency in New York that Marcia Nasatir had accepted and rejected. Before entering production, Smith had been a successful publicist, with clients like Robert Redford, Al Pacino, Liza Minnelli, Faye Dunaway, Barbra Streisand, and many others, and she had, by coincidence, worked on publicity for *The Deer Hunter*. Albeck enthusiastically approved her joining UA as part of a strategic turn I wanted to take toward bigger names, our "little" pictures having for the most part fared badly. Lois had a maternal sort of access to her former clients, who not only liked her but trusted her, as did Wunsch, Sylbert, and Parks. She would spark our future.

On October 28, just before I returned to California to vote, Albeck invited me to his office to discuss that future.

"I've been doodling around," he said brightly, "and I'd like you to look at my doodles and tell me what you think." He spread a sheet of paper on the desk and turned it around for me to study. It was an organizational chart, and at the top was the name of the chairman of the board: Andy Albeck. To my considerable relief, the letters "CEO" were also there. Descending directly from the chairman's box were the smaller boxes for the financial and administrative officers of the corporation. Angling left and right were two other tiers of positions. On the left was written "United Artists Productions," and on the right "United Artists Distribution." In the uppermost production box was my name, with "president" penciled beside it. On the distribution side the name was "Auerbach," followed by the same designation.

It was basic reorganization and a distinct reversal of the philosophy with which Andy had taken over the company almost three years be-

fore. Not only were production and distribution separated cleanly and
clearly, but there was another major change, one that not only seemed
sensible but resolved a situation that had rankled for two and a half
years and had, I believed, much to do with David Field's frustrations at
UA: Business affairs would now report to production, instead of being
equal with it. Domination of production by both distribution and business affairs was at an end.

Perhaps this was what Jack Beckett had meant back in August,
when he had decided to change the company's name to Transamerica
Films but allowed me to dictate the office layout. "You're the one who'll
be living there," he had said.

Andy broke my study of the chart. "This will not take effect until
January first," he said, "and we won't announce it until just before
Christmas—that is, if you agree it works."

I did. I went to California and voted against an actor, and even the
depressing news that he had won and my uneasiness over *Heaven's Gate*
couldn't dent my elation, for I was surely one of the most elated people
in show business.

For at least two weeks.

CHAPTER 20

PREMIERE

In order for any event, public or private, to become a major news story, a story that dominates the media for weeks or months, the event and the coverage of the event must acquire a key ingredient. Without that ingredient, the story drifts and eventually withers. The ingredient is reaction—broad public reaction. . . . Some events are sufficiently momentous to compel substantial and varied reaction from the time they occur until far into the future. Just as often, though, reaction develops gradually, and then is sharply accelerated by some form of catalyst—a particular news article or a subsequent event.

—David McClintick,
Indecent Exposure (1982)

"He's a genius!" Mike Nichols declared. "Woody has made his own Fellini film *and* a parody of 8½ at the same time!"

Anthea Sylbert asked crisply, "Are you sure he hasn't made a Diane *Arbus* film?"

"It's brilliant," stated Nichols unequivocally. Sylbert batted her eyelashes "uh-huh" and looked sharply around, casing the room. We were at Elaine's after attending the first screening of "Woody Allen No. 4," now revealed as *Stardust Memories*, and Woody might be there. Mike hoped so; I hoped not.

I kept quiet. I had approved the script after all, had found it funny and sad, but thought Woody's most unguarded and autobiographical movie had soured in execution: Woody as filmmaker, artist in angst, simultaneously rejecting and exploiting celebrity, sending up pretentious critics, satirizing gaga fans. It read fresh and funny and frank, but the gaga turned grotesque, and Pauline Kael was not alone in feeling it was a "horrible betrayal" full of "contempt for the public," as she wrote in the *New Yorker*. Kael overstated wildly, but more moviegoers agreed with her than with Mike Nichols's delight. To many, the studio executive in the film (played by Andy Albeck) called the shot with ominous clarity in his single (Allen-authored) line: "He's not funny anymore."

Stardust Memories found its audience, though it was a commercial disappointment after the triumph of *Manhattan*, and it signaled the end of the four-picture deal that had begun with *Annie Hall* and *Interiors*. The time had come to talk.

Whatever Albeck's private expectations of keeping Woody, his openly declared determination to do so was staunch. My own desire to entice Woody into staying and working within the new company structure that would take effect in January far outdistanced any realistic hopes I had of doing so.

We met at the nearly deserted Russian Tea Room late on a Friday afternoon. Woody greeted me with polite attentiveness, as always, but his bland expression betrayed no expectations, no content whatever. It seemed best to be direct.

"You know we want you to stay at UA, Woody, and frankly I don't know how to bring that about. We can frame an economic offer difficult to refuse, and we'll do that when we meet with Sam [Cohn, his agent] and Jack and Charlie in a few days. But I doubt if that's the issue. We can meet any money offer, but so can others. Andy and I have been searching the company to see what we can offer we don't already happily give, which is, well . . . total freedom."

"You've been wonderful," he said. "Everybody's been wonderful."

"The sales department had fabulous success with *Manhattan* and spared no efforts with *Interiors* and *Stardust Memories*. Our respect for the movies and our loyalty to you are unquestionable, I think, and aside from Pauline Kael's head, I can't think of anything more we can offer."

He smiled and fooled with a teaspoon. "I don't know what to say. You and Andy and Hy and Sol [Lomita] and everybody else have been wonderful to me. I can honestly say there isn't one thing I've wanted or needed that I haven't gotten. If I had to name a way in which you or Andy failed me, I couldn't. . . ."

But?

"But it's not about business, exactly. . . ."

"It's about loyalty."

He nodded thoughtfully. "It's not possible sometimes *not* to disappoint *some*body. I don't want to disappoint *any*body."

"I know. And I'd rather that it not be me. Or Andy. I'm not sure you know the respect he has for you, the admiration."

"He's, uh, not a demonstrative man."

"No, he isn't. But he wants to be now."

"Why do I feel this growing more difficult?" he asked.

"I'm not trying emotional blackmail," I said. "I would if I thought it would work, but I don't, so I won't. I only want you to know that Andy and I are determined to find a way to keep you and your movies at UA, and when Sam and Jack and Charlie tell us what you're looking for, I hope that won't be just courtesy, just some perfunctory gesture. Because we are determined to demonstrate our sincerity. Maybe we can only do that with money and love and loyalty and respect and commitment, but you can't have everything."

He laughed, and we said friendly good-byes.

I had no illusions. The relationship with Woody was so laissez-faire it hardly existed. It was mostly definable by negatives: He didn't give us problems; we didn't give him problems. His filmmaker freedom was as total as anyone could make it. Money could be equaled; so could respect and commitment. But the personal history, the shared experiences, confidences and years with Arthur Krim were *hors de combat*; they just *were*, and there was no way we could compete with them directly. Still, we would try.

Albeck, Stolber, and I met repeatedly before Sam Cohn arrived with his précis of the deal he was presenting to UA and to Orion. (Twentieth Century-Fox was also trying to interest Woody, and maybe others were as well, but Sam privately admitted there were only two serious competitors allowed, and everybody knew who they were.)

Andy, Dean, and I exhaustively researched the files, studied every deal memo, every letter, every doodle; we asked for detailed written histories of the relationships between Woody and ad-pub, Woody and sales, Woody and foreign, and we gradually anticipated what we thought Sam might ask and how "demonstrative" we were prepared to be (economically and otherwise) not only to Woody but to Rollins and Joffe, too.

"Gentlemen, I'm just the messenger in this thing," said Sam as he pushed back the sleeves of his pullover and slipped his feet out of his Guccis in Andy's office. "This is from Jack and Charlie, with Woody's knowledge and approval, and I have virtually no influence in the negotiation or the final outcome. I just want that understood before I get to the terms."

We understood. We also understood that Sam wanted to take himself off what his disclaimer clearly hinted was a hopeless hook. He read us the terms. We had done our homework well. There was hardly an item in the dozen requests we hadn't anticipated with some degree of clarity and correctness.

We quickly prepared a counteroffer which was essentially better than had been asked: We were negotiating *up* but not recklessly. Albeck had precisely worked out our proposals with a series of very sharp yellow pencils. Still, the demonstration of intent was generous, insightful, and dramatic.

Sam, a most unflappable man, looked flapped. He jotted notes as we talked and when we finished, he said, "Gentlemen, when I came here to discuss these terms, I thought you had no chance whatever of competing with Orion. But you have stepped forward like mensches with a very generous and—in my opinion—sensible offer, and I'm impressed. I said I have no influence in this situation, and that's true, or it is marginal at best. But I intend to make my strongest recommendation that your offer be seriously considered, and you may recall from our past dealings"—he nodded gratefully to Albeck—"I can sometimes be persuasive." He bent to retrieve his shoes. "I think you're back in the ball game, fellas!"

When I returned to New York on November 14, a Friday, I did something movie executives seldom have time to do (and should be required to do): I went to the movies. I stood in line for an hour on East Fifty-seventh Street, waiting for the doors of the Sutton Theater to open. I listened to lobby talk, studied the eager eyes that go to the movies at noon on a weekday, tried to get some sense of the expectations of people for whom, in fact, we were doing what we did for a living.

It was opening day at the Sutton for *Raging Bull,* and I wanted to be there not for a premiere but for a paid public screening. I bought a ticket and noted happily that a Sold Out sign was quickly posted. It might have been because that morning's *New York Times* had carried Vincent Canby's review, saying " 'Raging Bull' . . . is a big film, its territory being the landscape of the soul," but then he had called *Stardust Memories* "a marvelous movie," and that hadn't made it a marvelous hit. In the lobby, I noted, was a poster for *Heaven's Gate,* which would open in four days a few blocks away. The poster, a mysterious-looking photograph of Kristofferson standing in shafts of mote-filled light, featured the words adorning the screenplay when it had been approved almost two years before: "What one loves about life are the things that fade." It was Cimino's personal ad campaign, the only one he would approve after turning down dozens from the ad agencies over which he had also exercised approval. I was ruefully certain that I would love *Heaven's Gate* most when it had faded away.

I settled into the crowded Sutton with the other moviegoers, braced with surprise at how good it felt to be "audience" again. The viewers that day fed back to the screen all the passion that had been invested in getting it up there. They were not silent, as we had been in our screening room; they screamed and yelled and laughed and howled and rolled with the brutal punches and drew collective breath and participated with the characters in a way that reinforced for me the real power movies sometimes achieve and the reason for making them.

Canby's review was followed by others equally good. Jack Kroll in *Newsweek* called it "the best American movie of the year," and I sent clippings at Albeck's suggestion to Jim Harvey in the Transamerica pyramid in San Francisco, hoping to open at a high point a dialogue that would be useful for the future.

Negotiations continued over Woody's deal. Sam had been right: Our willingness to step forward with an unprecedented offer had had its effects, if not on Woody, then on Jack and Charlie. There were additional rounds of talks, refinements of deal points, and finally, there was nothing more to say or hear. Woody asked for time to think and would let us know.

Sam said, "It's gone from being a foregone conclusion to being a call too close for me to make. I want you to know that if I were UA's own agent, I wouldn't be able to recommend to you a single course of action you haven't taken. If you don't make the deal, you can console yourselves that it wasn't for lack of trying. And, gentlemen . . . I congratulate you—win or lose."

There was nothing to do but wait.

And see *Heaven's Gate*.

Tuesday, November 18, was busy but quiet at 729. We were patiently waiting for Woody's response, assuming that the longer he took to decide, the more reason for wary optimism. *Raging Bull* continued to do sellout business where it had opened and was going on almost every important critic's "ten best" list in America. *The Idolmaker*, which had opened the same day, collected mostly appreciative reviews, and first business was good. We at 729 noted these facts gratefully, but the calm efficiency of that Tuesday was not that of any other day, and a quiet tension pervaded the building, most apparently in the offices of ad-pub on the twelfth floor.

No one in the company had seen as much of *Heaven's Gate* as I had—or as often—and most had never seen it at all. The publicity department, busy with the afternoon press screening, would see before I did the version Cimino brought from California in the early morning, a so-called wet print, fresh from the lab. They would scan critical faces at that press screening, searching for clues to report back to 729 about early reactions.

They were ambiguous. Silent. Ominously so, even though the critical press habitually conceals reaction from movie companies—and from each other. First reports back to 729 were worried, guarded, and it did not feel good. Still, the evening premiere performance and the party after required activity, the kind of keeping busy that masks anxiety. Or tries.

I left 729 early to go home and change clothes for the premiere, which was not, however, black tie, as a show of glitter seemed inappropriate for a movie that had been so widely, so long criticized for extravagance. It had been a long day, full of meetings and telephone calls and unexpressed nerves, but in some aura of utter calm I dressed almost happily, because tonight's official screening would write finis to two years that had exacted exorbitant tolls, extravagant costs of many kinds. It was over.

I had a vodka and waited for the doorman to announce the arrival of the rented limousine. When he did, I rode the elevator to the lobby, suddenly realizing I had forgotten my topcoat. I didn't go back for it in spite of the November wind and sleet; I would go from apartment to limo to theater to limo to party to limo to bed, and it seemed silly to delay by going back upstairs. I wanted to get on with it, to get it over.

I climbed into the limo, which had already picked up Lois Smith, my friend and colleague-to-be. Lois scrunched the softest shoulder in town next to mine, and as the driver headed with funereal pace toward Third Avenue, she chirped, "Don't worry, ducks! It's almost over." I smiled and looked for wood to knock. There wasn't any.

We pulled into Third Avenue behind a long row of limousines, black lacquered tanks, their roofs like ebony mirrors reflecting the lights of the theater marquees lining the block, including the one over both the Cinema I and the Cinema II announcing *Michael Cimino's "Heaven's Gate."* Traffic was jammed. Nothing moved, except the crowd on the sidewalk behind the ropes, peering curiously from chapped faces with runny noses at the celebrities filing into the theater, umbrellas whipping in the sleety wind, veiling their views of the rich or famous or important who threaded through lobby photographers, being nudged and directed by anxious publicists. One of them called out to Lois and me to pause on our way into the theater; we smiled grimaces against the cold—*flash!*—greeted friends, associates, colleagues, faces we knew that were attached to people we'd never met. I nodded to New York's most famous autograph hunter, a pleasant-faced, stout young man who always recognized me as someone he'd seen before and whose perennial question—"Are you anybody?"—doubtless seemed less philosophical to him than it did to me.

Someone from publicity nervously asked us to go directly to our seats in the roped-off section of the balcony because it was going to be a long evening. Almost four hours of movie, followed by more sleet, colder cold, and a party that had to start before midnight. "Please clear the lobby," someone yelled.

We fought the crowds and finally found the section reserved for the company's executives and the picture's stars and director and producer. We filed past Kris Kristofferson, looking jumpy next to Isabelle Huppert. Kristofferson had been in the theater all day, had seen the picture for the first time at the press screening, and had been embarrassed after the screening, when he changed clothes in one of the theater's private rooms for the evening premiere, to discover that he had no pants. Since he was to leave the theater by the back door, enter a limo, and rearrive at the front door for the photographers, the one-piece suit presented a problem. Words were exchanged, taxis dispatched, pants retrieved. He was wearing them now. I nodded to leading man and leading lady, and they nodded back. "Are you anybody?" their expressions asked. Christopher Walken and his wife were down the row, and so was Jeff Bridges. Directly in front of us was Joann Carelli. To my left was a man in a brown wool suit, someone I didn't know. I turned and introduced myself. He explained he was somebody's lawyer from New Jersey. He'd been given tickets by his client, who hadn't cared to attend. Did I know anything about this movie? "Not anymore," I said, which caused him to nod seriously, pondering. Am *I anybody?* I wondered. I turned to Lois, whose head was swiveling and bobbing with professional cheer as she waved and gestured and smiled greetings to friends and acquaintances scattered through the theater. I followed her glance as she nudged me with a powerful elbow to the ribs. There, just a few rows away, sat a distinguished-looking man in his late sixties, dressed in a dark blue business suit which failed to Westernize the buddhalike calm with which his unsmiling face surveyed the audience: Arthur Krim, chairman of a rival picture company, former chairman of this one. *He* was somebody, and it showed. Anonymous lawyers from New Jersey, former chairmen of the board. Finally, Joann Carelli turned in her seat in front of me and said, laughing, "Do you believe it? It's *over.*"

"Not for another three hours and thirty-nine minutes," I said.

She smiled back. "Yes, it is," she said consolingly. "It's over."

The lights dimmed, and the seven-minute overture began. Lois pat-
ted my hand, and I jumped. "Relax, ducks," she said, but I knew I
couldn't. I felt like 170 pounds of guy wires over which a business suit
had been draped. The movie began, and for the next four hours, possibly the longest four hours of my life, I studied the screen, able for the
first time in months to follow the images, the action, the characters
because there was an audience there to follow them with. But something was wrong. *I couldn't hear anything.* The sound track . . . No, it
couldn't be the sound track, not that expensive, endlessly reworked,
and Dolbyized sound track—it must be my *hearing.* . . . "Whatdide-
say?" asked the lawyer from New Jersey, and then I heard the important
sound, the deafening one there in the audience, the silence. The audience was either speechless with awe or comatose with boredom. I
began sweating icy rivulets in that silence that roared with quiet disdain. I sat there sweating and hyperventilating and composed myself
with words I repeated like a mantra: *It's over, it's over, it's over.* . . .

Intermission came, and with it a desperation to have a cigarette.
Lois and I pressed through the strangely silent crowd, and she moved
away to chat up a publicist friend she saw leaning against the wall,
observing the crowd with narrow, slitlike eyes. I headed for the curiously uncrowded bar, where waiters were poised with plastic glasses and
bottles of champagne. I took a glass and scanned the crowd. Why did
they look so unfamiliar? I wondered. *Where is everyone? Why are they so
quiet?*

Lois returned. "Listen, ducks," she said, "don't be too surprised to
see a lot of empty tables at the party after."

"Why?"

"I think they're going to be too exhausted after this. I mean, this is
some long movie."

"What did whosits say?" I asked, indicating the publicist.

"I shouldn't laugh," she said, doing so, "but he said he just saw
Michael and Michael came over and asked, 'Why aren't they drinking
the champagne?' and he answered, 'Because they hate the movie, Michael.'" She enjoyed the gibe.

"'Hate'?" I asked. "Isn't 'hate' a little strong?"

"Well, you win some, you lose some. Let's go back in."

The aisles were crowded. It was as if people didn't want to be in the
lobby and have to talk, but neither did they want to resume their seats.
I felt a hand on my arm and turned to a familiar face. It was David
Brown, whom I had seen rarely since our breakfast at the Sherry
Netherland a year and a half before to discuss this picture.

His normally self-assured and smiling face seemed to register shock. "My God, Steve," he said. "I'm so sorry I wasn't more help to you. Now I see what you meant." He moved quickly away into the theater.

"What did that mean?" asked Lois brightly.

"Tell you later," I said, knowing I wouldn't.

The picture began again, and so did the silence. The battle sequence was a third its original length, but felt just as long. Nothing was working. No one cared about Averill or Champion or Ella or the plight of the immigrants, who continued to caterwaul unintelligibly. No one cared about the magnificent photography or the majestic scenery or the authentic costumes with their authentic fabrics or the perfect settings or the meticulously re-created buggies and wagons and pushcarts or the nuances of composition or performance or editing. I was sitting in a room full of hundreds of people, most of them professionals, who worked just that hard to create just such feelings of authenticity every day of their lives and neither demanded nor received any special credit for it. They were not about to give special credit either, for not one of them had been made to *care* about what was happening on that screen. They were kept in their seats not from courtesy to the filmmakers and actors present, or reluctance to brave the sleety avenue outside, or even because they knew it was too early to head for the Four Seasons and the party after. They stayed there mesmerized by the spectacle, the enormity of the miscalculation, the perfection that money can buy, the caring that it can't. They were stunned into submission by the sheer weight of the thing, the luxuriant wastefulness, the overbearing sound, the relentlessness of its self-importance, its self-love.

Finally, Averill and Ella packed their things silently (blessed silence) in Ella's cabin. Then Canton ambushed them, and Ella died, her pretty white dress full of pretty scarlet bullet holes, and we were suddenly in 1900, and there was a pretty yacht and a pretty sunset and some pretty music, and the audience stopped being silent. It began to make little bewildered noises as Averill looked out at the pretty sunset, and the noises got louder as he descended into the salon of the yacht and— "Who the hell is *that?*" asked the lawyer in the brown suit next to me. There on screen was a beautiful woman lounging against satin pillows. When she said to Averill, "I'd like a cigarette, please," someone in the theater laughed, and Averill went back on deck and looked out in pretty sorrow and heard Ella's pretty music and tears crept into his eyes, and the audience began creeping, then rushing into the aisles. Tiny and pathetic pockets of polite applause were drowned by the sound of people rushing for the exits as the music surged for the eight intolerable minutes of end credits and the angry babble of the crowd was mercifully masked by the music. The music saved me; I had always liked the music.

Everything about the Four Seasons gleamed. The marble floors, the bronze fittings, the oak paneling in the Grill Room, the lethal-looking metal sculpture suspended over the bar, the maître d'. Pale faces moved in and out of the downlights over the bar; I recognized none of them, though this was our party, the invitation-only *Heaven's Gate* buffet supper in an elegant, gleaming space. Empty space.

"I told you not to be surprised," said Lois cheerfully as we surveyed the almost empty room, where David Mansfield's music was playing softly on a sound system installed that afternoon by United Artists. Lois and I had shared our limo from the theater to the restaurant with producer Gabriel Katzka and his wife. We all were old friends and normally had much to say. That night we talked about traffic, about sleet.

The party had been planned as something tasteful and low-key to counter the publicity about costs that had continued unabated for months, but this party was so tasteful and low-key it wasn't happening. Cimino was there, looking tired and defensive. Carelli was there, looking relieved. Chris Walken and his wife were there; Cimino's new lawyer (Eric Weissmann had been fired) was there, too, looking dazed and polite, telling Lois, "I'm glad I've already made Michael's next deal"; and a famous New York party crasher was there, bubbling gaily in *Heaven's Gate*'s wake, and it seemed pointless to eject him. It was such a tiny crowd, and the tables were heaped with so much food in so many silver chafing dishes.

I saw the personal manager of one of the actors in the picture across the room and tried to wave cheerily. He lumbered across the carpet, a glass in his unsteady hand, and pulled me by the elbow out of Lois's earshot. He slurred something breathy and gin-scented in my ear. I couldn't have heard what he said correctly, so I asked him to repeat it. He did, louder. He said, "Now I can tell you what I've always wanted to tell you, which is what a *shit* you are."

"My God," I said to Lois. "is the movie *that* bad?"

"Don't pay attention to trash," she said.

"I think it comes with the job," I said.

American Airlines flight 3 to Los Angeles departed at noon the following day, leaving me plenty of time to read and reread Vincent Canby's review in the *New York Times*, with which I had seared my eyeballs since early morning. "'Heaven's Gate' fails so completely," he began, "you might suspect Mr. Cimino sold his soul to the Devil to obtain the success of 'The Deer Hunter,' and the Devil has just come around to collect.

"The grandeur of vision of the Vietnam film has turned pretentious. The feeling for character has vanished and Mr. Cimino's approach to his subject is so predictable that watching the film is like a forced, four-hour walking tour of one's own living room."

It got worse. "Mr. Cimino has written his own screenplay, whose awfulness has been considerably inflated by the director's wholly unwarranted respect for it." And worse. "Nothing in the movie works properly. For all of the time and money that went into it, it's jerry-built, a ship that slides straight to the bottom at its christening." And worst: "'Heaven's Gate' is something quite rare in movies these days—an unqualified disaster."

I hadn't expected ecstatic reviews, but I hadn't been prepared for "unqualified disaster" either. Boring, yes; too long, yes; pretentious, yes; overproduced and inflated, yes. Short on content, drama, meaning? Yes, yes, yes to all the complaints one could legitimately make, but *unqualified disaster?* Well, they'll certainly get a laugh out of that one at the Polo Lounge, I thought, * and buckled myself into my seat. The stewardess began distributing copies of that morning's *Times.* I wanted to burn them all but reflected instead on that sad, defensive maxim that today's review wraps tomorrow's fish and sank back in my seat, grateful that except for tomorrow night's Los Angeles premiere, I would never have to sit through *Heaven's Gate* again. I would never have to fight with Michael Cimino again. *This strange thalidomide movie has been born and will likely suffer a quick and merciful death, but at least it's over,* I thought.

I tried to sleep on the plane, but *unqualified disaster* kept me awake. It flashed on and off like neon on my eyelids.

I let myself into the house in Los Angeles, wanting to get on with all the other projects and people that had been neglected for so many months. The scripts and manuscripts unread, the telephone calls unreturned, the people uninvited, the invitations unaccepted, the locations unvisited, the dailies unseen—all of them deserved more than they had gotten, and now I could get back to them in something approximating routine and order.

There was a stack of phone messages waiting for me: Andy Albeck,

* Later Jean Vallely in *Rolling Stone* reported they didn't laugh in the Polo Lounge: "[T]he room erupted in cheers."

somebody at *Time*, Gene Goodman, Joann Carelli, Hy Smith, Nan Leonard in UA publicity in New York, Tom Gray in UA publicity in Hollywood, Sam Cohn, Stan Kamen, Dean Stolber, somebody from the AP, the UPI, the *Los Angeles Times*. I called Andy.

"You and I have got a bit of a problem," he said, his voice strong but subdued, lacking its usual chirrup.

"I know," I said, but I didn't.

"We've been kicking it around here while you were in the air, and we've been considering something radical which Michael and Joann have asked us to do. . . . What would you say to withdrawing the picture?"

I was too stunned to say anything. Withdraw $35 million from release because of Vincent Canby? Withdraw to spare Michael's sensitive feelings over bad reviews? Withdraw? What the hell did it mean?

"Michael and Joann called from their hotel in Toronto. They want us to withdraw the picture and let Michael reedit, so we can release it at some reasonable length. I want your vote on the matter because this is such an unusual thing. I won't do it unless I have one hundred percent agreement from everyone involved, and that means Gene and Norbert and Hy and Dean, but mostly it means you, because if we do this thing, you will be in charge, you will be responsible for the result, and if Michael can't or won't do it, you'll have to."

The pile of phone messages was now clearer. "What do the others say?"

"They're in favor."

"The other reviews are that bad?"

"Yes. Think it over, and call me back," he said, and hung up.

I was reeling. There was some sort of precedent for such a measure, I knew. The Judy Garland *A Star Is Born* had been cut after its first release; so had *Cleopatra* and *The Shining* and *Star!*; and even a little Disney picture that summer called *The Watcher in the Woods* had been withdrawn, a new ending made, and the picture rereleased. There were probably others, too, but they had been cut quietly and without being yanked from exhibition. With *Heaven's Gate* there was no way to do anything quietly now if anything could be done anyway. And there was little chance anything could be done without Cimino, or at least without Bill Reynolds, somebody who knew all that footage, that $35,190,718 worth of footage, all but four hours of which was in storage someplace. And how much more money would it take? How much more time? How much unquantifiable cost to everyone involved?

I felt time-warped. During a five-hour plane ride I had arrived not in Los Angeles but in October 1978. I felt as if a Mack truck had just run me down and were going into reverse to retrace the tire treads printed across my back. *But wait a minute. It isn't 1978,* I thought. I had taken the two-year Cimino cure for auteur worship and laissez-faire "vision." Cimino had asked for this unthinkable step. He was at last prepared to do what he had been begged to do all along: cut the movie. Maybe he was so bludgeoned and bloodied by Canby and the rest that he would listen to reason, would be malleable enough to admit someone else into his presence and process, open the door to his secretive isolation, stop talking about how wrong Universal had been when they tried to get him to cut *The Deer Hunter.*

Maybe.

To gain a little time, I decided to return calls. The press people could be avoided and fielded by the publicity department. What was I going to say to them anyway? *I think Canby's* right? The others in the company would want to discuss the withdrawal proposal, but I needed to have an attitude of my own before I talked with them. Stan Kamen probably wanted to push for Joann and Michael's request, so he could be postponed. Sam Cohn. Wise Sam, who represented nobody and nothing connected with *Heaven's Gate.* I would call Sam.

"It's an appalling thing that's happened," he said on the line from New York. "Even if the critics are right, it's terrible and shocking, and I want you to know that if there's anything I can do to help, I will. We can't let this thing destroy United Artists."

Destroy United Artists? My God. How bad *were* the reviews? I fleetingly thought of asking him to help me find another job if things were that bad, but instead, I asked his silence and advice over the withdrawal issue. As usual, Sam didn't equivocate.

"It's brilliant! It's offensive instead of defensive. It will throw the press for a loop and give them something to talk about besides how awful the movie is. It's also the only hope you've got of salvaging the thing. It's a terrible, boring movie but not totally without merit."

"That'll look good on a marquee," I said. "'Not totally without merit'—Sam Cohn.'"

"Maybe you can find something in all that footage if you have a little time. At least it makes it look like you're doing something. Do it."

I brooded awhile longer before calling Andy back. I told him how fearful I was that there might be no remedy; the whole process might result in a shorter, not a better, movie. "Shorter will be easier to book," he replied. I also voiced my concerns that I would not have the stamina to go through another six or eight months of daily contact with Cimino, with or without Joann's constant, counterproductive backstop-ping. "Only you can decide that." Then there were the cost, the public relations problems, the unpredictability of Cimino's cooperation—or energy.

"I understand all your fears," said Albeck, "and I don't want you to be railroaded into this by the others. You are the one who will bear most of the burden. I don't want to rush you either, but we need to make the decision tonight, because if we withdraw the picture, we will cancel the Los Angeles premiere tomorrow."

We continued to debate. We decided the minimum amount of time necessary would be six months, the maximum amount of money another $1 million, possibly less. We could take control of the advertising campaign in the meantime and attempt publicity that would counteract the reviews. If Cimino couldn't or wouldn't cooperate, we could find someone to help us reedit and pare it down. *Save* it. Finally, wearily but firmly I voted with the others.

"Get some rest," Andy said before hanging up. "You're going to need it."

I looked at my watch. At that very moment Michael and Joann and Kristofferson and Huppert would be sitting in the University Theater in Toronto, watching the second of the three premieres, hostages to ritual. Tomorrow, when the third was canceled and the withdrawal announced, Cimino would be on a plane flying west, perhaps booked as "Mr. Michael," and I would be in the midst of chaos. Suddenly and urgently I wanted to speak to David Field.

I finally reached him and explained what had happened and what was going to happen. It was likely that he would be receiving flak, too, if not snide remarks from his new colleagues at Fox, then from the press, and I felt he needed to be warned and prepared. I also wanted him to see the picture. I wanted someone else with whom I could share my outrage, my fury, to know what all the time and energy and care had amounted to. It didn't occur to me until later that I simply wanted someone with whom to share the misery, and who more appropriate than Field?

I also wanted his advice for recutting, and thought he might have the objectivity I knew I had lost. He would like to see it, he said, and I promised to arrange a private screening at MGM for the next evening at seven or whenever he could get there from Fox. I would see it with him, and we would talk later.

The next day took place underwater. My own phones didn't ring, and the office staff whispered, walked on tiptoe, floated through a considerate but appalled silence, as if somewhere someone were dying. Certainly they were speculating on my fate within the company and wondering just how awful the movie could be.

Down the hall, out of earshot, things were chaotic. The publicity department, headed by Tom Gray, had been given the task of announcing an unprecedented action to a press already rapacious for statements and reactions to the critics. New York would handle most of that, while in Los Angeles Tom and his associate, Lili Ungar, canceled the premiere, sending out thousands of telegrams, one to each invited guest, stating:

AT MICHAEL CIMINO'S REQUEST, UNITED ARTISTS IS CANCELLING THE SCREENING OF HEAVEN'S GATE THAT WAS SCHEDULED AT THE PLITT THEATRES IN CENTURY CITY, THURSDAY, NOVEMBER 20, AT 7:30 P.M.

YOU WILL RECEIVE ANOTHER INVITATION WHEN WE ARE ABLE TO RE-SCHEDULE THE SCREENING.

WE SINCERELY REGRET THIS LATE NOTICE AND ANY INCONVENIENCE IT MAY CAUSE YOU.

In a macabre typo the return address on the telegrams was "UNITED ARTIST." United's artist returned to Los Angeles after working out with the UA publicity department, at UA's insistence, a "statement," a letter to Albeck that would be both a *mea culpa* and an attempt to alter the movie's reputation from "unqualified disaster" to a film of "clouded . . . perception." UA's lawyers, seeking to avert probable exhibitor legal action against the company, insisted furthermore that the letter stress unequivocally that the decision to withdraw was Cimino's. The finally approved text was typed on *Heaven's Gate* stationery, signed by Cimino, sent out as part of the press announcement, and printed as full-page ads in *Daily Variety* and the *Hollywood Reporter* on Monday, November 24. The text read:

Dear Andy,

As you know, for many months we have been locked in an around-the-clock effort to meet the November release date which we all wanted for "HEAVEN'S GATE." My editorial crew has adhered to this schedule valiantly, with dedication and without complaint. And, forgoing the usual time-tested work-in-progress previews, we were able to meet our commitment to exhibitors.

It is painfully obvious to me that the pressures of this schedule and the missing crucial step of public previews clouded my perception of the film. Thus, unable to benefit and learn from audience reaction, we rushed to completion.

So much energy, time and money have gone into the making of "HEAVEN'S GATE" that I am asking you to withdraw the film from distribution temporarily to allow me to present to the public a film finished with the same care and thoughtfulness with which we began it.

I am only too aware of the emotional difficulty and various complications of such an extraordinary step, but I believe that we have learned an invaluable lesson from our very first public showing. I want to do everything possible for "HEAVEN'S GATE" to achieve its widest audience around the world. Once again, I call on your remarkable faith, understanding and cooperation.

It was signed "Sincerely, Michael Cimino" and dated "November 20, 1980," the day of the premiere that never was.

Late that funereal afternoon my phone finally rang. It was David Field, who said he was calling from the airport, was on his way out of town, and wouldn't be able to make the screening.

"Call when you get back," I said. "I'll reschedule."

"Yeah," he said, and hung up. He never called back. As far as I know he has never seen the original version of the movie, but he saw the cut version and had something to say.

His screening had been scheduled and would have to be paid for. I walked into the quiet corridors and asked the staff to gather at my end of the hall. It had finally occurred to me that these dazed, wounded people weren't worrying only about my job future but about their own; that their loyalty to the company was large enough to encompass wishing even Cimino well, in spite of their widespread resentment of him, their unamused clucking over ironies they read in his open letter to Albeck; and that none of them had the faintest idea what the movie was except what Vincent Canby had told them. I invited them all to the "Field" screening, husbands, wives, partners, too. I told them we were planning to recut and rerelease and asked them to try to view it unemotionally, for its virtues as well as its faults, and I voiced some hollow confidence we would survive this devastating public humiliation with hard work and a little luck.

The next morning my desk was covered with letters, some typed, some scrawled, all marked "personal" or "confidential"—from the staff, of course. They were thank-you notes, awkward and mostly sincere strivings to be supportive. One or two even professed to like the movie, and almost all found something to praise. It was a touching effort to lift spirits they knew were low. It was sentimental and moving, and I wanted to tell Albeck because the support was for him, too. He would need it in the days ahead, for it was only then that the full public impact of *Heaven's Gate* began to be clear; the private impact, too.

It was the not quite unprecedented act of withdrawing the picture from exhibition and canceling the Los Angeles premiere that turned *Heaven's Gate* from merely a failed movie into the "media event" the *New York Times* called it and helped create. Pauline Kael was undoubtedly correct when she wrote in the *New Yorker* that "the press had been waiting to ambush Cimino. His public remarks over the past couple of years since 'The Deer Hunter' had invited it, and so had the cost of 'Heaven's Gate,'" but press reaction went beyond ambushing Cimino and the movie, to encompass finally the company and the industry in which *Heaven's Gate* had happened. Only ten days after dubbing it "an unqualified disaster," Vincent Canby would be referring to it in the *Times* as "'Heaven's Gate'—the phenomenon not the movie," and a phenomenon is precisely what it had become.

The often fractious critical fraternity at last agreed on something. The *Times* referred to the relatively few printed reviews as "an avalanche of critical derision," with "blistering and almost universally negative reviews." Canby's own was not merely the first and most devastating but was highly quotable, and it was reported around the world as if the review itself were news. *Time* quoted it; *Newsweek* quoted it; the wire services and television networks quoted it. B. J. Franklin, Hollywood correspondent for Britain's *Screen International* quoted it after reading it quoted in the *Invercargill* (New Zealand) *Southland Times*. "Unqualified disaster"—accurate or not—was simply irresistibly quotable, and the news traveled fast.

John Chancellor announced it on NBC's nightly network news on November 20, which he rightly called "a bad day for United Artists." Tom Brokaw continued the theme the next morning on the *Today* show in conversation with the *Daily News'* Kathleen Carroll, who did not quote Canby but offered her own variant with "all-out disaster." She told Brokaw and America, "The more you saw, there was nothing on that screen—nothing at all."

Nor was there anything to show on television, no film clips, no stills, because of Cimino's obstructionism in releasing such visual material. As an ironic consequence, all three television networks and many independent metropolitan television stations ran for their viewers the UA-prepared television spot commercials—in prime time as hard news. Those that didn't gave wide coverage instead to the eight-page color spread in the current issue of *Life* magazine. Jim Watters of *Life* had not planned "Return of the Epic Western" (as the article was titled) for the November issue at exactly the moment Cimino was returning his epic western to the cutting room, but a scheduling conflict caused its appearance on the stands then and, as a result, on television. Rumors quickly circulated that this embarrassment had compromised Watters's job, but he later characterized *Life*'s reaction as "mostly joking."

The critics weren't joking, though one suspects they had their share of fun. Archer Winsten in the *New York Post* wrote under a headline that read "GATE" GOES ON AND ON AND ON AND ON, each *on* in a smaller typeface, making reading of the review superfluous. Andrew Sarris in the *Village Voice* called it a "ponderous spectacle" made by a "tiny talent" of "dubious sensibility." He was among the first to sound the revisionist theme that recurred and built over the coming months. "I am a little surprised," Sarris wrote, "that many of the same critics who lionized Cimino for *The Deer Hunter* have now thrown him to the wolves with equal enthusiasm," but he distanced himself from such "captious critics" with "I was never taken in. . . . Hence, the stupidity and incoherence of *Heaven's Gate* came as no surprise since very much the same stupidity and incoherence had been amply evident in *The Deer Hunter.*"

Critics seemed to feel obliged to go on record about *The Deer Hunter*, to demonstrate that their critical credentials were unbesmirched by having been, as Sarris put it, "taken in." After dusting off the old clippings to review what they had said, they emerged warily. David Ansen admitted to retaining "a great if uneasy respect" for the earlier film in *Newsweek*, where his *Heaven's Gate* review began with "An epic vision isn't worth much if you can't tell a story" and went on to describe Cimino as a cross between Aleksandr Dovzhenko, David Lean, and Bernardo Bertolucci, who "has lost all sight of day-to-day reality—and all sense of dramatic truth." Jack Kroll in an article titled "'Heaven' Can Wait" in *Film Comment* stated, "I remain convinced that *The Deer Hunter*, despite its own flaws, is a genuine and powerful achievement," but he added that perhaps De Niro's contribution to that achievement had been underappreciated at the time. Jean Vallely, writing in *Rolling Stone*, noted that "the amount of revisionism at work regarding *The Deer Hunter* [which she had termed "great" in *Esquire*] would make any good Stalinist proud. The critics seem to have used *Heaven's Gate* as a way to rereview *The Deer Hunter*, and to point out that they never really liked it." Commenting on the "vituperative attacks" against *Heaven's Gate*, she wrote that "you get the feeling that these folks are not going to rest until they see Cimino behind bars."

Stanley Kauffmann in the *New Republic* found it all predictable: "On the basis of *The Deer Hunter*, there was no reason to believe that

Cimino could make an organically sound film." *Films in Review* was gleefully self-congratulatory: "[S]ince there was no end to the talk of his genius back in *The Deer Hunter* days, many of us who saw that film for the dreck that it was are heartily enjoying ourselves as his former admirers eat their words." The *Nation*, which had published Gloria Emerson's "Oscars for our Sins" denunciation two years before, reminded readers that *The Deer Hunter*, "whatever its popular success, was a grotesquely self-indulgent film" with "an unacceptably biased view of the war in Vietnam." David Denby, who had praised *The Deer Hunter* as "an epic" in *New York* magazine, wisely refrained from remarking on that evaluation and noted that "the [*Heaven's Gate*] fiasco caused almost as much joy as dismay." He divided blame for it between Cimino, "who has been vain, foolish and wasteful beyond belief, and an inept leadership at United Artists—a group of men who apparently cannot read a script, who lack the confidence to act on their intuitions and doubts, and who watched Cimino dissipate a fortune on nonsense."

Other such attacks swiftly followed. Movie reviewers enjoy feeling some economic power over pictures they review, though they are quick to disclaim this. They enjoy seeing their names on marquees like movie stars, or in boldface type decorating movie ads with their quotes. By withdrawing *Heaven's Gate*, UA and Cimino left reviewers out in the cold, reviewing a movie that would never be seen, except by the relative handfuls who could make it to the Cinema I in New York during the one (sold-out) week that the picture remained on exhibition. By the time the weekly reviewers were in print, the movie was nowhere watchable, and it became, as a movie, irrelevant. The critics wrote not about the aesthetic questions raised by *Heaven's Gate* but about the "disaster" and "phenomenon" it had become. Perhaps a measure of the notoriety was the *New York Times* itself, which ran major hard news stories about *Heaven's Gate* in November alone on the twentieth, the twenty-first, the twenty-second, the twenty-fifth, and the thirtieth, when Canby took another swing, this time on the front page of the Sunday Arts and Leisure section, in which he reviewed the many limousines on Third Avenue the night of the premiere, using them as metaphors for "The System That Let 'Heaven's Gate' Run Wild."

Most of that system—and most of the movie press—are, of course, in Los Angeles, where no one at all had seen or would be allowed to see the picture (save the UA staff for whom I screened it and a few friends for whom Cimino screened it). This did not stop the Hollywood community's "cackles of contumely," as Richard Corliss called them in *Time*, or "cackles of glee," as Jean Vallely called them in *Rolling Stone*. No one had seen the picture; but this was the biggest news story since

Begelman, and no one wanted to be left out, though in typical ax-
grinder fashion, all wanted anonymity, a desire noted with curiosity by
both Canby and Aljean Harmetz in the *New York Times* and by Dale
Pollock in the *Los Angeles Times*. "Their shyness," the latter wrote, "in
a business not known for reticence, comes less from a desire to avoid
ridiculing their unfortunate UA counterparts than the fearful thought
that in six months they, too, might have a 'Heaven's Gate' on their
hands." This fear proved to be uninhibiting, as was the absence of facts.
"There is almost always something pleasing in the failure of any com-
petitor," one (anonymous) studio head told Aljean Harmetz, "but
'Heaven's Gate' is a catastrophe of such proportions that it's beyond
laughing." Well, yes. And UA's one official statement (from Albeck)
did nothing to alter that dramatic assessment. "We believe that
Heaven's Gate is going to be an excellent film in its shortened version
and that it has tremendous worldwide commercial potential," he said,
and the cackles continued. UA made no attempt to "defend" itself or
answer its critics, for to have done so would have been further to damage the movie's reputation. This left the press with very little to report,
but a great deal over which to speculate or attitudinize, including the
picture's cost because of UA's long-standing policy of not announcing
such figures. The range of speculation began at an almost accurate $36
million (the cost at the time of the premiere had been $35,190,718)
and spiraled upward to $40, $50, even $60 million. (As recently as
April 12, 1984, the *New York Post* "reported" the figure as $100 mil-
lion.)

Claudia Cohen unsheathed her uninhibited imagination (and
kept it unsheathed for months) in the *New York Daily News* on November 21:

*All over Movieland, top studio bosses, major producers and show biz observ-
ers, all shell-shocked from the mindboggling "Gate" debacle, are worrying
about what it means for the industry. . . . And they are mostly blaming the
power that UA gave to the arrogant Cimino. . . . Why didn't UA tell
Cimino to stop? For one thing, UA had been suffering the loss of its top film
execs [here it was again], who left to form Orion Pictures, and was reportedly
afraid to offend its remaining stars: Cimino and Woody Allen (whose
"Stardust Memories" reportedly went over $10 million beyond budget, with-
out a peep from UA).* *

This was errant nonsense and irresponsible gossip started in the

---

* A neat trick, if true, for $10 million was the movie's *cost*.

Village Voice in October by Stuart Byron, who had written that Woody had gone over budget. "[E]stimates start at $20 million," he said, adding that Woody had done so "without one peep [apparently an in word among the literati] from production head Steven Bach or president Andy Albeck." While Claudia Cohen gaily continued carving up Cimino and UA in the *Daily News*, Byron dusted off his Charles Schreger file, the seeds of which were now bearing distinctly poisonous fruit. Byron changed "office boy" to "office manager" and let fly: "Any of the five other major studios is capable of producing a disappointment or a flop, but only United Artists, at this point at least, could produce a disaster." All because of Albeck and Transamerica, of course. Byron's call for "a change in top management at United Artists" had perhaps come as the result of special insight he had gained into the decision-making process at the company, where only weeks before he been relentlessly promoting himself for the job that went instead to Lois Smith.

Misinformation and harsh judgments were spreading beyond the popular press to the financial press. Joy Gould Boyum in the *Wall Street Journal* announced:

The studio, United Artists, interfered so little with Mr. Cimino that the production cost was allowed to escalate from its original budget of $11.6 million to the $40 million figure. The studio's executives apparently saw almost nothing of the film's footage during the entire 18 months of its production in Montana. [Who feeds them this stuff?] When they were finally shown a five-hour, uncompleted version last September they saw problems but remained supportive.

Having presented her creative version of the facts, Boyum proceeded to judgment. "One surely has to blame United Artists' executives for their extraordinary lack of judgment." The reason lay in "the recent history of United Artists"—i.e., the Transamerica-Krim feud of three years before. Boyum quoted me in an interview she had done earlier for the *Journal* as stating (ruefully, I thought), "The industry has to a degree abdicated to directors." She claimed, "This is the victory that those of us who care about films have always wished for, but it turns out now not to be precisely what we had in mind." Well, no.

Business Week turned to such motion-picture production experts as "Harold L. Vogel, entertainment analyst with Merrill Lynch, Pierce, Fenner & Smith," who "pointed an accusing finger at United Artists President Andy Albeck. . . . United Artists should have scrapped *Heaven's Gate* sooner,'" said Mr. Vogel.

Vincent Canby's overview may have been Olympian, but it was well informed. "'Heaven's Gate'—the phenomenon not the movie—has been a long time coming, but to blame it on any one director or corporate management is vastly to oversimplify what's been happening to commercial American movies over the last several decades . . . the cost of making a movie, even a modest one, has soared even faster than the cost of everything else in the economy," he wrote, correctly pointing out that "the hits make more money than ever, while people won't go to see a flop even if it's free. The pressure to find movies with some kind of built-in appeal grows greater day by day. Thus the emphasis on sequels, on 'properties' that have been pre-sold as best-selling books or hit plays, by name writers, by casts with great film or television celebrity, or by the reputations of those directors who have become 'bankable.'" In observing that "the pattern of the smash-hit film followed by the smash-flop film is a familiar one in today's Hollywood," Canby was calling up reminders (quickly trotted out by the rest of the press) of *The Blues Brothers, Raise the Titanic!, The Shining, The Wiz, 1941, Flash Gordon, King Kong, Apocalypse Now, Ragtime, Star Trek, Sphinx, The Black Hole, Popeye, Wolfen, Altered States, Honeysuckle Rose, The Legend of the Lone Ranger,* and, waiting in the wings, *Reds* and *One from the Heart.*

The weaknesses and foolishness of an entire industry had been focused and exposed by *Heaven's Gate* and United Artists, and the press and the industry were going to let neither director nor corporation forget it. Cimino took the sensible position that he would not read his reviews, which Carelli had told him were "devastating." I could not afford that luxury, and reading the press barrage that continued for the next six months was never unpainful. Transamerica read the press, too, and remained calm and dignified. It was, after all, a strong company the revenues of which had risen to $4.04 billion in 1979 and the stock of which, true to form, responded to the fire storm in the press with a temporary dip of three-eighths of a point. Jim Harvey, responding to rumors, told the *Los Angeles Times,* "We're absolutely not going to sell. We have turned numerous inquiries down," and added that "one movie is not going to affect any management changes or restructuring." It did, though. Albeck's new structure for the company was swept away on the tide of negative publicity, and Albeck asked me to stay on in my present job, reporting to the man who would replace Albeck as UA president, Norbert Auerbach.

I had a choice, but didn't feel as if I did. There had been so many allusions in the press to the *Titanic* that UA had developed a not altogether inappropriate shipwreck solidarity as we pulled together for the painful editing task ahead. It was our only opportunity to redeem UA, redeem *Heaven's Gate*, and redeem ourselves. I agreed to stay.

November 20, the day of the canceled Los Angeles premiere, Bob Wunsch reminded me of *The Fountainhead*.

"What about it?" I asked.

"Well," he said, "in *The Fountainhead* Howard Roark blows up his housing project rather than let it be defiled by Philistines. Think about it."

"Cimino as Howard Roark? Just because he wanted to make *The Fountainhead*?" Then I thought about it. I remembered the published rumor that he had threatened to kidnap *The Deer Hunter* negative rather than let Universal cut it. "I felt I could have killed somebody if they mutilated it," he had told *Horizon*. I made a quick call to the legal department in New York. Gary Schrager, UA's attorney on *Heaven's Gate*, wrote Technicolor, reminding them, "The negative [in Technicolor's possession] and all other . . . material . . . shall be held in the name and under the control solely of United Artists."

I also called Roger Mayer, who was in charge of the physical studio at MGM, where Cimino's cutting rooms were located. We arranged to meet the following morning.

Mayer arrived, looking pale. He listened politely as Wunsch and I told him that we were concerned about Cimino's ever-present armed guard, that UA had no access to the cutting rooms because the locks had been changed. Could MGM change the locks again, providing UA with duplicate keys?

"Of course, of course," Mayer said, his voice and hands trembling.

"What is it, Roger?" I asked.

"Look," he said, "no matter what bad feelings have existed between MGM and UA, I want you to know how sorry we are about your problems with this movie. But we have problems, too."

His face was ash-gray, lined with tension.

"This morning the MGM Grand Hotel burned," he continued, his voice faint and wavering. "At least seventy-five people are dead— maybe more. They're still . . . counting bodies."

After he had left, Bob and I sat in silence longer than is appropriate in a busy office. Finally, I said, "You know something? 'Ingrid,'" I began and he, recognizing the quote, nodded toward the shelf where the pictures of his family stood, and finished it for me, trying to imitate the famous Hitchcock tone, "'. . . it's only a mooovie.'" But it came out mournful.

Soon after that Woody Allen called. With regrets.

His, and mine.

CHAPTER 21

BLOODBATH

"Muggers know who to mug"

—Joann Carelli,
   in conversation, New York (May 31, 1984)

Norbert Auerbach wasn't wearing his pussycat smile or any kind of smile at all. He was wearing a fur hat with earflaps that merged with his beard and a car coat with some sort of furry lining that looked synthetic. He was thought around 729 to be a man of style, but style wasn't conspicuous at eight o'clock in the morning on December 19, 1980, in the yellow breakfast room at the Pierre Hotel. Maybe it was the beard, I mused, that kaiserish gray luxuriance that made people call him presidential, a term then spoken admiringly at 729. To me he looked merely anxious.

I was leaving that night for a brief Christmas vacation in Hawaii, taking with me videotapes of *Heaven's Gate*, which in the month since the disastrous New York premiere, when not one more frame could be cut, had swiftly been trimmed by a full hour and was now slightly more than two and a half hours long. Everyone at UA was to see it that afternoon at its newly reduced length and agree to let Michael Cimino (with Bill Reynolds's help) continue working on it, paring it down, adding narrative connectives to explain confusing action, adding titles to tell the audience when, where, sometimes who—or the film would be taken from him. I was to continue in any case to study the movie in Honolulu on videotape machines, making notes, recommendations, my life on rewind and fast forward.

"I want you to support me in San Francisco," said Auerbach, rubbing together hands still cold from the freezing weather outside.

"You have my support," I said.

"I mean, about Andy."

"What about him?"

"This company can't survive with Andy as chairman."

"And chief executive officer, you mean."

He nodded. "This company is on the brink of disaster."

"Really? Twenty-two million dollars of net profits, even with *Heaven's Gate?* How disastrous is that?"

"I want to turn this company around. We may have to let a few people go, make a few changes—*if* I can get Andy to agree. Farber, Goodman, a few others . . ."

"Who'll be left?"

"You will," he said reassuringly. "And I will. I plan to take a much greater interest in production, you know."

"I figured," I said.

"Andy has no production background." He paused and smiled. "Did I ever mention that my father produced *Ecstasy* with Hedy Lamarr?"

"Many times," I said.

"She was called Hedy Kiesler then," he said, warming with reminiscence. "He knew them all. Did I tell you what he used to say about Dietrich? 'I knew her before she was a virgin'?" He laughed as he always did at this line.

"Many times," I said.

"We need new producers at UA, too," he said. "We can't afford people like Chartoff and Winkler anymore. They're too expensive."

"How expensive *is* a *Rocky?*" I asked.

"We need people like—like the Mirisch brothers," he said.

"New?" I asked. "They made many fine pictures . . . before Harold Mirisch died. I think you're barking up the wrong decade."

"Walter and Marvin Mirisch have had successes," he countered. "*Same Time, Next Year,* for example."

"I know all about *Same Time, Next Year.* I was one of its coproducers on Broadway."

"So you've said. Many times."

"Touché."

"There's no reason you and I can't work closely together. But I need your support with Jim. In San Francisco."

"To get rid of Andy."

"I wouldn't put it that way."

"No? I don't think you should count on me, Norbert."

"No?"

"No. I think Andy should stay right where he is, as chairman. It's called loyalty. It should be reassuring to you as the new president that your employees have some."

"But his *style,*" he said, grimacing.

"Style isn't everything. Anyway, it's a very clear style. No hidden

agendas on Andy's desk. They're all right there, like the follow-up
sheets. I like that kind of clarity."

"Do you find me unclear?"

"Not now," I said.

I went to Hawaii.

It seemed that everyone in America knew how to fix *Heaven's Gate*
except Pauline Kael and me. Kael remarked in the *New Yorker*, "While
watching the three-hour-and-thirty-nine minute 'Heaven's Gate,' I
thought it was easy to see what to cut. But when I tried afterward to
think of what to *keep*, my mind went blank." Such candor was not
permitted me, for a key facet of my job—perhaps *the* key facet now that
Auerbach had assumed the presidency on January 1 (and greater interest in production)—was to reassure a still-avid press and a puzzled public that *Heaven's Gate* was shrinking down nicely, thank you, and
would, after all the critical carnage, be just dandy.

At two and a half hours on December 19 *Heaven's Gate* was both
leaner and clearer. Virtually no narrative scenes were removed in the
excision of more than an hour of footage then or ever, and very few
were shortened, except for the elimination of many artful pauses.

It had always been true that Cimino's screenplay had a striking lack
of narrative incident. There were no subplots, few characters subsidiary
to the central trio, and those there were, were more decorative than
dramatic in their script and screen functions. The paucity of character
and narrative detail was not enriched by the inundation of production
detail—however authentic—but was buried by it, contributing to the
widespread notion that there *was* no story, no "there" there. Merely
cutting away millions of dollars of "production value" to expose the
story line didn't make the story any better, but it gave the picture a
discernible dramatic line and made it less "intolerable" (Kael's word) a
display of excess. The beauties of photography, music, settings, costumes, and geography remained; there were just less of them, and less
was, if not *more*, then more watchable.

The cutting room floor after only a month was littered with picturesque peasants, roller-skating immigrants, Ukrainian and Polish folk
songs, and considerable nudity formerly on soft-focus display as "this
little French mouse" (Kael again) cavorted or bathed or practiced her
trade on screen. Also missing was the epilogue, which had become
incomprehensible even to those of us who had championed its "poetic
value," and John Hurt's valedictory address in the prologue was halved.
The nineteenth-century language in which it was composed (it was
based on actual valedictory addresses of the period) was bewildering to

contemporary audiences, and the sound track of the film was so over-wrought, with so much Dolbyized "presence," that dialogue here and elsewhere was often unintelligible. A film in which nothing much seemed to happen until the climactic battle sequence was not helped by dialogue that couldn't be understood when something *was* happening. A remix would be performed.

The world had suggestions. My desk became and remained heaped with sheaves of written suggestions from staffs in New York and California, as well as letters from well-wishing strangers who had no end of suggestions (some good, some crackpot) in spite of never having seen one frame of the movie, except perhaps the television spot commercials on the nightly news. One of the more notable and curious suggestions (Auerbach's) was to make *Heaven's Gate* . . . longer. With 200 hours of film, wouldn't it make a great miniseries for TV? Well, no. Another suggestion deemed not without merit was to cut the footage into individual frames and sell all that Montana scenery as picture postcards. This, too, was rejected.

By January 5, 1981, additional changes had been made: Some offensive dialogue cherished by its writer was dropped ("You look like a man about to shit a pumpkin," for example); written titles appeared to clarify the movie's often confusing changes of locale; a brief narration was written for Kristofferson to speak, explaining his trek west from Harvard and his continued presence there, twenty years after the graduation scene and waltz, which still opened the picture, still stunningly. Considerable length and violence had been removed from the battle sequence, partly at the suggestion of the American Humane Association, which continued to send newsletters and press releases denouncing the film's treatment of animals. Finally, there was nothing left to do to the movie without audience guidance, previews. Getting audience reaction on so highly publicized a movie—still attracting major news stories in the press—could be dangerous, as Coppola had learned with *Apocalypse*, and as Columbia, whose "sneak" of *Close Encounters of the Third Kind* had sneaked swiftly and loudly onto the pages of *New York* magazine, could testify.

A sneak preview schedule was prepared with the help of Joseph Farrell, whose National Research Group had taken on market survey and campaign plans for the picture months earlier. Farrell, a low-key but extremely articulate man (he has a law degree from Harvard), had been with both the prestigious Carnegie Corporation and the Harris Poll before entering movie research. He had shaped the marketing policy on *Apocalypse Now*, persuading a skeptical Francis Coppola that the $10 ticket price Coppola hoped to impose on the movie, making it seem "something special," would instead make it seem a rip-off to moviegoers. Farrell also focused the campaign on the image and name of Marlon Brando and calmly, patiently earned the plaudits he received for the marketing success of that picture.

Joe's work on *Heaven's Gate* had been severely limited by Cimino and Carelli's lack of cooperation, but now, with the clamor in the press hardly abated, the producer and director were listening to advice or at least hearing it. That Farrell was an artist himself (a sculptor) and came with Coppola's recommendation perhaps made his advice easier to hear than that of the executives at UA, all eagerly offering two cents, often with conflicting recommendations and confused loyalties, in a new administration in which tension at the top was widely rumored, if not yet plainly visible.

In December Farrell had written an acute ten-page analysis of the movie and the troubled event it had become, noting that "what is called for now is a very carefully calculated exploitation of the attention," which, negative as it was, would require strictest cooperation of all involved, particularly Cimino, who was the focus of the attention, though UA was still attracting its share of space (and lumps) in the general and financial presses. Albeck's moving to the chairmanship was widely interpreted as a kick upstairs, enabling Beckett and Transamerica to save face for having installed him in the first place. But nobody noticed much that Beckett himself had, on January 1, retired, turning control over to the new chairman, James Harvey, and that Albeck, far from being stripped of power, still remained chief executive officer to Auerbach's chief operating officer. As long as Albeck remained in place, the power that derived from San Francisco was his, and so were the unpleasant attentions of the press.

Auerbach's "presidential" qualities began operating almost at once. Bart Farber's was the first head to roll, on January 23. Farber had been with UA for twenty years and like all UA executives (except Auerbach), had no contract (even Albeck didn't have one). That Farber had had less to do with *Heaven's Gate* than any other major executive in the company was read internally as an irrelevant irony. Axes were falling in the bloodletting predicted by the press in November, or a power struggle between styleless CEO and presidential COO was shaping up. Or both.

Albeck allowed Auerbach to fire Farber (whether in agreement or not), but after twenty years of service Farber was not entitled to the full benefits of early retirement because at fifty-three he was sixteen months too young to qualify. Albeck insisted that a settlement in payroll form be continued until Farber's fifty-fifth birthday to protect those benefits, as we had seen him do before for others.

Gene Goodman, in his position as head of domestic distribution for only a year, was next. Auerbach, had chosen his replacement, a sales executive from Paramount named Jerry Esbin, whom Auerbach described to me as "not exactly our style. Wears too much cologne and too pointy shoes, but he's dynamic." He had also had heart surgery, and Albeck, mindful of Danny Rissner's similar surgery and convalescence—and the train of events that had been set in motion almost three years before—said no.

I felt burdened by Auerbach's confidences about Goodman and Albeck's refusal to approve Esbin because I liked Gene and was scheduled to make the rounds of *Heaven's Gate* previews with him as well as to travel with him to San Francisco in late February for sneak previews of *Caveman* and *Eye of the Needle*. If he truly was going to be replaced, what was the point of sending him on all this traveling to see how pictures played he would never have a chance to sell?

I carried my guilty knowledge uneasily, hopeful Albeck would prevail. I had been ordered by Auerbach to do some bloodletting of my own that seemed transparently symbolic and weighed more heavily on me than whether or not Auerbach would win his candidate in the "too pointy shoes."

My New York secretary, Anne Harkavy, was the first to go. Anne, in her early seventies, looked back in sadness. "I worked for Alexander Korda here," she said, "and Ilya Lopert and Mr. Benjamin, too, but I'm not sorry to leave. This used to be a company"—she stressed—"not a kingdom or whatever the heck this is."

Then there was Craig Zadan, whose sparking of the West Coast with youthful enthusiasm and ideas seemed to Auerbach somehow inconsistent with the atmosphere he wanted to bring back—with the Mirisches—to UA. And while we were at it, Richard Parks in New York could go, too, because now with Lois ("Loeeeese" he pronounced it), why did we need Parks? And as long as I didn't have a secretary or an assistant in New York, why did I need an office? The mayhem of the battle sequence in *Heaven's Gate* was beginning to look understated.

Not just people went. Projects did, too. *Iceman, Swing Shift, Pope of Greenwich Village, Splash,* the little musical idea Craig Zadan had been working on with lyricist-screenwriter Dean Pitchford, which later was called *Footloose.*

Screening *Heaven's Gate* secretly—with Farber bounced and Goodman, all unawares, bouncing—would indicate what further work it needed, and such privacy and "civilian" audiences could only be found far from New York and Hollywood. Pittsburgh, Denver, Calumet City (outside Chicago), Kansas City, Seattle, and Portland were selected for a series of secret sneak previews in mostly middle-class neighborhood theaters at the end of January and early February.

I missed Pittsburgh because I had had to fly to Cortina to check in on For Your Eyes Only, then shooting there, but I was back in time for the other five previews. We learned from them that the violence of the battle sequence was still far too brutal for most moviegoers and that the rape sequence before it—graphic in the sense of violation it imposed on the audience as well as Isabelle Huppert—was everywhere accompanied by (mostly) female walkouts. Those hardier viewers who sat through it and through the battle sequence at the end saw differing conclusions. In the "happy ending" version (Auerbach's), for example, the images of Ella and Averill froze as they left Ella's house, in what was a full-circle return to Cimino's old, original The Johnson County War screenplay of 1978. Another variation featured a pared-to-the-bone epilogue, but in none of the versions tested was President Benjamin Harrison's quote— "I can do nothing except act with the state to prevent violence"—used as in the original screenplay. Harrison made the seemingly damning statement all right, however, not in 1891, as the script had indicated, but in 1892. It was, in fact, his response to the Johnson County War as it was occurring, when the situation out West must have seemed far murkier than it does even today.

Virtually none of the daily or weekly reviewers who wrote about the New York premiere had commented on the historical basis of the screenplay, other than to note it had one. Pauline Kael, whose New Yorker review did not appear until the December 22 issue, was one of the first to note that as Cimino had warned, "one uses history in a very free way." Suddenly, it seemed, every journalist in America was intimately familiar with "History's Most Expensive Minor Footnote" and rushed authoritatively into print to condemn not only Cimino's indulgence and ego but his scholarship as well. It didn't really happen! As if that were what was wrong with the movie and Cimino. And The Deer Hunter, too.

"Historical deformations," charged Rutgers's Michael H. Seitz in the Progressive, flailing away at The Deer Hunter to demonstrate "Cimino's wholesale abuse of historical fact," though in a spirit of fairness, perhaps, Seitz did note that Tolstoy and Stendhal had not actually palled around with Napoleon on the Russian front or at Waterloo.

How much of the various controversies—economic, aesthetic, historical—were filtering back to the general public was impossible to

know, but by Seattle and Portland, the last two stops on the six-city
preview tour in early February, it was clear that if audiences didn't love
the picture, they didn't hate it either, and the very secrecy with which
the previews were conducted (audiences were usually told they were
going to see *Thief* with James Caan, and even the UA fieldmen were
unaware the cans marked "THIEF" actually contained the reels of
Heaven's Gate), mitigated against any definitive conclusion: Would
those who disliked (or liked) the movie ever have bought tickets to it
had they known what they would be seeing? All that was beyond con-
jecture was that at two hours and twenty-eight minutes there was a
shorter movie that had some sort of unknowable chance at the box
office.

Gene Goodman, still unaware of his imminent dismissal, but knowing he needed a bid print to show to exhibitors, thought by Seattle
there was a chance of success. We decided to "lock" the picture and
send it back for resounding and reprinting for a spring rerelease.

Now it really is over, I thought as I returned to my hotel room in
Seattle. I had known since breakfast at the Pierre in December that my
fate at UA was inextricably bound up with *Heaven's Gate*'s—and with
Albeck's—and I was once again so relieved that I wasn't even very
shocked to discover, there in that dark hotel in Seattle, that I was
bleeding internally. Somehow it even seemed appropriate.

Tuesday, February 17, I was back in New York, working out of
cardboard boxes in the small conference room attached to Albeck's office. A United Artists board meeting was scheduled that week, and I
was expected to make a production report to the board, on which I sat
as a formality only. A sudden call had been placed that morning for all
senior vice-presidents to report at nine-thirty to Albeck's office for an
unscheduled meeting. I left the cardboard boxes and their disarray
where they were and strolled down the hall to Dean Stolber's office a
few minutes before nine-thirty. Dean was chronically late to meetings,
and I often stopped in to bring him along punctually.

He was ready that morning. "What's it about, do you think?"

"Andy's resigning," he said without missing a beat.

I felt the floor drain away from under me. Dean marched ahead and
down the corridor to Albeck's office. Somehow I followed, past that
procession of UA posters, dazed and unseeing.

Andy welcomed us in quietly. Goodman, me, Stolber, Auerbach,
and Nathaniel Kwit, Farber's assistant who had replaced him just three
weeks before. Andy made a quiet, dignified announcement about early
retirement, wished us all well, particularly Auerbach, who would as-

sume the role of chief executive officer, though the chairmanship would remain vacant. Andy gently excused us, and I walked back into the conference room and looked at my own career, appearing haphazard and disorderly in boxes marked "Bekins." The questions careening and colliding in my brain were not ones that I could answer or maybe even pose.

Nor could I work. Anne was long gone, unable now to help me field the phone calls I knew would start pouring in. Above all, I needed to see Albeck, to say . . . *something*.

I knocked on his office door and opened it without waiting, as was the custom on the fourteenth floor. He was pacing on the middle of the beige wool carpet, his arms folded across each other in the small of the ramrod back. The usually upright head was staring at the floor, and it seemed his face had flushed beyond red, to black. He appeared not to have expected me or anyone but quickly lifted his chin and forced a cheery smile. He welcomed me to a chair as he took his familiar place behind his immaculate "Hollywood" desk, his familiar unbowed posture restored.

He waited for me to begin, and I realized I had nothing to say. Or so much that no articulation would come. Finally, I said, "I'm sorry, Andy. Truly and terribly sorry."

He looked through the windowpane spectacles at the graceful palm, shuddering softly in the corner, and then back at me, his face no longer dark with whatever emotion I had surprised him in. He smiled. "We had a bad year last year," he said evenly. "And when you have a bad year, you fire the boss. That's the way it is in business."

He smiled again, but I couldn't. He bade me good-bye and good luck, and when I shook his hand, the firm grip spoke to me not of style, but of substance.

The news reports all attributed the "early retirement" to the *Heaven's Gate* fiasco. The press had never known Albeck and wasted no time in looking back. Besides, Albeck's firing wasn't the only big movie story that week. Two days later Twentieth Century-Fox announced it was buying back its own stock, going "private." There was another story, too. Norbert Auerbach, newly appointed chief executive officer of United Artists, announced, as Aljean Harmetz reported in the *New York Times*, "Dean Stolber, senior vice-president for business affairs, was named today to the newly created position of executive vice president and second in command to Mr. Auerbach." Harmetz observed that "Mr. Stolber's appointment was viewed [in Hollywood] as implying a lessening of authority for Steven Bach, the company's [senior] production vice president."

Dean and I were close friends, and he and his wife, Jackie, and I had sailed together on the *QE2* to Europe that summer for business meetings, Jackie's first trip abroad. Dean called me to say that he regretted the press interpretation being placed on his appointment. I shrugged it off and congratulated him. He volunteered, in his elation, that he had been given a contract.

I spent that weekend in San Francisco at the *Eye of the Needle* and *Caveman* sneaks. They went well, though not spectacularly, and Goodman and I and several others stayed up until two or three in the morning in my suite at the Stanford Court, doing postmortems and marketing discussions, though Gene had to catch the early plane back to the East just after dawn.

When I arrived in Los Angeles early Sunday, I called Auerbach at his home in Chappaqua to report on the sneaks.

"What did Gene say?" he wanted to know.

"He thought the pictures played well."

"Not about *that*," he said. "About *Esbin*."

"*Esbin?* Nothing, of course. Do you think I would have *told* him?"

"It's been on the street all week." He sighed. "I was hoping he had heard."

"*Hoping?*"

"Well," Auerbach said wearily, "he lives only fifteen minutes from here. I suppose I'll have to drive over there and tell him."

"It's better than letting him hear it on the street," I said.

The next morning I told Gene I knew and was sorry. He surprised me by saying he had agreed to stay on, reporting to the new appointee.

"Well," I said, "at least Norbert had the courtesy to tell you in person."

"In *person?*" he said. "He did it on the telephone."

Jerry Esbin, Goodman's new boss, was shown the newly deflated *Heaven's Gate* and announced dynamically, "This picture is going to turn this company *around*." He felt so confident of it he called Jim Harvey in San Francisco, to tell him so.

Getting rid of Hy Smith in ad-pub would not be so easy, not only because he had an ex-wife and two children to support and a brand-new beautiful wife he had not planned on carrying across the threshold to insolvency, but also because he saw it coming. When Hy was ordered, as I had been, to fire valued staff members, he agreed under duress, but he

demanded a promotion at the same time, to counteract the inevitable
rumors that would quickly circulate in the press and "on the street." He
got it. He was named "*first* senior vice-president of advertising and publicity," a title that puzzled everyone (perhaps including Hy) because
there was no longer any "second" anything since Ed Siegenfeld, Hy's
former second-in-command and others had been terminated at Auerbach's order. Hy was later to quip that the moment the dubious promotion was granted, "I *knew* I was out," but he didn't, and the title looked
to many gallows humorists as if Hy were negotiating a way to stay in the
papers but not in the company.

The end came on Good Friday, April 17, a week before the scheduled and booked national rerelease of the picture that would "turn this
company around," on which Smith had labored long and thanklessly.
He agreed to have lunch that day with Auerbach's longtime assistant
Mel Danheiser because Danheiser was in a quandary. He had been assigned the task of ensuring the presence of movie stars at the testimonial banquet to be given for Auerbach in the fall by Variety Clubs
International, a splashy annual charity event, for which Auerbach had
consented to be named Man of the Year.

Danheiser, a timid and diffident man, didn't *know* any movie stars,
but Hy Smith did, and would Hy help him guarantee a star-studded
dais?

"Well, star-sprinkled anyway," said Smith.

The two went to Vesuvio's around the corner from 729 for lunch,
there running into Cubby Broccoli, producer of the James Bond movies
and an old friend of Smith, with whom he had been working on marketing plans for the summer release of *For Your Eyes Only*. Cubby
seemed strangely, atypically nervous to Smith and left the restaurant
quickly to return to his own permanent office at 729. Smith and
Danheiser drew up lists of stars for the testimonial dinner ("to *testify*,"
Smith later deadpanned).

Back in his office after lunch Smith looked up from his desk, flocked
with the miniature penguins he collected, to see his new superior, Jerry
Esbin, head of domestic distribution, standing in the open doorway,
from which he announced—for the entire twelfth floor to hear—"Hy,
the time has come to talk!"

After they had talked, Smith realized why Cubby Broccoli had
beaten so hasty a retreat from Vesuvio's, and after Esbin had left, Smith
called him. Broccoli confirmed that he had known Hy was fired and was
shocked to realize—by both Hy's usual quip-a-minute manner and the
curious purpose of the lunch with Danheiser—that everyone "on the
street" but Hy knew that Hy was out of a job. Broccoli asked Hy to stay

on with him as special marketing consultant on *For Your Eyes Only*, if
Hy thought he could emotionally survive daily contact with the administration that had so casually fired him.

Smith agreed and went to Dean Stolber's office to discuss a settlement. As he left Stolber's office, Mel Danheiser was waiting outside,
sent to see Stolber on some errand for Auerbach. As Hy emerged, pale-
faced and grim, Danheiser said, "Hy, you look *terrible.*"

"So would you if you'd just been fired," snapped Smith.

"*Hy!*" said Danheiser, clearly unapprized. When the news registered, he asked fearfully, "Does this mean you—you won't get me any
stars?"

"Good thinking, Mel," said Smith.

CHAPTER 22

BUSINESS AS USUAL

". . . The film studio of today is really the palace of the sixteenth century. There one sees what Shakespeare saw: the absolute power of the tyrant, the courtiers, the flatterers, the jesters, the cunningly ambitious intriguers. There are fantastically beautiful women, there are incompetent favorites. There are great men who are suddenly disgraced. There is the most insane extravagance, and unexpected parsimony over a few pence. There is enormous splendor, which is a sham; and also horrible squalor hidden behind the scenery. There are vast schemes, abandoned because of some caprice. There are secrets which everybody knows and no one speaks of. There are even two or three honest advisers. These are the court fools, who speak the deepest wisdom in puns, lest they should be taken seriously. They grimace, and tear their hair privately, and weep."

"You make it sound great fun."

—Christopher Isherwood,
Prater Violet (1945)

When Woody Allen announced his decision to rejoin his former patrons at Orion, he did so with a gracious and considerate nod to United Artists, "whose new management continued to treat me wonderfully." The sadness at watching Woody go transcended simple business considerations, but it accentuated UA's need to enhance its product with star names, and there was no name more celestial than that of Barbra Streisand.

UA had tried to find or develop a project for Streisand off and on for the last two and a half years. One notion was somehow to refashion the Harold Arlen-Truman Capote musical *House of Flowers* (which UA had bought in the fifties but never made), but the idea of Streisand's playing either the part originated on Broadway by Diahann Carroll or that played by Pearl Bailey was finally recognized for the nonsense it was. Then there was Colette's autobiographical novel, *La Vagabonde*, about her early theatrical career, which I proposed to Sydney Pollack, who had directed Streisand in *The Way We Were*. He agreed that it might work if we could persuade Arthur Laurents (who had written *The Way We Were*) to write the script and get Stephen Sondheim (who had written a wonderfully "French" film score for Alain Resnais's *Stavisky*) to write the music and lyrics. The idea never got beyond wishful thinking because the charming Frenchwoman who owned the movie rights to the book (but had never produced a film in her life) wanted to know who was this Sydney Pollack, anyway, that he should want to produce the movie as well as direct it?

There was Sarah Bernhardt. Streisand had long talked of playing the great French star, but this idea, too, came to nothing. We continued sifting ideas, stories, manuscripts, screenplays, searching for something that might attract her to UA, and when finally we were offered a Streisand picture, we turned it down out of hand.

Not we. I.

Everyone in Hollywood knew about *Yentl*, and everyone in Hollywood had turned it down. It wasn't just that Streisand intended to play Isaac Bashevis Singer's teenage heroine who disguises herself as a young man in order to study at yeshiva. This seemed an unpromising enough premise for a musical, true, unless one remembered that one of the biggest musical successes in history concerns a Jewish milkman trying to marry off his three unbeautiful daughters before the pogrom arrives at the *shtetl*. A far greater problem with *Yentl* than its subject was its intended director: Barbra Streisand. Who was also the intended producer and had written (or was writing) the script. The songs she had left to Alan and Marilyn Bergman and composer Michel Legrand, but the functions of star, director, screenwriter, and producer seemed at least one too many, even for so protean a talent as Streisand's.

There was no star in the world with whom UA wanted to work more and hardly any project more risky at the estimated $15 to $18 million budget that had caused the picture to be placed in turnaround by Orion. There seemed little doubt to anyone that Barbra Streisand could direct a picture (though she never had, Hollywood legend of her interference with directors notwithstanding), and a big-budget musical from a first-time director seemed doubly unlikely at UA, still suffering through the looming unknowns of the shortened *Heaven's Gate.* When Stan Kamen, representing *Yentl,* called for my reaction to the script, I told him I hadn't even read it. It was being rewritten anyway, I knew, and I told Stan that as he was only too aware of UA's problems with another of his director clients, perhaps he could understand the inappropriateness and imprudence of UA's entertaining any notions about *Yentl.* He understood.

Still, I wanted the company to know we had been offered the project, and I announced this at the March production meeting in the boardroom of the Occidental Tower in downtown Los Angeles. I expressed my skepticism about the subject, though I stressed the same point made above about *Fiddler on the Roof,* for UA had made many millions on the motion picture based on it. I stated that the notion of building a relationship with a creative artist *at any cost* had an ominous and familiar ring. The time had come to make the right decisions for the right reasons, and *Yentl* was a wrong decision, an attitude which the production staff unanimously shared.

President Auerbach chuckled in amusement at the hubris of a forty-year-old actress/singer/producer/writer/director playing an eighteen-year-old girl playing an eighteen-year-old boy. Jim Harvey, down from San Francisco for the meeting, nodded in agreement. "What if she turns out to be the female Michael Cimino?" he asked.

One, we agreed, was enough.

More than enough. As the newly shortened *Heaven's Gate* reels went to the lab, Cimino began pressing for the final $45,000 due him by contract on delivery of the finished picture. The UA legal department had been withholding the payment on the ground that the picture had not been literally delivered, while it searched for some technical breach of contract that could legally justify not adding that $45,000 to the $25 million the picture had already gone over budget. In spite of bitter internal feeling at UA that the cost overrun per se constituted failure to deliver the picture as agreed, this was simply a moral position without force, as "merely" going $25 million over budget did not legally, as we have seen, constitute "breach."

As rerelease of the picture on April 24 drew nearer, the momentum of Joe Farrell's campaign to alter the negative image of the picture (and its creator) was abruptly slowed by Cimino's communicating his financial squabbles with UA to Farrell. On February 18 an embarrassed Farrell wrote Cimino (and Carelli), "It is not my place to take a position on these financial matters both because it is not my right and I simply do not know the issues. But I do know," he continued, alluding to the threat that the dispute might be made public, "that the success of the movie is in everyone's best interest and concomitantly negative statements can only harm the direction the campaign is designed to take."

Cimino decided he would take no part in publicity and promotion at all until, perhaps, the time of rerelease in April, causing Farrell to suggest that "regrettable and baffling behavior on Mr. Cimino's and Ms. Carelli's part" would make their aiding the promotion campaign to save their own picture "almost impossible."

Cimino's behavior may have baffled Farrell, but the rest of us thought it a direct result of the financial controls which had been imposed on him ever since November. A strict policy had gone into effect that no charges whatever, of any kind, could be incurred without a purchase order presigned by UA (usually by Kavanagh or me). Costs incurred without a UA signature were to be borne personally by Cimino himself or any member of his staff who had so acted. The system generally worked, though there were slips and at least one occasion on which a purchase order was altered (not by Cimino but by a member of his staff) after the signature had been obtained.

The system was annoying to everyone involved, but Cimino viewed it as harassment, and it led to a paper war between Cimino and Kavanagh, the tone of which was fast becoming familiar to everyone at UA. Much of the warring centered on Carelli. Cimino wrote: "I take the greatest exception to the adversary tone of your memos and your continued . . . petty harassment of Joann Carelli. . . . She has been working longer on this film than anyone else, selflessly and for the last year without one cent of renummeration [sic]. . . . Please be advised that I have informed [UA] of the urgency of this situation and the rapidly eroding morale of my staff." Kavanagh responded:

I have [not] harassed Joann . . . and I take great offence that you more than infer otherwise. . . . I have been unaware of Joann's activities since last August, so any request for payment . . . is always referred to Steven Bach. You should know that Steven is not inclined to agree to [these] payment[s].

Finally I am pleased to note that you have advised [UA] of the urgency of the needs. . . . A great deal of time [has been] spent in discussing "HEAVEN'S GATE," and how best we can . . . ensure that the picture is released appropriately so that it may receive the accolades to which it may be ultimately entitled and perhaps this may do something to bolster the morale of your Staff.

When limousine bills incurred by Cimino for Isabelle Huppert during rerecording in New York were sent to Kavanagh's office for payment with no accompanying purchase order, Kavanagh's secretary, Kathi Page, properly questioned them. "If Mr. Bach or Mr. Kavanagh think [paying these bills] is inappropriate," Cimino wrote back, "I will of course inform Miss Huppert of this in Paris, and I am sure that she will be only too thrilled. . . . And I am further certain you may not count on her services in connection with publicity for the movie . . . nor may you count on my own."

Cimino's venting his frustrations on secretaries did little to relieve the growing ill will, and his refusal to speak to the press was viewed, given his mood, as a perhaps ironic advantage. Still, it meant that I became the corporate voice of harmony and confidence to the press, sounding more hollow to myself with each press statement or television appearance as I predicted ultimate success for the recut picture. Most of the press seemed politely subdued by the immensity of the *Heaven's Gate* phenomenon, though there was open speculation about my longevity on the job. *Variety*, with the directness for which it is famous, openly (and correctly) questioned the candor of my public pronouncements. BACH GUSHES read a headline, and the headline was right.

The gushes of hot air with which I was inflating my hollow optimism were mostly predictable corporate statements. Privately I simply didn't know and was falling back on that wishful optimism well known before opening night that "the cow might fly." The picture was shorter, clearer, and more watchable, but whether it was "better," I didn't know. Cimino had been right to assert he had built rhythms into the picture from the start of production, and they showed in the movement of a crane shot, the deliberation with which the actors walked or spoke. The recut epic was a masterful job of editing by Bill Reynolds, but there were odd moments when it seemed almost meager, like a man whose crash diet has left him with a baggy wardrobe, or too tight, like a face lifted to a new and not quite natural configuration. I also knew the movie too well, knew what wasn't there as well as what was, and I also knew that whether the movie was "better" or not was irrelevant to the company and my place in it. "Would it sell?" was the critical question, with or without Cimino's help.

Joe Farrell felt his purpose being undercut at every turn by lack of cooperation from Cimino and Carelli, and he made a surprising suggestion: Fire him. Do not run the risk that he will walk away from the picture and attack UA in the press. The picture was now finished, after all, except for lab work. I doubt there was a person at UA aware of this suggestion who did not feel emotionally drawn to it as what Farrell called "a final decision," but I argued against it.

The foreign department, now headed by Michael Williams-Jones, was hoping to persuade Gilles Jacob, of the Cannes Film Festival, that the picture should be entered in competition for prizes, and the Los Angeles Film Exposition had asked for it as the closing-night attraction of the two-week Filmex, a prestigious slot at a prestigious Hollywood event. Both exposures could help the picture, and both events could boomerang if firing Cimino after all the work had been completed appeared merely an act of corporate vindictiveness.

Management agreed with me, but firing Cimino and being done once and for all with his obstructionism became a very real contingency plan. A press release was written in advance and still exists. It began: "United Artists announces with very deep regret that Michael Cimino, director of *Heaven's Gate*, has been relieved of any further responsibilities with the production." And it ended: "We are heartily sorry to have reached the conclusion that Mr. Cimino's continued association with us is in conflict with the best interests of *Heaven's Gate*." If it had to be released to the press, it was ready.

Departing executives continued to wave their last farewells to Julie, the doorman at 729, when I received a call from Auerbach.

"I'm in love," he announced kittenishly from New York.

I was not surprised to hear this since he made no secret of his appreciation of feminine charms, but it seemed distinctly out of character that he should confide in me.

"With Yentl," he added coyly, pausing to let it sink in.

"With Yentl or with *Yentl*?" I asked as nonchalantly as I could.

"Both," he said. "I have just spent the day at Barbra's apartment with Loeees," he said, "where Barbra sang the entire score for me. I am in love with Yentl and with *Yentl*."

Having duly noted that it was already "Barbra," I agreed that the songs were undoubtedly wonderful. The Bergmans and Legrand were wonderful writers, and God knows there is no one alive who can ingratiate herself or romance a listener with a song like Barbra Streisand.

"But—"

"No buts. I think we should do it," he said quietly. Too quietly. "Besides," he added, "there's someone else already cast. The father in the picture."

"Oh?" I replied, not very interested in a small supporting role. "Who?" I asked out of courtesy.

"Me," he replied, out of breath.

So we had not only the Mirisches but *Yentl.*

"You're making it up," said Anthea, aghast.

"He doesn't have a clue," said Wunsch. "Not a clue."

"He doesn't need one," I said. "He has the power."

Lois Smith explained via long distance. "He wanted to meet Barbra," she said. "What could I do?"

"Ever hear of no?" asked Anthea sweetly.

"He knew I had a coffee date with her, and he asked to come along. You don't say no to the king."

"It's been done," I muttered.

"Anyway, we went up to her apartment and she played him a tape—"

"She didn't play him a tape," I contradicted. "She sang him the whole goddamned *score.*"

"'The whole goddamned score' isn't written yet," said Lois calmly. "She played him a tape. The score isn't finished; the script isn't finished. It'll probably never happen. Probably."

"Is it the speakerphone that makes your voice sound so hollow," I asked, "or *guilt?*"

"Oh, stop it, ducks. Anyway, Barbra wants to make the picture in Czechoslovakia or Yugoslavia or someplace, and that triggered 'Hedy Lamarr' and 'my father' and 'my youth on the sound stages of old Prague,' and before I tuned back in—I mean, it's not that I haven't heard these stories before, right?—he was offering not only to make the movie but to be her interpreter in whatever country it is, and she just sort of said, 'Oh, good, and you can play my father, too,' and . . . *you* know," she concluded.

"We know," I said.

Marathon negotiations began with Streisand's agents and lawyers. Jon Peters, her longtime friend whom I had never met, called to tell me how lucky I was to have the project. *If I'm so lucky,* I thought, *how come you're not producing it, the way you produced* A Star Is Born, *which made everybody rich? Richer.* Finally, the negotiations were finished, and *Yentl,* the picture nobody wanted, was ours.

I was treated to the songs (on tape) at her funk-nouveau "ranch" in Malibu, all rusticated walls and giant ferns, and they were wonderful. I was hooked by melody and charm. She gave me the tour of her Art Deco house on the adjoining property, all burgundy, rose, black, and gray, down to the teacups in the cupboard and the soaps in the bathrooms. Even the closets were hung with authentic Deco period clothes in burgundy, rose, black, and gray, and if nothing else demonstrated the visual sense she would exercise as a director, that house did. It was also reassuring from another point of view: She conducted the tour with a connoisseur's appreciation of its details (many custom-made from photographs she had taken herself while scavenging Europe for authentic Deco work). Her tour spiel also had the slightly put-upon tone of a businesswoman complaining knowledgeably about the greed and incompetence of contractors. In spite of the fact that at this time she was immensely successful and owned seven different residences, she was also famous as a slow woman with a dollar, and this, coupled with the fact that production overages on *Yentl* would come out of her personal compensation, boded well for the budget.

Like Auerbach, I fell in love. She is intelligent, funny, professional, obsessive-compulsive, a perfectionist with a soupçon of parsimony, and far more attractive off screen than on. Telephone conversations with her about the script tended to go on rather longer than it took to lay the Atlantic cable and rarely required more than the occasional "uh-huh" from me to indicate I was still listening; but I liked her, and the force of her personality and common sense persuaded me that if anyone in the world could make *Yentl* work, it was she.

No one and nothing in the world could convince me—or Wunsch, Sylbert, or Smith—that *Romantic Comedy*, from the Broadway play by Bernard Slade, could work. Ours was a regretted but real conviction, and the Mirisches were gracious gentlemen about it and logically went directly to Auerbach, who approved it for production over the unanimous objections of the production staff.

If it hadn't been clear before that Auerbach had taken over production, it was now. We had become an advisory group and a control group. We got all the problems, and none of the fun.

Like *The National Lampoon Picture Show*, whose high commercial promise was dashed when its two directors delivered three good, funny segments and a fourth that rendered the other three pointless because it was of an awfulness that made the whole picture—too short with merely three sections—look unreleasable. The director of the frankly terrible and distended sequence had his agent come to argue for it in the Thalberg Building, from which the agent was asked to leave after the abusiveness of his remarks about UA caused the meeting to degenerate into a worse—and more hysterical—shambles than the director's botch of his material. Then there was Bette Midler, who was no less professional and obsessive about her work than Streisand but who lacked Streisand's experience in the movie business. Midler had had director approval and had mysteriously chosen Don Siegel, who had made good, tight action pictures in the past (including the original *Invasion of the Body Snatchers*) but almost always with male stars, most-recently Clint Eastwood. It quickly became apparent that he had no taste for the picture, which had acquired the prophetic title *Jinxed*, or any very clear notion of his star's unique appeal. When I asked him why he didn't quit, he coolly informed me, "Because then I wouldn't get my fee. Why not fire me?"

The French Lieutenant's Woman looked wonderful; *For Your Eyes Only* looked hugely commercial (and was); *Rocky III* looked bigger than the previous two bouts (and was); *True Confessions* looked beautifully made and problematical commercially (and was). None of them mat-tered: Only one picture at United Artists mattered—to the press, to the public aware of such things, to the company, and to me.

Press interest in United Artists and *Heaven's Gate* remained high as the picture's release grew nearer. The Filmex closing-night presentation of the picture had been announced with hesitantly favorable specula-tion in the community. Gilles Jacob arrived at MGM, saw the movie, and told me over lunch in the commissary that he didn't like it person-ally, but he agreed to enter it in competition at Cannes, hoping its presence there would have much the same effect *Apocalypse* had had two years before. The *New York Times Magazine* had assigned Aljean Harmetz to write a major piece on the movie, held up by demands of its director, who insisted (according to a letter from his personal press rep-resentative, Michael Maslansky):

1. [on] full text approval

2. [on] full photo approval, including the selection of the photogra-pher

3. that no one, other than Joann or Michael, be mentioned in the piece and that all of Aljean's subsequent explorations with UA executives not be included in a story that would be only about Michael

More practical and to the corporate point, Auerbach agreed to a joint interview with me for Bob Thomas of the Associated Press. It took place on March 16, and the two of us were photographed in friendly harmony, though Thomas observed in the printed piece that "Auerbach-Bach make an odd corporative couple, yet they seem com-plementary." Well, maybe. Auerbach allowed for attribution "If the

picture is sucessful, a lot of credit for the turnaround goes to Steve."
And if not? I wondered, but I knew.

If the picture worked as *Apocalypse* had, I could probably resign with
some dignity, the way Tom Gray in publicity did, just after setting up
the Bob Thomas interview, because he "just couldn't stand the terrible,
oppressive, despotic atmosphere any longer." But if *Heaven's Gate*
failed, the company could coolly remove from its midst the last vestige
of the regime responsible for it. It felt odd being a vestige.

The desire for publicity control implicit in Michael Cimino's demands to the *New York Times* and Aljean Harmetz became clearer to
me as I had my breakfast coffee while watching the *Today* show on
NBC on April 23, the morning of the Filmex evening presentation.
There on the television screen in my den was Michael Cimino, speaking softly with Gene Shalit, of the eccentric hairdo. Cimino, who had
refused to cooperate with UA or Joe Farrell in any press or promotion
on the picture, had secretly (I later determined) flown to New York to
tape his own personal press and promotion with Shalit on April 16,
thereby sabotaging appearances Joe Farrell had prearranged with David
Brinkley on the same network and the Filmex "exclusive" promised to
Rona Barrett for ABC.

Cimino looked weakened and nervous. He had never had Coppola's
grandly expansive "come and get me" daring and seemed to be receding
into himself as Shalit posed hard questions. "Is it obscene to spend that
much money" on a movie? Shalit asked, having calculated that "a hundred American families making twenty-five thousand dollars each could
live fourteen years on thirty-five million dollars."

"No," answered Cimino, seeming shocked by the word *obscene*.
Motives must be examined. To spend $35 million just to make money
would be obscene, but not "to present a portrait of a period the way it
really was . . . if one's *intentions* are honorable . . ." His voice faltered.

"Are you," asked Shalit, "obsessed with detail?"

"One is re-creating a period; one hopes that one doesn't make a
mistake."

"Will you have trouble getting financing after this? Don't people
consider you dangerous?"

At last a glimmer in those small, tired eyes. "I think they probably
always looked at me as a little dangerous." He seemed pleased.

Shalit announced that installment two of this interview would be
carried the following day, the day of *Heaven's Gate*'s national rerelease.

• • •

Filmex is a festive Hollywood event, largely supported by the industry in spite of widespread Hollywood mistrust of festivals as "too critical," "too arty." It is less a company town's self-celebration (the Academy Awards have long preempted that) than a nod to the muses that also induces a sense of cultural virtue. Opening and closing nights are traditionally considered the major events. Closing with *Heaven's Gate* attracted press attention with the Filmex imprimatur, which UA wanted, and could not damage the movie if the highly critical (mostly) industry audience hated it because the picture opened nationally the next day anyway. This time it really *would* be over.

The character of the event was, in many ways, unique. No one there was unaware of the troubled history of the movie, of the previous celebrity and honors of its director, and one suspects that few arrived without preformed attitudes about a film that had been denied them but that had everywhere changed attitudes in the industry in which most of them earned their livings, practiced their crafts, their arts.

Cimino made a statement for radio and television on entering Mann's Chinese Theater on Hollywood Boulevard, where the event was held, his voice faltering and unsure, saying he hoped tonight's screening would "reflect well on all of us."

All of us entered and took our seats, settling back for what would truly be the last picture show. The audience was agitated with anticipation, bubbling with an energy entirely absent from the New York premiere six months before. I saw David Field enter across the auditorium and exchange nods with Bob Wunsch. I decided not to speculate on David's reactions.

The movie began. It was shorter. Maybe better. No one saw it. They saw, instead of the movie on the screen, the movie they had been told about by forests of newsprint, by cascades of critical condemnation, by front offices that had altered their own lives and careers in tightening screws not because of *this* movie but that other one, that "unqualified disaster" they tried to discern through the lights and shadows of the truncated one before them. No one in that industry audience had been unaffected by this movie—however temporarily—and they seemed to feel cheated somehow, for all it was, was . . . a *movie*. A kind of odd western, which began for some reason in a Harvard they all knew was Oxford and then went to Wyoming, where not much of anything happened, though people talked about what was *going* to happen, and then, finally, it *happened*, and what happened gave a hint of all the "intolerable excess" those New York people had talked about, and then it was over, on a kind of depressing and nihilistic note. The cavalry saved the bad guys. The girl got killed. The hero lost everything but his memories and his yacht. The phenomenon *reduced* was, well, no phenomenon at all. It was just a *western*, and not so thrilling at that.

"Oh, it's a *horror*," one viewer told a radio reporter, and he chuckled with glee when he said it. *Well, chuckles are better than cackles*, I thought grimly.

David Field wasn't chuckling when he passed Bob and Judy Wunsch on his way out of the theater, not lingering for the credits. "You guys should be ashamed of yourselves," he said, and negotiated his way through the lobby, becoming quickly lost in the Hollywood crowd.

The press reaction wasn't much. So few critics had seen the original version that they were mostly trying to vie with the New Yorkers in bons mots and, like the audience, trying to figure out what all the furor had been about, so they reviewed that.

The picture received one authentic rave, from Kevin Thomas in the *Los Angeles Times*, who later declared, "I don't think in twenty years of movie reviewing I've ever been so . . . *totally alone.*" He was so alone, in fact, that Charles Champlin, arts editor of the *Times*, who had retired from movie reviewing, came out of retirement to shove Thomas's piece to an inside page, so he could himself blast the movie on the front page of the "Calendar" section.

National reviews weren't much better. Most—by no means all—found it "an improvement," as did David Ansen in *Newsweek*, but he decided "Cimino has chosen the wrong story to tell . . . it's a mood piece improbably disguised as a political passion play," full of "spurious authenticity." He noted that "Cimino does have a real eye for epic images, and there are ravishing painterly effects . . . that are worthy of comparison with the best nineteenth-century luminist paintings," but "Cimino aches for greatness, and his film aches from the discrepancy between his prodigious pictorialism and his primitive grasp of character and drama." Richard Corliss in *Time* announced, "Well, it's shorter . . . the story makes some sense." But he mourned the loss of the "brazen visual virtuosity . . . a vision of the American West as a place too vast and mysterious for man to conquer . . . that was [the longer version's] folly and its grandeur."

Stanley Kauffmann in the *New Republic* wrote, "Now, *Heaven's Gate* can at least be sat through," and "its generally failed ambitions are at least now lucid, but its few virtues are much stronger." He rejected what most found the film's principal virtue, finding Vilmos Zsigmond's photography a major mistake. He wrote it added "an aesthetic shimmer that [fought] the hard material" and concluded that "a long bore has been converted into a tolerable non-success."

These were not what are called in show business money reviews, and Cimino's second *Today* show appearance the morning after Filmex, and the day of the picture's national release, didn't help much. Shalit asked if he expected better reviews this time around, and Cimino was dubious, saying that "so many have gone so far" he thought them "unlikely to come back from such an extreme position." He added sternly that critics have "a responsibility, an absolute responsibility" to deal with a film's subject matter.

Which was what? "*Heaven's Gate*," he said somberly, "in its own way has more to do, in my opinion, with the kind of ethic that produced Vietnam than *The Deer Hunter*." Not the poetry of America, not the education of a nation, not the things that fade. Vietnam. Well, I thought, as I sipped my coffee in the den, 20 million television viewers just decided to forget about *Heaven's Gate*, but I continued to watch the performance.

Shalit confronted Cimino with Joann Carelli's remarks about him to Jean Vallely, who had printed them in *Rolling Stone*. "Michael was a little crazy up there in Montana," Carelli had said. "He won those two Academy Awards and really believed they meant something. He was definitely out of control." As Shalit read these remarks, Cimino's eyes looked wounded and then softened. He decided to forgive her. She's a person of "rather remarkable courage and intelligence," he said. If there was one thing he would have done differently, he admitted, "I would have paid more attention to my producer, Joann Carelli."

In its first weekend of release, in 810 theaters nationwide, *Heaven's Gate* grossed $1.3 million, averaging just over $500 a night for each theater. The *New York Times* announced in an article headlined RE-VISED 'HEAVEN'S GATE' COLLAPSES AT BOX OFFICE that "At Loew's Astor Plaza in New York, it grossed $10,105—less than half of that theater's operating expenses for a week." The long Sunday magazine piece the *New York Times* had planned never ran. This wasn't "an unqualified disaster" or "a phenomenon." This was just—a flop.

The last word came in the *Los Angeles Times*, where Jerry Esbin told Dale Pollock, "It's as if somebody called every household in the country and said, 'There will be a curse on your family if you go see this picture.'" He added dynamically, "I've never seen anything like this in my life."

Heaven's Gate was over except for Cannes in mid-May. Perhaps European reaction would be more enthusiastic. It is well known, after all, that the French revere Jerry Lewis.

I wasn't invited to Cannes, but Dean Stolber was. Stolber was spending a lot of time with Auerbach that year. When the two were in California, they stayed together at the condominium on Wilshire Boulevard in Westwood that Transamerica had bought at Auerbach's suggestion. They brought their wives out for the Academy Awards, but Auerbach overslept in the condo and missed seeing Robert De Niro win his Best Actor award for *Raging Bull.*

Auerbach seemed undaunted by the failure of *Heaven's Gate.* His conversation was liberally sprinkled with "Barbra this" and "Barbra that," and finally in the first week of May he suggested that the production staff and he and Stolber should take Barbra to dinner at Ma Maison, so we all could get better acquainted.

Anthea and Bob, Dean, Auerbach, and I met at Barbra's Art Nouveau house in Beverly Hills for drinks before going on to the restaurant. Leaving the house in private cars, Auerbach suggested I myself drive Barbra, a gesture which I appreciated but which still seems curious in view of what came four days later.

We arrived at the restaurant, were ushered upstairs by Patrick Terrail, the sleek, smart owner of the famously unlisted bistro. Patrick arranged us at a round candlelit table in the private dining room. Just like friends, we began to chat of this and that. Inevitably conversation got around to "my childhood on the sound stages of old Prague," and as Anthea, Bob, and I exchanged glances, Barbra looked up in surprise and said, "I didn't know you were from Prague."

There was a moment of hushed silence before Auerbach began to stammer. "But—but we discussed all that in New York *weeks* ago," he reminded her smilingly.

"We did?" she asked.

And he launched yet again into the story, the studio, Hedy Lamarr née Kiesler, all of it.

Barbra's face reflected true interest as she listened to this autobiographical recital she clearly had no memory of. Either that or she's an even better actress than I think. The more Auerbach talked, the more strained his voice became. It was hard to tell if the strain came from his realization that his impression on Barbra this and Barbra that had been less than indelible or from a genuine effort to prick her memory, so she wouldn't be embarrassed by her poor retention of this oft-repeated lore.

He finally ended with "That's why you asked me to play your father, remember?"

"My *father?*" she said, astonishment in face and voice. "Morris Carnovsky is going to play my father!"

In the end Nehemiah Persoff got the job.

CHAPTER 23

GIFT WRAP

Studio executives are intelligent, brutally
overworked men and women who share
one thing in common with baseball managers: They wake up every morning of the
world with the knowledge that sooner or
later they're going to get fired.

— William Goldman,
Adventures in the Screen Trade (1983)

My first sharp awareness that I had to get out of show
business came on a shuttle flight from Washington to New York. Anthea Sylbert and I had flown down to catch the matinee of a play in
out-of-town tryout, and the flight back was one of unusual turbulence
and stark white knuckles.

Because my career required a great deal of flying, I had the habit on
takeoffs and landings of reciting to myself the Lord's Prayer. I did so
now, as lightning flashed outside the windows of the plane, which was
bouncing like a yo-yo. I stopped in mid-phrase, when I realized that
what I had recited was "Our Father, which art in Heaven, Hollywood
be thy name." It was time to go, time to get out.

Others agreed, of course, and I must have had some premonition of
unusual clarity the Monday morning of May 11, for I rose calmly, had
coffee, read the newspaper with interest, and drove to Culver City with
the top down.

I called my lawyer, Barry Hirsch, and had a brief chat, telling him I
thought it was over. He asked to be kept posted. I then called London
on a whim, spoke to a friend, saying I might be over soon. The morning passed with routine business. Bette Midler was in Lake Tahoe, making a movie she hated with people she hated, but behaving like the
professional she is; Barbra Streisand was in Malibu preparing the *Yentl*
script with her assistant and coproducer, Rusty Lemorande; Nathaniel
Kwit, Bart Farber's replacement in New York, had come up with a dim

scheme to pay two young editors $5,000 to cut *Heaven's Gate* down to ninety minutes and release it with a new ad campaign and a new title he had dreamed up: *The Johnson County War.*

Shortly after two o'clock Rita buzzed me to say that Dean Stolber was on the line. His voice, when he said hello, was calm, mellow, warm, as if inviting my respect and sympathy for the task he defined as "the hardest call I've ever had to make in my life."

Then why make it? I thought, but I only said, "Oh?"

"Can you come to New York and talk about it?" he asked, rather as if asking for a favor.

"Couldn't you have handled it while you were here?" I said. They had had the whole week. But then, of course, they had had the bankers, too, and applecarts that needed to remain upright, however temporarily.

There was a long pause as he framed his response. "This is the way we wanted to handle it," he said.

After we hung up, I made one private phone call to pass on the news, then asked Rita to get me Barry Hirsch again and London again. Barry offered to go to New York with me to negotiate a settlement, but I declined his offer with thanks and told London I would be arriving sooner than expected—at the end of the week, in fact, for a few days' sightseeing and theatergoing.

I told Rita, who made sure the door was shut before she began to cry, and I asked her please to stop that, cancel the rest of the day's appointments, and help me clear out the desk. Most of this annoying chore had been done, and we sorted out a few personal things as Rita booked me on a plane first to New York and then to London and made discreet calls to the West Coast executives, asking them to gather in my office at four o'clock.

I met privately with Bob and Anthea, who had remained loyal and supportive to the end. At four o'clock I told the rest of the staff, "I have been fired. I am going to New York tomorrow to settle things with Dean, and I am going home now. I won't be back, so this is my only chance to say thank you to all of you."

I left. I didn't want to hang around and cast them in the roles of emotive sympathizers. Besides, they themselves had been through enough these past months, through all the losses of friends and colleagues, the distortion of the human consideration with which Andy Albeck had tried to infuse the company, the daily battering by the press, the heaping of that special scorn Hollywood reserves for its own. They were hardworking, dedicated, uncynical people, and I left so they could get on with it.

I drove home in the convertible that would be repossessed for my replacement to drive in two days, said hello to Margo, the old English sheepdog, whose playfulness seemed odd and happily more real than the events of the day. I made only one phone call, to my parents. I thought they should hear the news from me instead of from Rona Barrett on *Good Morning, America,* which I knew they watched each day at breakfast. I swam in the pool, had a quiet drink with a friend who understood the therapy of silence, and I went to bed, where dreams did not intrude.

Tuesday, May 12, I was in an airplane for most of the day and arrived at my apartment in New York to meet the embarrassed eyes of the elevatorman, who had read the *New York Times,* in which a story alerting him to my arrival in the city had appeared. I asked him for it, read it, and watched a movie on TV. The phone did not ring.

Wednesday, May 13, I had an appointment to see Dean Stolber and try to settle with the company. Before that, however, I had a lunch date with a lawyer friend who had called that morning and insisted that he see me before I saw Stolber. It was urgent, he said. I assumed he wanted to advise me on my settlement, for he knew, as few outsiders did, that UA did not give contracts, except for those held by Auerbach and Stolber. I had worked for three years and three days without one, and I had no legal entitlements whatever. My lawyer friend had added, "I'll buy."

We met at the Russian Tea Room, where a number of people waved and smiled and mimed sympathetic support. My lawyer friend asked for a table away from the front booths full of movers and shakers, and after I ordered a bloody Mary and my invariable eggplant orientale, he said firmly, "You are never to reveal we had this conversation to anyone under any circumstances. I'm not sure, but I could be violating some pissant law about disclosure, and much as I want to help you, I don't want to find myself twisting in the wind."

"You won't," I said, wondering what could be so dramatic.

"The company's being sold," he whispered.

I was stunned. "When?"

"Right now. This very minute. And nobody at Seven-twenty-nine *knows.*"

He looked around warily before continuing. "All last week," he said, "while Auerbach and Stolber were in California for the bankers' meetings you guys had, Seven-twenty-nine was up to its tits in a twenty-four-hour-a-day antitrust research trying to find some way to prevent Transamerica from selling the company to"—he smiled cutely—"the *buyer.*"

"Who is?"

"Kerkorian." He grinned.

"MGM?" I asked, astonished.

"You got it. And United Artists thinks they licked it, that Kerkorian backed off, but he didn't."

"Where's the money coming from? Not the hotels."

"He's got all that stock in Columbia that the feds ordered him to get rid of because of antitrust; but that was the old feds, and this is the new feds, and the *new* Justice Department doesn't give diddleysquat about antitrust."

"So he sells the Columbia stock and buys UA in order to have the distribution company."

"You got it."

"Are you sure?"

"I'm sure. I can't tell you how—I *won't* tell you how—but I'm sure. I'm so sure I could probably be disbarred or some goddamn thing for telling you."

"What do you mean nobody at Seven-twenty-nine knows?"

"*They don't know,*" he said, a certain glee in his voice. "I don't know if they even suspect anything. Do you think Jim Harvey is going to ask Norbert Auerbach's advice about whether or not Transamerica should sell the fuckin' company?"

"Well, they can't keep it a secret forever. I mean, sooner or later even *Norbert* will figure it out."

"San Francisco. Harvey is going to ask him to go to San Francisco for a meeting, and they'll tell him there."

"How do you know?"

"I *know.*"

"When?"

"Tomorrow, I think."

"I thought he was going to Cannes with Dean at the end of the week."

"So he'll go to San Francisco, and *then* he'll go to Cannes. Or he *won't* go to Cannes. Who the hell cares?"

"Listen," I said, "this is fascinating stuff and all that, but what's it got to do with me? I don't work there anymore."

"What does it say in your contract?"

"I haven't got one, and you know it."

"Auerbach does. Stolber does." He smiled. "Why should they give a fuck what happens to the rest of the company? Frank Rosenfelt can come into Seven-twenty-nine and fire the whole goddamn company for all they care because *they've* got the contracts."

"What are you saying?"

"I'm saying that Dean leaves for Cannes at four o'clock tomorrow afternoon, and if you haven't made your settlement by three o'clock, baby, you ain't going to get one."

My bloody Mary had arrived. I drank it slowly.

It made some kind of sense, I reflected, as I walked down Seventh Avenue to 729 after lunch. Andy told me that MGM made periodic attempts to buy the company every year, sometimes through its attorney, Greg Bautzer, sometimes by Rosenfelt himself. David Begelman had not long before suggested the companies be merged, and Andy had said, "I have a film library, a production company, a music company, and the best distribution company in the world. What do *you* have to merge, Mr. Begelman?"

I knew what Begelman had now: He had a long string of big pictures that would soon be ready for release: *Buddy, Buddy, Whose Life Is It, Anyway?, Yes, Giorgio, Cannery Row, All the Marbles, Pennies from Heaven.* Begelman would want to control their distribution, but he couldn't do that without controlling UA, still reeling from the *Heaven's Gate* fiasco.

It could be the right moment in San Francisco, too. Harvey had probably had it with the movie business, I thought, and why not? Transamerica had finally achieved its goal of being identified with United Artists through one of the most public film failures of all time. Still, the price would have to be right, but Kerkorian had never been known as a *low* roller. They had a previous relationship, too, one that went back to 1968, when Kerkorian had sold Transamerica his airline for $85 million. Now maybe Transamerica would return the favor, but the number would have to be a far larger one than that. At least $250 million, I thought.

As I neared 729 for my meeting with Stolber, I felt a wave of irrational destitution pass over me, probably not uncommon to men who have just been fired, and I suddenly turned in the direction of the Pussycat Theater, looking for "the drummer of Forty-ninth Street," but he had evidently moved on.

I entered 729, wondering if my lawyer friend was right. He was someone I trusted implicitly, and he had been persuasive. He had spoken of midnight meetings and secret phone calls and draft briefs and hidden agendas and had told me most of them. He had long been a good friend, and I knew him to have what he boasted of as "an infallible shit detector." He had shared secret information with me out of no motive more harmful than friendship, and as the elevator rose to the fourteenth floor, I decided to bet on friendship. But whose? His? Or Stolber's?

Annie Garrett, the tiny, birdlike fourteenth-floor receptionist, looked up from the newspaper she was reading, suddenly startled to see me, but then she was always suddenly startled to see anyone. I smiled as I passed, and she mispronounced my name as she had every day for three years, in her fragile, trembly voice. She turned back to the lurid pages of her tabloid as I wandered past the framed posters to Stolber's office.

Dean was notorious for keeping people waiting, and he kept me waiting, but not for long. He wanted someone to tell how unhappy and morose he felt over the burdens of firing a close friend, and who better than the close friend? I listened with some interest to the psychology at work; it must have looked like sympathy because he kept on. I didn't need to spend a May afternoon in New York listening to how sensitive Dean was to the difficulties of his job or even how sad Jackie was and how nothing would ever be the same again. I knew all that, and while I didn't want to question his sincerity (is there anything more sincere than self-regard?), I wondered how he could deal with the situation in which he had been placed.

"Norbert has a theory," he explained. "He believes it is necessary in business to be *tough*." He said it without irony, and I thought maybe the room was bugged. "And he knew that there would be nothing *tougher* for me than to make that phone call I made to you on Monday. He thinks I'll be a better executive because of it."

"Curious theory of executive training."

He smiled indulgently. "You never did like him."

"What does that have to do with anything? If he fires everybody around here who doesn't like him, you and he are going to be pretty lonely." Then, truly wondering, I asked, "Do *you* like him?"

"I've gotten to understand him," he said.

"That isn't what I asked."

"Do I like him? *Yes*," he said assertively.

I nodded. I assumed that he did. I hoped he did, for I knew well the strain of pretending.

"So what happens now?"

"You mean your settlement?"

"No," I said. "We'll get to that. I mean what happens now with you and the company?" He might say nothing; but he wouldn't lie, and I needed to know what he knew or if there was anything *to* know, if my lawyer friend had been right.

"Well," he said, visibly relaxing and warming, "I've been thinking about it a lot, and Jackie and I have been talking. Norbert has changed my life, you know. Once, when I was working for Bill Bernstein, I thought: *Maybe someday I can be head of business affairs.* That was a kind of *dream*. But now"—he smiled modestly—"I will work with Norbert as executive vice-president for two or three years until Norbert retires or becomes chairman, and then . . ." He let his future hang there for me to admire.

"Really?" I said, impressed.

Again the modest smile and nod. "There was a time when I would have been afraid of being president of a major company—well, not *afraid* exactly . . ."

"Diffident?"

"Yes. But I've learned a lot about my own capabilities, and I'll learn more over the next two or three years with Norbert. It's really a wonderful opportunity."

"Unless the rumors on the street are true," I said casually.

He looked startled, then laughed. "The sale rumors? Forget it. That's all been put nicely to rest. I didn't think you *knew*," he said. "You didn't say a word last week."

"Neither did you," I said. "About much of anything."

"I don't deserve that," the executive vice-president said sadly.

"Probably not," I answered. "I'm happy for you and Jackie and this future you're describing, but I don't envy you. I suppose that if Norbert can toughen you up, maybe you can soften him up. You're in a position to have a very real, positive effect on the company. There are still a lot of good people here."

"I hope so," he said, beaming.

He was beaming less when he offered me two weeks' salary as a settlement.

I spoke quietly. "I came three thousand miles and three years to hear you say something else, Dean. I'll get back to you or Barry Hirsch will or somebody will."

"It will have to be before I leave the office tomorrow," he said. "We shouldn't let this thing hang."

"I agree. When are you leaving?"

"Three o'clock sharp."

"Somebody will call you before then. Maybe even me."

As I reached the door, he said, "Jackie would love to hear from you."

"She's probably busy packing and getting ready for Cannes. I don't want to bother her."

"It's only her second trip to Europe," he said.

"I remember the first one." I nodded.

"The *QE2*." He sighed nostalgically. "Wasn't it great?"

"Great," I said. Then, with what I hoped looked like a smile, I said, "Why do I worry for you, Dean?" and left.

My lawyer friend called me the next morning.

"The deal is done, and Auerbach is flying to San Francisco, maybe right now. *And he still doesn't know!*"

He knows, I thought, *he knows.*

"What did they offer you?"

"Two weeks."

"I don't believe it."

"I believed you; you can believe me."

"That's the fucking final humiliation!"

"You think it wasn't humiliating for Dean?"

"What are you prepared to accept?"

"Whatever I can get under the circumstances. You're *sure*?"

"Sure as sure."

I spoke to Stolber in the afternoon. He offered me six weeks' salary and some vague talk about possibly developing some projects for the company in the future. I wasn't much interested in more future talk and told him so. I wished him a happy voyage and a successful screening of *Heaven's Gate* at Cannes and asked him to give my love to Jackie.

He said he would and added a last-minute afterthought. "You know, Norbert's not here right now."

"I know. San Francisco called."

"How did you know?"

"I don't know," I lied. "Somebody mentioned something."

"He asked me to tell you that he was hurt and offended by you."

"Well," I said, "that makes us even."

"No, *seriously*."

"OK, Dean, *why*?"

"When you were in the building yesterday, you didn't go into his office to say good-bye."

There was not a trace of irony in his voice.

"Good-bye, Dean," I said.

When I checked into the hotel in London, Friday evening, May 15, there was a phone message marked "urgent." I called back Teddy Joseph, the UA production man in England, who rasped breathlessly over the line, "The company has been *sold*! To MGM!"

"I know, Teddy," I said. He was flustered and mystified and fearful for his own future, as I knew hundreds of others would be all over again in a cycle of anxiety that had begun three and a half years before and maybe now had an end in sight, one no one could have predicted. Teddy commiserated with me, and I with him, and we agreed to see each other for an old times' sake drink during my stay.

I asked the operator to get me the Carlton Hotel in Cannes, where I wanted to speak to Mr. or Mrs. Stolber.

Amazingly the call went through the usually jammed Carlton switchboard immediately. It was Dean who answered, his voice quiet and tentative. I told him Teddy had called to tell me the news that had been announced in California that day, when both Stolber and I had been in airplanes.

"Jackie and I got off the plane in Nice, and it was the first thing we heard," he said gravely. "I couldn't believe it, so I called Norbert. He couldn't reach *us*."

"Where is he?"

"In New York. He's coming over this weekend."

"What did he say?"

"I asked him if he wanted me to get on a plane and come back, and he said, 'No, no, everything's fine. Stay there and enjoy yourselves.'"

"Can you do that?" I asked.

"Of course. Sure. Why not? Everything's fine."

"What did MGM pay anyway?"

"Three hundred and fifty million. *More*. The Wall Street guys are saying they overpaid. Maybe as much as a hundred million."

"Who *would*n't sell? For a price like that at a time like this." I started to laugh.

"What's so funny?" he asked.

"Nothing. It just occurred to me that *Heaven's Gate* led to a lot. It crippled the company and made it easy prey, but because the guy who wanted it most—Kerkorian—is such a high roller, it didn't go at a distress price but at a premium if Wall Street's right. So deduct forty million dollars for the picture, and there's still a net profit of sixty million dollars. *Heaven's Gate* made money after all."

"For Transamerica," he said dubiously.

"For Transamerica," I agreed.

I put the phone down and smiled unhappily, feeling no satisfaction. I sat in my hotel room feeling disoriented with no scripts to read, no phone calls to make, no release to worry about except my own. I reflected that the costs of *Heaven's Gate* had now, with the sale of the company, become truly incalculable, forever unknowable. *Good-bye, Doug and Mary*, I thought. *Good-bye, Charlie and D.W., Jim and Andy, and everybody else. And yes, good-bye, Norbert.*

Let's call it a wrap.

CHAPTER 24

STRINGS

I give you the end of a golden string;
Only wind it into a ball,
It will lead you in at Heaven's gate,
Built in Jerusalem's wall.

—William Blake,
Jerusalem (1820)

The big attraction at Cannes that year turned out to be not Michael Cimino, or Isabelle Huppert, or even *Heaven's Gate*. It was Leo the Lion. At the press conference following the press screening of *Heaven's Gate*, Norbert Auerbach mounted the podium, wearing a Lacoste shirt with an alligator on the pocket and a stuffed lion under his arm.

There had been some booing reported at the morning screening, but there was courteous applause for Cimino as he, too, took his place on the stage of the *presse salle*. Auerbach was too much the realist not to know that whatever the critics thought of *Heaven's Gate*, MGM's purchase of UA was the bigger story, and he played to it with humor and style.

When a reporter's question suggested that UA's sale had resulted directly from the movie screened just minutes before, Cimino announced that "actually UA has been for sale for the last two years." Auerbach gently corrected him and admitted that if *Heaven's Gate* had not directly caused Transamerica's retirement from show business, it certainly hadn't prevented it.

Cimino faced his critics, saying, "I don't feel this is a trial," but a British reporter thought the words were hollow and wrote that he sounded "out of it, rather than above it all. Not quite with us, somehow." Cimino supported his film with the familiar litany about authenticity and painstaking efforts to get it right. Asked about critical reaction to his film, he continued to claim that he hadn't read the

critics and explained them away with "When John Kennedy was assassi-
nated, a lot of people felt better. Because he was so brilliant he gave
them bad consciences about their own lives. I don't compare myself to
Kennedy, of course," he added. "But certain journalists have been waiting to destroy me for similar reasons. Because I represent success and
talent." Tony Crawley, one journalist who quoted this remark, thought
Cimino's ordering of his attributes revealing, perhaps about Hollywood
in general: success first, talent second.

If Crawley and others were skeptical or snide, there were enthusiasts
among the critics, and gossip traveled the Croisette that the jury might
give the film le Palme d'Or, just to show its contempt for American
critics. *Figaro* thought *Heaven's Gate* "enrich[ed] the anthology of cinema," and *Libération* called it "ε beautiful spectacle, beautifully produced and directed." One French critic referred to Cimino as "*le Tolstoi
de la caméra,*" but *Nice Matin* found the movie "mediocre," and in the
end it won no prizes at all. Jury president Jacques Deray made a statement: "We found a lack of understanding of the story and the characters."

International postmortems were either angry, like *Films Illustrated*'s,
or appalled, like the Swiss-German *Cinéma*'s "The Height of Folly"
("only the film technique is real," it reported), or mournful, as in
French *Cinéma*'s lengthy elegy, "Requiem for a Still-born Poem." None
of them cited Wallace Stevens's poem "The Worms at Heaven's Gate,"
but they didn't have to; it was dead. Even *with* the French reviews and
a handful of supporters in England, the picture failed to attract an audience in either country and was quietly pulled from exhibition. Or, as
Auerbach neatly put it, "the public pulled it for us. We didn't have to
do a thing."

Everybody went home, and MGM discovered it couldn't use the
expensive worldwide distribution company it had just bought, because
CIC, the international distribution company headquartered in London
which distributed its films abroad (as well as those of Paramount and
Universal), would not let MGM out of its contract. Various foreign
laws governing corporate behavior precluded just dumping UA's international offices and firing the overhead. Finally, a way was found to
merge CIC with what and who was left of UA distribution, and when
David Begelman decided to take over UA in Culver City (relinquishing
MGM), Norbert Auerbach was invited to London as copresident of the
merged distribution company, now called UIP International. Begelman
named Paula Weinstein president of UA production. Soon after, Bob
Wunsch was let go, and eventually Anthea Sylbert, too. All vestiges of
Heaven's Gate were gone in little more than a year.

• • •

On December 6, 1982, a year and a half after the short version's failure, the French film magazine *Cahiers du Cinéma* (in which, appropriately enough, the auteur theory was born) and the *Cinémathèque Française* presented the long version to what *Le Monde* described as "an enormous crowd." Isabelle Huppert introduced it, announcing that "a miscarriage of justice," which "posterity will one day redress," had been perpetrated. Two days later *Le Monde* solemnly announced, "It falls to France to reverse the unhappy judgment of an ill-inspired American press," and did not fail to allude to Erich von Stroheim, *Greed,* or "the air-conditioned Hollywood nightmare."

The screening was something of a sensation, and an American who was there told the *Los Angeles Times,* that "twenty-five minutes into the projection, roughly 150 people literally *swarmed* into the theater. . . . Costa-Gavras (president of the *Cinémathèque*) . . . had to plead with the invaders to leave the balcony . . . because it was in danger of collapsing." The *Times'* unnamed correspondent put it into perspective with "So as not to get *too* lofty in realms cinematic, be it known that the hospitalization of Jerry Lewis was a major news story here. . . ."

But something was stirring stateside, too, perhaps curiosity or love of movies. Jerry Harvey and Fred Grossbud at Los Angeles's pay-cable Z channel persuaded MGM/UA (as the combined companies were called) to allow them to exhibit the long version of the film on television starting on Christmas Eve, the first time Hollywood had ever seen the film in its fuller length.

Charles Champlin, the *Los Angeles Times* arts editor, who had written his own denunciation of the short version, saw the long one and wrote in the *Times* a few days before the Z channel airing that "it seems to me a pity bordering on tragedy that the longer version was not shown [originally]." He found John Hurt's oratory "subtle . . . a wonderful piece of acting and credible graduate foolishness," found "the central character of Kris Kristofferson . . . clearer," and he thought Isabelle Huppert's Ella "not so much . . . the stereotyped whore with the heart of gold but . . . an independent woman with her own code." He announced, "Not a damned thing was gained commercially by forcing [sic] Cimino to eviscerate his work, but audiences were denied the chance to see fully whatever it was that Cimino had in mind." He concluded sternly that "the moral of *Heaven's Gate* seems to be that the then-executives at United Artists poured bad judgment after bad judgment in a futile effort to make the earlier judgments look less bad." *

---

* The *Times,* it should be noted, could be sharply critical and also generous, as it was to one of those executives in a long article called "Bachgate: The Firing of an Executive" in the summer of 1981.

Not long after, the Library of Congress scheduled the long version
as part of its series on "The American Cowboy on Film," running the
copyright deposit print on June 16 and June 17 in its small sixty-four-
seat theater. It was forced to turn away film enthusiasts and curiosity
seekers. The library's film programmer, Scott Simmon, later said that
"the film had a cult following, even then," and he told the Associated
Press, "I think they should re-release the thing."

In England critical reaction to the short version had ranged from
Tony Crawley's scathing commentary to Nigel Andrews's enthusiasm in
The Financial Times, who called it "not merely a fascinating Western
but quite possibly the greatest American movie of the last 10 years." In
June the National Film Theatre of the British Film Institute ran newspaper ads illustrated by a bleeding film can marked Heaven's Gate, from
which a knife protruded. ON NOVEMBER 4TH 1980 [sic], ran the headline, NEW YORK'S CRITICS MURDERED HEAVEN'S GATE. Then, in
smaller type: "Was the critics' treatment of 'Heaven's Gate' justifiable
homicide?" The ad was membership promotion, announcing that the
uncut seventy-millimeter version of Heaven's Gate would have six performances at the NFT August 13–16.

These screenings, preceded by an appearance by the director,
opened perhaps the last startling chapter in the long saga of Heaven's
Gate. The critics came, and their response was extraordinary. Derek
Malcolm in the Guardian wrote, "The full version, I can assure you, is
quite an experience—an extraordinary attempt to make a major American movie at a time when only the minors hold sway." Philip French,
who, like Andrews, had praised the short version, called the long one
"only an amplification of the shorter one, and not in any sense a substantially different work, as many have claimed. I hope this masterpiece
will now get the support it deserves." Geoff Brown in the Times found it
"a delirious spectacle," thought "most of the performers work wonders,"
and cited Huppert as "touchingly natural." He added, "One emerges
from the complete Heaven's Gate dubious perhaps, about its intellectual
worth, but dazzled and moved by cinema's magnetic power."

The Sunday Telegraph reported, "The restored version is little short
of magnificent," and Nigel Andrews rereviewed the film in the Financial
Times and declared unequivocally, "The film is a masterpiece."

With such reviews the newly formed UIP decided in September
1983 to release the long version theatrically for the first time in England (or anywhere, since the disastrous New York opening in 1980) at
London's Plaza 2 cinema. The reviews and the commercial run stimu-
lated news stories in America, like Ed Blanche's AP story in October,
titled "'Heaven's Gate' Triumphs in Uncut Version," and the New York

Times' "Conflict, Revisionism and Harmony: The Arts in England," which generously quoted the most laudatory English reviewers in a Sunday "Arts and Leisure" piece.

In spite of the critical praise, however, the "triumph" was not sufficient to inspire a full rebirth or even extended exhibition in England. Hy Smith, now overseeing the film for UIP in London, where he had settled after working on *For Your Eyes Only*, reported that "after a run of a couple of months, with expenses deducted, the engagement yielded a profit of maybe two thousand pounds. This is a triumph?" Further distribution plans were shelved.

It may be that the extreme divergence of critical views on *Heaven's Gate*, from "unqualified disaster" to unequivocal "masterpiece," reveals only that critics are as various as the rest of us or that they are subject, like us, to the mood of the moment, the temper of the times, those relevant but irrelevant motes that get in the eye of the beholder. That Vincent Canby's response to the picture was swayed by the attitudes of the industry of which he is an acute observer is likely; that he called it as he saw it is unquestioned. Perhaps, too, the French and English overreacted in some reverse chauvinism to their New York counterparts, or maybe it was simply that three years later the film could be viewed as just a film, with no (or hardly any) commercial stakes riding on it, no personality or broad industry issues hovering between viewer and screen. There was some distance now, and legends are, almost by definition, better viewed from afar.

One thing is certain: I believe there to have been not one day or one moment in the turbulent history of *Heaven's Gate* in which Michael Cimino intended anything other than to create "a masterpiece," a work of lasting art. His certainty that he was doing so conditioned that history and much of the behavior of those around him. He did not set out to destroy or damage a company but believed he would enrich it, economically and aesthetically.

Cimino implied in his interview with Gene Shalit that judgment should be tempered by a consideration of intentions, and surely the pursuit of perfection is an honorable, if expensive, goal. But just as surely perfection implies discipline, and there can be no art without it. The most disciplined period of production on *Heaven's Gate* was that of the prologue, and following its shooting, cinematographer Vilmos Zsigmond noted, "This brings up a question in regard to future production. I'm sure that once it becomes known that . . . [the prologue] was shot in this way, people will question why we spend ten million dollars on a film when it can be done for two million dollars. . . . We did it

because we were pushed to do it, but I feel that directors and cam-
eramen should have the luxury of shooting schedules that give them
room to think a little bit, to create. I don't believe this is the way to
shoot important sequences—but we did it."

The key word there, it seems to me, is *luxury*, and the obvious
question it suggests is "What price creativity?" and it is far from academic. Movies matter. Because they do, and because they are created
and manufactured in both artistic and industrial contexts, their costs
matter, too. Signs that those costs are once again escalating wildly and
could one day make movies simply a prohibitively expensive "luxury"
should be deeply sobering to those who care about them and most sobering of all to those who make them, the auteurs and artists whose
assiduous pursuit of final cut or this or that other contractual advantage
is a meaningless, even destructive luxury unless accompanied by the
salutary force of discipline which no union, management, or conglomerate can impose. Like art, it comes from within.

I think it likely that audience and critical perception of *Heaven's
Gate* as a failure (in America, anyway) came not only from awareness of
the scandalously undisciplined method of its manufacture but also from
a deeper, more disturbing failure of discipline in the picture itself. Not
only the filmmaker but the film, too, was "out of control" (to quote
Carelli). Characters and story were sacrificed to the filmmaker's love of
visual effect and production for their own sakes. The "look" of the
thing subsumed the sense of the thing and implied a callous or uncaring
quality about characters for whom the audience was asked to care more
than the film seemed to. Whether those characters were well or ill
conceived, they seemed sabotaged by their creator's negligence of them
as he pursued the "larger, richer, deeper" things that surrounded them,
obscuring them, making them seem smaller, poorer, more shallow.

The larger failure of *Heaven's Gate* is not that the "golden string"
finally stretched to an irrecoverable $44 million (the figure at which it
was written off, including promotional costs) but that it failed to engage
audiences on the most basic and elemental human levels of sympathy
and compassion, and this failure is finally cardinal.

But *Heaven's Gate* left few viewers merely cold. There was something else there that aroused antipathy in many, and the anger of the
critics is still discernible in their condemnation of it (whether they are
right or wrong). That something else, I think, is a pervasive nihilism
that runs through the film from its advertising slogan—"What one
loves in life are the things that fade"—to its climactic and violent reworking of history. That nostalgic-sounding slogan is finally reductive:
It narrows the world instead of enlarging it. When it is pictorialized in

the closing moments of the film, as Averill stands on the deck of his yacht and his eyes brim over with recollection of faded things, we feel untouched, and Averill's sorrow smacks of self-pity because only he can feel it. We have never been made to understand or feel that there was—or is—anything in life to love, anything worth our efforts to prevent its fading. Such a world, whatever its spectacle, viewers (this one anyway) finally found wanting in the very values, the very respect for human life that had made the story seem worth telling in the first place.

Perhaps there is something about the movie business itself, the industry as it is constituted today, that mitigates against the kind of humanism that might have transformed *Heaven's Gate* from an essay in exploitation to what John Gardner called at various times "moral" or "generous" fiction. Perhaps the conditions in which careers are forged and films constructed partake so little of those qualities that we should not expect to find films imbued with them. But occasionally we do, and that is what justifies continuing to make them.

In one two-week period in the summer of 1984 the top managements of three major motion-picture companies changed personnel completely. Within three years of the *Heaven's Gate* debacle, with only one exception noted below, the management of every major company in the motion-picture industry had changed. Not one production head in Hollywood today is where he was three and a half years earlier. Such instability precludes continuity and development not only in the industry but in "the art form of the 20th century" itself, and one might fairly ask how discipline and responsibility can be expected from artists who know that the only continuities in the business are those of their own work and those derived from conglomerates who, for the most part, own Hollywood and are not, as we have seen, afraid to walk away.

But continuity of the art depends on discipline of the art, because without it, it could fade away. Ultimately what one loves about life are the things that *last*, because those who care, see to it that they do.

Movies might.

EPILOGUE: END CREDITS

Andy Albeck still grows Christmas trees on his farm in New Jersey and still sells them only to families with children. "Christmas trees are *for* children," he maintains. He is working on two books, one for his grandchildren and one for the rest of us, and is successfully reconverting Manhattan brownstones back into one-family dwellings. His wife, Lotte, is still a broker.

With characteristic honesty and self-scrutiny he stated recently that "the failure of *Heaven's Gate* was the failure of three people: David Field, Steven Bach, and Andy Albeck," and with characteristic generosity he still thinks of Michael Cimino as "a remarkably talented man."

Norbert Auerbach eventually resigned as copresident of UIP in London and recently appeared on Austrian television as one of the international set who live at least part time in Salzburg. He is reportedly preparing a picture to be produced in Paris.

John Beckett still retains an office in the Transamerica pyramid in San Francisco, where he is chairman of the executive committee.

David Begelman resigned from United Artists in 1982. His expensive slate of pictures for MGM that, in part, triggered the purchase of UA failed: *Buddy, Buddy, All the Marbles, Whose Life Is It Anyway?, Yes, Giorgio, Cannery Row,* and *Pennies from Heaven.* The last named picture alone cost $22 million and returned perhaps three. It is likely that the aggregate losses to MGM equalled or surpassed those sustained by UA with *Heaven's Gate.* All was not bleak, however: In acquiring UA, MGM also acquired UA's pictures, and that same year had two block-busters—*For Your Eyes Only* and *Rocky III.*

Bart Farber is a successful cable television executive in Manhattan.

David Field left Twentieth Century-Fox in 1983 and, after writing a screenplay for that company, joined Tri-Star as a production executive. When Tri-Star changed management after less than three years in business, Field became an independent producer for the new regime. He is reportedly preparing to produce there the screenplay he originally wrote for Fox.

Al Fitter died peacefully at his home in Old Greenwich, Connecticut, in the summer of 1983.

Gene Goodman resigned from United Artists in the summer of 1981 and joined AMC (American-Multi-Cinema) in Jacksonville, Florida, one of America's largest theater chains. Instead of booking pictures, he now buys them, often from former UA fieldmen who used to work under him.

James Harvey is chairman and president of Transamerica and generously shared the wealth Transamerica derived from the sale of United Artists in the form of bonuses to a score of executives who had served UA long and loyally. The telescope given him by Francis Coppola is still in place on the twenty-fifth floor of the Transamerica building, still trained on Zoetrope's offices below, though their proprietor "does not seem to be at home."

Lee Katz is an executive in Beverly Hills for the Completion Bond Company, for which he roams the globe, protecting wide-ranging film investments.

Derek Kavanagh has made the transition to life in Southern California "quite happily, thank you," and is back to what he likes best, production management in the field.

Arthur Krim remains chairman of Orion. It is perhaps not insignificant that Orion is the only major company in the motion picture business that has the same top management it had at the time of *Heaven's Gate*. Box office for Orion has been mixed, but the company has been successful with such pictures as *The Terminator* and *Amadeus* and, of course, Woody Allen's *Zelig* and *Broadway Danny Rose*. Krim remains the *éminence grise* of the motion-picture industry.

Charles Okun is still a production manager. He recently worked with director Jonathan Demme, who calls him "just the best."

Jerry Paonessa is writing and producing independently, having briefly worked for Michael Cimino and Joann Carelli following *Heaven's Gate*.

Richard Parks is a partner in a New York production company, engaged in film and television production. He made his film producing (and writing) debut on *Blackout*, for HBO Premiere Films.

Hy Smith is senior vice-president of advertising and publicity for UIP International in London. He remains quip-a-minute.

Lois Smith has returned to public relations, with her own firm based in New York. She still calls people ducks.

Dean Stolber left New York for California when UA was sold to MGM. He is still with the company as executive vice-president.

Anthea Sylbert supervised production of *Yentl* for United Artists and is now an independent producer in partnership with Goldie Hawn. She produced *Swing Shift* and *Protocol*, both for Warner Brothers.

Robert Wunsch has returned to the agency business in Beverly Hills, specializing in writers.

Craig Zadan produced *Footloose*.

Michael Cimino worked on many projects after *Heaven's Gate* and turned many down, including *Bounty*, the picture that resulted from David Lean's never-made duet of *Mutiny on the Bounty* pictures. He also worked briefly on *Footloose*, which was subsequently directed by Herbert Ross. He has developed numerous projects for himself, including a life of Dostoevsky with poet and short-story writer Raymond Carver and a version of *The Yellow Jersey*, a bicycle marathon-themed novel, for Dustin Hoffman. When he and Hoffman visited the Tour de France in the summer of 1984, Cimino told Samuel Abt of the *International Herald Tribune* that he was thirty-eight and had begun working on *The Yellow Jersey* in 1975. He began his first directing assignment since *Heaven's Gate* in the fall of 1984 for producer Dino de Laurentiis on *The Year of the Dragon*, which will be released by MGM/UA. In February of 1985, Cimino agreed to make his next picture for that company, in a deal made by (then) MGM executive Danton Rissner: a movie based on Truman Capote's *Handcarved Coffins*.

Joann Carelli continues developing motion-picture properties both with and without Cimino. She is the mother of a beautiful baby girl, whose father is David Mansfield, to whom Carelli reports she is happily married.

MGM/UA has, like other Hollywood companies, gone through a succession of executive personnel in the last three years. Management has included such well-known Hollywood figures as Freddie Fields and Frank Yablans. In mid-March of 1985, Alan Ladd, Jr. (whose Ladd Company did not survive its Orion-like establishment at Warner Brothers) was named chairman of MGM/UA. Each company has its own president but, significantly perhaps, their separate staffs report directly to Ladd. The combined companies remain under the majority ownership of Kirk Kerkorian.

729 was sold in 1983 and gutted. Reconstruction has erased all traces of the office in the northwest corner of the fourteenth floor, formerly occupied first by Mary Pickford, then by Arthur Krim, and finally by Andy Albeck (though never by Norbert Auerbach). It is available from a Manhattan real estate firm for $27 per square foot.

Steven Bach wrote this book.

Index